Casebook of Psychological Disorders

The Human Face of Emotional Distress

Steven S. Schwartzberg
McLean Hospital
Harvard Medical School

Allyn and Bacon

Boston ■ London ■ Toronto ■ Sydney ■ Tokyo ■ Singapore

Executive Editor: Rebecca Pascal
Vice President Director of Marketing: Joyce Nilsen
Full Service Production Manager: Joseph Vella
Project Coordination and Text Design: York Production Services
Electronic Page Makeup: York Production Services
Cover Administrator: Jenny Hart
Manufacturing Buyer: Megan Cochran

Copyright © 2000 by Allyn & Bacon
A Pearson Education Company
160 Gould Street
Needham Heights, MA 02194

Internet: www.abacon.com

Library of Congress Cataloging-in-Publication Data
Schwartzberg, Steven.
    Casebook of psychological disorders : the human face of emotional
distress / Steven S. Schwartzberg.
        p.   cm.
    ISBN 0-321-01171-6
    1. Psychology, Pathological Case studies.   I. Title.
    [DNLM: 1. Mental Disorders Case Report.   WM 140 S399c   1999]
RC454.S3614   1999
616.89—dc21
DNLM/DLC
for Library of Congress   99-15004
                                                                                       CIP

Printed in the United States of America.

ISBN 0-321-01171-6

10 9 8 7 6 5 4 3   03 02 01

CONTENTS

PREFACE

T he study of abnormal psychology is a journey into the mystery and breadth of human experience. Few fields open such a fascinating window into the inner workings of people's lives; few disciplines examine so carefully how people adapt to the complexities of modern society, or falter in their attempts to do so. By mapping the particular ways in which people experience emotional turmoil, behave maladaptively, react to stress, or struggle to achieve meaningful relationships, we learn as much about psychological health as we do about dysfunction.

Yet, because abnormal psychology is based in science, this essential humanness easily can be forgotten, the suffering diminished amid scholarly rigor. And so for this reason, a casebook offers a valuable complement to the traditional abnormal psychology textbook. Whereas a textbook succeeds to the extent that it organizes and conveys the prodigious wealth of knowledge we have accumulated, a casebook highlights how psychological distress is experienced and treated in real life. A textbook covers the breadth of a phenomenon; a casebook delves into the rich specifics of individual lives.

The aim of *Casebook of Abnormal Psychology: The Human Face of Emotional Distress* is to bring to life, in a humane and realistic manner, an array of the psychological difficulties that people currently encounter. Because the DSM-IV (American Psychiatric Association [APA], 1994) has become the most prominent model for conceptualizing mental disorders, the fifteen cases in this collection each exemplify a specific DSM-IV disorder.[1] Each focuses on the life of a particular individual (or

---

[1]*DSM-IV stands for Diagnostic and Statistical Manual of Mental Disorders, fourth Edition*. The impact of this manual is greatest in North America. The diagnostic scheme of the World Health Organization (1992), the ICD-10 (International Classification of Disease, 10th edition) is the psychiatric manual of note for much of the world.

individuals), while also addressing the more global and generalizable features of the disorder.

Four principles have guided the creation of this book. First is a commitment to the scientist–practitioner model of clinical psychology. Good clinical work must be embedded in sound research, and these cases make ample use of data regarding treatment, etiology, epidemiology, and prognosis. But clinical work also is more than science. We have learned much about the mechanics of effective psychotherapy, but the precise alchemy that sparks therapeutic change still remains a mystery. And so the psychotherapists in these cases are theoretically grounded but also at times rely on a dash of art in their craft.

Second, a danger in the study of psychopathology, for students and seasoned professionals alike, is adopting an "us versus them" attitude. How tempting it is to pathologize what we find anxiety-provoking, upsetting, or just plain different! With this in mind, these vignettes strive to portray people as respectfully as possible. I try to communicate not only the "facts" of each case but also the toll on life quality, and the person's subjective experience of his or her own distress.

The third and fourth principles relate to diversity. Cultural diversity is interwoven throughout the book in several ways. The cases themselves feature people from a variety of backgrounds and heritages. When relevant, the impact of cultural issues on treatment, etiology, and epidemiology is discussed, with supporting research. Several cases examine how sociocultural factors shape the experience or prevalence of a disorder. Particular issues are addressed as they arise, such as how cultures may clash in conceptualizing and defining a disorder (as with Conchita Morales, a Puerto Rican woman with panic disorder), or how treatment is affected when the client and therapist come from different ethnic backgrounds (as when Sharleen Washington, an African-American woman with dysthymia, meets with a white psychotherapist).

And fourth, these cases also are diverse in the theoretical orientations that guide treatment. *Casebook of Abnormal Psychology* is unique in that it does not favor any one perspective but instead samples from among the rich tapestry of theories that shape modern clinical work. As such, these vignettes feature cognitive-behavioral, psychodynamic (especially object relations and self-psychology), feminist, systemic, biological, and humanist-existential perspectives. Treatment modalities include individual, couple's, family, and group psychotherapy, hypnotherapy, psychopharmacology, psychoeducation, and case management. Several of the therapists use an integrative or eclectic treatment approach. This, too, reflects real life, where the majority of clinicians do not describe themselves as strict adherents of any one perspective (Garfield & Bergin, 1994).

When a specific modality or orientation has been demonstrated in the research literature to be most effective, that treatment is featured. Thus Jonathan Martell, who suffers from posttraumatic stress disorder, works with a cognitive-behavioral clinician. Brian Hamilton, with narcissistic personality disorder, enters into a long-term psychodynamic therapy. Joel and Brenda Mahoney work with a couple's therapist, with an eclectic orientation, to treat Joel's erectile difficulties. And Roger Larkin, a young man with paranoid schizophrenia, does not receive any individual psychotherapy but benefits from case management, psychopharmacology, psychoeducational groups, and the structure of a psychiatric day program.

The cases all follow a similar format. Each begins by describing the person's current functioning and psychological difficulties. A *psychosocial history* then provides relevant information regarding childhood, family-of-origin dynamics, social, academic, and occupational functioning, how the disorder has evolved or been manifest over time, and any other related issues. A brief *conceptualization* follows, presenting the rationale for diagnosing the person with his or her disorder(s) using DSM-IV criteria, explaining relevant terms, and examining questions regarding differential diagnosis. Next is a detailed account of the person's *treatment*. This includes, as relevant, assessment, prior treatment history, and the specifics of how the disorder is currently being addressed. A *multiaxial DSM-IV diagnosis at the time of termination* (or *multiaxial DSM-IV diagnosis at this point in treatment*) concludes the treatment section, providing diagnostic information on all five DSM axes.

A *discussion* follows. These sections vary somewhat, shaped by the particular disorder. But as a general rule, each includes a brief history of the disorder, a review of relevant research, reflections on the person's treatment, a look at the disorder and treatment from various perspectives, current controversies, and cultural or subcultural issues. A *prognosis* then returns to the case, providing follow-up data (when available) and speculations about what the future might hold for the person, based on current outcome research. Finally, *critical thinking questions* address conceptual issues regarding the disorder and the specific case presented.

I have chosen these particular vignettes for several reasons. Some are included because they so crisply illustrate the diagnostic issue at hand. Others capture more of the ambiguities and diagnostic complexities that typify real life. Most feature a "typical" representative of the disorder (such as Jenny Landau, a 21-year-old female with bulimia nervosa), while a few do not (such as attention-deficit hyperactivity disorder in a six-year-old girl, Sally Howard, even though this disorder is more common in boys than girls). The cases also have been selected to sample from a broad spectrum of diagnostic categories. And in keeping with real life, some of the treatments are more successful than others.

Each vignette stands on its own, and the chapters may be approached in any order. Yet the cases vary in some key ways, including the primary theory guiding treatment, the complexity of the presenting problem(s), and treatment outcome. As such, the chapters accrue to something greater than the disparate parts: a balanced and broad-based introduction to how we currently understand and treat psychopathology. In this regard, *Casebook of Abnormal Psychology* is useful for undergraduate students encountering their first brush with the field, as well as those seeking a more nuanced application of theory, or in the process of clinical training.

All these vignettes originate in real lives and real psychotherapies. However, I imagine that any actual person would be hard-pressed to recognize him or herself, his or her life, or his or her psychotherapy (or psychotherapist) from these pages. Because of the paramount ethical importance of confidentiality, all identifying characteristics have been altered. Often, the person presented is a composite of several individuals. Pedagogical considerations also have influenced the structure and presentation of certain cases.

I hope that these fifteen vignettes resonate at more than an intellectual level. If alleviating emotional and mental distress is the guiding hope and purpose behind the study of abnormal psychology, then detaching ourselves too fully from people's distress is to miss a crucial component of education. To the extent that this book helps foster a union for the reader between the science of psychopathology and the soul of human turmoil, I will have accomplished my intent.

I greatly appreciate assistance of all sorts I received writing this book. The following colleagues, many of whom read cases drafts in their particular field of expertise, offered sage advice and information: Donald Davidoff, Ph.D., Frances Frankenburg, M.D., Aurilee Jones Goodwin, Ph.D., Martin Kafka, M.D., Lori Kaplowitz, M.D., Melanie Katzman, Ph.D., Elizabeth Murphy, Ph.D., Doug Needles, Ph.D., Lawrence Rosenberg, Ph.D., Joseph Rubin, Psy.D, Elizabeth Torres, Ph.D., Steven Tublin, Ph.D., and Virginia Youngren, Ph.D. The suggestions and comments of C.P. Bankart, Wabash College; David Berry, University of Kentucky; Jack Blanchard, University of New Mexico; Alan Butler, University of Maine; James F. Calhoun, Univeristy of Georgia; Sarah Cirese, College of Marin; E.M. Coles, Simon Fraser University; Lani Fujitsubo, Southern Oregon State College; Marc D. Henley, Delaware County Community College; Fred A. Johnson, University of District of Columbia; Joseph Lowman, UNC—Chapel Hill; David J. Lutz, Southwest Missouri State University; Bronna D. Ramanoff, Russell Sage College; Joan Devlin Rykiel, Ocean County College; Louis W. Stamps, University of Wisconsin—La Crosse; and Carol Thompson, Muskegon Community College made during the peer review process were tremendously helpful in honing the text into its current form. I also am indebted to Alice Clark, Ph.D., and Aida Khan, Ph.D. (dissociative identity disorder), Donna O'Connell, LICSW (male erectile disorder), and Dana Weaver, Ph.D. (bipolar disorder and attention-deficit hyperactivity disorder) for giving clinical and thematic shape to these chapters and sharing the writing. Patricia Yi provided much needed assistance with the bibliography. Richard Halgin, Ph.D., first sparked the idea for the project and encouraged me to do it. Robert Feldman, Ed.D., offered continuous good advice. Eric Stano and Becky Pascal infused the project with their enthusiasm and support. Finally, thank you to Kevin Cathcart, Nat and Marilyn Schwartzberg, and to the many psychotherapy clients who have honored me by sharing their lives in such an open and trusting manner.

Steven Schwartzberg, Ph.D.
Associate Psychologist, McLean Hospital
Assistant Clinical Professor of Psychology,
Department of Psychiatry,
Harvard Medical School

Posttraumatic Stress Disorder

Jonathan Martell was a 23-year-old graduate student studying European History. He had always done well academically and socially; peers, family members, and teachers regarded him as a bright, likeable, and easygoing young man. He started graduate school directly after college and did well his first semester. But his ability to function academically and socially collapsed precipitously after a traumatic incident that occurred over the winter break.

Jonathan had gone out dancing to a gay nightclub with a friend. Walking back to his car alone late at night, he was assaulted by three teenagers. The attackers punched and kicked him repeatedly in the face, stomach, and groin. They stole his wallet and threatened to stab him. Throughout, they taunted him with threats: "You stupid faggot scum. We should kill your fairy ass. I hope you get AIDS and die."

The assailants fled when they heard other people walking down the street. Jonathan was wounded but fortunately without severe bodily injury. He was sore for several days and sustained a black eye, a split lip, and bruised ribs. Nothing was broken or permanently damaged—at least not physically. But now, several months later, after his body had healed, the psychological impact of the assault continued to haunt him.

Jonathan often replayed the assault in his mind. Starting immediately after the attack, the memory of his fear, and his assailants' rage, intruded into his thoughts. Sometimes, it was as if he were reliving it. Certain cues in his environment would bring the terror of that evening vividly and instantaneously back, such as walking down the street and seeing a group of male teenagers, or hearing one of the songs he had danced to before leaving the club. Once, working at his job in the university library, he caught an unexpected whiff of the same distinctive cologne his friend had worn that night. He immediately felt paralyzed with a wave of fear.

These intrusive memories of the assault were typically accompanied by feelings of helplessness and panic. Yet, at other times, Jonathan recalled the event and felt very detached, as if it had been unreal, or as if he were watching it happen in a movie to somebody else. Jonathan also purposely avoided any experiences or activities connected with the assault. He had not returned to the club where he had been dancing, or even to that part of town, since that evening. In general, he went out less and became more isolated. He withdrew from his friends and spoke to his family less frequently.

In addition to these symptoms directly related to the assault, Jonathan's overall ability to function suffered. When he tried to study, he could not concentrate on the words in front of him. His mind drifted, no matter how hard he tried to focus. He slept fitfully at night, had occasional nightmares, and overslept many mornings, often missing class. Several times a day, a sudden surge of anxiety overcame him, seemingly out of the blue: his heart raced, his breath became labored, he felt dizzy. He was easily startled and felt "on edge" most of the time. When he went outside alone, he was preoccupied with the fear that a similar attack might happen again.

Jonathan's difficulties also affected his part-time job at the library. Unable to muster enough interest or stamina to work, and fearful that he would again experience such a paralyzing fear in public, he began to avoid going to work.

By mid-semester, Jonathan was in danger of failing his courses and losing his job. His ability to function had been steadily deteriorating since the assault. His supervisor let him know his job was in jeopardy. But she also expressed concern and wondered what was troubling him. She was puzzled: Jonathan had been a conscientious and friendly worker the previous semester but now seemed to be depressed, anxious, and distracted (when he bothered to show up at all). She did not understand what was going on.

Jonathan had not told her, or anyone else, about the assault. But deciding finally that he needed to confide in someone, he responded to his supervisor's repeated solicitations of concern and told her what had happened. At first when he spoke to her about the assault, he seemed distant and matter-of-fact, as if the event were not such a big deal. But then he started crying and became overcome with feelings of terror and fear. He admitted how frightened he was that his assailants were going to kill him.

The supervisor encouraged Jonathan to speak with someone at the University Counseling Service. Even though he had previously been against the idea of counseling, he agreed to do so. Somewhat reluctantly, he met with Dr. Harlan Litwack, a staff psychologist, to discuss the assault and his subsequent decline in functioning.

PSYCHOSOCIAL HISTORY

Jonathan grew up in a working-class neighborhood in southern Florida. He was the youngest of two children, with a sister three years his elder. His father worked as a mechanic; his mother was a secretary. Jonathan was the first member of his extended family to attend and graduate college; his decision to attend graduate school was greeted with pride by his parents, although they also felt skeptical about its value. But then, in various ways Jonathan's parents had always seen him as being somewhat "different."

Prior to the assault, Jonathan had not demonstrated any major evidence of maladaptive or disturbed psychological functioning. His childhood and adolescence were fairly ordinary. He was a good student and had a steady circle of friends. If anything, he was considered somewhat of an overachiever in high school: In addition to working hard in his studies, he wrote for the school newspaper, participated on the debate team, and sang in the school's glee club.

The primary life stressor Jonathan had faced prior to the assault was coming to terms with his sexual orientation. In retrospect, Jonathan knew at least since puberty, and perhaps earlier, that he was gay. But he did not acknowledge this to himself until high school. When he did privately admit to himself that he was gay, his sexuality felt uncomfortable and shameful. He quietly wished his desires "would just go away" and tried to fight off his sexual attraction to other males. Outwardly, he remained gregarious, social, and popular, but he felt he harbored a major secret that separated him from his peers. He chose not to date and avoided any girls who expressed romantic interest in him.

When he arrived at college, away from home for the first time, Jonathan felt more courage to explore his sexuality. He learned that his school had a gay student organization and attended a few of their meetings. He began to socialize with other gay students, relieved to meet other people who revealed that they had similarly grown up feeling alone and isolated. He had his first brief relationship with another male during his sophomore year. As he gradually gained more exposure to being with other gay people, he developed a much greater level of comfort and acceptance about himself.

By the time Jonathan graduated from college, he had made a lot of progress in his process of "coming out" to other people. He had told many of his friends that he was gay—most of whom greeted the news with an acceptance that surprised him (he had feared their rejection or condemnation). Amid great anxiety, he also made the decision in the summer before his senior year to tell his sister and parents. His sister expressed support and affirmation; she told Jonathan that she had a couple of gay friends, and his being gay did not affect how she felt about him. She also was willing to help their parents cope with the news. Although they responded by telling Jonathan that they still loved him, they were upset and confused. They said they would try to understand—but was there something he could do to change? Was there anything they had done wrong?

Jonathan's increasing comfort with his sexuality throughout this process of coming out stood in sharp contrast to how he felt about being assaulted. From as soon as the assault occurred, Jonathan felt ashamed and insecure. He believed he would only be ridiculed if he spoke about it. In fact, at the hospital emergency room he went to immediately after the attack, one of the nurses asked him, "Why are you gays always looking for trouble?"

So in the days immediately after the incident, Jonathan kept to himself. After going to the emergency room for medical treatment, he did not heed the physician's advice to follow up at the Student Health Service. He also chose not to report the event to the police for fear of not being taken seriously or being humiliated by them. He did not seek any sort of counseling or support. He avoided going out in public until his black eye and swollen face had healed.

Jonathan had hoped to put the event behind him quickly by pretending it had not happened. He believed that this was the best way to cope. It was only several months later, with the mounting evidence of his declining functioning, that Jonathan realized the limitations of this strategy.

CONCEPTUALIZATION

According to the Diagnostic and Statistical Manual of Mental Disorders, 4th edition (DSM-IV) (American Psychiatric Association, 1994), posttraumatic stress disorder [PTSD] is "characterized by the reexperiencing of an extremely traumatic event accompanied by symptoms of increased arousal and by avoidance of stimuli associated with the trauma" (APA, 1994, p. 393). The DSM-IV specifies six diagnostic criteria for PTSD:

A. The person has been exposed to a traumatic event in which both of the following were present:
    1. the person experienced, witnessed, or was confronted with an event or events that involved actual or threatened death or serious injury, or a threat to the physical integrity of self or others
    2. the person's response involved intense fear, helplessness, or horror
B. The traumatic event is persistently reexperienced in one (or more) of the following ways:
    1. recurrent and intrusive distressing recollections of the event, including images, thoughts, or perceptions
    2. recurrent distressing dreams of the event
    3. acting or feeling as if the traumatic event were recurring (includes a sense of reliving the experience, illusions, hallucinations, and dissociative flashback episodes, including those that occur on awakening or when intoxicated)
    4. intense psychological distress at exposure to internal or external cues that symbolize or resemble an aspect of the traumatic event
    5. physiological reactivity on exposure to internal or external cues that symbolize or resemble an aspect of the traumatic event
C. Persistent avoidance of stimuli associated with the trauma and numbing of general responsiveness (not present before the trauma), as indicated by three or more of the following:
    1. efforts to avoid thoughts, feelings, or conversations associated with the trauma
    2. efforts to avoid activities, places, or people that arouse recollections of the trauma

3. inability to recall an important aspect of the trauma
4. markedly diminished interest or participation in significant activities
5. feeling of detachment or estrangement from others
6. restricted range of affect (e.g., unable to have loving feelings)
7. sense of a foreshortened future (e.g., does not expect to have a career, marriage, children, or a normal life span)

D. Persistent symptoms of increased arousal (not present before the trauma), as indicated by two (or more) of the following:
1. difficulty falling or staying asleep
2. irritability or outbursts of anger
3. difficulty concentrating
4. hypervigilance
5. exaggerated startle response

E. Duration of the disturbance (symptoms in Criteria B, C, and D) is more than 1 month.

F. The disturbance causes clinically significant distress or impairment in social, occupational, or other important areas of functioning.

Jonathan Martell met all these criteria: He experienced, with intense fear, a traumatic event (criterion A); he reexperienced the assault with recurrent and intrusive recollections (criterion B); he avoided stimuli associated with the event (criterion C); he demonstrated persistent symptoms of increased arousal (criterion D); and the symptoms lasted longer than one month and resulted in significant distress or impairment (criteria E and F).

Before arriving at this diagnosis, Jonathan's psychologist, Dr. Litwack, also considered the possibility of two alternative diagnoses: acute stress disorder and adjustment disorder with mixed emotional features. *Acute stress disorder* is much like posttraumatic stress disorder, with a similar array of symptoms that develop in response to a traumatizing event. However, with acute stress disorder, the symptoms abate within one month after the trauma. By the time Jonathan sought help, his symptoms had already persisted for over three months.

Similar to PTSD and acute stress disorder, *adjustment disorders* develop in response to experiencing a stressful event. The stressful event may be a specific trauma (such as assault, injury, or bereavement), or it may be a difficult life passage (such as divorce, the end of a relationship, unemployment, or moving). Jonathan fit the criteria for an adjustment disorder: the DSM-IV's description of "clinically significant emotional or behavioral symptoms in response to an identifiable stressor or stressors" certainly applied to him (APA, 1994, p. 623). However, while the descriptions of PTSD and adjustment disorder overlap somewhat, the diagnostic criteria for posttraumatic stress disorder are considerably more precise. Given that Jonathan meets these more specific requirements, PTSD is the more accurate diagnosis. Jonathan's PTSD is further specified as "chronic," an indication that his symptoms have lasted three months or longer.

TREATMENT

When a person is faced with a cataclysmic event, some sort of psychological counseling, no matter how brief, can be of great assistance in coping with the trauma (Brom, Kleber & Defares, 1989; Rothbaum & Foa, 1996). Often, psychotherapy is seen as a supportive endeavor, providing an outlet for the traumatized person to speak about the event, express the strong emotions associated with it, and try to come to terms with what has happened. Some of these benefits are *transtheoretical*—that is, they cut across the details or benefits of any one particular theoretical orientation. Among various specific treatment modalities for PTSD, cognitive-behavioral therapies are currently believed to have the greatest success rate, but a range of theories and styles of intervention also have proven to be effective (Rothbaum & Foa, 1996; McFarlane, 1994; Shalev, Bonne & Eth, 1996).

Dr. Litwack worked primarily from a cognitive-behavioral orientation. His approach to psychotherapy with Jonathan included two main goals: 1) to offer Jonathan a supportive environment in which to discuss his emotional reactions to the assault; and 2) to help Jonathan manage his anxiety and become less reactive to the many stimuli that had come to evoke fear in him.

Toward the end of their first meeting, Dr. Litwack explained to Jonathan the nature of posttraumatic stress disorder. Jonathan's symptoms, although of course undesirable, were understandable in the context of what had happened. In particular, Dr. Litwack highlighted Jonathan's intrusive thoughts of the assault, his avoidance of upsetting stimuli, and his occasional flashbacks as typical reactions to a life-threatening traumatic event (flashbacks are highly evocative sensory experiences, as if one is reliving a prior event).

Dr. Litwack made several recommendations. First, he recommended that he and Jonathan meet for a course of brief psychotherapy, perhaps ten to fifteen sessions, with an explicit focus on beginning to recover from the trauma of the assault. Second, he recommended that Jonathan consult with a psychiatrist to determine if a short-term course of anti-anxiety or antidepressant medication might improve Jonathan's difficulties with sleeping and concentrating. And third, he wanted Jonathan to meet with a primary care physician, as he had not returned for a follow-up examination after his visit to the emergency room.

Jonathan agreed to this treatment plan but also brought up two additional concerns. First, he asked what Dr. Litwack's beliefs were regarding homosexuality; he wanted to make sure that the therapist would not try to "treat" his being gay as something wrong. The psychologist assured him that this would not be his intention. Relieved by this response, Jonathan then mentioned that he was in danger of failing all four of his classes and being placed on academic suspension. This had become a great source of anxiety in itself. After discussing a few options, Dr. Litwack suggested that Jonathan consider withdrawing for the semester. If Jonathan requested, Dr. Litwack could write a letter to the dean supporting the need for a medical withdrawal.

Over the next week, Jonathan contemplated this decision. He spoke with his academic advisor, stating the general nature of his difficulties but choosing not to reveal the specifics. Jonathan decided that he could probably get back on track in two of his classes but would be unable to catch up in the other two. Dr. Litwack agreed to help Jonathan seek a medical withdrawal from those two classes.

In his initial psychotherapy sessions, Jonathan talked a lot about his symptoms and his memories of the assault. He repeatedly expressed disbelief that the attack had actually happened. He was surprised that it had affected him so greatly. He also began to experience many conflicting and strong emotions about that evening. Now, in contrast to his earlier reaction of minimizing the assault, Jonathan felt barraged with fear, sadness, guilt, and anger. Interestingly, he did not feel anger toward the three young men who attacked him, but instead he felt angry with other people—a bystander whom he believed saw the assault but did nothing, the emergency room nurse who made disparaging comments—but most of all with himself.

Jonathan felt a great deal of self-blame for what had happened. He told himself that he should have known better. He should have been more prepared. He should have taken care to avoid it. Jonathan castigated himself for being so "stupid" and "careless." Yet, in response to questions and comments by Dr. Litwack, he admitted that he could not think of anything he necessarily could have, or should have, done differently, perhaps other than not to have gone out at all.

Related to this, Jonathan also discussed how the assault felt like "taking ten steps backwards" in feeling comfortable with his sexual orientation. He assumed he was targeted for the assault because he was gay, given the anti-gay invective of the assailants. Since the attack he often thought to himself, "this wouldn't have happened if I wasn't gay." He knew how irrational this thought was, but he could not stop feeling that being the victim of an attack made him "unmanly" and "weak."

Dr. Litwack attempted to normalize Jonathan's doubts and worries. He told Jonathan that people who have suffered a trauma often try to find some way to explain the traumatizing event—perhaps out of a wish that the trauma could have been avoided, or out of a desire to regain a sense of personal control. He supported Jonathan in taking whatever steps he needed to regain this sense of control, including whom he chose to tell about the assault. But Dr. Litwack also wondered if Jonathan's secrecy about the trauma—he still refused to mention it to anyone outside of treatment—was hindering his ability to recover. He posed a challenging question to Jonathan: Was Jonathan so secretive about the assault because it was gay-related? Had he been assaulted in a different context—the victim of a mugging, for example—would he still keep it so quiet?

At first Jonathan denied this was the case, but then agreed that his desire not to tell people *was* based mainly on his fear that others would blame him for what happened, and connect it to his sexuality. Treatment then focused on helping Jonathan overcome his shame regarding being the victim of an assault. He had done nothing wrong; the assault was not his fault. Based on these discussions, Jonathan began to rethink his decision not to tell other people about the event. (It also helped that the one person he had told, his work supervisor, continued to offer support and reassurance.)

Jonathan told a few friends about being assaulted and then decided to tell his parents. He had refrained from telling them because he worried that this would confirm their fear that being gay was a dangerous and unsafe way to live. But, in fact, telling them had an unexpected effect. Although they were greatly disturbed by the news, Jonathan's revelation opened the door for the family to engage in more positive and honest discussions of Jonathan's sexuality than they had before.

After six or seven sessions of psychotherapy, Jonathan's functioning began to improve. As is often the case, Jonathan was uncertain what led to this improvement—Was it his meetings with Dr. Litwack? His changed attitude about telling people? Or perhaps it was the medication? (After consulting with a psychiatrist at the start of treatment, Jonathan started taking a small dose of anti-anxiety medication.) Regardless of what was helping him, alone or in combination, Jonathan felt better and was in the process of getting back on his feet. He was again attending work regularly and catching up in his two courses.

However, Jonathan was still bothered by PTSD symptoms. He continued to suffer from nightmares, intrusive thoughts, and occasional flashbacks of the assault. To address these specific symptoms, Dr. Litwack introduced a second component of treatment, a modified version of the behavioral technique *systematic desensitization*. This technique involves imagining anxiety-provoking situations, in a graded fashion, while simultaneously engaging in muscle relaxation exercises. The principle is one of *counterconditioning*—that is, pairing a relaxation response with anxiety-provoking thoughts to help break the learned association between a conditioned stimulus and anxiety.

Dr. Litwack first trained Jonathan in progressive relaxation techniques (Jacobsen, 1938). In progressive relaxation, a person learns first to tense and then to relax various muscle groups throughout the body, usually starting at the head and working down. After Jonathan was able to use these techniques to relax himself, he and Dr. Litwack then wrote out a hierarchical list of anxiety-related images from the assault. These moved from minimally stressful memories (such as dancing earlier in the evening) to moderately stressful memories (e.g., walking back to the car) to very stressful memories (e.g., the assault itself). Over the course of several weekly sessions, Dr. Litwack then guided Jonathan through these images, pacing them so that Jonathan was able to imagine increasingly stressful scenes while maintaining a relaxation response.

Over the course of several meetings, Jonathan progressed in his ability to tolerate these fearful images. Dr. Litwack also began encouraging him to counteract his avoidance responses in real life. They generated a list of *self-statements* that Jonathan could repeat to himself to reduce anxiety when confronted with the inevitable environmental triggers that might spark memories of the assault, such as the time in the library when he smelled his friend's cologne.

After working on these cognitive-behavioral strategies for several weeks, Jonathan decided he was ready to confront his fears more directly by returning to the club where he had been dancing. (This is an example of *in vivo* exposure, in which a person confronts his or her fears in the actual experience, not only in a therapist's office. *In vivo* exposure, most often in a planned and systematic manner, is often a key component of treating anxiety disorders, especially when it is part of a more broadly based treatment [Craske & Barlow, 1993]).

Multiaxial DSM-IV Diagnosis at Time of Termination:

Axis I:	Posttraumatic Stress Disorder, chronic
	CONDITION: IMPROVED
Axis II:	No diagnosis
Axis III:	None
Axis IV:	Victim of assault
Axis V:	*Treatment Onset:* 55 (moderate to serious impairment with academic and occupational functioning)
	Termination: 80 (transient symptoms, slight impairment in academic and occupational functioning)

Jonathan still felt he needed to avoid walking down the street where the assault had occurred, and he was too frightened to go to that section of town alone. But after thinking about it and discussing it in therapy, he called a friend (whom he had told about the assault) and they made plans to go together. Being able to accomplish this successfully meant a great deal to Jonathan. Later, looking back on the assault and its aftermath, he came to regard that decision as a major turning point in his recovery.

Jonathan met with Dr. Litwack for 17 sessions over a five-month span. He did well in the two courses he completed that semester and continued with his job at the library. Three months after terminating psychotherapy, in consultation with his psychiatrist, Jonathan opted to discontinue taking anti-anxiety medication. This transition also went smoothly. He was able once again to sleep soundly and concentrate on what he was doing, with only slight interference in his life from PTSD symptoms.

DISCUSSION

Posttraumatic stress disorder entered our diagnostic nomenclature with the DSM-III in 1980, but the notion that a traumatic event can lead to psychological impairment is not new. Historically, the first version of the DSM included a diagnosis called traumatic neurosis, highlighting the lingering impact of a traumatic event (APA, 1952). DSM-II included disorders labeled gross stress reaction and transitional situational disturbance (APA, 1968). These DSM-II disorders acknowledged the potentially devastating immediate nature of trauma but minimized the role of long-lasting impairment. Now, since the introduction of PTSD in DSM-III (APA, 1980), we have returned to the earlier diagnostic understanding of trauma having far-reaching implications, this time with a clearly articulated, specific constellation of symptoms absent from the earlier diagnostic manuals.

The validity and reliability of PTSD have been documented by a great deal of empirical research. Little dispute remains over the existence of the disorder. Yet some researchers and clinicians question whether PTSD belongs among the anxiety disorders, where it is currently classified. Anxiety symptoms are prominent in PTSD—but so are other symptoms (depression, psychosomatic impairment, the defense mechanism "dissociation," and sometimes maladaptive personality functioning). And some critics argue that since the disorder results from an external trauma, why even consider it a mental disorder at all?

Regarding this last point, the DSM-IV (APA, 1994) does not differentiate between disorders that result from external trauma from those that do not—all are considered to be "mental disorders." However, the diagnostic system of the World Health Organization, the International Classification of Diseases (ICD-10; World Health Organization, 1992) takes a different approach, distinguishing PTSD, and other disorders with clearly trauma-based etiology, from other psychological disorders.[1]

PTSD can result from a wide range of traumatic experiences, including natural disaster, war, victimization, accident, or human-wrought atrocity. Depending on the event, it can affect vast numbers of people in entire communities or an individual in a quick but impactful experience of terror. Within the general category of trauma, researchers have delineated several more specific traumatic stress responses.

For example, a "rape trauma syndrome" has been identified among victims of sexual violence (e.g., Burgess & Holmstrom, 1974; McCann, 1988). This may include posttraumatic difficulties in emotional, cognitive, physical, behavioral, and social functioning (McCann, 1988). Similarly, the concept of a generalized "disaster syndrome" is supported by evidence gathered from a wide variety of catastrophic events. For example, studies with victims of the Mount St. Helens volcanic explosion in 1980, Hurricane Andrew in Florida in 1992, a school bus kidnapping, and several plane crashes all point to a similar profile of psychological disturbance, marked by short-term, long-term, and delayed effects of anxiety, depression, and heightened autonomic arousal (Perlberg, 1979; Shore, Tatum & Vollmer, 1986; Terr, 1990).

Perhaps the most comprehensive data on posttraumatic stress disorder come from a large-scale epidemiological study of Vietnam War veterans, called the National Vietnam Veterans Readjustment Study (NVVRS) (Kulka et al., 1990). In this landmark investigation, a team of researchers documented the extent and nature of war-related trauma among returning Vietnam soldiers. The results dramatically indicate the stressfulness of war and the profound impact of PTSD on many peoples' lives. Among returning Vietnam veterans, the lifetime prevalence of PTSD was estimated to be approximately 31% for male veterans and 27% for female veter-

---

[1]Like the DSM, the ICD is a diagnostic manual of psychiatric disorders. The DSM is the official diagnostic scheme of the American Psychiatric Association; the ICD is the official manual of the World Health Organization. Although these two diagnostic systems have many overlaps, there are also some significant differences in how psychological disorders are conceptualized and categorized.

ans (most of whom served as nurses). These rates were significantly higher among African-American and Hispanic soldiers (Kulka et al., 1990). All told, these data suggest that nearly one million soldiers who served in Vietnam have met, currently meet, or at some future point will meet, diagnostic criteria for PTSD.

Who Develops PTSD?

Are some individuals more prone to the disorder than others? This remains a controversial issue and is one of the most important questions that current research on PTSD is attempting to address.

Some research indicates that preexisting personality traits, such as low self-esteem, interpersonal skills deficits, or emotional insecurity, may heighten the likelihood of developing PTSD (McFarlane, 1988). Yet not all the data support this. In a review of available studies of disaster-related trauma, Rubonis and Bickman (1991) concluded that the strongest predictor of subsequent distress was not any preexisting personality factor, but the severity of the trauma. Other researchers suggest that preexisting factors may matter more with low or moderately stressful events than with extreme stressors (Ursano, Boydstun & Wheatley, 1981). In other words, it may be that the more severe the trauma, the less a person's prior functioning is relevant.

One important variable in developing PTSD may be a person's beliefs regarding the danger or degree of threat in a traumatic situation. In some cases, the *perception* of threat is a more reliable predictor of PTSD than the actual threat involved, which may explain why some people develop PTSD and others do not when faced with the same event (Foa, 1997; Foa & Steketee, 1989). Yet this still does not fully address the question of preexisting personality factors, given that an individual's perception of how threatening a situation is may also be linked to pre-existing personality factors.

The role of personality factors in PTSD was also examined in the NVVRS. Among all those who served in Vietnam, who was most likely to develop PTSD? The data from this large study indicate that although personality likely played some role in the development of a posttraumatic stress reaction, it was *not* the most important determinant. Far more influential was one's actual degree of combat experience. Among returning Vietnam veterans, the men most likely to develop PTSD were those who served the longest and had the greatest exposure to combat. Soldiers who saw more war-related action were four times as likely to develop PTSD than those whose stay of duty exposed them to low or moderate war-zone stressors (Kulka et al., 1990).

So what can be made of all of this? Not all people exposed to traumatic situations will develop PTSD—but many will. Further, events that may lead to the development of PTSD vary from person to person—what traumatizes one person may barely affect another. And no matter what the nature of the trauma is, other factors must be involved in the etiology of this disorder, at least to some extent. Learning more about these factors will help us design more effective treatments, both of a long-term nature and in the immediate aftermath of a traumatic event.

Theoretical Perspectives

Each of the major theoretical frameworks highlights specific aspects of PTSD to explain its etiology and approach treatment. From a psychoanalytic viewpoint, Horowitz (1976) proposes that PTSD symptoms result from the ego's failure to manage an event that is too stressful or overwhelming for a person to assimilate. The ego (the part of the psyche responsible for managing stress and negotiating reality tasks) becomes overloaded. Horowitz theorizes that the alternating phases of "intrusion" and "denial" frequently seen in trauma survivors—a traumatized person often oscillates between being flooded with intrusive memories and feeling emotionally numb—represent the ego's inadequate attempts to regulate the powerful affect associated with the trauma.

Behaviorists focus on how posttraumatic symptoms are perpetuated once they are established. They emphasize the role of *two-factor learning* (Mowrer, 1960) or learning that involves both classical and operant conditioning. Theoretically, in the aftermath of a traumatic event, many previously neutral stimuli can suddenly lead to a strong autonomic fear response through classical conditioning. We see this in Jonathan, and how following the assault he responded with fear to the dance songs he heard, to seeing a group of male teenagers, and to smelling his friend's cologne— these have become conditioned stimuli. Then, through operant conditioning, avoiding these fear-provoking stimuli is reinforced because the avoidance stops the person from needing to re-experience the terror and distress of the trauma (Keane et al., 1985).

Several cognitive psychologists employ an *information-processing* model to explain why PTSD symptomatology affects so many areas of functioning (Foa, 1997; Lang, 1979). According to this model, the brain functions in a manner similar to a computer. Related bits of information are clustered together into "networks." As such, stimuli associated with a traumatic event are mentally encoded as belonging to a "fear network" or "trauma network," consisting of words, images, and sensory perceptions all connected to the memory that one's life or physical integrity was threatened. Because of the profoundly frightening nature of traumatic events, these networks are activated quickly and easily, leading to PTSD symptoms in a wide variety of situations.

Finally, theorists from a cognitive or existential perspective (Frankl, 1959; Lifton, 1980; Janoff-Bulman, 1992) emphasize trauma's impact on a person's prior ways of seeing the world or life as meaningful. Janoff-Bulman (1992) argues that a traumatizing event may shatter previous ideas about the safety, benevolence, or justice of the world. As such, the primary cognitive challenge for traumatized individuals is how to regain a set of viable "assumptions" about ascribing meaning to life. Some data indicate that traumatized individuals see the world as more random, less benevolent, and less meaningful than do their non-traumatized peers (Janoff-Bulman, 1992).

A Note on Homosexuality

In reviewing Jonathan's case, it is also important to discuss the issue of Jonathan's homosexuality. Note that Dr. Litwack did not attempt to make Jonathan's homosexuality a focus of treatment. In fact, when Jonathan raised concerns himself about the role of his sexual orientation in the assault, Dr. Litwack helped Jonathan understand this as his need to regain some control over the traumatizing event.

Homosexuality was declassified as a mental illness in the early 1970s. Despite long-standing assumptions and biases about the aberrant nature of homosexuality, the vast majority of empirical research supports the contention that homosexuals do not differ in psychological functioning from heterosexuals (Gonsiorek, 1991; Hooker, 1957). Gay men and women face some unique psychological challenges, but these relate more to *homophobia,* or the fear, hatred, and social stigmatization of homosexuality, than to a homosexual orientation itself (Gonsiorek, 1995).

To some extent, psychologists and other mental health professionals considered homosexuality abnormal until the 1970s because of what the early 20th-century philosopher Charles Sanders Pierce called "the method of tenacity": We assume some things to be true because we have long heard they are true, even in the absence of any supporting evidence that they *are* true (Rosenthal & Rosnow, 1984). Once clinicians and researchers began to question the underlying assumption that homosexuality was a mental disorder, this long-held belief appeared not to deserve the merit it had been granted.

The declassification of homosexuality as a mental disorder also raises some important issues about the cultural relativity of psychiatric diagnosis. How do we determine what is considered "pathological," what is "normal"? Until the early 1970s, homosexuality was a mental illness, a disease—and then it stopped being one. It is hard to contemplate a similar process occurring with physical illness. Could you imagine seeing a newspaper headline proclaiming, "Doctors determine that cancer is no longer a disease"? With the concept of mental illness, the role of culture must always be taken into account when regarding what is healthy and what is sick.

Violence against gay men and lesbians is a problem that has received increasing attention in the past several years. In the United States, anti-gay violence is believed to be the most prevalent kind of "hate crime," or crime motivated by the race, ethnicity, or other personal characteristic of the victim (Klinger & Stein, 1996). No adequate statistics are available on the incidence of such crimes, in large part because they often go unreported or undocumented. However, most documented anti-gay hate crimes are perpetrated by young men or teenagers who are typically acting in a group (Berrill, 1992).

Like any other assault, victims of hate crimes are highly vulnerable to experiencing PTSD or acute stress disorder, or symptoms thereof. In addition, victims of anti-gay violence are at risk for particular difficulties, such as the *secondary victimization* (Herek, 1995) that may result from disclosing one's sexual orientation, and the nature of the assault, to other people.

PROGNOSIS

Given the range of possible PTSD responses, Jonathan's experience could have been far more debilitating, and his was a good outcome. His impairment was severe for a brief period of time, but he then regained his pre-trauma level of functioning.

After those difficult first few months, his improvement continued with no major setbacks. One year after the assault, he felt that the worst of his ordeal was behind him, even though unexpected environmental triggers could still elicit strong anxiety and he still had occasional nightmares.

Jonathan's decision during therapy to shed his secrecy and tell selected people about the assault may have been quite important in his recovery. Ample research indicates that social support can play a crucial role in coping with traumatic life events (Janoff-Bulman, 1992).

Eighteen months after the assault, Jonathan read a newspaper article about an anti-gay attack that resulted in the death of the victim. Learning of this murder was extremely distressing to him. Immediately, it initiated a renewed burst of intrusive thoughts and vivid flashbacks of his own assault. He became anxious. However, his reaction to this assault included additional, newer responses. He felt a sense of identification with the victim, rage toward the assailants, and a deeper awareness that his was not an isolated event. The newspaper article mentioned an anti-gay violence project that had recently started in his city. Jonathan contacted them and offered to do volunteer work. He found this volunteer work quite helpful in his own residual process of healing from his assault.

Jonathan's choice to join a group combating anti-gay violence is one example of a strategy many traumatized people follow in a process of recovery: becoming involved in altruistic activity, often related to their particular traumatization (Janoff-Bulman, 1992). For example, the organization Mothers Against Drunk Driving was formed by parents with children who had died in alcohol-related car accidents; similarly, many people become involved in volunteer or charity work for a particular cause that has affected their lives.

Data on the course of PTSD suggest that, like Jonathan, many individuals recover from posttraumatic symptoms. But others maintain a chronic course, and still others have a long-delayed onset of impairment (Harvey, 1996; McFarlane, 1988; Ronis et al., 1996). Yet even with Jonathan and others for whom the symptoms subside, an important question remains: What does it mean to recover from a trauma?

Did Jonathan "recover"? Was he "cured"? Yes and no. On the one hand, he did recover: His maladaptive symptoms disappeared. He regained his ability to function well socially, at work, and at school. He stopped avoiding going out (as he had in the months after the assault) and became more re-engaged in life.

But even after he got better, the assault continued to have more subtle long-lasting, unwanted effects. For Jonathan, the world had changed. Even as the distressing intrusive images of the assault faded, the memory of that evening's unexpected terror, and the unforgettable knowledge of the rage and hate in his attackers' eyes, did not completely leave him. He had survived. His life was back on track. But a degree of wariness now entered into almost everything he did. He no longer felt so youthful or carefree as he once did, and he suspected that might never return.

CRITICAL THINKING QUESTIONS

1. Why is posttraumatic stress disorder a more accurate diagnosis for Jonathan than acute stress disorder? Generalized anxiety disorder?

2. If Jonathan's symptoms started one year after his assault, how, if at all, would this affect his diagnosis? Would this still be considered posttraumatic stress disorder?

3. What do you think might be important in the immediate aftermath of a traumatic event to help a person cope with the trauma?

4. Imagine that Jonathan was with a friend that evening, and both he and the friend were assaulted. However, what if Jonathan developed posttraumatic stress disorder, but the friend did not. What factors would you think might help to explain this?

5. Adolescent males are the most frequent perpetrators of anti-gay violence. What factors might contribute to this?

Panic Disorder with Agoraphobia

Conchita Morales was a 35-year-old research chemist who held a good job with a small pharmaceutical company. Despite her professional success and a comfortable income, Conchita lived a rather quiet, narrow life. In part, this was because she valued order, routine, and stability over excitement or adventure. To a greater degree, however, her small range of activities resulted from the profound anxiety she experienced whenever she attempted to step beyond the safe confines of her home and work environments.

Conchita suffered from frequent panic attacks—sudden episodes of uncontrollable anxiety that left her crippled with fear. She had endured these attacks on and off for years. She estimated that since her first panic attack at age 24 she had survived hundreds of recurrences, yet their frequency offered little comfort. In this case, experience was a poor teacher.

With each new attack, Conchita invariably felt the same terrible sensations. It started with a twinge of anxiety, followed by a half-hearted attempt to calm herself and pray that it would go away. Sometimes this worked, but far more frequently she only felt increased anxiety and a sinking, hopeless dread about what was to come. Within moments, she would be flooded with a terrifying panic. She felt dizzy and lightheaded. She gasped for air and could not catch her breath. Her body trembled all over and she perspired profusely. Her arms and legs tingled with painful, needle-like sensations. Everything seemed as if it were far away, distorted, and unreal. She hyperventilated so severely that she thought she was being strangled, and might faint or even die. And each time she faced the same catastrophic and paralyzing thoughts, as if she had never been through it before: What if this time it's a true medical emergency? What if it doesn't end? What if no help is available? Am I going to die?

Conchita considered herself fortunate in that she never experienced a bout of panic at work, so at least her anxiety did not jeopardize her job. On the contrary, work was a refuge for her: She felt most calm and at ease when in her laboratory or office, absorbed in a challenging problem or interacting with colleagues. She also felt safer when she was with one of her few friends or with Gregg, her boyfriend of the past several years. Instead, the vast majority of her panic attacks occurred when she was alone and driving. This was particularly true when Conchita drove on a new or unfamiliar road, or ventured just a few miles beyond her home or office.

When she had a panic attack, Conchita would most often pull off the road until the terror subsided, or would turn the car around to head home. Sometimes it took her all day to run a necessary errand, starting and stopping repeatedly as her anxiety dictated. In severe instances—perhaps a dozen times over the past several years— Conchita felt compelled to forego her planned destination and instead rushed to the nearest hospital. She would enter the emergency room and sit there, as quietly and unobtrusively as she could, to wait out the storm. She was too embarrassed to ask for medical attention, but it soothed her to know that help was available if she needed it. When the worst had passed, she would quietly get up and leave.

Over the years, Conchita had grown to tolerate these attacks, as unpleasant and debilitating as they were. Sometimes, to her relief, they would disappear for months on end. But they would then resurface, most often during times when work was particularly stressful, or if she hit a difficult patch with Gregg, or when a major life change seemed imminent. She also frequently felt depressed but could not determine whether it was the panic attacks themselves that caused her low mood.

Years earlier, a physician had prescribed her an anti-anxiety medication, Xanax, to treat the disorder. This helped to some degree. However, Conchita chose not to use the medication for two reasons. First, she did not feel comfortable with the possibility of becoming physically or psychologically dependent on Xanax or any other benzodiazapene (a class of drugs with the potential for addiction). Second, the panic attacks occurred intermittently and suddenly; Conchita did not see much purpose in taking medication on days when no attack would be happening, and what good was it to take a pill while driving, once an attack had already started?

Conchita finally sought psychological help for her panic when a crisis, in the form of a promotion, developed at work. The company was expanding, and her boss asked Conchita to assume more responsibility. This would include travel—both to other cities by airplane and (even more disturbing for her) frequent car trips, by herself, to towns several hours away. Conchita did not want to turn down this good career opportunity, but her anxiety became more severe as the promotion date moved closer. She felt anxious all the time, and her panic attacks became more frequent, occurring at least once daily. A few times she awoke at night gasping for breath, as if having an attack in her sleep—a new occurrence for her. She also developed a deeper, more pervasive feeling of general, "free-floating" anxiety that never seemed to leave.

Conchita recalled having seen an episode on a television news magazine about psychological treatments for anxiety disorders. She recognized that she probably had panic disorder and *agoraphobia* (a debilitating fear of being in places and situations from which escape would be difficult or embarrassing). Finally determining that she needed help, Conchita contacted a local clinic that specialized in anxiety disorders.

PSYCHOSOCIAL HISTORY

Conchita was born in Spain and spent the first years of her life in a poor rural Spanish town. When she was three years old her father left the family to emigrate to Puerto Rico; eighteen months later, Conchita and her mother joined him. The family achieved economic stability, and Conchita's parents had a second daughter, six years her junior. Conchita stayed in Puerto Rico until her early 20s.

Since her early years, Conchita was a quiet, studious child with few friends and a shy disposition. Her parents were extremely overprotective of her. She described her mother as a timid, anxious, religious woman who seldom left home other than to go to church or take care of necessary chores. Mrs. Morales was always fretting about something and fearful of a great many dangers that could harm the family. Although her father was less of a worrier, he too was quiet, and her mother's anxieties and fears seemed to permeate the household.

This situation became more pronounced when Conchita was eleven years old and she developed an unusual seizure disorder. Although she was quickly put on an anticonvulsant medication that completely stopped the seizures, a physician warned her parents that she might have a seizure again, at any time—perhaps with serious repercussions. Because of this ominous warning, for many years Conchita's mother feared letting her out of her sight. Until she was 16 years old, Conchita was forbidden to spend any time on her own. Other than during school hours, she was invariably in the company of her mother, another immediate family member, or one of the few adults her mother deemed responsible enough to take swift action in case of sudden medical emergency.

The most satisfying aspect of Conchita's childhood and adolescence was her schoolwork. She excelled academically and was regularly considered among the brightest children in her class. She attended college, but still lived at home and developed little social life. However, she continued to achieve academic success, particularly in the sciences. She spent two years after graduation teaching courses at her university. With encouragement from her professors, she decided to pursue graduate school in chemistry at a university in the northeastern United States.

Conchita's first panic attack occurred several months before leaving Puerto Rico for graduate school. Driving by herself one day she was suddenly overcome with a feeling of terror, along with a host of physical symptoms. She became light-headed, her heart pounded, she felt nauseous, and her entire body began trembling. She had no idea what was wrong and was terrified that she was about to die—was this a return of the long forgotten seizures, which the family had so feared? She hurried to a hospital emergency room. An initial examination and subsequent tests determined that she had not had a seizure, and there was no medical explanation for her somatic symptoms.

A few weeks later Conchita had a second attack, this time while teaching a class. A student asked a question for which she could not provide a quick answer. As she mulled over how to respond, she began feeling the same symptoms as in the car—but this time with the added dimension of a deep embarrassment that onlookers might witness her loss of composure. After a few moments of trembling and hyperventilating in front of the class, she managed to whisper that she did not feel well and needed to leave. She hurried out of the classroom and sought the privacy of a bathroom stall, where she sat and hid for fifteen minutes until the terror passed.

In part because of these episodes, Conchita's parents tried to persuade her not to leave home. They feared she was suffering from *ataques de nervios*, or fits of sudden unusual behavior, perhaps caused by malevolent spirits. They encouraged her to see an *esperitista*, or spiritual healer. However, Conchita persisted with her plans and, perhaps surprisingly, experienced no other episodes before her departure. In fact, other than one attack the day after her arrival, she remained free from full-blown attacks for most of the four years she spent in graduate school.

Shortly before completing her doctoral degree, however, when Conchita's graduation meant that she needed to look for a job and perhaps relocate, the attacks returned. At first intermittent and sporadic—perhaps once every few weeks—her panic then became more steady and frequent. By the time she sought psychological treatment, and for several years up until then, she sometimes experienced several attacks a week, even several a day.

Conchita had been dating Gregg for four years. This was her first serious relationship. He, too, was a quiet and reserved man. They spent a lot of time together and occasionally talked about marriage, yet communicated very little about matters of emotional or psychological importance to them. Gregg knew about Conchita's panic attacks, but they were seldom discussed. For her part, Conchita felt safe when around Gregg, as if his presence inoculated her against having an attack. She rarely experienced a panic attack in his presence. But she also refrained from mentioning her anxiety too frequently, both out of shame and a fear that he would end the relationship if he knew the severity of her problem.

CONCEPTUALIZATION

Conchita suffers from panic disorder with agoraphobia. As detailed in the DSM-IV, this diagnosis has several components.

First, a person with panic disorder experiences "recurrent, unexpected panic attacks followed by at least one month of persistent concern about having another panic attack, or worry about the possible implications or consequences of the panic attacks, or a significant behavioral change related to the attacks" (APA, 1994, p. 397). In specifying what constitutes a panic attack, the DSM-IV includes a long list of possible somatic, cognitive, and emotional symptoms. *Somatic* symptoms include palpitations, pounding heart, or accelerated heart rate; sweating; trembling or shaking; sensations of shortness of breath or smothering; feeling of choking; chest pain or discomfort; nausea or abdominal distress; feeling dizzy, unsteady, lightheaded, or faint; parathesias (numbness or tingling sensations); and chills or hot flashes. *Cognitive* symptoms include derealization (feelings of unreality), depersonalization (being detached from oneself), and the terrifying belief that one is dying, going crazy, or losing control. The primary *emotional* component of panic is an intense fear or discomfort.

For a bout of anxiety to be considered a panic attack, at least four of these somatic and cognitive components must be present. The symptoms escalate rapidly, usually peaking within ten minutes. They last for a discrete period of time—at least several minutes and rarely longer than half an hour.

There are three types of panic attacks. In *unexpected* (or *uncued*) attacks, a person experiences an attack as occuring suddenly, "out of the blue," with no known trigger. In *situationally bound* (or *cued*) attacks, certain environmental situations or cues almost invariably lead to an attack. This is often the case in specific phobias, such as when a person with a specific profound fear—of heights perhaps, or snakes, or flying in airplanes—almost always experiences panic in the feared circumstance. *Situationally predisposed* attacks are most apt to happen in specific situations yet do not always occur. This was the case for Conchita, whose panic attacks were most likely to occur while driving, even though she was often able to drive without an attack occurring.

Not all individuals who experience panic attacks have panic disorder. The disorder is diagnosed only when the attacks occur on a recurrent basis or when a person's functioning is severely impaired due to the fear of having a panic attack.

Agoraphobia, the second part of Conchita's diagnosis, relates to avoidance behaviors that develop in response to anxiety. There are three main criteria for agoraphobia (APA, 1994 pp. 396–397):

A. Anxiety about being in places or situations from which escape might be difficult (or embarrassing) or in which help may not be available in the event of having an unexpected or situationally predisposed panic attack or panic-like symptoms.

B. The situations are avoided (e.g., travel is restricted) or else endured with marked distress or anxiety about having panic attack or panic-like symptoms, or require the presence of a companion.

C. The anxiety or phobic avoidance is not better accounted for by another mental disorder.

Panic disorder is classified as either with or without agoraphobia—in other words, the person does or does not develop avoidance behaviors in response to the panic attacks, or is able to engage in anxiety-provoking activities but only under great duress. Conchita may be considered to have panic disorder *with* agoraphobia in that her panic attacks lead her to restrict her sphere of travel, she suffers "marked distress" when driving alone, and she drives more comfortably when with a companion.

For some people, agoraphobia is much more restrictive than it is for Conchita. In situations of severe agoraphobia, a person may become extremely incapacitated, perhaps to a point that he or she is completely housebound or unable to venture more than a few blocks from home.

Although it may not warrant a formal diagnosis, it is important to note that Conchita also has symptoms of *generalized anxiety disorder*, characterized by a diffuse sense of anxiety and worry.

TREATMENT

In the last two decades, much research has been conducted regarding panic disorder, particularly in regard to treatment options. In large part, this is because panic disorder, with or without agoraphobia, seems particularly well tailored to behavioral and cognitive-behavioral interventions (Barlow, 1997). Several such treatment models are available (Craske & Barlow, 1993; Michelson & Marchione, 1991). Medication has also proven helpful in the treatment of panic disorder—although in the absence of psychological treatment, medication alone is apt to lead to relapse after the medication is discontinued (Clark et al., 1994; Klerman et al., 1993).

Conchita's treatment, which spanned seven months, was primarily a cognitive-behavioral psychotherapy. It also included two additional components that Conchita pursued on her own—yoga and meditation.

Conchita had a lengthy intake assessment when she arrived at the Anxiety Disorders Clinic. This included a thorough review of her symptoms, a review of her childhood and family history, and a physical examination to determine if her panic disorder was related to an underlying medical condition (which it seemed not to be). Conchita was then assigned to work with Dr. William Roberts, a cognitive-behavioral psychologist. She also was given the option of concurrent treatment with medication. She decided to leave this open as a future possibility but preferred to try addressing her problems, at least at first, psychologically.

Initial weekly psychotherapy sessions focused on educating Conchita about her disorder. Dr. Roberts explained what was known about some of the physiological and cognitive mechanisms relevant to panic attacks. He recommended two books for her to read—one a more "hands-on," practical self-help approach, which they would refer to throughout her treatment, and the other a more scientific work, which Conchita found helpful given her interests and background. Over the first few weeks Conchita read these books eagerly.

The early sessions of psychotherapy also focused on building a rapport between Dr. Roberts and Dr. Morales (this is how they addressed one another, at least in their first meetings). Regardless of theoretical orientation, an important foundation of any treatment is the *treatment alliance,* or the collaborative working relationship between the two individuals. In this situation, Dr. Roberts was particularly interested in learning about Conchita's cultural background, which differed from his. His aim was to understand her better as a person, as well as to learn about any culturally related issues or conflicts that might be contributing to Conchita's distress.

For example, he asked what it was like for Conchita to be living away from home, on the mainland. What were her parents' values, and how were they the same or different from hers? Did she feel tension between her traditional, religious upbringing and her current life? How did being involved in an interracial relationship affect her and her family relationships? Conchita had mentioned *ataques de nervios* during the intake—did she see this as a relevant description of her difficulties? (She said she felt more comfortable instead with the concept of panic disorder). They agreed that it was important to keep these cultural considerations in mind, and Dr. Roberts invited Conchita to inform him about particular cultural issues whenever they seemed relevant. He would do the same.

Looking then at the specifics of Conchita's anxiety problems, Dr. Roberts identified three interrelated components: 1) the role of *anticipatory anxiety* in fostering panic attacks; 2) managing the panic attacks themselves; and 3) counteracting the avoidance behaviors that Conchita developed in response to her panic.

Regarding anticipatory anxiety, Dr. Roberts helped Conchita see the role that "fear of fear" played in perpetuating her disorder. Recall that once Conchita experienced a minor twinge of anxiety, she immediately began to worry that another panic attack was imminent—and this worry then often became a prime contributing factor. To begin combatting this vicious cycle, Dr. Roberts worked with Conchita to help her become more aware of her *automatic thoughts* (thoughts that come to us so quickly and habitually that we may take them for granted, or not even recognize their presence).

Conchita came to realize that whenever she was in the throes of a panic attack or felt that an attack was imminent, she could not shake the belief that she might die or be stranded alone without help. Not only was she frightened by her physical symptoms, but as she thought about it, she realized that the vivid image of her mother's reaction, years ago, to her unexpected seizures had never left her. She had not had a seizure since she was nine years old, and the medical evidence suggested that a seizure would now be no more likely for her than anyone else, but Conchita had never fully relinquished her fear that another one might happen.

Conchita at first bemoaned that her terrifying thoughts about dying or becoming stranded were "uncontrollable." She told Dr. Roberts that even though she *knew* they were maladaptive, she was unable to stop them—"how can you simply change what you think?" Dr. Roberts acknowledged that these automatic thoughts would not go away so easily—but neither need they be given the full, unchallenged power that Conchita usually granted them.

Using a method of *cognitive restructuring*, Dr. Roberts helped Conchita begin slowly to counteract these irrational ideas with more reasonable ones. In sessions, they practiced self-statements that Conchita could use when she was anxious, or when she recognized she was thinking irrationally: "Yes, this *is* frightening, but I'm not dying . . . ." "This is only a panic attack, it will end soon . . . ." "I am *not* having a seizure . . . ." "I can survive this."

Dr. Roberts also helped Conchita devise and implement several pragmatic strategies to increase a sense of security when driving. For example, they made a cassette tape together, which detailed what Conchita could do when she started feeling anxious. The tape was quite specific, and Conchita kept it in her car. It outlined a series of actions she might take in case of mounting anxiety, such as opening the window for fresh air; practicing deep breathing exercises; listening to soothing music; pulling over for a few moments if it was safe to do so; and focusing on specific details of driving or the road or her trip, rather than allowing her thoughts to stray. The tape also emphasized the new self-statements Conchita could repeat to herself to counteract her irrational automatic thoughts.

To address Conchita's fear of being stranded while driving, Dr. Roberts encouraged her to buy a cellular telephone for her car and to prepare a list of numbers to call in case of emergency, so that in the event of actual peril she could quickly attain help. Conchita agreed with these suggestions and put them into practice. As it turned out, she rarely used the phone, but just knowing it was there further reduced Conchita's concern that a crisis situation would arise over which she had no control.

These interventions began to have an impact relatively quickly. Conchita's panic attacks did not stop altogether, but more often than in the past she succeeded in halting what would have been, just weeks earlier, another attack. Perhaps as important as these specific strategies, Conchita started to feel a change in her attitude about her anxiety. Previously, she had felt that panic was something beyond her control, that she was helpless to fight it. Even though she still continued to experience attacks, a new perception was evolving: She was beginning to feel that this was something over which she could exercise more control than she thought previously, that she was not powerless. This belief itself became an important and useful tool.

Once Conchita started feeling more secure in her progress, Dr. Roberts introduced a new phase of treatment, one that would further emphasize this issue of control. He indicated that the next step was for Conchita actually to induce panic attacks in herself, during their meetings. By imagining frightening situations and forcing herself to simulate the physiological sensations of panic—by hyperventilating, or spinning rapidly in her chair, or shaking her head rapidly side to side—she could trigger a panic attack. They would then have the opportunity, together, to see how Conchita reacted in the actual situation and what she might be able to do to calm herself.

Just the mention of this possibility made Conchita so anxious that she did not think much additional imagination would be necessary to induce a panic attack—she could feel one starting right at that time! When she questioned the necessity of this aspect of treatment, Dr. Roberts explained a current theory of panic, which Conchita had already learned from her reading.

For some people, the central nervous system may misinterpret normal physiological functions as if the person were in the midst of a grave, life-threatening crisis. These sensory over-reactions are then further exaggerated by a person's learned fear of fear—i.e., feeling anxious becomes a trigger to feel *more* anxious, and so on. In this manner, anxiety may quickly snowball into huge proportions, even though it started simply as an over-reaction to everyday, expected physiological events.

By inducing panic attacks in a safe and controlled setting (a process called *interoceptive exposure*, because "interoceptive" refers to a person's reactions to his or her own internal bodily sensations), Dr. Roberts could help Conchita learn that while her body was reacting as if she were in great danger, any real threat to her was probably far smaller. He reminded her, for example, that as frightening as it was for her to hyperventilate, people did not die from hyperventilation.

Conchita continued to be uneasy about proceeding with this phase of treatment, but agreed with Dr. Roberts about its potential benefit. In fact, the process was not nearly as upsetting as she worried it might be. Without much effort, she was able to induce panic attacks in front of Dr. Roberts. With his assistance in talking her through it, Conchita began training herself to think that the anxiety that was flooding through her did not indicate a real threat, and she could survive it. This realization was of great help, and she continued to gain mastery over her panic.

Given that the goal of treatment was to help Conchita's panic disorder in real life, not in the therapy office, she also understood the necessity of the next aspect of treatment: to induce these panic attacks on her own, at home. Here, too, Conchita was anxious about moving ahead, but in time found this a key exercise, and she forced herself into, and then down from, a panicky state several times per week.

Three months into treatment, Conchita mentioned that she had always been curious about stress-reduction techniques such as yoga and meditation but had never pursued these. She wondered if these would be a helpful adjunct to psychotherapy. Dr. Roberts encouraged Conchita to explore these interests (some research [Kabat-Zinn et al., 1992] indicates that meditation-based stress reduction programs can provide substantial relief from agoraphobic and panic symptoms). After learning these skills, Conchita began practicing them on a daily basis. At first she was uncertain if they made any difference. In time, however, she began to feel a lessening of anxiety in general, not just panic, and assumed that these practices were contributing to this change.

As therapy continued, Dr. Roberts and Conchita began to expand the material they covered to include other topics. They talked about the pride and anxiety Conchita felt about being a successful Latina woman in a field where most of her colleagues were white men. Conchita also talked some about her complicated emotions about having moved to the mainland. She liked the "openness" of American culture and the career and personal opportunities she had here. But she also felt guilty about being a "bad" daughter because she had moved far away from home and was breaking away from the values she was raised with. She had not fulfilled the role that her family, and her cultural tradition, expected of her: to get married, raise children, and stay near home to take care of her aging parents. Conchita did not know if these issues related to her panic disorder but saw how they created a constant "hum" of underlying stress that was always with her.

Conchita and William (this is how they referred to each other now) also talked about Conchita's early family history, and in particular the impact her parents' overprotectiveness might have had on her. More generally, Dr. Roberts helped Conchita see the generally anxious and worried tone of her family's style—something she had never previous thought about. With these discussions, it sometimes became confusing for Conchita to separate cultural issues from familial issues, and it took a while for Conchita to realize that hers was an anxious *family*, regardless of her cultural background.

Conchita made good progress in mastering her symptoms. With increasing success, she was able to apply her new skills in most situations, even in particularly stressful ones. She experienced panic attacks far less frequently and was more adept at curtailing her anxiety before it mushroomed into an attack. Five months after treatment started, she was able to fulfill her new work responsibilities (driving and flying to new destinations) with relative comfort. She had broadened the length of time and distance she could drive on her own. She was still often anxious, but to a far less degree than she had been, and now only rarely to the extent of a full-blown attack.

Conchita decided to terminate psychotherapy, with William's support. As is not unusual, this decision led to a brief resurgence of her symptoms. Two days after deciding to end treatment she experienced her most severe panic attack in months and worried that all her gains had been lost. However, William told Conchita that such a brief setback sometimes happened, and she renewed her decision to try and make it on her own. They formulated a plan for termination, which included meeting every other week for six weeks, with follow-up appointments at one month and three months. When Conchita stopped treatment, she continued to practice her new skills, along with meditation and yoga, and remained largely symptom-free for the next several years.

Multiaxial DSM-IV Diagnosis at Time of Termination

Axis I:	Panic Disorder with Agoraphobia CONDITION: IMPROVED
Axis II:	No diagnosis
Axis III:	History of seizure disorder in childhood
Axis IV:	Job promotion
Axis V:	*Treatment Onset:* 60 (symptoms causing moderate difficulty in life functioning) *Termination:* 80 (slight impairment in social and occupational functioning)

DISCUSSION

Perhaps the poet W. H. Auden was correct when he labeled our era "the age of anxiety" (Auden, 1947)—anxiety is a common and often distressing part of modern life. Along with depression it is the most frequent presenting problem for individuals who seek psychotherapy. Yet despite its commonness in the commotion of our fast-paced society, anxiety is not new—as is made clear in the ancient roots of our many words that describe shades of being anxious.

"Anxiety" derives from the Latin "angere," meaning to choke or strangle—an apt description of the visceral experience of being caught in anxiety's grip. Greek mythology provides the source for "phobia" and "panic." Phobos was an attendant of Ares, the god of war, who provoked fear in his enemies so that they would flee from him. Panikos of Pan, the playful god of woods and shepherds, had the ability to inspire a tremendous sense of terror, disorder, and chaos in others—hence, words such as panic and pandemonium. And agoraphobia literally means fear of open spaces, dating back to the open-air Greek market, the agora.

Modern classification of anxiety disorders underwent a major change from the DSM-II (APA, 1968) to DSM-III (APA, 1980). With the DSM-III, for the first time, different subcategories of anxiety—panic, generalized anxiety, simple phobias, social phobias, and posttraumatic stress—were separated and defined, allowing for more precise research and treatment design. Until then, the DSM classification system highlighted two types of anxiety disorders: an "anxiety neurosis" and a "phobic neurosis."

Panic, with its fits of sudden, overwhelming terror, is distinct from the free-floating, pervasive worry of generalized anxiety. Panic disorder is thought to affect between 3% and 5% of the general population (Kessler et al., 1994), but the actual experience of isolated or occasional panic attacks is likely much higher. In one study (Norton, Dorward & Cox, 1986), thirty-five percent of a nonclinical sample had experienced at least one panic attack in the previous year. Similarly, many people experience "subthreshold" or "limited symptom" panic attacks—distressing bouts of intense anxiety that, while disruptive, do not meet full diagnostic criteria for panic (Klerman et al., 1991). Among those who suffer from a full-blown panic disorder, roughly one-third also develop agoraphobia (Robins & Regier, 1991).

Panic disorder most commonly begins in late adolescence through the mid 20s. It is more common in women than men, for reasons that are not fully understood. Most people with the disorder report that their first panic attack occurred spontaneously, with no clearly identifiable antecedent. Yet this spontaneity may not reveal the complete story—on careful inspection, it is often the case that a person has experienced a major life stressor some time in the year preceding a first attack (Craske & Barlow, 1993; Roy-Byrne, Geraci & Uhde, 1986).

Theoretical Perspectives

Psychoanalytic theories have much to say about the nature and function of anxiety in general but little to say about panic in specific (Josephs, 1994). This is because psychoanalytic theories tend not to differentiate between panic and more general anxiety. However, a psychoanalytic approach to thinking about Conchita's case would look for unconscious connections between Conchita's early years and her subsequent development of panic. In particular, a therapist with an Object Relations orientation would explore how powerful fears reaching back to Conchita's infancy and early childhood—fears of separation, abandonment, or helplessness—might unconsciously perpetuate her disorder. (Object Relations is a branch of psychoanalytic theory that highlights the centrality of relationships, and our unconscious models of relational patterns, in psychological functioning. These unconscious relational patterns are believed to be rooted in very early experiences.)

For example, Conchita panicked almost exclusively when she was by herself, without a companion. Did this have roots in childhood events, such as her early, lengthy separation from her father, her lack of any independence or privacy as an adolescent, or her parents' grave fear of the "serious repercussions" of another seizure? Despite the competence that she had demonstrated in her school and work life, did she unconsciously see herself as helpless when on her own? Possible, if circumstantial, support for these unconscious connections comes from the timing of Conchita's early attacks, in how they occurred during periods of impending or actual separation—first when preparing to leave home, and then again when preparing to leave graduate school.

Similarly, a learning theory approach would also turn to Conchita's childhood to determine if certain anxious behaviors were modeled and reinforced. For example, we know that Conchita's mother was anxiety-ridden. She may quite possibly even have had an undiagnosed case of agoraphobia, given the limited scope of her activity. Did Conchita's mother provide a model for Conchita to react with fear or avoidance to new or foreign situations? Did Conchita experience a *secondary gain* to her markedly overprotected adolescence—in other words, was there something inadvertently reinforcing about being the focus of so much concern and worry, such as her parents' attention?

One prominent cognitive theory of panic disorder proposes that panic attacks have more to do with distorted thinking than with behavioral reinforcement. According to this theory, panic results from the "catastrophic misinterpretation of certain bodily sensations" (Clark, 1986, p. 461). In other words, external cues may be less relevant than internal distortions. For example, a person may misinterpret minor heart palpitations as a potential heart attack or confused thinking as indicating that he or she is going insane. These misinterpretations then lead to greater anxiety, leading to more heart palpitations, leading to greater anxiety, and so on, in a manner that can quickly spiral out of control. Support for this theory comes from the success of cognitive therapies that seek to correct and counteract these catastrophic misinterpretations (Clark et al., 1988), and we can certainly see the influence of these ideas in Dr. Roberts's approach to treatment with Conchita.

Biological theorists emphasize the neurochemical aspects of panic, along with evidence that supports a genetic component to the disorder. In one study, first-degree relatives of individuals with panic disorder were almost 12 times more likely to experience panic attacks themselves than were first-degree relatives of non-panic disordered controls—a finding that did not extend to generalized anxiety disorder (Crowe et al., 1983). Twin studies (Perna et al., 1997; Torgeson, 1983) also support a biological component to the disorder, with monozygotic (identical) twins more likely to share a diagnosis of panic disorder than dizygotic (fraternal) twins. Perhaps Conchita was biologically predisposed to panic disorder (we know of her mother's anxious nature, but this fact by itself could indicate either a biological or environmental etiology).

Three neurotransmitters—norepinephrine, serotonin, and GABA (gamma-aminobutric acid)—have been heavily studied to determine their roles in escalating or inhibiting a physiological fear response. One current theory implicates a portion of the brain stem, the locus ceruleus, in panic disorder. Relying primarily on norepinephrine as its messenger, the locus ceruleus functions roughly like an alarm system, indicating an impending threat to the rest of the central nervous system; panic disorder may arise from dysregulation of this system.

It is worth noting that the same neurotransmitters related to panic—particularly serotonin and norepinephrine—also are crucial in regulating mood and depression. This may help to explain why depression and panic disorder have a high degree of *comorbidity*—many individuals with panic disorder also suffer from depression, either concurrently or in the years following the onset of panic (Robins & Regier, 1991). Some theorists even suggest that panic disorder is more closely related to depression than to generalized anxiety.

In fact, the medications that are often most helpful in the treatment of panic disorder are antidepressants, not anxiolytics (anti-anxiety agents). Although the effectiveness of some newer benzodiazapenes in treating panic disorder has made the puzzle more complex, most psychopharmacological treatment of panic involves the use of several classes of antidepressants—monoamine oxidase inhibitors (MAO-I's), tricyclic antidepressants, and the newer selective serotonin reuptake inhibitors (SSRI's) such as Fluoxetine (Prozac)—instead of the benzodiazapenes that help in the treatment of generalized anxiety. Over the past several years, the SSRI's have emerged as the leading psychopharmacological intervention with panic disorder (Jefferson, 1997; Sheehan & Sheehan, 1996).

Panic and Agoraphobia

The relationship between panic disorder and agoraphobia remains yet to be fully understood. Despite some interesting theories, it remains uncertain why some individuals with panic disorder develop agoraphobia and others do not.

One view regarding the etiology of agoraphobia places primary emphasis on the role of *two-factor learning* (Mowrer, 1960), or learning that involves both classical and operant conditioning. In this view, recurrent panic attacks, in a variety of situations, serve as multiple unconditioned stimuli that lead to avoidance behavior. Through classical conditioning, external cues associated with an attack become conditioned aversive stimuli. For example, a panic attack while food shopping may result in grocery stores becoming a conditioned stimulus for a response of fear. Another panic attack while banking may lead to bank machines becoming another conditioned stimulus for fear, and so on. Avoidance of shopping and banking is then maintained by operant conditioning because escaping anxiety by avoiding these activities serves as a negative reinforcer.[1] Accruing bit by bit, it becomes easy to see how a person's world may thus become very limited.

Such a model seems logically plausible. However, its validity has been questioned (Thorpe & Hecker, 1991), in part because it does not accurately match the experience of most people with agoraphobia. Avoidance behaviors do not develop in such a specific orderly manner, with various pieces systematically piled on top of one another. Nor can the two-factor model answer the question of why some people with panic disorder develop agoraphobia while in the same circumstances, others do not.

To examine these differences, various linkages have been proposed between childhood disorders and adult agoraphobia. Some data suggest that adults with agoraphobia are more likely to have a childhood history of separation anxiety disorder, overanxious disorder, or school phobia, in comparison with people with panic disorder without agoraphobia (Gittleman & Klein, 1973; Shear, 1996). Similarly, perhaps those who develop agoraphobia are more dependent, more generally fearful, or less able to cope with anger. Or agoraphobia may be most likely to develop from panic disorder among individuals who label all arousal states as anxiety or fear, who have a poor ability to connect feelings with external events, and who have panic attacks that take on arbitrary cues (Goldstein & Chambless, 1978).

As of yet, no conclusive data have resolved these questions, in part because such studies tend to rely on subjective self-reports about childhood, which are easily subject to distortion. However, learning more about this important question is apt to further hone our understanding and treatment of both panic disorder and agoraphobia in the years ahead.

---

[1]Recall that *negative reinforcement* is not the same as *punishment*. The goal of negative reinforcement is to increase the likelihood of a certain behavior or response by removing a noxious stimulus. In this case, the person's goal is a reduction of anxiety, and avoiding anxiety-provoking situations increases the likelihood of reaching the goal.

Cultural Considerations

Cultures vary in the expression of psychological distress, and diagnoses that are known in one culture may be described—and experienced—differently across the world. A disorder known as *ataque de nervios* (Conchita's parents' explanation for her distress) is prevalent in many Hispanic cultures (Rivera-Arzola & Ramos-Grenier, 1997). In an *ataque de nervios*, a person experiences sudden, discrete episodes of dramatically changed behavior accompanied by a host of somatic symptoms, such as hyperventilation, heart palpitations, and trembling. As this description indicates, many features of *ataques de nervios* overlap with the DSM-IV description of panic attacks. However, an important difference between the two is that fear, the central emotional feature of panic, may be completely absent in an *ataque de nervios*.

Because Conchita saw her own situation as panic disorder, she was able to participate in a psychotherapy that aimed to alleviate her symptoms. But this is not always the case; in order to be effective, psychological treatment must fit with, and be respectful of, the cultural beliefs of the person seeking help. For example, in Puerto Rican communities, *esperitistas*, or traditional spiritual folk healers, play a central role in the culture. These spiritual healers are not considered to be psychotherapists. Yet much of what *esperitistas* do—inquire about emotional and physical distress, offer support, and suggest pragmatic solutions—may not be all that different from what mental health practitioners do (Garrison, 1977). In general, the more that an individual or family has been "acculturated" into the mainstream society, the greater the likelihood of seeking help from a psychologist or psychiatrist (Canino & Canino, 1993).

PROGNOSIS

Conchita remained symptom-free for approximately two years, at which time she recontacted Dr. Roberts. She had again begun experiencing panic, following the break-up of her relationship with Gregg. She met with Dr. Roberts for a few months to help weather this major transition. When she felt the worst had passed and again gained control over her panic attacks, she stopped treatment.

Conchita's outcome was a good one: With her two periods of psychotherapy, the ongoing practice of the skills she learned, and her now regular routine of meditation and yoga, she was able to greatly reduce the interference of anxiety and panic in her life. For many people, however, panic disorder becomes a chronic ailment, with marked periods of impaired functioning over a long period of time.

Several longitudinal studies suggest that while a substantial minority of individuals (perhaps up to 40%), like Conchita, are symptom-free years after treatment, many others remain incapacitated by anxiety, continue to experience occasional panic attacks, or develop major depression (Klerman et al., 1993, Pollack & Otto, 1997). One typical pattern is for a person to enjoy extended periods of improved functioning, only to be followed by renewed episodic bouts of panic. Poorer prognosis is associated with more severe and debilitating symptomatology at the onset of the disorder, a history of trauma, or a comorbid mood or personality disorder, (Klerman et al., 1993, Marchand et al., 1998; Michelson et al., 1998). Still, with active new developments in both psychopharmacological and psychological interventions, the treatment of panic disorder is one area in which clinical psychology has made great strides, and holds even greater promise, in bringing relief to those who suffer.

CRITICAL THINKING QUESTIONS

1. How is panic disorder similar to generalized anxiety disorder? How is it different?
2. If Conchita's panic attacks began a few weeks after witnessing a terrible car accident, what other possible diagnoses would you consider?
3. What factors might contribute to panic disorder being more prevalent in women than men?
4. Conchita grew up in a culture quite different from mainstream American culture. What significance, if any, do you think this has in her panic disorder? How, if at all, should it affect treatment?
5. How does the concept of "fear of fear" relate to agoraphobia?

Dysthymic Disorder

As is often the case, Sharleen Washington thought about seeing a psychotherapist for a long time before she actually did anything about it. She had gone through the same discussion in her head many times. Yes, she had problems—but were they really bad enough to seek help? Wasn't therapy only for people who were "sick"? Why share one's dirty laundry with a stranger? Shouldn't a 32-year-old woman be able to solve her difficulties on her own?

It was only with constant prodding from her older sister, Janette, that she finally decided it might be worthwhile to speak with a professional. Janette had started psychotherapy one year earlier, and Sharleen was impressed with the changes she saw in her—she seemed more confident, more self-assured, less self-demeaning. And Sharleen realized that even though she somehow always managed to get along alright in life, she was unhappy, lonely, and isolated—and had been feeling the way she did for several years, with barely any relief.

As she half-heartedly joked with Janette, her life looked fine "on paper." She had been married for seven years to Roland, whom she met while at college. Together they had a three-year-old daughter, Danielle. Until becoming a mother, she had worked as a loan officer in the financial aid office of a university. She now stayed at home and raised Danielle, hoping to return to work when Danielle started school. Sharleen and Roland were financially stable and owned their own small home in a safe, pleasant neighborhood.

But something was clearly wrong. Sharleen could not recall the last time she felt happy. In fact, when she reflected back, she had to admit that she had been feeling somewhat depressed for years. Nostalgically, she remembered her high school and college days, and her early twenties—in comparison, how content she had been! What had happened? Those times seemed so long ago.

Now, in most everything she did, Sharleen felt apathetic, sad, tired, or simply "flat." Things did not seem to matter that much to her, or mean what they used to. She and Roland rarely socialized, and drifted away from the few friends they had made earlier in their courtship and marriage. They still belonged to the church they had joined years earlier, but now rarely worshiped there or took part in other aspects of church life.

Activities and hobbies Sharleen once found pleasurable had lost their appeal. For example, she had previously enjoyed going to classical music concerts and taking long walks in the countryside near their home. But now when she went for a walk, her mind would drift off and lodge on some current unhappiness or worry. She would spend the entire time ruminating about some minor household irritation, or a conflict with Roland, or simply her own unhappiness. The same thing happened the last few times she attended a concert—she could not concentrate on the music. In fact, she had a hard time concentrating on anything, even losing interest in the brief magazine articles she once relied on for pleasant distraction. Sharleen gradually started withdrawing from the things she once enjoyed.

At the same time, her self-esteem plummeted. Sharleen said she had "never ever felt great" about herself, but now things were far worse. She constantly berated herself for being "stupid" or "lazy." She saw herself as a failure as a wife, mother, and daughter. When she was in contact with other mothers of young children, she inevitably compared her parenting skills to theirs, and came to the conclusion, "They're better mothers than me." When her old supervisor at work once telephoned to see if she would be available to return to work, she mistrusted his sincerity—she assumed only that "they must be really desperate" to find somebody.

As might be expected, these difficulties affected Sharleen's marriage and family life. For a while, she and Roland seemed to be constantly irritable with one another, with many of their interactions ending in bickering or a larger fight. But for the past year or two, these disagreements had given way to an uneasy, distant quiet. They fought less often than they did but also now spent little time communicating with each other or doing things together. For his part, Roland spent an increasing amount of time with a few friends he had made on his own, through work. And Sharleen found herself increasingly impatient with Danielle, despite daily reminders to herself to be patient and monitor her temper.

In general, Sharleen described her life as "drudgery." She knew she was down but was she "depressed"? Sharleen remembered a co-worker, years ago, who had suffered from a severe major depression. That woman had needed to leave her job, and even spend time in a psychiatric hospital, because her depression had become so serious. Sharleen did not see herself like that: She had never missed a day of work, or other important responsibility, because of her down mood. Her sleeping and eating habits were basically normal. And even though most mornings she would wake up feeling blue, she never really thought about committing suicide or dying. But at the same time, she could not understand why she did not feel better than she did.

And despite her chronic unhappiness, Sharleen could not pinpoint exactly what was wrong. Maybe it was all in her own mind, and she was just being a complainer. She chastised herself for being so negative—a voice echoed in her head, "grow up, you're a big girl." Yet inevitably these "pep talks" failed and she continued to be sad, with her self-criticism only making her feel worse.

Janette had been gently pressuring Sharleen to speak with a therapist for a long time. So had Roland—although when he said it, she took this as an insult or criticism, rather than sympathetic concern. Finally, acknowledging that her difficulties were worse than she could handle herself, and feeling hopeless that things would ever change, Sharleen agreed to seek professional help.

PSYCHOSOCIAL HISTORY

Sharleen was the second of four children, born into a middle-class African-American family in a stable, predominantly African-American neighborhood in Philadelphia. Her sister Janette was a year older than she. Her two other siblings were a brother and sister, seven and eight years younger. Because of this age difference, Sharleen felt that the family actually had two sets of children—Janette and she, and then her younger brother and sister.

Sharleen recalled her early years as happy. She idealized her mother when she was young. She was rather shy and had few friends but was content to stay at home and help out around the house, enjoying the role of "mother's little helper." However, when she was twelve years old the family moved across the country. For Sharleen, this was a difficult and unwelcome change. For one thing, the move took them away from extended family. Sharleen missed the regular contact she had grown accustomed to in her neighborhood with her grandparents, aunts and uncles, and several cousins.

Further, Sharleen felt she did not fit in with the other children in her new school and community. There were few other nonwhite families in the new town. Sharleen was teased, and sometimes bullied, by other children. For the first time, she was subjected to schoolyard racial epithets. In fact, the entire family felt that they were not made to feel welcome in their new neighborhood, and assumed that race was a factor in their cool reception.

Compounding these stresses, her father's new job did not work out well financially. The family began to struggle economically, and Sharleen's mother went to work for the first time. This combination of economic difficulty, social isolation, and racism began to take its toll on the family. Mr. Washington, whom Sharleen had earlier regarded as easy-going and relaxed, grew more withdrawn and depressed. Mrs. Washington, on the other hand, lost some of her merry disposition and frequently made bitter, angry comments about their situation.

Because of her mother's new job, Sharleen was given much more responsibility around the home. In particular, she started shouldering the burden of caring for her younger siblings until her mother came home from work. After school, she was obligated to return home to babysit. Now, rather than enjoying her role as mother's helper, she began to see this as an unfair imposition—especially since Janette, who was involved in after-school athletics, did not have to make the same sacrifices. Still, Sharleen rarely complained—and why bother? When she expressed any dissatisfaction or annoyance, her mother scolded her. Mrs. Washington more than once responded to Sharleen's complaints with a pointed, "Life ain't a picnic for me, either."

Academically, Sharleen was consistently an attentive, average student, responsible and competent in her work. Throughout school she usually had one close girlfriend, but these friendships did not last long. In her sophomore year, she joined the high school orchestra, and this activity became the highlight of her school life. Through the social connections she made there, she felt like she was becoming more a part of things, and began to enjoy her high school years. After graduating she attended a two-year college, where she earned an associate's degree. She then went to work and continued taking courses at night school, hoping one day to earn her bachelor's degree. She had worked at the university financial aid office for several years before her daughter Danielle was born.

Before meeting Roland, Sharleen had a few other dating experiences, none of them serious. She and Roland dated for several years before deciding to get married. Sharleen was never sure that she was in love in Roland but agreed to marry him because she felt safe and comfortable when she was with him. She also worried that if she did not marry him, nobody else would be interested in her.

Over the years, Sharleen was aware of how her feelings toward her parents had grown more sour. Characteristically, she felt guilty about this. She was unsure what had happened—had they actually changed as people, or did she now simply see them differently? Was she being ungrateful? She now viewed her mother, whom she had so revered in childhood, as a critical, negative woman, quick to blame others for any difficulty. Her father seemed uninterested in much of anything and seemed to spend all his time immobilized in front of the television (Sharleen thought she was more like him than any other member of the family). Over the past few years, she had less and less contact with them or with her younger siblings. She no longer had friends from her high school or college years. Only she and Janette had remained close.

CONCEPTUALIZATION

Sharleen meets diagnostic criteria for dysthymic disorder (or dysthymia), one of the mood disorders described in DSM-IV (APA, 1994). Dysthymia is conceptualized as a chronic, low-level depression. It lacks the intensity or severity of Major Depressive Disorder, but habitually leaves a person feeling blue or "down in the dumps." This is reflected in the following DSM-IV criteria (APA, 1994, p. 349):

A. Depressed mood for most of the day, for more days than not, as indicated either by subjective account or observation by others, for at least 2 years.
B. Presence, while depressed, of two (or more) of the following:
    1. poor appetite or overeating
    2. insomnia or hypersomnia
    3. low energy or fatigue
    4. low self-esteem
    5. poor concentration or difficulty making decisions
    6. feelings of hopelessness

C. During the 2-year period (1 year for children and adolescents) of the disturbance, the person has never been without the symptoms in Criteria A and
B for more than 2 months at a time.

D. No major depressive episode has been present during the first 2 years of the
disturbance (1 year for children and adolescents); i.e., the disturbance is
not better accounted for by chronic major depressive disorder, or major depressive disorder, in partial remission.

These traits are characteristic of Sharleen. She has been depressed for at least
two years (Criterion A); she experiences low energy, low self-esteem, poor concentration, and feelings of hopelessness (Criterion B); and, based on her report, the
symptoms are almost always present, with no evidence of major depression in the
first two years of the disorder (Criteria C and D).

Dysthymia is further categorized as early onset, late onset, or with atypical features. *Early onset* dysthymia begins prior to age 21, and *late onset* dysthymia starts after age 21. This distinction is regarded as important because individuals with early
onset dysthymia are believed to be at elevated risk for major depressive episodes
later in life (APA, 1994). In dysthymia *with atypical features*, a person's chronically
depressed mood occasionally brightens in response to positive life events. In
Sharleen's situation, we can see evidence of periods of unhappiness prior to age 21
but not a chronic dysthymic disturbance. In fact, she can recall extended periods of
time of feeling happy and contented. She would therefore be diagnosed with dysthymic disorder, late onset.

Individuals with dysthymia may also suffer periodic exacerbations of their mood
disorder, becoming more severely depressed. In other words, a person may develop a
major depressive episode superimposed onto the more chronic dysthymic disorder.
This is referred to as *double depression*. Although this was not the case for Sharleen,
it is often double depression that ultimately leads someone with dysthymia to seek
psychotherapy—perhaps because despite the discomfort of dysthymia, a person
grows accustomed to his or her chronically down mood and begins to regard it as
normal or expected.

TREATMENT

Once Sharleen decided to give psychotherapy a try, she assumed that she would
simply become a patient of Janette's therapist—after all, he had been helpful with
her sister, so why not her? However, in an initial telephone contact, Janette's
therapist explained that this might not be suitable. Since he continued to work
with Janette, he thought this might compromise each of the women's confidentiality. But after obtaining Janette's permission, he agreed to meet with Sharleen
for a one-time assessment. He then referred Sharleen to a colleague of his, Dr.
Amy Bergman.

Sharleen also worried about the finances required for treatment. She and
Roland were making ends meet but did not have much money left over for extras.

Sharleen's insurance policy only covered a small number of psychotherapy visits annually. She was uneasy about spending too much of their carefully budgeted income on psychotherapy.

In part to meet these concerns, Dr. Bergman proposed that Sharleen participate in a short-term treatment option. Dr. Bergman had originally been trained as a therapist in long-term, psychodynamic psychotherapy. *Psychodynamic* models of psychotherapy are derived from the theories of Sigmund Freud and his followers, and emphasize the impact of the unconscious on human behavior. Traditionally, psychodynamic psychotherapy was regarded as requiring at least one year of treatment, and often much longer. Over the past few years, however, Dr. Bergman had adapted her technique to provide shorter-term care. She felt this was the best solution for a problem she faced as a psychotherapist—staying true to the psychodynamic principles she believed in but also meeting the needs of the growing number of people who, like Sharleen, desired treatment but whose health coverage provided only minimal coverage, and who did not have the resources to pay for longer-term psychotherapy.

Interpersonal psychotherapy (IPT) (Klerman, Weissman, Rounsaville & Chevron, 1984) is a treatment for depression derived from psychodynamic principles, especially from the work of interpersonal theorists such as Harry Stack Sullivan. However, IPT differs from traditional psychodynamic therapies in a few key regards. First, it is short-term, usually lasting no more than 15 sessions. Second, the emphasis is on the "here and now" of a person's relationships. Although past relationships are examined to identify current maladaptive patterns, they are not the focus of treatment. Third, the therapist plays a more active role than in traditional psychodynamic psychotherapy.

ITP has three phases. With Sharleen, the first phase spanned four meetings. During this time, Sharleen described her symptoms to Dr. Bergman, who was particularly interested in hearing about the nature and quality of Sharleen's interpersonal relationships. What had led to the distance she felt from Roland in their marriage? What did they fight about, when did she feel closest to him? How did Sharleen understand her growing isolation from her family and friends? What had been the nature of her relationships with coworkers—what did she currently miss from those relationships, what was she relieved to be free of?

As part of this assessment phase, Sharleen also was offered the possibility of trying antidepressant medication. The SSRI's (selective serotonin reuptake inhibitors), such as Prozac and Zoloft, have proven effective in the treatment of non-severe depressions such as Sharleen's and gained widespread popularity in this regard. However, Sharleen felt strongly that she did not want to take medication. She did agree to leave open the possibility of trying medication at some later point if her symptoms did not improve.

Also in these early sessions, Dr. Bergman raised the topic of race. How did Sharleen feel about working with a white therapist? In response to this question, Sharleen shrugged her shoulders noncommittally and said it did not really bother her. Yes, perhaps she would have preferred an African-American therapist—but then again, "I don't think my problems have anything to do with race." In fact, Dr. Bergman suspected that racial issues might somehow be relevant in Sharleen's depression. For example, she wondered if perhaps Sharleen was resigned to the effects of racism and prejudice in her life because they were easier to ignore than to fight. But at that point, Dr. Bergman responded simply by acknowledging and accepting Sharleen's answer and telling her that she should feel free to talk specifically about this, or any other, aspect of their relationship.

The second phase of treatment involved ten sessions, spread over the course of four months. During this time, Sharleen and Dr. Bergman explored Sharleen's difficulties in more depth. They attempted to find solutions or new options for some of her concerns and to learn new ways to combat her chronic depression.

One specific area of focus was on what Dr. Bergman labeled "role transitions." In IPT, therapists pay particular attention to major changes in a person's life that might relate to depression, such as marriage, divorce, starting or ending a new job, moving, bereavement, or the birth of a child. Dr. Bergman observed that Sharleen's chronically low mood had steadily gotten worse after the birth of Danielle. Were the two related? Together, they examined the profound impact that becoming a mother had on Sharleen's life. For one thing, motherhood meant leaving her job. As they talked, Sharleen realized that she missed working. Her job had been one of her few sources of positive self-esteem, and she looked back wistfully on her accomplishments there. Work also had provided her with a ready-made forum for easy social contact with other people—similar to the orchestra in high school—something she had a hard time initiating or maintaining on her own.

Having a baby also affected her marriage with Roland. Sharleen realized that many of the fights they had had related to Danielle, in terms of sharing the responsibility of caring for her, and their different ideas about how to raise a child. And for the first time, Sharleen openly expressed her own sense of inadequacy and her mixed feelings about motherhood. When she was growing up, she had always assumed that becoming a mother would be the most important and wonderful thing in her life, but the reality was different. She loved Danielle but admitted she sometimes felt "too tied down" caring for her, and at other times, she was "overwhelmed" with the responsibility. She realized that sometimes when she felt angry with Roland, it was because she resented his ability to continue leading a fuller life.

Fortunately, Danielle was an easy-going child, quiet and rarely needing to be disciplined. But Sharleen felt tremendously guilty about her negative thoughts about motherhood. And didn't having those thoughts, by their very existence, confirm that she was a bad mother?

Dr. Bergman and Sharleen approached these concerns in two ways. First, Dr. Bergman responded to, and empathized with, Sharleen's feelings of sadness, confusion, and resentment. In fact, she encouraged Sharleen to grieve her losses—for Danielle's birth *did* entail loss. For one thing, it meant giving up some of her independence by relinquishing her most rewarding outlet for social interaction. It also meant taking on the enormous responsibility of raising a child. It was understandable and "normal" to have the strong, conflicting feelings she did. But Dr. Bergman also helped Sharleen see all the ways in which she was behaving like a caring, responsible, and loving mother.

Second, together they looked at pragmatic, realistic ways that they might be able to change Sharleen's situation. Dr. Bergman believed that Sharleen needed to have more satisfying interpersonal contact in her life. Could she return to work part-time? Could she join a local parents' support group? Were there women with whom she might develop friendships? Dr. Bergman listened compassionately to Sharleen's difficulties but also emphasized that unless she took some initiative to change things, it seemed unlikely she would feel any better.

Sharleen thought about returning to work. She decided against this option because she felt strongly that a mother should stay home with her children, if at all possible (which Dr. Bergman further highlighted as an expression of maternal concern). However, she agreed with Dr. Bergman that she needed more social contact. She knew a few other mothers who were also in her situation. Perhaps she could organize a weekly mother/child group for get-togethers?

With encouragement from Dr. Bergman, Sharleen started putting energy into forming this group. This helped her mood; it gave her a lift to have a new project to work on, and she was pleased to find interest among some of the other women she contacted. One particularly enthusiastic neighbor suggested they try to organize their plans through the church. The church agreed to provide a meeting space for the get-togethers and to help find new members through their newsletter.

As therapy continued and this project started getting off the ground, Sharleen still felt down, although not as deeply or frequently. She often found that she had more energy and more patience with Danielle. Communication with Roland also improved. They decided to spend more time together by themselves as a couple, hiring a babysitter so they could sometimes go out for an evening alone. She started developing friendships with a few of the women in the mother/child group.

The third and last phase of treatment, lasting four more sessions, was the termination phase. Sharleen was fearful about therapy ending—she had come to rely on Dr. Bergman's support and guidance. She worried that she would become depressed again. Together, she and Dr. Bergman looked at how the ending of therapy might feel similar to previous endings and transitions in Sharleen's life. Endings seemed to be painful for Sharleen, and old memories came back to her about earlier losses. For example, she recalled, for the first time in many years, how difficult it was to move across the country when she was twelve years old. What a terrible time that was—the broken interpersonal connections, the new financial hardships, the toll the move took on her parents, the racism she began to experience first-hand.

Dr. Bergman acknowledged the sadness and fear involved in having the psychotherapy relationship end, but also reminded Sharleen that she had learned helpful new skills in stopping herself from feeling so isolated. They also looked at some of the ongoing issues that had not been addressed but which might also be relevant—Sharleen's strained relationships with her parents and other family members, her disappointment that she never earned her bachelor's degree. Perhaps at some point in the future, when Sharleen was interested in doing so, or felt more financially secure, she could return to psychotherapy to work on those issues.

Treatment ended after eighteen sessions, which spanned the course of six months.

Multiaxial DSM-IV Diagnosis at Time of Termination

Axis I:	Dysthymia, Late Onset
	CONDITION: IMPROVED
Axis II:	No diagnosis
Axis III:	None
Axis IV:	Inadequate social support
Axis V:	*Treatment Onset:* 65 (mild-to-moderate difficulty in social functioning)
	Termination: 80 (slight impairment in social functioning)

DISCUSSION

Current estimates suggest that approximately one out of every fifteen people in the United States will meet diagnostic criteria for dysthymia at some point in their life (Kessler et al., 1994). Add this to the high incidence of major depression—some community studies place the lifetime risk for a major depressive episode as high as one in four for women, and one in seven for men—and the magnitude of the issue becomes clear (Kessler et al., 1994). Whether it be the acuity of a single deep depressive episode or the chronic lethargy and sadness of dysthymia, depression has a powerful, pervasive presence in our society.

Dysthymic disorder was first introduced in DSM-III (APA, 1980), echoing most closely the earlier psychoanalytic concept of "depressive neurosis." Despite ongoing attempts to refine appropriate diagnostic criteria, this disorder remains somewhat hard to pin down. On the one hand, it lacks the severity of major depression. Even though it sometimes includes the *neurovegetative symptoms* (such as disturbed eating or sleeping patterns) that are a common aspect of major depression, it represents a milder form of impairment.

Yet on the other hand, it can be challenging to distinguish this "milder form of impairment" from the ordinary sadnesses and challenges of everyday life. Typically, distinguishing between ordinary sadness and dysthymia is based on variables such as the intensity, duration, and impact of a person's mood. Yet this, too, can be a gray zone, and the DSM-IV (APA, 1994) acknowledges this difficulty in always knowing exactly when unhappiness is a disorder and when it is "normal." With each revision of the DSM, the criteria for dysthymia have changed. Still new criteria are currently under investigation.

Further complicating the picture, several related but distinct conceptualizations for this type of depression have been proposed. Possible new diagnoses to be included in the next version of DSM include minor depressive disorder, recurrent brief depressive disorder, mixed anxiety-depressive disorder, and depressive personality disorder (APA, 1994). In part, these diagnostic complications arise because important questions about dysthymia remain unanswered: Is it best viewed as a sub-type of major depression, on a continuum with major depression, or as a completely distinct entity? To what extent are the biological underpinnings of dysthymia and major depression the same? With individuals who suffer from chronic, low-level depression, how can this be distinguished from their personality?

This last issue—the overlap of mood and personality—raises intriguing conceptual issues about how we view mood disorders. If a person chronically holds a negative, pessimistic, and sad outlook on life, couldn't this be thought of as a depressive personality? Some researchers (Akiskal, 1989) theorize that this may be the case. For example, some people may be biologically predisposed to a *dysthymic temperament*—a characterological tendency to experience life through the darkened veil of many of the depressive symptoms that characterize dysthymia. From this perspective, it is not that these people have a disorder; it may just be who they are. Conversely, some other people have a *hyperthymic temperament*—a tendency toward a constant mood and energy level that is characteristically high-spirited, optimistic, and self-assured.

These issues have become more relevant with the increasingly common prescribing of mood-altering medications, particularly the SSRI's. Unlike earlier antidepressants, SSRI's are now routinely prescribed for individuals with dysthymia—and often even for individuals who suffer from dysthymic *symptoms*, but who do not meet diagnostic criteria for dysthymia, other mood disorders, or any psychiatric disorder at all (Knutson et al., 1998). The widespread popularity of these medications attests to the benefits many individuals experience from their usage. But here too, important conceptual issues are raised: If medications are now used to treat individuals who do not meet the criteria for a disorder, at what point do we distinguish the "illness" of a mood disorder from daily unhappiness, disappointments, or a person's personality, even if it that personality features qualities such as gloominess, low self-esteem, or a tendency to feel blue?

Theoretical Perspectives

Traditionally, psychodynamic theory regards depression in two primary ways. First is the notion of depression as "hostility turned inward." In other words, feelings of anger or aggression toward others go unexpressed, but then are directed internally, resulting in harsh, critical attacks on oneself. This notion dates back to the work of an early psychoanalyst, Karl Abraham (1911), and to an influential paper of Sigmund Freud's, "Mourning and Melancholia" (1917), in which he compares depression with the process of grieving the death of a loved one.

Second, other psychoanalytic theorists see depression as related to an unconscious sense of abandonment, disconnection, or aloneness, with roots in very early life experiences (Bemporad, 1985; Bowlby, 1980; Klein, 1940). According to this view, disturbances in important relationships during infancy or childhood have a tremendous impact, leaving a person vulnerable to depression later in life. These disturbances may reflect actual events, such as a prolonged separation from one's caretakers—perhaps due to a parent's death, divorce, or another event that interferes with the continuity of the parent–child relationship. Conversely, the disturbances may primarily be an unconscious experience on the part of the infant or young child, or based on a more emotional sense of abandonment, without such a dramatic life incident.

As with many psychodynamic concepts, empirical support for the validity of these ideas is hard to come by. Studying them is difficult. This does not mean that the ideas are untrue, but devising tests or measures to assess them scientifically is no easy matter. Yet even without empirical support, certain concepts continue to live on. For example, the notion of depression as "hostility turned inward" holds widespread appeal in psychoanalytic treatment as well as in many popular views of depression, perhaps because it seems to resonate with many people's experience.

Cognitive-behavioral theorists contend that certain thoughts and cognitive styles play an important causal role in depression (Bandura, 1986; Beck et al., 1979; Rehm, 1984). Beck (1976; Beck et al., 1979) describes what he labels the *cognitive triad:* depressed individuals have a negative view of themselves, the world, and the future. As the cornerstone of treatment with depressed individuals, cognitive-behavioral therapists attempt to help clients identify and challenge their *automatic thoughts*—cognitions that a person experiences so routinely and frequently that they often go unnoticed or unquestioned, even though they may exert a great influence on such issues as optimism, self-esteem, and confidence.

Cognitive-behavioral therapists examine how a depressed person's automatic thoughts tend to be (1) negative and (2) overly generalized. For example, in response to a minor setback, a depressed person's automatic thoughts might be "I always fail," or "I'm a complete idiot," or "Everybody hates me." In cognitive-behavioral therapy, the therapist first helps a client identify these automatic thoughts, and then, in a manner akin to a benevolent but firm lawyer conducting a cross-examination, subjects them to rational scrutiny.

From a more strictly behavioral perspective, depression is seen, primarily, as resulting from a lack of positive reinforcers in a person's life, or from an overload of punishing events (Lewinsohn, 1974). A person may become depressed after the loss of positive reinforcers, whether these are externally derived (e.g., money, praise from others) or internally derived (e.g., a sense of accomplishment, pride, or self-worth). Because of how stressful life events can affect positive reinforcement, depression may result from stressors such as bereavement, the loss of a job, or another significant transition. Or, less tangibly, depressed people may lack the necessary skills to create and maintain adequate positive reinforcers in their life in the first place, perhaps lacking the necessary social skills or self-motivation to engage in activities that could potentially be rewarding.

In addition to these psychological perspectives, a vast body of evidence highlights the key role of biology in depression. Family and adoption studies repeatedly indicate a genetic component in unipolar and bipolar mood disorders, including dysthymia (Rice et al., 1987). Biology may indeed play a role in Sharleen's dysthymia, supported (correlationally, but not causally) by evidence of what appears to be a possible depressive disorder in her father as well.

The success of various antidepressant medications indicates that neurotransmitters (primarily the *catelcholamines,* such as norepinephrine, dopamine, and serotonin) are crucial in modulating human moods, even though the exact mechanisms are not yet well understood. Hormones are also known to play a role in depression, particularly *cortisol*, a hormone more generally involved in the physiological management of stress.

It is important to note that biological models of depression need not contradict other theories. For example, biologically-oriented theorists with a psychodynamic perspective are now studying ways in which early life losses may result in neurological changes that affect personality functioning later in life (Kramer, 1993; Shear, 1996).

Finally, a feminist perspective seeks to answer a fundamental question: Why is it that depressive disorders are so much more common in women than men? The rate of depression in women appears to be at least twice that of men, regardless of race or cultural background (Culbertson, 1997; McGrath et al., 1990; Nolen-Hoeksema, 1990; Steele, 1978). Epidemiological studies suggest that this not due to biases in diagnosis, but reflects the actual state of affairs: In community samples, more women are depressed than men, and women may be depressed more severely.

It seems likely that several factors contribute to this. A National Task Force on Women and Depression (McGrath et al., 1990) emphasized the importance of cultural and economic factors, along with psychological and biological ones, in understanding womens' increased risk for depression. The Task Force noted that women are disproportionately affected by poverty (more than 75% of poor adults are women) and are more likely than males to suffer early physical and sexual abuse, both of which are known to contribute to depression. In the realm of individual psychology, women may be more apt than men to favor certain cognitive styles, such as negative or pessimistic thinking, and to demonstrate personality characteristics of avoidance or dependence, rather than engaging in the "action and mastery strategies" that can sometimes help alleviate depression (McGrath et al., 1990, p. xii).

How do these perspectives apply to Sharleen's situation? A traditional psychodynamic clinician would highlight Sharleen's early experiences and how these may have set the stage for later depression. In particular, in addition to events during infancy and early childhood, perhaps Sharleen still had lingering, unconscious reactions about her family's relocation in childhood, a move that resulted in many losses and broken interpersonal connections. (Dr. Bergman believed this to be the case, even as she kept the actual treatment focus on the "here and now.") In a longer psychodynamic psychotherapy, a therapist might also examine the link between Sharleen's harsh tendency towards self-criticism and what seems to be her mother's critical style. Is Sharleen, who has withdrawn from contact with her mother in adulthood, directing hostility she feels toward her mother inwardly, toward herself?

Interestingly, behavioral, cognitive-behavioral, and feminist perspectives also seem to match Sharleen's treatment. The goals of treatment were to increase the degree of Sharleen's interpersonal connections and to strengthen the quality of her relationships—goals that, in the language of behaviorists, could easily translate into increasing the positive reinforcers in her life. And as we saw, part of how Dr. Bergman worked was to challenge (gently) some of Sharleen's distorted, self-critical thoughts—a central feature of cognitive-behavioral treatment, and one of the ways in which feminist clinicians seek to empower female clients.

The fact that Sharleen's treatment could be seen through each of these lenses points to how the main psychological theories of abnormal psychology can be seen to inch toward one another as they continue to develop. Each has a differing central focus, but there is increasing overlap. This merging together is reflected in the "real world" of psychotherapy, where more clinicians define themselves as "eclectic" than as strict adherents of any one model (Garfield & Bergin, 1994).

A Note on Race and Psychotherapy

Did Sharleen's working with a white therapist affect psychotherapy? Because of the pervasive racism in our society, white therapists may be inadequately sensitive to the realities of life for African-Americans or other individuals from nondominant ethnic cultures (Comas-Diaz, 1992; Williams, 1996). Therapists (and clients) can hold harmful prejudices and misconceptions about each other, subtly or overtly, that interfere with building the trust necessary for a psychotherapy relationship. Conversely, therapists may bend over backward *not* to appear bigoted, acting on an overly strong sensitivity not to be racially offensive—and by so doing, fail to address important issues (Greene, 1985). Another potential pitfall is a therapist's assumption that someone's difficulties are exclusively determined by his or her ethnicity and not by the externals stressors or psychological conflicts that may affect anyone (Jenkins, 1996).

In Sharleen's case, race may not have been a central factor in her treatment, even though it still may have been relevant. Sharleen and Dr. Bergman were able to establish a strong therapeutic alliance. Dr. Bergman addressed the topic of race in one of their early sessions, allowing Sharleen to voice her concerns, apprehensions, or questions. Perhaps in a longer, less-focused treatment, Sharleen would have explored more of the impact that race had no doubt played in her life—or Dr. Bergman may have more strongly expressed her belief that Sharleen's experiences of racial discrimination, which she tended to downplay, were of psychological importance.

In psychotherapy, the issue of race is but one example of a broader question: How similar do a psychotherapist and client need to be for treatment to be effective? Although many individuals desire to see a therapist with certain characteristics or experiences—often, characteristics or experiences familiar in their own life—data on psychotherapy outcome indicate that treatment can be beneficial in a range of situations, regardless of the exact demographics of the therapist and client (Lambert & Bergin, 1994; Sue, Zane & Young, 1994). What may matter more than specifics such as race, gender, age, or sexual orientation are issues such as trust, respect, and the client's perception of the therapist's willingness and ability to help (Beutler, Machado, & Neufelt, 1994; Lambert & Bergin, 1994).

And if Sharleen *had* wanted to work with an African-American psychotherapist, unfortunately she may have had difficulty finding one. Despite aggressive efforts on the part of graduate training programs in psychology and other mental health disciplines to recruit students of diverse ethnic backgrounds, the vast majority of mental health professionals in North America are white men and women.

This situation may even be worsening, rather than improving: Between 1996 and 1997, the number of African-American students enrolled in graduate psychology programs fell by 30%, and enrollment for Hispanic students fell by 23%, mirroring a decline in minority graduate school admissions across a wide range of disciplines (American Association for The Advancement of Science, 1998).

PROGNOSIS

Immediately after termination of psychotherapy, Sharleen felt that her mood was better than it had been for several years. She looked forward to the weekly get-togethers with other mothers, felt more confident about her parenting skills, and less guilty and self-critical about her relationships with Roland and Danielle. She began again to experience some pleasure in taking walks and other old favorite activities.

These gains lasted for many months. By one year after termination, however, Sharleen noticed that her progress had gradually slipped away. She was again depressed much of the time. Her marriage slipped back into its familiar uneasiness. The weekly mothers' meetings first became more sporadic, and then fell apart—one woman moved away, another had a schedule conflict, and bit by bit the whole idea just lost steam. Sharleen briefly considered returning to work part-time at the university but was dismayed to learn of a hiring freeze. She did not feel any initiative to look for work someplace else. Eventually, she found herself back almost to where she began—not quite miserable but far from content.

Does Sharleen's relapse to chronic, low-level depression mean that her treatment was ineffective? Unfortunately, such a course may not be uncommon. In one large-scale, controlled study of treatment outcome for individuals with mild to moderate depression (Elkin et al., 1989), the short-term benefits of both interpersonal therapy and cognitive-behavioral therapy were quite impressive. In fact, in many such cases, these psychotherapies can be as effective as medication. But these gains may not have long-lasting effects. Although some research indicates the sustaining power of these brief interventions (Hollon, Shelton & Davis, 1993), other reports indicate that the gains of ITP may not hold up with the passage of time (Shea et al., 1992).

It may be that for people who suffer from dysthymia, as contrasted with those who suffer from isolated bouts of depression but who otherwise enjoy a stable mood, short-term psychotherapy might not be the most appropriate treatment option. If the comparison between dysthymia and a personality disorder is apt, then short-term treatment may only be of limited utility. With personality disorders, longer-term, in-depth treatment is typically required to produce substantial change (Andreoli et al., 1989). The same may be true of the chronic, pervasive, low-level impairment of dysthymia.

Perhaps what may ultimately be effective for Sharleen will be several short-term treatments, each focusing on a specific area of concern. Over time, such brief therapies may have a cumulative effect in chronic disorders such as dysthymia—an idea that is accepted by some clinicians but has not been adequately tested in controlled studies. And if Sharleen were to return to treatment, it may be worthwhile for Dr. Bergman, or Sharleen's new therapist, to reopen a discussion about antidepressant medication, with the hope that such an intervention might offer more sustained relief than she has thus far been able to find.

CRITICAL THINKING QUESTIONS

1. Why is Sharleen diagnosed with dysthymia and not major depression?
2. What are some differences between "normal" sadness and dysthymia?
3. How might a clinician with a cognitive-behavioral orientation approach Sharleen's treatment? A more traditional psychodynamic orientation?
4. Dr. Bergman thought that racial issues might be relevant in Sharleen's dysthymia, but Sharleen did not agree with her. What do you think?
5. If Sharleen experienced periods of time when she did not feel as downcast as she does, would this affect her diagnosis? How?

Bipolar Disorder

T hirty-year-old Audrey Samson briskly paced the short length of the psychiatric evaluation unit of her local hospital. "Where's my manuscript? Where's my pen? Dr. Spock is obsolete! Child-raising, child-rearing, experts, experts, and more experts! I'm rewriting it all, for mothers everywhere! Revamping patriarchal society's version of bringing up baby. It takes a village, I know that much, Hillary Clinton. They're expecting me in Washington, and I've got work to do, I'm the one for the job!"

Mark, Audrey's husband, stood outside the evaluation room, rubbing his forehead. His eyes were red-rimmed from lack of sleep. A social worker with the hospital's psychiatric crisis service watched Audrey through the window panel in the door. "I've never seen her get this bad," Mark told her. "She didn't want to come to the hospital, obviously. The past month has been rough, since our baby was born. She only came after her psychiatrist called the police, you know, to bring her here against her will."

When Mark and the social worker entered the evaluation room, Audrey barely took notice. She continued to pace and rave excitedly about her manuscript until the social worker interrupted. "Mrs. Samson, I'd like to speak with you for a moment."

"Oh, you think you have all the answers! I've got your number, little missy. Twelve, and thirteen others like you! You just stay away, we won't be talking. You have red hair, but that doesn't make you smart. You look like Red Buttons. Call your own mother, I'm Mother Theresa, that's who I am!"

Mark stood by helplessly. He knew it was useless to try to reason with Audrey, so he felt relieved when the social worker suggested instead that he go with her to her office to talk. "We'll be back, Audrey, so you just wait for me here," he said gently. He cringed to see that a security officer was standing outside the evaluation room door, but he knew that otherwise Audrey would never stay put.

PSYCHOSOCIAL HISTORY

Audrey Samson was raised in a midwestern university town and had happy memories of her childhood. Her father was a painter, and her mother was a professor of biology. Both parents enjoyed modest acclaim in their chosen field, and they encouraged Audrey and her younger brother to pursue scholarly endeavors. To Audrey's way of thinking, her mother was particularly supportive and attentive, perhaps to compensate for her father's inconsistencies.

Occasionally, her father would seclude himself in his bedroom for days at a stretch, only to emerge later with no outward acknowledgment that anything was amiss. He often drank to excess during these times, worsening his moodiness. Always mercurial, however, he could just as easily be exuberantly charming and funny. And when working on a painting, he would become so engrossed in it that he might spend two or three days and nights painting feverishly, barely taking a break. Audrey was fearful of her father's swings into melancholy, having heard many stories about her great aunt, who spent her last years of life institutionalized before finally committing suicide.

In keeping with her family's standards and expectations, Audrey was a driven student, even as a young girl. At times her parents worried that she was too pressured and perfectionistic about her schoolwork—her drive toward achievement seemed endless.

During her freshman year at a prestigious university, Audrey fell into a deep depression. By mid-semester, she was sleeping 14 to 16 hours per day. She had retreated into her dorm room and could barely find the energy to shower. She could not concentrate or read. Alarmed by a call from her roommate, her parents came to the campus to find their once vivacious daughter drawn, pale, and in bed. They immediately brought her to the student health center, and after it was clear that nothing was wrong physically, she was seen by a psychiatrist. Audrey confided to him that she constantly ruminated about killing herself.

Despite the severity of this depression, Audrey was able to return with her parents to the safety of her home. On medical leave from school, she spent the remainder of the semester recovering, in outpatient treatment with a psychiatrist who prescribed antidepressant medication and provided some short-term, behavioral psychotherapy. Feeling better, Audrey returned to college in the spring with renewed hopefulness. Her quick rebound was seen as "proof" that she had weathered the storm of this depressive episode, and her psychiatrist gradually discontinued her medication. But Audrey was secretly left with the realization that she, like her father, had a capacity for terrible despair.

For the remainder of her college years, Audrey resumed her energetic pace, much to her advantage. During midterms or finals week, she could function on only three or four hours of sleep each night. Her mind raced with endless ideas, which she poured into papers, impassioned classroom discussions, and her senior honors thesis. Rather than raising concern, others saw her late hours and boundless energy as adaptive, even enviable. By graduation, Audrey was being courted by several publishing firms, and with the depressive episode far behind her, she launched a promising career in publishing.

Following the death of her grandfather when she was 24, Audrey experienced her first full-blown manic episode. Despite her deep love for him, at his death she experienced not grief, but instead a curious sense of elation. In fact, in the days and weeks following his funeral, she started feeling more confident and witty, even more attractive, than ever before. She began arriving at work at the crack of dawn and staying up most of the night, enthused over a new idea or project. As this continued, her ideas became more grandiose and then increasingly disorganized. She spun off on tangents during work meetings and flew into a rage if anyone tried to interrupt her.

Audrey then started dressing provocatively at work and initiated an affair with a junior assistant. She openly flaunted this relationship in front of her colleagues, detailing her sexual advances to anyone who would listen. When faced with a reprimand (not to mention shock and confusion at the change in her demeanor), Audrey threatened to quit and take her "case for love" to the American Civil Liberties Union. Instead, her boss took her to a nearby emergency room, and she was ultimately admitted to a psychiatric unit.

In retrospect, Audrey was grateful that someone had convinced her to go to the emergency room and relieved that she had enough clarity of thought left to agree to hospitalization. She would later reflect that she knew she was "about to crash," and indeed her mania quickly spiraled into severe depression after her admission. She spent four weeks in the hospital. She was treated by a psychiatrist, Dr. Donna Torrisi. Audrey was placed on lithium, a commonly used mood stabilizing medication. When she was discharged, she returned to work to face her co-workers with shame and humiliation over her bizarre behavior.

For the next three years, Audrey continued to see Dr. Torrisi as an outpatient. She remained on medication despite her misgivings. She complained that she had lost her "mental razor" and felt less incisive or creative at work. She often was tempted to discontinue taking the drug, "just to give it a go without it." But her implicit trust in Dr. Torrisi's judgement, as well as her sobering fear of swinging into bleak depression, prevented her from doing so. Dr. Torrisi steadfastly reminded Audrey that she had successfully picked up the pieces of her life and resumed her impressive career, all while on lithium.

Ultimately, Dr. Torrisi was able to point to another success as well. When she was 27 years old, Audrey was introduced to Mark Samson by a colleague at work. Over the ensuing year, she experienced all of the normal excitement and fears associated with falling in love, none of which tipped the balance of her emotions toward the extremes of unrealistic euphoria or depression. Not long after her 28th birthday, Audrey and Mark were married.

Audrey's second manic episode occurred soon after her honeymoon in Mexico. Dr. Torrisi was surprised when Mark brought Audrey into her office for an emergency session shortly after their return. However, she learned that Audrey had forgotten to bring her medication with her on the trip, and had hoped she would be alright for the brief time away. Although Audrey's symptoms were reminiscent of her first episode, they were not quite as severe, and Dr. Torrisi was able to correct her lithium level and manage her mania on an outpatient basis.

One year later, when Audrey realized unexpectedly that she was two months pregnant, she decided to stop taking her lithium. Dr. Torrisi concurred that this was probably wise, due to a concern that lithium treatment during pregnancy can sometimes harm a developing fetus. Fortunately, Audrey experienced no episodes of either mania or depression for the duration of her pregnancy. Only a month after she gave birth, Mark wistfully described the birth of their son, Noah, to the hospital social worker as the most joyous occasion of their marriage.

Mark had expected Audrey to resume medication after Noah was born. Dr. Torrisi had warned them that the postpartum period is an especially vulnerable time for women with mood disorders. But Audrey had insisted that she felt fine—blissful, in fact—and she did not want to miss one minute with Noah, not even to see her psychiatrist.

About one week after delivery, Mark began to notice changes in Audrey's behavior. She talked to friends and family members for hours on the phone, usually about her overflowing love for Noah, or about her "supreme" feelings of attunement to his needs and moods. During a call to a children's retail mail-order company, she kept a manager on the phone for thirty minutes, giving elaborate, rambling suggestions about improving the workmanship of the infant clothing line. She voraciously read parenting magazines and books on child development and began to think of herself as a "homegrown" expert on babies. She wrote copious notes, recording in detail her disagreement with the "sexist male bias" in child-rearing attitudes. She tracked down a prominent feminist theorist at the nearby university and left long, incoherent messages on her voice mail about maternal instincts and raising sons from a "womanist" perspective.

Audrey did not sleep much during this time. She was up frequently with Noah and would not return to bed once he was fed. Mark soon realized that she was accruing massive credit card debt during these late night hours. Packages began arriving daily—children's clothing, toys and furnishings, even in-line skates and ski equipment ("Just planning ahead," Audrey explained). Audrey exploded in anger when Mark refused deliveries and returned cartons. She accused him of depriving Noah of "essential pleasures" and threatened to leave with the baby to protect him against Mark's "testosterone poisoning."

Audrey's threat frightened Mark into action. He also realized that despite her feelings of "supreme attunement," Audrey was becoming increasingly inattentive to Noah's needs. He had already tried to persuade his wife to seek help, but did not push the issue. Alarmed now by Audrey's worsening condition, he hastily called Dr. Torrisi, who urged Mark to bring Audrey to see her.

Together, Dr. Torrisi and Mark appealed to Audrey's sense of maternal responsibility in a successful effort to convince her to resume medication. Dr. Torrisi warned Audrey that her mania would ultimately harm her ability to take care of Noah—or worse, land her in the hospital where she would be separated from him. Audrey loudly disagreed and argued that she had never felt so "cosmically alive." Speaking so rapidly that Dr. Torrisi could not interrupt, she described her "treatise" about "effective mothering in the age of postmodern feminism" and pulled from the baby's diaper bag a notebook filled with her rambling, digressive notes on the topic. But she acquiesced when Dr. Torrisi whispered to her, "mother to mother," that taking her medicine was the best thing for Noah. Dr. Torrisi prescribed both an anti-psychotic medication to help organize Audrey's thinking and lithium to stabilize her mood.

Two days later, Mark sat in the social worker's office and shook his head. "Too little too late, I guess," he said. Audrey's condition had only worsened, so much so that she could no longer care for the baby. She had stopped sleeping and bathing, and barely seemed to notice that Mark had assumed total responsibility for Noah's care. She became enraged when her mother-in-law came to take Noah to her house, and frenetically threw a mishmash of belongings into a suitcase. Dr. Torrisi notified the police after a frantic call from Mark: Audrey was heading to the bus station, suitcase in hand, on her way to meet with the president about directing the Children's Defense Fund. Fortunately, when Audrey saw the police arrive, she acquiesced at least to the point of allowing Mark to bring her to the hospital, although he was not at all sure what she would do once they got there.

CONCEPTUALIZATION

Audrey Samson suffers from bipolar disorder, an illness characterized by the cycling of mood between extremes of depression and elation. Widely known as manic-depressive illness, hallmarks of this mood disorder are episodes of euphoria, grandiosity, abundant energy, torrentially pressured speech, and runaway thoughts. But just as extreme is the flipside of the cycle—the immobilizing, even life-threatening, despair and isolation of major depression.

Several concepts and definitions are important in understanding and distinguishing bipolar disorder from other mood disorders. These include manic, depressive, and mixed episodes; mania vs. hypomania; unipolar vs. bipolar depression; bipolar I vs. bipolar II disorder; and psychosis.

As defined by DSM-IV, a *manic episode* is "a distinct period of abnormally and persistently elevated or irritable mood. . . . The period of mood disturbance must last at least one week, or any duration if hospitalization is necessary" (APA, 1994, p. 332). Three or more of the following symptoms are present:

A. inflated self-esteem or grandiosity
B. decreased need for sleep (e.g., feels rested after only three hours of sleep)
C. more talkative than usual or pressure to keep talking
D. flight of ideas or subjective experience that thoughts are racing
E. distractibility (i.e., attention too easily drawn to unimportant or irrelevant external stimuli)
F. increase in goal-directed activity (either socially, at work or school, or sexually) or psychomotor agitation
G. excessive involvement in pleasurable activities that have a high potential for painful consequences (e.g., engaging in unrestrained buying sprees, sexual indiscretions, or foolish business investments)

The mood disturbance must also result in marked impairment in social or professional functioning, or require hospitalization to prevent harm to oneself or to others.

A manic episode is typically preceded or followed by a *major depressive episode*, as was true for Audrey during her first psychiatric hospitalization. During a major depressive episode, five or more of the following symptoms must be present for two consecutive weeks, with at least one of the symptoms either (1) depressed mood, or (2) loss of interest or pleasure in activities:

A. depressed mood most of the day, nearly every day, as indicated by either subjective report (e.g., feels sad of empty) or observation made by others (e.g., appears tearful)
B. markedly diminished interest or pleasure in all, or almost all, activities most of the day, nearly every day (as indicated by either subjective account or observation made by others)
C. significant weight loss when not dieting or weight gain (e.g., a change of more than 5% of body weight in a month), or decrease or increase in appetite nearly every day
D. insomnia or hypersomnia nearly every day
E. psychomotor agitation or retardation nearly every day (observable by others, not merely subjective feelings of restlessness or being slowed down)
F. fatigue or loss of energy nearly every day
G. feelings of worthlessness or excessive or inappropriate guilt (which may be delusional) nearly every day (not merely self-reproach or guilt about being sick)
H. diminished ability to think or concentrate, or indecisiveness, nearly every day (either by subjective account or observed by others)
 I. recurrent thoughts of death (not just fear of dying), recurrent suicidal ideation without a specific plan, or a suicide attempt or a specific plan for committing suicide.

Again, the symptoms must result in clinically significant impairment in personal or occupational functioning.

While manic and depressive episodes may appear quite distinct, *mixed episodes* also occur. A mixed episode includes symptoms of both mania and depression, and a person's mood may oscillate rapidly between euphoria and profound despondency. A milder form of mania, called *hypomania*, involves many of the same symptoms as mania but to a less pronounced or dangerous degree. The distinction between mania and hypomania is one of duration and severity. In hypomania, a person's functioning is rarely impaired to such an extent that hospitalization is required. Through careful and thorough history-taking, Dr. Torrisi realized that Audrey's "highs" during college, complete with enjoyable bouts of productivity and decreased need for sleep, were actually hypomanic episodes.

The experience of major depressive episodes with no history of manic, hypomanic, or mixed episodes signifies the presence of *unipolar depression*, listed in DSM-IV as major depressive disorder. During her freshman year at the university, Audrey's first psychiatrist treated her for this disorder. His misdiagnosis was understandable, for it was only after the polarity of her illness began shifting that the diagnosis of a bipolar disorder became clear. This is not uncommon among women, who often first experience a major depressive episode rather than a manic one, and so are likely to be misdiagnosed (APA, 1994). On the other hand, the first episode among men with bipolar disorder is usually manic. The reasons for this gender difference are not well understood. Misdiagnosing bipolar disorder as unipolar depression can have serious repercussions, because certain antidepressant medications can precipitate mania in people with an underlying bipolar disorder (Goodwin & Jamison, 1990).

Finally, the DSM-IV distinguishes between two types of bipolar disorder: *bipolar I disorder* and *bipolar II disorder*.[1] In both disorders, a person experiences major depressive episodes. But whereas the highs of bipolar I disorder reach the point of mania, in bipolar II disorder they stay within the realm of hypomania. Audrey has bipolar I disorder, with full-blown manic episodes. Had she continued with psychiatric follow-up during college, and her hypomania been formally diagnosed, she would at that time have met criteria for bipolar II disorder.

It is not surprising that Audrey stopped her treatment during college, because her hypomania felt good. She was happy, energized, and successful. Like many people with a bipolar disorder, she welcomed the relief that her elevated mood offered from feeling so miserable. Indeed, she later even lamented to Dr. Torrisi the loss of the "edge" that her mood sometimes provided. But for some individuals, hypomania signals an impending manic deterioration. Audrey's worry about this, as well as the potential for depressive episodes, kept her on her lithium.

During her second psychiatric hospitalization, Audrey's mania had progressed to the point of *psychosis*, or impaired reality testing. Her self-perception was grandiose to the point of being delusional, with a grossly distorted and dangerous sense of her own self-worth and capabilities. When mania reaches these reality-distorting proportions, it can sometimes be hard to distinguish from other psychotic illnesses, such as schizophrenia or schizoaffective disorder (a disorder that involves a primary mood disturbance *and* a primary thought disturbance). Often, knowing a person's history, such as Dr. Torrisi's knowledge of the course of Audrey's illness, can help in determining the appropriate diagnosis.

The content and structure of her speech when she was in the emergency room also conveyed the severity of Audrey's mania. Not only was Audrey's speech pressured, as is often the case in mania, but it was also marked by *flight of ideas*, or abrupt changes in topic that are based on personal associations, wordplay, or distractions in the environment. Flight of ideas is characteristic of manic speech, and in Audrey's case it left her unable even to engage in the psychiatric evaluation. Dr. Torrisi knew that the severity of this episode called for an aggressive treatment approach.

TREATMENT

Treatment for bipolar disorder almost always involves psychotropic medication. Although psychotherapy can be useful in providing support, education, and personal understanding, the weight of evidence suggests that psychotherapy alone cannot control the mood swings or prevent relapse (Colom et al., 1998).

By the time she was hospitalized, Audrey was so agitated, impulsive, and psychotic that she punched the nurse who tried to escort her to her room. Her rantings

---

[1]A third mood-cycling disorder, called *cyclothymia*, also involves fluctuations in mood but to a less severe degree than either Bipolar I or Bipolar II disorders. In cyclothymia, a person cycles between periods of hypomania and periods marked by at least some depressive symptomology.

escalated to include threats to hurt anyone who tried to stop her from leaving for Washington, and she refused to take medication orally. Dr. Torrisi prescribed haloperidol (Haldol), an antipsychotic medication, to be administered by injection.

Antipsychotic medication, in addition to a mood stabilizer, is sometimes necessary during the *acute treatment phase* of bipolar disorder. In this phase, intervention is aimed at ending the episode, and for Audrey this included alleviating psychotic symptoms. Unlike lithium, Haldol can be injected and works relatively rapidly. After 24 sleepless hours, during which her ravings and frenetic behavior kept other patients awake and the nursing staff busy, Audrey was exhausted. The physical toll of the past few weeks, combined with the effects of the Haldol, left her sedated and finally able to sleep. The pace and volume of the entire ward subsided as Audrey slept, almost without interruption, for 24 hours.

Within two days, Audrey agreed to take oral medication. Still agitated and irritable, with pressured speech and racing thoughts, she nevertheless no longer claimed to be Hillary Clinton's confidante and stopped talking endlessly about her "treatise." She recalled how helpful her first hospitalization had been for her and agreed to attend therapy groups held on the unit. Her behavior remained disruptive, however. She often interrupted others with rambling advice about child-rearing or other family matters, and her mood was *labile* (subject to rapid, dramatic changes). She could be gregarious and humorous one moment, only to lash out in irritation in the next.

Although she immediately reinstituted lithium, Dr. Torrisi continued the Haldol during the first two weeks of Audrey's hospitalization, before tapering and stopping the dose. This helped calm and organize Audrey's thinking and behavior until the lithium was able to take effect. But as Audrey's thinking cleared, she grew despondent as she reviewed her behavior since Noah's birth.

Perhaps inevitably, Audrey's previous energy and expansive optimism gave way to despair and ruminative concerns about her ability to take care of her son. From her manic high, she plummeted into a depression reminiscent of the episode she experienced in college. She refused visits from Mark and Noah and stopped attending psychotherapy groups on the unit. She continued to take her medication only because she could not muster up the energy for resistance. "Why bother with me?" she asked Dr. Torrisi. "I'm hopeless. No pill will correct the damage I've done." Audrey even felt that Noah "would be better off if I was dead." Things had now come full circle: No longer a danger to herself from manic impulsivity, she was at risk of killing herself out of hopelessness and despair.

Audrey remained in the hospital for a total of one month. Psychopharmacological medication was a cornerstone of her treatment, but there were other components as well. For example, the *therapeutic milieu* of the psychiatric unit provided Audrey with much needed support and direction as her depression began to clear. In *milieu therapy*, the entire environment of a hospital unit is considered part of the treatment, with the assumption that all interactions and behaviors, no matter how seemingly insignificant, can have therapeutic value.

In a twice-weekly psychotherapy group, Audrey gained a broader perspective of her psychiatric illness and its impact on her feelings about herself as a new mother. She continued to feel guilty about her neglectful behavior during her manic

> ## Multiaxial DSM-IV Diagnosis at the Time of Hospital Discharge
>
> | | |
> |---|---|
> | Axis I: | Bipolar I Disorder, Most Recent Episode Manic, Severe with Psychotic Features, with Full Interepisode Recovery
CONDITION: STABILIZED |
> | Axis II: | No diagnosis |
> | Axis III: | None |
> | Axis IV: | Childbirth |
> | Axis V: | *Time of admission:* 25 (serious impairments in communication and judgment, some danger of harming self or other)
Time of discharge: 65 (mild to moderate symptoms) |

episode, and about the extended separation from Noah during her hospitalization, but her feelings no longer dipped into suicidal melancholy. Mark attended several of Audrey's individual sessions with a staff psychologist, where the focus was on addressing both of their concerns regarding the long-term course of bipolar disorder, Audrey's ongoing treatment needs, and prevention of further episodes.

By the time of her discharge from the hospital, Audrey's depressive symptoms had diminished to the point that she was no longer at risk of harming herself. Her sleep and concentration were closer to normal and, although she continued to feel fatigued, she was motivated to return home, continue with her medication, and resume responsibility for Noah's care. Based on her work in individual and group psychotherapy, she focused on clear and attainable goals, such as beginning a photo album and "baby book" and reconnecting with family and friends.

On the recommendation of the hospital psychologist and Dr. Torrisi, Audrey also scheduled an outpatient appointment with a psychotherapist. In contrast to the self-confidence she felt prior to her manic episode, Audrey now doubted her adequacy as a parent. In weekly therapy, she could continue to examine this concern and develop skills to meet the challenges of parenting. Audrey agreed that psychotherapy also could provide additional support for her in facing the realities, and fears, of living with her disorder.

DISCUSSION

Bipolar disorder typically first strikes in early adulthood, although it can begin at any age, from childhood to middle age or later. Equally likely to afflict both men and women, the lifetime prevalence of the illness is approximately 1% to 2% (Kessler et al., 1994). This prevalence rate is far lower than that of unipolar depression (which may be as high as 24% for women, 15% for men; [Kessler et al., 1994]), but it does not render the disorder rare—as many as 2.2 million Americans will suffer from the illness in their lifetimes. Moreover, in almost all cases, bipolar disorder runs a recurrent course. More than 90% of the time, a single manic episode is a harbinger of episodes to come.

The life disruption caused by bipolar I disorder often is tragically severe. This sometimes results directly from the symptoms, but just as often springs from the potentially devastating fallout from manic or depressive behavior, such as broken relationships, legal difficulties, or the dire financial consequences of massive impulsive spending. Before lithium treatment was introduced in the 1970s, the suicide rate for people with manic-depressive illness was distressingly high, with perhaps as many as one in five people with the disorder committing suicide (Goodwin & Jamison, 1990). Today, the risk for suicide still remains high, particularly during the initial years of the illness. Adolescents with bipolar disorder are at especially high risk for suicide, and overall perhaps between 25% to 50% of bipolar I patients attempt suicide at least once (Goodwin & Jamison, 1990).

In the past few decades, the use of lithium has revolutionized the treatment of bipolar disorder. A natural element, lithium's mood stabilizing properties were first noted in 1949 by Australian psychiatrist John Cade, but it took until the 1970s for this treatment to gain widespread popularity. In the past few years, several other mood stabilizing medications, such as carbamazepine, valproic acid, and gabapentin, also have proven effective. In many cases, valproic acid (Depakote) is now considered to be the treatment of choice, because it may produce fewer side effects than lithium. Appropriate use of these medications can often curb, or even prevent episodes of relapse (Maj, 1992; Suppes et al., 1991). But unfortunately, despite the help these medications can offer, a significant complication with bipolar disorder is that many affected people refuse or discontinue treatment. Estimates vary, but perhaps more than 50% of people with bipolar disorder at some point do not comply with medication regimens (Goodwin & Jamison, 1990).

Why is treatment noncompliance such a problem? As may be evident by this point, one primary reason has to do with the very nature of the illness. As was true for Audrey, there can be a pleasurable side to the symptoms. Feelings of euphoria, financial or interpersonal omnipotence, mental sharpness, and professional and sexual competence are certainly invigorating, especially in sharp contrast to the lows that accompany depression. How hard it can be to contemplate giving these things up! A lifetime of commitment to preventive medication requires a level of acquiescence and acceptance that some people may find unwanted and unfamiliar, if not intolerable. This is heightened by the fact that many people, like Audrey, report that lithium has an undesirable "flattening" quality (Millet, 1990).

Nevertheless, there are compelling reasons to comply with preventive treatment, not the least of which is an elevated risk of relapse with each subsequent episode. In other words, if left untreated, or if medication compliance is only sporadic, the illness often worsens over time—the more episodes of mania or depression a person experiences, the more likely he or she is to have an ever-worsening course of the disease.

Theoretical Perspectives

Almost all theories regarding the etiology of bipolar disorder assume that biology plays a fundamental role. More so than with any other psychiatric disorder, the pre-ponderance of evidence suggests that bipolar disorder has a strong genetic compo-nent (Gershon, 1990; Torrey et al., 1994). Twin studies show a very high concor-dance rate for manic depression among identical (monozygotic) twins—from 70% and even as high as 100% in one study—compared with an estimate of 20% concor-dance rate for fraternal (dizygotic) twins (Jamison, 1993).

We can see this familial connection in Audrey's life. Based on the description of her family, it seems likely that Audrey's father also had a mood disorder, perhaps bipolar II disorder. Although the evidence is scanty, the fact that a paternal great aunt committed suicide raises the possibility of a unipolar or bipolar depression.

It also is worth noting a couple of additional points of interest regarding Au-drey's father. First, he drank heavily and may have had an alcohol abuse disorder. This is not unusual: Nearly half of individuals with a bipolar disorder also have a co-morbid substance abuse disorder at some point during their lifetime (Regier et al., 1990). Second, he was an artist. This, too, is not unusual: Among artists, writers, poets, and other creative individuals, there is a higher prevalence of bipolar disor-ders than is found in the general population. This raises fascinating questions about the relationship between creativity and psychological functioning, especially with mood disorders (Goodwin & Jamison, 1990).

Still, even with the assumption of a biological basis, the exact genetic or chem-ical mechanisms involved in bipolar disorder are not well understood. One current biological explanation for how bipolar disorder develops is called the *kindling theory* (Post, 1992). Imagine a fire that starts small, with only a few twigs. As more kin-dling wood is added, the fire grows. At some point, the fire then takes on a life of its own and becomes much more difficult to extinguish. At a biochemical level, this may occur in bipolar disorder. Like kindling wood, each episode accrues to raise a person's biological susceptibility to subsequent episodes. At some point, if "kindled" enough, the disorder takes on a life of its own—and, like a large fire, becomes much harder to put out.

Indirect support for this theory comes from the fact that over the course of time, a person's cumulative mood episodes become less and less responsive to medication. In other words, a manic or depressive episode is more easily "kindled." This may be the result of permanent biochemical changes over time, caused by the sharp mood swings (Post, 1992; Young et al., 1994). Further support comes from the difficulty of treating a certain subtype of bipolar disorder called *rapid-cycling*. "Rapid cyclers" ex-perience frequent and pronounced mood changes (at least four manic or depressive episodes in a given year). This type of bipolar disorder is much more difficult to treat—perhaps because, as the kindling model suggests, the increased number of episodes quickly renders medication unhelpful. This subtype is more common in women, for reasons not yet well understood (Leibenluft, 1996).

Even assuming a predominant biological component, a *diathesis-stress* model is relevant in understanding bipolar disorder—that is, psychological and environmen-tal factors are also important. Stress may play a key role in potentiating a manic episode, particularly in the onset of the disorder (the first episode). Most often, stressful events, such as beginning college, bereavement, or having a baby, directly precede a first manic episode. Subsequent episodes also may be triggered by stressful life events or other psychological factors, although these later episodes may occur spontaneously.

Another biological factor that may trigger recurrences of mania is sleep disruption or deprivation. Lack of sleep disrupts a person's *circadian rhythms*, the body's natural biological "clock." These disturbances cause neurochemical changes which, in turn, can lead to mania (Wehr, Sack & Rosenthal, 1987). Alcohol abuse also may lead to recurrences. Substance abuse can weaken a person's commitment to treatment, worsen manic or depressive symptoms, and complicate the use of medications.

From a psychodynamic perspective, mania is conceptualized as a defensive reaction against thoughts, feelings, or impulses that are too anxiety-provoking or painful to tolerate (Baruch, 1997; Freeman, 1971; Klein, 1940). For example, the not uncommon experience of manic episodes following funerals may represent a psychic need to disavow the reality of a beloved person's death, or an inability to deal with feelings of grief, because acknowledging the loss would be too difficult.

Mania also has been conceptualized psychodynamically as a defense against dealing with other painful affects, such as a fear of abandonment or separation. In this regard, it is interesting to observe that each of Audrey's manic and depressive episodes occurred following stressful and developmentally significant times—her first separation from her parents, her grandfather's death, her wedding, and the birth of her son.

Cognitive and behavioral theorists tend to have little to say about the etiology of bipolar disorders. Whereas depression is relatively easily conceptualized in cognitive or behavioral terms, it is more difficult to account for the phenomenon of mania from these perspectives. However, cognitive-behavioral strategies may still be implemented in the treatment of bipolar disorder, particularly in terms of managing symptoms, coping with life stresses, and addressing distorted cognitions about oneself or the illness.

Special Considerations for Women with Bipolar Disorder

Like Audrey, women with bipolar illness are extremely vulnerable to a mood episode during pregnancy and after the birth of a child. The postpartum period requires careful attention to treatment and prevention (Leibenluft, 1996). According to one large study, the risk of psychiatric hospitalization within 30 days of childbirth is dramatically higher for bipolar mothers than for depressed or schizophrenic mothers (Kendall, Chalmers & Platz, 1987). Further, if a woman who has already experienced a postpartum mood episode decides to have more children, the risk of relapse is greater than 50% with her subsequent deliveries (Dean, Williams & Brockington, 1989). Marital problems also may increase a woman's postpartum risk (Marks et al., 1992). In ways that are not yet fully understood, psychological factors can combine with rapid changes in hormonal, gastrointestinal, and central nervous functioning to kindle a postpartum decompensation (Cohen et al., 1995).

Complicating matters further, expectant mothers with bipolar disorder face difficult decisions regarding medication. For many years, practitioners warned mothers against taking lithium during pregnancy, for fear of causing cardiac abnormalities or lithium toxicity in the baby (Cohen et al., 1995; Weinstein, 1976). Concerns about the danger of secreting lithium into breast milk also dissuaded practitioners from prescribing lithium after childbirth for women who chose to breastfeed their infants (Cohen et al., 1995). More recently, however, Cohen and colleagues (1994) reviewed the relevant data and concluded that the risk to babies of lithium-treated mothers was considerably lower than previously thought. They recommend that women carefully weigh the risks and benefits of lithium treatment before and after delivery, compared with no treatment at all.

For example, Audrey's postpartum episodes of mania and depression were devastating and potentially dangerous. Her impulsive behavior, along with her suicidal despair, might have resulted in great harm. Audrey was fortunately spared from this, and she was able to find her way (albeit initially against her will) back into treatment. But this is not always the case. For some mothers, prolonged periods of impaired judgment result in loss of custody of their children. Decisions regarding the management of bipolar disorder during and after childbirth remain a difficult challenge and must be made on a case-by-case basis.

PROGNOSIS

Audrey left the hospital with a much deeper appreciation of the impact of her illness on herself and those she loved. She now acknowledged that bipolar disorder is a lifelong illness, with the potential for an ever-worsening course if not treated consistently and effectively.

Audrey was still in psychotherapy several months after her discharge from the psychiatric unit, and she grappled with her fear of a relapse. Her psychotherapist, sensing Audrey's feelings of helplessness, recommended that she become a more active participant in the management and treatment of her illness. Following this advice, Audrey learned as much as she could about bipolar disorder and how to live with it. Previously, she had not wanted to spend much time educating herself, with the rationale that she did not want to "dwell" on her illness. Now, she read books and attended lectures. She went to local meetings of a national organization called the Depressive and Manic-Depressive Association, where she heard others' experiences of how to prevent or cope with symptoms and live with the disorder.

The more she learned, the more Audrey realized she needed to make lifestyle changes to keep her moods balanced. Bipolar disorder was not something she could keep compartmentalized or separate from the rest of her life. She excluded caffeine and alcohol from her diet, started a regular exercise regimen, and made sure she consistently got plenty of sleep. Everything she did was geared toward reducing stress and keeping her life stimulating, but stable.

Mark joined Audrey in the effort to become better educated. They were heartened to learn that many people with bipolar disorder—perhaps as many as one in three—can stay free of symptoms, life-long, by consistent compliance with medication (APA, 1996). But they also wanted to prepare for the possibility of another episode. With Dr. Torrisi, they discussed the typical, early warning signs of mania. For Audrey, these included a sudden change in her sleep pattern, combined with an increase in restlessness and overabundant enthusiasm for a new project. Because medication adjustments in the early stages of an episode can be very effective in curtailing an episode before it is "full-blown," they agreed that these warning signs would signal the need to see Dr. Torrisi immediately (APA, 1996).

Audrey also agreed to take some additional steps to protect her family from the potentially harmful consequences of another manic episode. She arranged for all her credit card and banking privileges to require Mark's co-signature. She involved trusted family members in Noah's care. And although she had planned to return to work full-time after a six-month maternity leave, she made the difficult decision of rethinking her career and paring down her hours to half-time.

Mark's ongoing supportive role in Audrey's treatment is a good prognostic indicator for her future. Evidence suggests that recurrence of a severe episode following hospitalization is less likely among people with bipolar disorder who have uncritical, supportive families than it is among those who lack this interpersonal support (Miklowitz et al., 1988).

We leave Audrey as she is beginning to use psychotherapy to discuss her wishes and fears regarding having another child. As with any woman with bipolar disorder, Audrey's situation is not unusual. She has learned to manage her illness through medication and lifestyle modifications, and she knows the severity of what can befall her should she choose to reduce or stop her medication for another pregnancy. Both she and Mark are worried about what they know about the risk of genetic transmission of the disorder. But they balance these concerns with the knowledge that this is a well-studied and treatable illness, and with their certainty that they can provide a supportive and loving home for their children. Together, Audrey and Mark must now include her illness into their decisions, plans, and hopes regarding how to build their future together.

CRITICAL THINKING QUESTIONS

1. How is Audrey different from a person with bipolar II disorder? Cyclothymia?
2. Based on the limited information available, do you think Audrey's father also suffers from a mood disorder? What additional information would you want to know to help with this decision?
3. What are some of the benefits associated with the psychopharmacological treatment for bipolar I disorder? What are some of the costs?
4. Audrey voluntarily admitted herself to the psychiatric hospital. Had she not done so, Dr. Torrisi was prepared to use her legal authority to commit Audrey to an involuntary hospitalization, given that Audrey's judgment had become so impaired. What would you do if you were Audrey? If you were Dr. Torrisi?
5. If somebody close to you had bipolar disorder and confided that he or she wanted to discontinue taking medication, what would you do? Would you advise him or her to do so? Why?

Conversion Disorder (Hysterical Blindness)

K urt Petrowski was led into Dr. Lerbin's office on the arm of his 16-year-old daughter, Patricia. He walked hesitantly, reaching out and moving his free hand to make sure nothing blocked his path. When they reached Dr. Lerbin's door and the psychologist verbally introduced himself, Kurt extended his right arm for a handshake. Although his hearing was intact, Kurt seemed to misjudge where Dr. Lerbin stood and offered his hand several feet away from the sound of the doctor's voice.

Dr. Lerbin asked Patricia to wait in the anteroom, and then led Kurt to a chair in his office. Kurt's manner was pleasant and genial. As he sat down, he made a half-joking comment about his annoyance at having to meet with a psychologist and quickly dismissed the implication that his recent problems were all "in his head." But the eye specialist at the hospital had insisted on a visit to a psychologist, along with a host of other medical and neurological tests, and Kurt had decided magnanimously to go along.

Ten days earlier, Kurt had woken up unable to see. Although he had no previous difficulties with his vision other than nearsightedness, he was now almost completely blind. He reported that at best, he could make out dim shapes and sharp contrasts of light and dark. The intensity of his lack of vision was not constant—some moments were slightly better than others. He said it was like looking through a dense, shifting mist in the middle of the night.

So far, a range of opthamological tests had failed to explain his sudden and dramatic loss of vision. Medically, his eyes registered as normal. Similarly, an MRI (magnetic resonance imagery) and CAT scan (computerized axial tomography)—two sophisticated techniques to chart brain functioning—failed to produce any neural explanation for his blindness. Yet he was not simply "faking it." His wife Lurleen (who was concerned but also skeptical—she didn't know what to think) had watched him a few times, secretly, from another room in the house. She saw that he acted no differently when alone than when with other people. And in his physician's office, he did not involuntarily blink or shut his eyes in response to tests with a bright light, as would a person with normal eye functioning.

As they spoke, Dr. Lerbin was struck by Kurt's seeming lack of concern about his sudden blindness. The only minor glimmer of distress was when Kurt called it "a bother" to face this disability that sprang from nowhere. But, he added rather casually, "What's done is done. Besides, there's no use crying over spilled milk, now is there?" Dr. Lerbin also noted that Kurt's memory seemed to be quite poor for the days preceding the onset of his blindness: He remembered working as usual but not the details of what happened during the days.

Dr. Lerbin's special area of expertise was *hypnotherapy*, psychotherapy that involves the use of hypnosis. He had been asked by the opthamologist to meet with Kurt to help determine the reason for his blindness. Was it *psychogenic* (i.e., caused by psychological factors)? Could anything in Kurt's life or psychological functioning explain it? Or was Kurt intentionally acting blind in order to stop working and collect disability payments, as his impatient and disbelieving employer claimed?

PSYCHOSOCIAL HISTORY

Kurt Petrowski was a 35-year-old married white male, the father of two children. His daughter Patricia was 16 years old, his son Kurt Jr. was 14. The family lived in a small, rural, economically depressed town in the Midwest. Kurt worked as the manager of a fast food restaurant. He and Lurleen had gotten married immediately after graduating high school because Lurleen was pregnant.

Kurt had grown up on a farm in the town where he still lived, the second youngest of six children. His father had an erratic temperament. He often was quiet, noncommunicative, and seemingly indifferent to the financial hardships of their life. Other times, however, he would become verbally and physically abusive to the children. These outbursts occurred particularly when he was drinking, which he did episodically. When Kurt was eight years old, his father took off without explanation and was gone for several months. He then returned home just as suddenly as he left, also without explanation. After a tense period of settling back in, the incident of his unexplained departure was never discussed again. His father died from a heart attack when Kurt was 29.

For as long back as he could remember, Kurt's mother was afflicted by some unusual medical ailment. She was an obese woman and often stayed in bed for months at a time, relying on her children (particularly her two oldest daughters) to tend to her and run the household. A host of doctors were unable to diagnose or treat her many varied somatic complaints. She frequently referred to her medical troubles simply as her "condition."

Shortly after Kurt's father left and then returned to the family, his mother underwent a religious conversion. She embraced an evangelical, fundamentalist Christianity. Mrs. Petrowski forbade the children to listen to music or watch television, both of which she labeled (among many other things) "the work of the devil." She reminded her children daily that the Lord saw all that they did and would punish them for any sins they committed. These punishments were often described in vivid detail, and included such things as being struck mute, deaf, or blind.

Following his mother's lead, Kurt also became active in the local fundamentalist church. Throughout his adolescence, he was involved in the church's youth organization. He found great comfort in the strong, clear-cut views of right and wrong behavior the church put forward; this felt like a welcome contrast to what often seemed like the chaos at home. As time continued, however, Kurt's religious beliefs were increasingly at odds with his developing sexual relationship with Lurleen. When Lurleen became pregnant, Kurt felt he had no choice but to marry her.

Before his sudden blindness, Kurt had no history of major psychological difficulty. In the first few years of his marriage, he tended to complain a lot of physical ailments, but Lurleen usually chided him to "quit your bellyachin'—and don't go being like your mother." Lurleen had a rather no-nonsense manner about her, and Kurt learned long ago that he could not count on her for sympathy if he was feeling ill.

CONCEPTUALIZATION

Dr. Lerbin strongly suspected that Kurt's sudden blindness was a conversion disorder, one of six *somatoform disorders* described in DSM-IV (APA, 1994). These disorders share one dominant feature: the translation of psychological distress into a physical expression (*soma* is the Greek root for "body"). Often, the physical symptoms of a somatoform disorder fly in the face of medical reality—that is, they can not be substantiated by any available laboratory or neurophysiological testing, and may even contradict known physical mechanisms by which the body works.

To be diagnosed with conversion disorder, an individual must meet the following criteria (APA, 1994, p. 457):

A. One or more symptoms or deficits affecting voluntary motor or sensory function that suggest a neurological or other general medical condition.
B. Psychological factors are judged to be associated with the symptom or deficit because the initiation or exacerbation of the symptom or deficit is preceded by conflicts or other stressors.
C. The symptom or deficit is not intentionally produced or feigned.
D. The symptom or deficit cannot, after appropriate investigation, be fully explained by a general medical condition, or by the direct effects of a substance, or as a culturally sanctioned behavior or experience.

As Criterion A states, the conversion symptom may be either a motor or sensory impairment. Examples of motor difficulties include poor balance or coordination, paralysis or weakness of a specific body part, aphonia (the inability to talk or make sounds), difficulty swallowing, and an inability to urinate. Sensory impairments include loss of touch or pain sensation, blindness or double vision, deafness, or visual hallucinations.

Individuals with a conversion disorder may exhibit a marked lack of concern about their difficulty. To the disbelief of onlookers, the affected person may seem completely indifferent to the fact that he or she is paralyzed, blind, or unable to move his or her arms, legs, hands, etc. This phenomenon, called *la belle indifference*, is present in Kurt's situation.

When a person demonstrates *la belle indifference* along with a sudden motor or sensory impairment, diagnosing a conversion disorder may be relatively straightforward, because most people who suddenly develop a severe medical difficulty feel great distress. However, either with or without *la belle indifference*, the accurate diagnosis of conversion disorder often presents a significant challenge because the possibility of actual physiological impairment always needs to be considered. Medical science is not infallible, and even if an ailment cannot be confirmed by current laboratory tests or technology, this does not automatically mean it is of psychological origin. In some cases, individuals with a conversion disorder later prove to have actual neurological impairments that were undetected at the time of their conversion symptoms (Kent, Tomasson & Coryell, 1995).

TREATMENT

Treatment for conversion disorder can be approached from a variety of perspectives. However, no matter what style or method of treatment is used, a general guideline is that the person's affliction must be accepted as genuine (Katon, 1993). Even though the physical impairments are assumed to have psychological roots, the symptoms are not under the person's willful or conscious control. As such, attempting to convince a person that his or her troubles are made up is apt to fail. In other words, individuals suffering from a conversion disorder cannot be told simply to give up their symptoms and move on.

In part because of this complex interplay of mind and body, hypnotherapy can be a useful therapeutic modality in the treatment of somatoform disorders. This is because hypnosis may be effective in gaining access to thoughts, feelings, and memories that are not in conscious awareness. The process of hypnotherapy itself can be used with a range of other psychotherapies, including behavioral, cognitive-behavioral, psychodynamic, and even family systems approaches (Brown & Fromm, 1987). As Dr. Lerbin practiced hypnotherapy, he integrated it with psychodynamic theory. In particular, he believed that a conversion disorder typically arises when a person is experiencing an unconscious conflict that cannot be expressed psychologically.

At first, Kurt was hesitant about participating in hypnotherapy. At the end of their first meeting, when Dr. Lerbin proposed this as part of their work together, Kurt responded by saying, "You gotta be kidding, doc! So you're gonna tell me how sleepy I am, and then get me to run around the room clucking like a chicken? You gonna wave a watch in front of my face? How can you do that if I can't even see?"

Dr. Lerbin laughed along with Kurt, but assumed that Kurt's joking probably hid the fact that he was nervous. Dr. Lerbin cleared up some misconceptions about what hypnotherapy did (and did not) involve. At no time would Kurt lose control of himself. The capacity to be hypnotized (called *hypnotizability*) resided within Kurt and not with the person conducting hypnosis. At no time would Kurt say or do anything he did not want to or reveal anything he did not want to reveal. Hypnosis was not mysterious or spooky, as it looked in old movies; Dr. Lerbin would not be waving a pocket watch in front of his eyes. Instead, he would simply begin by teaching Kurt relaxation techniques to help him feel calmer and more at ease, and they would take it from there.

Kurt remained skeptical, but then said he was willing to give it a try—"Who knows, it might even be fun." They agreed to meet again later that week. Dr. Lerbin assisted Kurt to the door, where he then left, gripping onto the arm of his teenaged daughter.

In the next session, Dr. Lerbin educated Kurt about some key aspects of hypnotherapy, particularly about *induction* and *trance*. Induction refers to the process a hypnotherapist uses to help a person reach an altered state of consciousness. This altered state, referred to as an hypnotic trance, is different from our usual sense of being awake, asleep, dreaming, or even meditating. It is a state of heightened yet relaxed concentration. Although experts disagree on exactly how to define or explain a trance, most agree that it is a distinct state of focused awareness, marked by enhanced suggestibility, increased access to personal memory and imagination, and decreased capacity for reality testing (Wall, 1984). When hypnosis is used in a therapeutic context, the process is effective only when it is interactive. That is, the patient needs to be a willing participant and not just a passive recipient.

To begin, Dr. Lerbin taught Kurt progressive relaxation exercises. He asked Kurt to make himself comfortable in his chair, focus on Dr. Lerbin's voice, and pay attention to his own breathing. Throughout the 20-minute exercise, he instructed Kurt to concentrate on and relax various muscle groups. He continually encouraged Kurt to allow himself to relax. Dr. Lerbin chose his words very carefully. For example, he repeated to Kurt, "you may allow yourself to become just as relaxed *as you like*," so Kurt would hear the message that he was in control of his own reactions.

In the next few meetings, Dr. Lerbin included these progressive relaxation exercises as part of their work together, along with more traditional face-to-face talking psychotherapy. They talked about Kurt's childhood and family history, his current situation, and the process of hypnotherapy. Kurt's demeanor was typically good-natured and even somewhat bubbly, as if he were enjoying going along for this novel ride. Still, throughout this time, he remained unable to see.

After Kurt had mastered progressive relaxation, Dr. Lerbin then furthered the process of hypnotherapy by using a *deepening* technique to create an hypnotic trance. He explained to Kurt a process called the "escalator technique." After Kurt was relaxed, Dr. Lerbin asked him to imagine riding on a series of escalators descending very slowly, bit by bit, to a serene, relaxing place (Dr. Lerbin had already discussed with Kurt what this place would be; Kurt had chosen an open meadow of wildflowers that he had often visited as a child). Dr. Lerbin verbally led Kurt through the imagery of riding the escalator slowly down, all the while becoming more relaxed. As always, he chose his words carefully because of Kurt's increased suggestibility in an hypnotic state. He mentioned that the meadow Kurt was heading toward might have special, healing properties—it might even allow Kurt to temporarily regain his vision.

As Kurt entered a deeper hypnotic trance, Dr. Lerbin suggested that if he were to open his eyes, he might be able to describe what he saw around him. In response to this *hypnotic suggestion* (telling a person in trance that a particular phenomenon or event may occur), Kurt accurately described the interior of Dr. Lerbin's office, down to naming titles of books in the bookcase and the color of the stripes on the therapist's shirt.

Dr. Lerbin now had evidence that Kurt's blindness was psychogenic; while in an hypnotic trance, his eyes could function normally. This confirmed that the cause of his disability was not physiological. This was crucial information, yet it by no means meant that Kurt was "cured." The goal of treatment was for Kurt to have his sight restored, and reaching this goal still involved a few central unanswered questions: What had caused this conversion disorder to occur? What would help Kurt recover his sight? And, most immediately, was Kurt ready to learn that he was not, in fact, actually blind? In part to address this last concern, Dr. Lerbin ended the hypnotic trance with the following *posthypnotic suggestion* (a statement offered when a person is under a trance to influence his or her post-trance behavior):

"It is now time, gradually, to leave the field of meadow flowers, and return to the escalator . . . to ride it slowly up . . . and come back to the office where we sit together. As you ride back up, you may find that *you remember all that you need to remember and forget all that you need to forget.*"

Dr. Lerbin and Kurt then discussed what had just occurred. When Kurt answered the therapist's questions about the details of his trance experience, he described the meadow of flowers but made no mention of seeing the office around him. Based on this, Dr. Lerbin assumed that Kurt was not yet ready to acknowledge the psychological nature of his blindness. This did not really matter. Kurt was responding well to hypnosis (not all individuals are equally hypnotizable, and Kurt's ability to enter a trance was better than average). And as a good prognostic sign, Kurt had permitted himself to reveal during the trance that he could, indeed, see. Before ending the session, Dr. Lerbin told Kurt that he was doing extremely well. He casually added that "sometimes people recall more from their hypnotic sessions the more they do it."

The next challenge of treatment was to determine, if possible, what had led to Kurt's sudden blindness. Most conversion disorders follow a significant or traumatic event. Kurt's conscious memory was sketchy for the days prior to the onset of his conversion disorder. Yet why had it happened just when it did?

Dr. Lerbin explained to Kurt that he would like to employ another hypnotic procedure, called *time regression*. After Kurt had entered an hypnotic trance, Dr. Lerbin would lead him back to the days and weeks preceding the blindness. Perhaps Kurt would recall something upsetting that had happened. As always, even when in trance, Kurt would only share information that he wanted to share. Kurt agreed to continue with the process.

After Dr. Lerbin induced Kurt into another hypnotic trance, he encouraged Kurt to imagine that he was at home, sitting in his favorite chair, and watching himself on television, as if he were the lead character on his own show. Kurt had the remote control in his hand and could change the channel or turn down the volume whenever he liked. In addition, the television included a "relaxation channel," featuring soothing images of the field of wildflowers. That way, any time an image or memory arose that was too disturbing, Kurt had the ability to switch "channels" away from it and turn to a relaxing image. After establishing this scene, Dr. Lerbin asked Kurt if anything unusual or out of the ordinary had happened in the days prior to his blindness. What was he watching on the television he "saw" in front of him?

Kurt responded that the Sunday prior to his blindness, he had been in the family's house by himself.

"Is that unusual?" Dr. Lerbin asked.

"Yes. Usually at least somebody else is there. It hasn't happened in a long time."

"So you're alone in the house. What are you doing?"

"I'm bored. There's chores that I know I need to do, but I don't want to. But I can't sit still."

"Is something in particular making you feel jumpy?"

"No . . . yes. I keep on walking to my kids' rooms, standing in the doorway. But it's not right to go in."

"Do you want to go in?"

"Yes. I know it's wrong, but I want to, you know, kind of spy on them."

Dr. Lerbin suggested to Kurt, "If you pay attention to that sense of spying on them, perhaps you will be able to describe more about it."

"Well, it's nothing serious. Nothing kinky or anything like that. But maybe, you know, I want to go through their drawers or closets or something. I don't know."

"What do you do?"

Kurt paused. "I go to the kitchen and make myself a sandwich. Then when I'm eating, Lurleen calls, and says they're going to be late. They won't be home for a couple of hours."

"So you know you have more free time by yourself."

"Yeah. . . . I don't know. I don't feel too good."

Kurt was getting anxious at this point. Dr. Lerbin said, "Remember, Kurt, you have the remote control in your hand. Would you like to turn back to the relaxation channel? We can come back to this anytime you're ready, if and when you want to."

Kurt decided he wanted to return to the field of wildflowers and then indicated he did not want to continue with the hypnotic trance at that time. Dr. Lerbin led him out of the trance. Afterward, he and Dr. Lerbin discussed what had transpired. This time, Kurt recalled most of what had happened during the trance. He still did not have a conscious explanation for his blindness or any sense that his blindness was psychologically caused. Nor did he remember any more details of what had actually happened in the scene he described while in trance. But he said he was interested in continuing with the process during their next session.

That evening, Kurt telephoned Dr. Lerbin in a high state of anxiety. He had a bad headache, and his vision had gotten even worse—he could now not even see the indistinct, misty shapes of the past few weeks. Dr. Lerbin speculated that Kurt's headache and worsening of vision were related to the hypnotherapy. Kurt was not sure he agreed, but agreed to come in for an emergency session early the next day.

In that session, again under trance, Kurt described the rest of what occurred on the day he was home alone. Although he felt wrong about it, he had decided to enter Patricia's room and look through her things. In the back of one of her desk drawers, he found her diary. After a moment's hesitation, he began to read it. He at first thumbed through it, feeling excited but also a little guilty. He was about to put it away but then saw a few entries that hit him with a tremendous shock. He read that Patricia had gotten pregnant the year before, when she was 15 years old. She had had an abortion. She had confided the information to Lurleen, who accompanied her to a health clinic for the procedure. Neither Patricia nor Lurleen had told him.

Kurt began sobbing as he described this scene to Dr. Lerbin. When Dr. Lerbin asked what was upsetting him, Kurt described his panic at feeling trapped. He did not know what to do. He felt he could not reveal learning about Patricia's pregnancy because he was too embarrassed to admit reading her diary. But he was very disturbed and angered by the news. And why hadn't she or Lurleen told him?

When his wife and children came home from their outing that afternoon, they (of course) acted like nothing was wrong. But for Kurt, everything seemed different. He suddenly developed a severe headache and went to bed early. It was the next morning that he awoke unable to see.

Before the trance ended, Dr. Lerbin once again told Kurt he would "remember all you need to remember, and forget all you need to forget." He added that Kurt had indeed experienced a great shock—"the kind of terrible event that your mother once warned you God punishes people for, maybe even by making them blind." But Dr. Lerbin also called the situation "very hopeful" because "once a shock like this is out in the open, it can pave the way to start making your eyesight better."

Out of the trance, Kurt was still emotionally shaken up. His typically cheery, superficial manner had given way to looking agitated and depressed. This time, he remembered all the details of the trance, and he now also remembered what had happened at home that afternoon. But what was he going to do? After weighing different options, he hesitantly agreed with Dr. Lerbin's recommendation that they schedule a psychotherapy session for the entire family (or at least with Kurt, Lurleen, and Patricia), so Kurt could reveal his discovery and his secret.

Scheduled for the next day, the family meeting went better than Kurt expected. He talked about what had happened that afternoon. After a brief period of embarrassment and finger-pointing, Lurleen, Kurt, and Patricia began the process of speaking about their reactions to Patricia's pregnancy and the abortion. They agreed to have a couple of meetings together with Dr. Lerbin as a family, including Kurt Jr. as well.

Over the course of the next several weeks, the family held three more sessions with Dr. Lerbin. Kurt continued to meet with him individually as well, although these meetings did not involve hypnosis. During this time, Kurt reported that his vision began steadily improving—not all at once, but as a gradual process. Two months after being afflicted with his sudden blindness, Kurt's sight had returned to normal. Although Dr. Lerbin offered him the option of continuing in weekly psychotherapy, Kurt chose to terminate his treatment.

DISCUSSION

It seems likely that the physical expression of psychological distress is as old as humanity; known descriptions of conversion reactions date as far back as 4000 years ago to ancient Egypt. And over the past one hundred years, the history of this

---

Multiaxial DSM-IV Diagnosis at Time of Termination

Axis I:	Conversion Disorder with Sensory Deficit (Blindness) CONDITION: RESOLVED
Axis II:	No diagnosis
Axis III:	None
Axis IV:	Learning of daughter's abortion
Axis V:	*Treatment Onset:* 50 (serious symptoms and impairments in functioning) *Termination:* 80 (no more than slight impairment in functioning)

---

unique disorder provides a fascinating glimpse into how specific psychological ailments wax and wane with changing times.

During the Victorian era (the mid 19th century to the turn of the of the 20th century), experiences such as Kurt's were not uncommon; today they are relatively rare. At that time, conversion reactions afflicted mostly women from well-to-do, educated families. Today, conversion disorders are still more common among women than men but tend disproportionately to affect individuals from lower socioeconomic strata, rural communities, and those who have less knowledge or sophistication about psychological and medical functioning (Guggenheim & Smith, 1995).

Conversion disorders were once so prevalent that much of the early history of modern abnormal psychology has its roots in attempts to understand this perplexing phenomenon. What is now called conversion disorder is closely related to the historical concept of *hysteria*. This linguistic usage lingers on, and conversion disorders often are referred to as "hysterical" conditions, such as "hysterical blindness" (in Kurt's case), or hysterical deafness, hysterical paralysis, and so on. More so than any other disorder, it is with hysteria that Sigmund Freud, and other early investigators, honed the theories that laid the foundations of psychoanalysis, modern conceptions of the unconscious, and the study of abnormal psychology.

Hysteria has interesting roots, dating back to ancient Greece. The word "hysteria" comes from the Greek word for "uterus." Greek physicians and philosophers believed that the cause of what we currently regard as conversion reactions was that a woman's uterus became dislodged and wandered throughout her body (they considered this to be exclusively a female disorder). The nature of the hysterical symptoms related to the location where the uterus had wandered.

The term "conversion" was introduced by Freud and one of his colleagues, Josef Breuer, to emphasize how a psychological conflict was converted into a physical ailment. In one of Freud's most influential early works, he described his treatment of "Anna O.," a young woman from a prosperous family who was overcome with a range of unusual symptoms following the illness and death of her father. She became partially paralyzed. She suffered visual hallucinations. She lost her ability to comprehend her native language, German, but remained fluent in English! Her symptoms defied medical explanation or treatment. And although she could not intentionally overcome these symptoms, they would sometimes disappear while under hypnosis.

Freud theorized that Anna O.'s symptoms resulted from her grief and unconscious conflicts regarding the death of her father. Anna O. regained her functioning as Freud helped her identify and verbalize these conflicts, first through hypnosis and then through his newly pioneered "talking cure," psychoanalysis. Freud's theoretical assumption was that by bringing Anna's unconscious conflicts into the realm of consciousness, she would no longer need to express them symbolically, through physical impairment. (As an interesting historical side note, "Anna O." was in actuality a woman named Bertha Pappenheim, who later became a prominent leader in the developing field of social work).

Most conversion reactions are brief, lasting several hours to several days. This is particularly true if the conversion symptom develops in response to an acute, specific, identifiable stressor. Yet in some instances, the symptoms can last much longer and develop into a chronic or recurrent condition.

This type of chronic impairment is the case with a particularly perplexing, widespread example of conversion disorder that came to light in the mid 1980s. At that time, researchers in California began documenting and treating an epidemic of hysterical blindness among a specific population: older Cambodian women refugees, who emigrated to the United States after surviving the brutal regime of Pol Pot, Cambodia's dictatorial ruler from the mid 1970s to mid 1980s (van Boemel & Rozee, 1992).

These researchers documented more than 150 cases of unexplained loss of vision among female Cambodian refugees who relocated to the United States. No medical explanation could be found, but all these refugees (most of whom did not know each other) had lost their ability to see. In common, all these women had experienced profound psychological stressors associated with years of forced labor and internment, including starvation, physical or sexual abuse, and multiple bereavements. Many had witnessed the execution or torture of neighbors, friends, or family members, or witnessed other atrocities. All had been able to see prior to their ordeal but lost their sight at some point during or after their internment.

These women tended to offer nonpsychological explanations for their blindness. One attributed her loss of vision to the smoke from the cooking fire in the tiny hovel where she and her family were made to live. Another believed she infected her eyes from rubbing them when her hands were dirty with soil from the fields of her forced labor (Wilkinson, 1994). It seems likely that these nonpsychological explanations relate to cultural factors—in other words, it made more sense to these women to attribute their affliction to "real," rather than psychological, causes.

These same cultural factors also may explain why the somatization of psychological distress is a more typical and widespread occurrence in Asian than Western cultures. For example, bodily symptoms and explanations for psychological difficulties, ranging from depression to eating disorders, are much more common in China than in North America (Katzman & Lee, 1997; Kleinman, 1988). In Western societies, conversion disorders are now most common among populations that have less sophistication about medical and psychological functioning, such as rural communities like that of Kurt and his family.

Theoretical Perspectives

Perhaps more so than any other cluster of disorders, the somatoform disorders defy plausible explanation from current theoretical viewpoints in psychology, given their complicated interplay of psychological and physiological mechanisms. Still, certain aspects of conversion disorder may be understood from our traditional models.

A social learning perspective emphasizes the role of learning and reinforcement in a conversion disorder. Of particular relevance here is the concept of the *sick role* (Parsons, 1951). Although rarely made explicit, we have certain guidelines and expectations in our culture for how an ill person is supposed to act. Being sick of course involves many limitations and losses, but it can also result in gains and privileges. For example, ill people are often exempt from obligations that would otherwise be expected of them, and they may receive a unique kind of sympathy or attention.

Terms related to this concept are *primary gain* and *secondary gain*. These terms have a psychoanalytic origin, but over time have been incorporated into a range of theoretical perspectives. Primary gain refers to the direct psychological "benefit" of an illness (or conversion reaction), which was originally conceptualized as a reduction of anxiety, given how the illness might serve to keep an intrapsychic conflict out of awareness. Secondary gain refers to the interpersonal benefits of adopting the sick role—the sympathy, attention, or special status a person may receive by being ill.

According to a social learning view, by translating psychological distress into a physical illness, a person may desire the sick role to reap the benefits of secondary gain. This can happen with or without a person's explicit awareness of the underlying motivation. In other words, acting sick may inadvertently be positively reinforced. Perhaps certain children learn in their family that illness (in themselves, a sibling, or parent) leads to the positive reinforcement of special attention. Or, through classical conditioning, acting ill becomes a conditioned response to dealing with a wide range of stressful situations. Both of these possibilities may apply to Kurt, who had the model of his mother's constant illnesses and the attention she received because of them.

Modern psychodynamic theory has remained true to Freud's original ideas about conversion disorder. Theoretically, conversion disorder results when an unacceptable, anxiety-provoking unconscious impulse is translated (converted) into somatic form. Usually, this impulse is of an aggressive or sexual nature. By translating this forbidden impulse into a physical symptom, the person is unconsciously freed from the guilt and anxiety of experiencing it. The specific symptom is thought to be related to the nature of the unconscious conflict.

How might this apply to Kurt? A psychodynamic theorist would likely see his hysterical blindness as an unconsciously motivated expression of both self-punishment and self-relief. Kurt might be punishing himself for sneaking into his daughter's room and reading her diary. Reading about her abortion may have also made him think of his daughter in a sexual manner, stirring anxiety in him or making him feel that he was doing something wrong or sinful (recall that Kurt's mother invoked the threat of blindness as part of God's wrath for sinners).

At the same time, Kurt's blindness provided him unconscious relief because he no longer had to experience the guilt and anxiety of his crisis. When he developed the conversion symptom of blindness, he *repressed* (put out of conscious awareness) his activities of that afternoon. His distress had found a physical, not emotional, expression.

It certainly seems that aspects of the psychodynamic model fit Kurt's situation. However, the usefulness of this perspective becomes more limited when we return to the phenomenon of the Cambodian women. To cast *their* conversion disorders in the light of unconscious conflicts about sexuality or aggression is to miss the central feature of their experience—the terrible trauma they have suffered.

So while social learning theory emphasizes principles of reinforcement that may help sustain a conversion disorder, and psychodynamic theory looks at the unconscious functions conversion symptoms may serve, neither theory can fully account for why some individuals translate psychological distress into a physical ailment. And neither of these theories touches an even more fundamental and mysterious issue: What actual physiological processes could be involved in creating a conversion reaction? Even as psychology and medicine move more and more toward appreciating the interconnection of mind and body, the exact means by which a phenomenon such as hysterical blindness occurs defies current explanation.

Bear in mind that an individual with a conversion disorder is not simply "faking it"—he or she is not intentionally pretending to have an ailment, as is the case with *malingering* and *factitious disorder*. In malingering, a person willfully pretends to be psychologically or medically ill for some explicit external benefit—perhaps to avoid school, prison, or military service, or to gain financially by collecting disability, worker's compensation, or insurance payments. In factitious disorder, a person also purposely acts ill, with either a medical or psychological disorder. But here, the motivation is exclusively to adopt the sick role; a person with factitious disorder is not seeking external gain. In contrast to both, a person with a conversion symptom truly believes that he or she suffers from that symptom. His or her impairment, despite the lack of medical validation, is real.

In this regard, conversion disorder overlaps with what are grouped in DSM-IV as the dissociative disorders, such as dissociative identity disorder (formerly multiple personality disorder) or dissociative amnesia. The thread common to both groups of disorders is that a central part of one's psychological experience operates outside the sphere of conscious control. In fact, in the latest revision of the International Classification of Diseases and Related Health Problems (ICD-10) (WHO, 1992), conversion disorder is grouped among the dissociative disorders, not the somatoform disorders.

Looking at Kurt's family of origin, it is interesting to speculate about the familial transmission of his conversion disorder. It seems quite possible (although uncertain, given the limited evidence) that Kurt's mother has *somatization disorder*—another of the somatoform disorders, where the primary symptom is a host of physical complaints and ailments, some of which may greatly interfere with a person's functioning. And in a symbolic way, her religious conversion may have modeled separating conscious ideals and beliefs ("goodness") from impulses that were regarded as "bad," such as those involving sex or pleasure.

A Note on Hypnosis

Hypnosis has been available as a treatment technique since the late 1800s and paved the way for Freud and others to use a nonmedical approach to solve psychological difficulties. At first, Freud relied on hypnosis as the primary tool to unearth the unconscious conflicts he believed lay at the root of his patients' distress. However, after he developed the process of psychoanalysis, he came to favor this newer method. In psychoanalysis, a person is encouraged to say whatever enters his or her mind through a process of *free association,* thereby slowly allowing access to the same unconscious material. As psychoanalysis gained popularity, hypnotherapy waned. It was then rediscovered as a treatment option during World War II, when it was employed to help combat soldiers' stress and battle exhaustion. In the years since World War II, hypnosis has earned respect as a key treatment modality in the realm of *behavioral medicine*—the application of psychological principles to the treatment of medical illness.

Hypnosis is currently used in many psychotherapeutic contexts, including pain management, smoking cessation, and the treatment of alcohol or substance abuse, sexual dysfunctions, and sleep disorders. It is also applied to the treatment of psychosomatic illnesses such as asthma, hypertension, and certain skin diseases. (Contrary to popular use of the word, *psychosomatic* does not mean that a person is faking an illness. Instead, like "somatoform," it refers to the interplay of psychological and somatic factors).

Hypnosis also can be beneficial for individuals who have dissociative disorders, who have been traumatized, or who wish to remember traumatic memories that they can not consciously recall. However, these applications of hypnosis are controversial. Without outside corroboration, there can never be any certainty that the "memories" uncovered in an hypnotic trance represent actual life events. Such corroboration did occur in Kurt's situation, with his wife and daughter acknowledging the truth of Patricia's pregnancy. However, hypnotic "memories" also may emerge that are influenced by a person's wishes, fantasies, or fears, and so it is only with great caution that the material elicited in an hypnotic trance should be regarded as "real."

PROGNOSIS

Kurt saw Dr. Lerbin for two follow-up meetings after he terminated psychotherapy, at six months and one year later. Throughout that time, Kurt experienced no subsequent episodes of blindness or impaired vision. He reported that family life had basically returned to normal.

Kurt never quite accepted the idea that his blindness was caused by psychological factors. Instead, he thought that the severe headache that he had suffered that afternoon, following the shock of his discovery and his own embarrassment and guilt, caused some "nerve damage." And now—even though he believed the psychotherapy and hypnotherapy had helped—he maintained that his vision returned because "the damaged nerve" had thankfully gotten better.

Kurt's good outcome is not unusual. Many individuals with conversion disorder appear to overcome their symptoms fairly rapidly (Folks, Ford & Regan, 1984; Kent, Tomasson & Coryell, 1995). A favorable prognosis is associated with situations such as Kurt's: a sudden onset of symptoms and a clearly identifiable stressor. In one recent study (Couprie et al., 1995), hospitalized individuals who began to recover quickly from a conversion disorder fared much better in the long run than those who failed to improve in the initial stages of treatment. The long-term outcome may be less hopeful for individuals who have maintained their conversion symptom for a long duration (Krull & Schifferdecker, 1990).

Perhaps because they are no longer as prevalent as had previously been the case (at least in Western culture), comparatively little research is now conducted on conversion reactions. Still, in the years ahead, understanding more about this unique phenomenon may shed new light on the fascinating interconnections between our bodies and minds, our "somas" and "psyches."

CRITICAL THINKING QUESTIONS

1. Do you think instead of a conversion disorder, Kurt has a factitious disorder (purposely pretending to be sick in order to receive the attention involved)? How would you distinguish between the two?

2. Hypnotherapy is an ethical and valid treatment approach for many disorders, but some psychologists consider it controversial. What might be some potential concerns about hypnotherapy? Some potential benefits?

3. Conversion reactions were far more common 100 years ago than now. What factors do you think might contribute to this?

4. What specific aspects of Kurt's treatment do you see as most helpful in his recovery? How would these have been the same or different if Kurt was treated by a therapist who did not use hypnotherapy?

5. What are some strengths and weaknesses of the psychodynamic perspective on conversion disorders? Why are somatoform disorders in general difficult to formulate from our current mainstream perspectives?

Dissociative Identity Disorder

M arie Warner was a kind, self-effacing 38-year-old woman who taught ballet at an elite dance studio in Manhattan. At first glance, the most striking thing about her was how *unstriking* she was. She dressed only in black dance garb, even when not teaching. She never wore makeup or jewelry and kept her hair simple and unadorned. Students enjoyed working with her; she was regarded as a talented teacher. And colleagues had long ago stopped registering surprise at the dramatic transformation she underwent when teaching a class: Her reserved manner then gave way to a commanding, energetic presence.

People also noticed other peculiarities about Marie. Often, she seemed to have no recollection of prior conversations. More than once, she passed a student or colleague on the street and looked startled and disoriented when the person said "Hello," as if she had never before seen the familiar face in front of her. And despite her eight years at the studio, nobody really knew anything about her personal life, other than that she was married to Pablo, a pleasant man several years her senior. Still, these peculiarities were accepted as part of who Marie was and were shrugged off as the quirks of an "artistic temperament."

Marie's life might have continued on in this routine manner indefinitely if not for a crisis. Pablo was hospitalized following a massive heart attack. Deeply shaken, Marie was terrified that he might die. Pablo was her sole confidante and companion; she had no friends and minimal contact with her family.

During Pablo's lengthy hospitalization and convalescence, Marie visited him twice daily. That is, she *thought* she visited him twice daily—but, much to her alarm, she soon realized that she was not sure of this! Alone in her apartment in the evenings, Marie increasingly had the chilling realization that she could not recall the day's activities. Had she been to visit Pablo? What had they talked about, how had he seemed? She could not always remember. Just as distressing, Marie also failed to recall what she did after her visits, or before.

At the same time, Marie began having other disturbing experiences. Certain commonplace events, such as passing well-dressed elderly women on the sidewalk, filled her with an inexplicable sense of dread. Twice, she was horrified to find herself in an unknown and dangerous part of the city, with no recollection of why she was there or how she had gotten there. She also began suffering various somatic problems, including frequent headaches, stomach pains, and a nearly constant fatigue.

Marie's functioning at the studio changed. After years of punctuality and reliability, she began showing up late for work. A few times, she did not show up at all. Her students did not know what had happened to her—her classes were now disorganized and lackluster, and she seemed *different*. Her colleagues tried to be supportive, given the stress of her current circumstances. But students and colleagues alike were flabbergasted one day when she arrived at the studio wearing not her typical black garb, but lipstick, mascara, and a flamboyant, low-cut red ballet outfit more suitable for the stage than for everyday life.

It was Dr. Zimmerman, the cardiologist treating Pablo, who first suggested that Marie see a psychotherapist, after a similarly bizarre incident. Visiting Pablo's hospital room, Dr. Zimmerman found Marie asleep in a chair at her husband's side and gently tried to awaken her. Marie was not easy to rouse. When Dr. Zimmerman finally succeeded, Marie did not appear to recognize where she was, who Dr. Zimmerman was, or even who Pablo was. She seemed like a lost and very frightened young child. Out of nowhere she cried out, "Not the basement, please, not the basement!" and began to sob. She curled up in her chair like a little girl.

Dr. Zimmerman was quite taken aback. Hoping that this behavior was the result of sleep deprivation or some inability to completely awaken from a dream, Dr. Zimmerman said she would get Marie a cup of coffee and be right back. But when she returned a few minutes later, there was no evidence of the frightened, childlike presence Dr. Zimmerman had seen only moments before. Marie was now striding about the room in a no-nonsense manner, tidying up. She rather tersely acknowledged Dr. Zimmerman's arrival and then launched into a series of well-informed technical questions about the results of Pablo's most recent tests.

Dr. Zimmerman stood stunned in the doorway, holding the cup of coffee, unsure of where to begin or how to respond to the transformed woman before her. After a few moments of awkward silence, she did the only thing she knew to do: She answered the questions. She then suggested they sit down the next afternoon to discuss Pablo's care. Marie dutifully made a note of the time, excused herself, and left the hospital room.

Dr. Zimmerman was confused and intrigued by what she had just seen. When she returned to her office, she contacted an old friend, a psychologist named Carolyn Lu, to talk over these strange events. Her friend recommended referring Marie for further evaluation, which Dr. Zimmerman did the next afternoon at their meeting. Marie's first impulse was to say no—she had already had a lot of contact with mental health professionals (in fact, far more than anyone would have guessed). But out of her respect for Dr. Zimmerman, and her own mounting distress about what was happening to her, Marie agreed to meet with Dr. Lu.

PSYCHOSOCIAL HISTORY

Marie Warner grew up in a wealthy suburb of Chicago. She was the youngest of three children, with two brothers eight and twelve years her senior. Her parents owned a successful nationwide business and were quite active in local civic affairs. Through much of Marie's childhood, the family had the luxury of full-time domestic help for childcare and household management.

It was soon after the family went through an immense business loss that Mrs. Warner learned she was pregnant with Marie. The pregnancy was unexpected, unwanted, and difficult in its course. Mrs. Warner was ordered to bed to "lie in" for the last five months of the pregnancy. During this period of forced inactivity, she became extremely depressed and angry. Mrs. Warner had never been easy to get along with; now, she was often irrational in her beliefs and behaviors. She became convinced that her husband had impregnated her to "get away" from her and to punish her for "becoming an old woman." She developed a strong resentment toward her unborn child, whom she blamed for her situation. Her irrationality grew to the extent that she even blamed the baby for the recent business failures.

During Marie's first years of life, her family sold off many assets to meet their mounting debts. Yet even with this financial decline, the Warners kept their home (without the former staff) and lived far more comfortably than most. Still, Mrs. Warner acted as if they were poverty-stricken. Many days she refused to buy food for fear of spending her "last dime." And without reason, her anger and resentment toward Marie continued to grow. This was Mrs. Warner's first experience of caring for an infant herself, and she did not like it.

When Marie was still an infant, Mrs. Warner began physically abusing her. At first sporadic, this abuse soon developed into a repetitive, unyielding, and horrific pattern. Mrs. Warner seemed to take pleasure in devising new ways to be cruel to her daughter. Marie was sometimes deprived of food and water for days on end; other times she was force-fed until she vomited. As punishment for something as trivial as spilling a glass of milk, she might be locked in the basement or a dark closet for a week. She was physically tortured with belt buckles, needles, and hot wax dripped onto her body. Once, after Marie soiled her underpants, Mrs. Warner made her eat her feces. Another time Marie nearly drowned, with her mother holding her head underwater in an unflushed toilet.

There seemed to be no escape possible from this nightmarish abuse. In public, Mrs. Warner effusively praised Marie and doted on her. And although Mr. Warner was aware that his wife had become emotionally unhinged, he responded only by working longer hours and taking more frequent, lengthier business trips. The two older sons lived at boarding school.

When still a young girl, Marie gradually learned to survive her mother's tortures with a kind of self-hypnosis. She started creating the illusion that these abuses were not happening—or at least not happening to *her*. At first, this self-hypnosis seemed to occur spontaneously, in response to her feelings of terror, pain, or exhaustion. But at some point Marie discovered she could induce this desired, detached state herself. By riveting her attention on some rote, routine task (such as rhythmically counting the flowers on the wallpaper), or by staring intensely at a lighting fixture, she could make herself "disappear" from the pain she was experiencing, and then "reappear" when it was over.

Without quite realizing it was occurring, Marie began to "disappear" more and more often. She became adept at slipping into this detached state at the start of any new abusive episode, or at the first awareness of any cue of possible harm, such as a tone in her mother's voice or the sound of her approaching footsteps. By her fifth birthday, Marie was entering into this altered state with frequency. And as she did so, she stopped remembering the traumas she continued to endure.

Also by her fifth birthday, the family business was once again thriving. The life of paid domestic help, travel, and civic involvement returned. Marie was now often left in the care of hired domestic help. No longer as frequently subjected to her mother's abuse, her next few years were relatively safe and less bleak. Marie forged strong, sustaining bonds with her new nanny.

Still, it was clear to most observers that something was terribly wrong. Marie rarely spoke, and she demonstrated limited understanding of events around her. She had an eerie, "spacey" quality. She had no friends and spent much of her time alone, rocking or cradling herself, or twirling in circles. Mr. Warner suggested that Marie be medically and psychiatrically evaluated for these oddities, but he deferred to his wife's opinion that "she'll grow out of it." Instead, Marie was enrolled in a small, private day school and placed in a special classroom.

Marie's teachers found that she was much less odd in some situations than others and that her behavior was inconsistent from day to day, or even moment to moment. I.Q. testing suggested she was below average intellectually, yet she occasionally surprised everyone with astute observations and flashes of quick-witted humor. She seemed most engaged and relaxed in activities that involved music and creative movement, leading one teacher to recommend that Marie take ballet lessons.

Marie's nanny, who was confused by her behavior at home, was grateful for the suggestion. From her first class, Marie loved dance lessons. Soon, the nanny could use the threat of taking away a ballet lesson, or rewarding her with extra ones, to help shape Marie's behavior (such as changing her stubborn habit of refusing baths—Marie was terrified of bathrooms, but she never could or would say why).

Learning ballet was a crucial turning point in Marie's development. She thrived under the nurturing support of her teacher, a kind, middle-aged Russian woman who recognized in her an unusual talent and potential. Marie took refuge in her ballet studies and entered the competitive world of ballet performance while still quite young. By age 13, she was winning scholarships and competitions, and she was invited to spend a summer touring with a professional ballet troupe.

Yet despite this success with ballet, all was not well. At home her mother continued to abuse her, cleverly out of others' awareness, just as cruelly but less frequently. Marie began experiencing panic attacks, or "waves of terror," as she called them. These attacks left her immobilized with fear. At age 14, she began drinking alcohol to quell her anxiety. By 16, she was using tranquilizers. Her substance abuse soon escalated to the degree that Marie was drinking and taking unprescribed sedatives daily.

Marie finished high school and won admission to a prestigious ballet school in Manhattan. She continued to abuse pills, alcohol, and other substances to manage her now constant feelings of anxiety or panic. She did well initially at school, but soon the competitive stress, and her own substance dependence, were too much. At 19, Marie took a nearly lethal drug overdose and was hospitalized. When questioned whether the overdose was intentional or accidental, she answered flatly, "I don't know."

After the overdose, Marie went through a precipitous decline that lasted for years. She stopped dancing and taking care of herself. In her early twenties, she made a series of suicide attempts, always followed by the same flat uncertainty about whether she actually wanted to kill herself. Her family gave her money to live on, but otherwise had little contact with her. She had several admissions to psychiatric hospitals and went through a range of psychotherapists, medications, and other treatments, none of which seemed to help.

Marie's condition baffled all the mental health professionals she encountered, and she accrued a wide range of diagnoses. All agreed that she had a substance dependence disorder, including abuse of alcohol, prescription medications, and street drugs. But she also was diagnosed at various times with schizophrenia (she sometimes spoke of hearing voices, or said odd things like, "I don't control my hands"); borderline personality disorder (her torso was covered with scars from self-inflicted wounds, and she had profound identity issues); major depression with psychotic features (depression sometimes debilitated her to the point where her reality testing was distorted); and bipolar disorder (her mood could vary from despair to periods of unbounded energy).

This pattern of frequent hospitalizations and marginal functioning ended when Marie met Pablo, the man who became her husband when she was 29 years old. Pablo was an extremely supportive and stabilizing presence in her life. He encouraged her to take dance classes again. Also with his support, Marie attended college to earn an associate's degree in dance and choreography. Pablo provided a loving acceptance that allowed Marie bit by bit to gain sobriety and stability, and even in some ways to blossom.

The next nine years were mostly smooth. Marie's frequent hospitalizations stopped. She continued to experience unusual symptoms, such as occasional unaccountable lapses of memory for a few hours, insomnia, and sudden urges to kill herself that seemed to spring from nowhere (but often surfaced in the days following any contact with her family). But Pablo took on the responsibility of caring for Marie during these odd lapses and was able to keep her safe and stable. Then, Pablo had his heart attack, and her ability to cope with daily life began to unravel precipitously.

CONCEPTUALIZATION

Marie Warner has dissociative identity disorder (DID), formerly known as multiple personality disorder. The DSM-IV specifies four criteria for this disorder (APA, 1994, p. 487):

A. The presence of two or more distinct identities or personality states (each with its own relatively enduring pattern of perceiving, relating to, and thinking about the environment and self).

B. At least two of these identities or personality states recurrently take control of the person's behavior.

C. Inability to recall important personal information that is too extensive to be explained by ordinary forgetfulness.

D. The disturbance is not due to the direct physiological effects of a substance (e.g., blackouts or chaotic behavior during alcohol intoxication) or a general medical condition (e.g., complex partial seizures). *Note:* In children, the symptoms are not attributable to imaginary playmates or other fantasy play.

As will become more evident, Marie has several distinct personality states, or "alters." Each has a separate identity with a distinct interpersonal, emotional, and cognitive style (Criterion A). Each identity sometimes takes control of Marie's consciousness and behavior (Criterion B). She has extensive memory lapses (often referred to as "losing time"; Criterion C). And despite her history of dependence on several substances, neither this nor a medical condition explains her symptoms (Criterion D).

DID is one of four dissociative disorders described in the DSM-IV. All of these disorders share the common feature of *dissociation*, which is defined as "a disruption in the usually integrated functions of consciousness, memory, identity and perception of the environment" (APA, 1994, p. 477). In the case of DID and the other dissociative disorders, the disruption caused by dissociation is profound and is often the central aspect of a person's experience.

In addition to DID, Marie also meets the criteria for polysubstance dependence, in remission. This diagnosis indicates that Marie has a history of substance dependence, and it is not currently an active problem. Some mental health professionals would also diagnose Marie with posttraumatic stress disorder (PTSD), given the childhood abuses she suffered. While such a diagnosis seems appropriate, her presentation does not match the specific criteria for PTSD described in the DSM-IV.1 [1]

TREATMENT

Psychotherapeutic treatment for DID is considered most effective when it is intensive and long-term, with three to five years a minimal reasonable estimate (Putnam, 1989). In many regards, the guidelines for treatment are the same as they are for other trauma-related disorders. Dr. Carolyn Lu, who worked from an eclectic perspective, followed a three-stage treatment model proposed by Herman (1992). The stages are 1) establishing safety and building skills of basic self-care; 2) recovering memories of past traumatic events, and mourning the losses and pain involved; and 3) coming to terms with one's own history, and reconnecting with the larger society. The model is particularly appropriate for individuals who have survived ongoing, severe abuse, such as Marie.

---

[1]A case study of posttraumatic stress disorder is presented in Chapter 1.

At the start of treatment, it is important to try to establish an accurate diagnosis. Based on Dr. Zimmerman's account, Dr. Lu hypothesized that one of the dissociative disorders might provide a plausible explanation for Marie's odd behavior. But there also were other possibilities to consider, including substance abuse, psychosis, an unusual sleep disorder, a personality disorder, a factitious disorder (in which a person acts mentally or physically ill for the attention involved), or even malingering (deliberately faking an illness for some explicit benefit, such as collecting insurance money or avoiding an unwanted situation).

And in fact, during their first two meetings together, nothing about Marie suggested anything as dramatic as DID. Instead, Marie seemed withdrawn, shy, and quite depressed. She told Dr. Lu about Pablo's condition but said nothing about her recent frightening experiences or troubled past. Most of the time, she stared out the window or appeared terribly engrossed in the patterns of the carpet. Dr. Lu gently asked many questions, but getting a whole sentence in response seemed a major feat. Dr. Lu even wondered if Marie might have a psychotic disorder, given the frequent long delays between her questions and Marie's monosyllabic responses. During these pauses it seemed as if Marie were listening to some internal dialogue, like the hallucinated voices often "heard" in psychosis.

However, the third meeting was remarkably different from the previous two. Marie finally revealed that most days she had no idea what she had done. She told Dr. Lu that she sometimes found herself carrying large sums of money, with no idea where it came from or what it was for. She had not felt this out of control since she had been hospitalized in her twenties—Oh, had she failed to mention that she had been hospitalized? Well, yes, eight times before meeting Pablo and getting sober. Oh—had she not mentioned her addiction problem? Yes, she had severely abused many substances. She thought she probably still attended a few NA (Narcotics Anonymous) meetings each week, but she was not completely sure. . . .

Dr. Lu was struck by Marie's parenthetical manner of relaying this information. She was further puzzled by other aspects of Marie's strikingly different presence. In contrast to Marie's prior withdrawn depression, she now spoke in fast, thoughtful paragraphs and watched Dr. Lu with a penetrating gaze. She seemed skilled at verbal sparring, and peppered her statements with curse words.

Dr. Lu explained her confusion to Marie, paying close attention to Marie's responses:

> DR. LU: "I was just puzzling over the marked change in your perspective today. You're talking a lot more and seem to be more alert. How do you make sense of that?"
>
> MARIE: "Listen, don't start that patronizing tone with me. You mention one word about psychosis or antipsychotic medication and I'm out of here. I watched enough of that shit the last time. *She* might be able to take that crap but I refuse."
>
> Dr. Lu paused, and then asked, "Who is she?"
>
> MARIE: "*She* is Marie. Maybe we'll talk about who I am some other time. I'm only here because somebody is planning to kill her again. I thought

> we were done with that crap. And I guess she needs help. So are you going to help or not?"

DR. LU: "How do you think I could help?"

And thus began the relationship between Dr. Lu and one of Marie's various alter personalities.

After several weeks of dialogue similar to the above, Dr. Lu was satisfied that she was witnessing phenomena consistent with dissociative identity disorder. She learned that "Elizabeth," the first alter to introduce herself, was often "in charge" when it came to dealing with the outside world. Later, it became clear that Elizabeth was the overseer of the personality system. Dr. Lu then met Pam, a little girl terrified of being hurt. (It was Pam who Dr. Zimmerman first encountered in Pablo's hospital room, and Elizabeth who greeted her on return). Dr. Lu also met Tony, a profoundly depressed male adolescent alter. In a state of despair, Tony wandered the streets after visiting Pablo. He was stockpiling money and scouting out unsavory neighborhoods in order to buy a gun and shoot "himself." Marie herself, or what Marie experienced as truly herself (in actuality, all these identities were part of "Marie") was quiet, timid, and unassertive.

Dr. Lu met these alters in a variety of ways. Sometimes a particular alter would enter the session from the waiting room, with a distinctive walk, style, and interpersonal manner. Other times during a session, Marie would abruptly become very withdrawn, silent, and unresponsive to Dr. Lu's voice. It was as if she had suddenly gone very far away. She would then emerge from such a state—which was, in fact, an episode of dissociation—in a changed identity.

Dr. Lu chose not to tell Marie about her diagnosis until she herself was certain what was going on. She then explained it first to Elizabeth, who agreed that Marie should know ("Marie" had no awareness at all of what any of the alters did or said when they interacted in the world, experiencing these episodes as empty time, without any sense of why this happened). Marie had a strong and contradictory reaction to the news. On the one hand, she was relieved to have, for the first time, an explanation that so clearly fit her odd experiences. As strange as this explanation sounded, it made sense to her. But she also was disturbed and frightened to think of herself as having different personalities.

And having this new diagnosis did not immediately help her get better. In fact, the opposite was occurring: Marie was spending increasing amounts of time in a dissociated state, and her functioning had deteriorated to the point that she could no longer work. Dr. Lu even recommended a psychiatric day treatment program, but Elizabeth refused this option, given Marie's past experiences with hospitals.

Once the diagnosis was established, Dr. Lu discussed her treatment approach with Marie (again, she first explained it to Elizabeth, who could participate in the necessary decision making; "Marie" by now seemed too disconnected and apathetic to care). Dr. Lu took the stance that Marie's capacity to dissociate had once been quite adaptive—it allowed her to survive the horrors of her childhood. When young children are faced with overwhelming and painful mistreatment at the hands of an adult caretaker, discovering ways to psychologically "leave" the traumatic experience is a creative, necessary strategy. But what had once been adaptive no longer was, and Marie's dissociation had significantly impeded her development as an adult.

Because Marie entered therapy in a state of crisis, the immediate goal was to create a safety plan to protect her from self-harm. Dr. Lu explained the importance of this to Marie, "and to any others who are listening and might want to participate." Over the next few sessions, two other alters, both of whom Dr. Lu had previously met, came forward to contribute to this plan. Tony, the most dangerous and self-destructive alter, agreed not to kill himself, "at least for now."

Marie and Dr. Lu met twice weekly during this initial stage. Dr. Lu placed maximal importance on creating a strong therapeutic alliance with Marie, including all the various "parts" of her. Because the foundation of an integrated identity or sense of self develops within a secure, trusting connection with early caretakers (an experience Marie lacked), a basic part of treatment for DID (and other trauma-related disorders) involves slowly establishing a capacity to trust the therapist.

After the immediate threat of crisis had passed, the focus shifted to improving Marie's self-care. In some very basic ways, sometimes even including personal hygiene, Marie appeared to be unable to care for herself. The first task to help overcome this was countering Marie's tendency to "lose time." To meet this end, Dr. Lu and Marie developed a detailed system of self-monitoring, including a wristwatch alarm set for every 30 minutes. When the alarm went off, Marie asked herself basic questions about time, place, and physiological state (e.g., "Where am I? Is this where I am supposed to be? What was I just doing? Am I hungry? Am I tired?"). This not only helped Marie to stay focused and become more aware of her body and needs for self-care, but it also gave her a more regular, continuous sense of time—an experience that most people take for granted but which for Marie was powerful and new, given that she had always experienced time as splintered and random.

Once Marie was able to do this self-monitoring consistently, the focus of psychotherapy shifted to helping the different alter personalities communicate with each other. At first, Elizabeth seemed to be the only alter aware of any of the others' existence. But as the various alters spent more time with Dr. Lu, each started indicating a readiness to learn about, or at least acknowledge the existence of, the others. Still, Marie had no direct access to any of these parts, and none wanted to communicate with her directly. Marie had to rely solely on Dr. Lu's feedback to learn what was going on inside of her. In time, however, the alters began to communicate with Marie in indirect ways, such as leaving messages for her on her answering machine, or notes for her to read. Eventually, Elizabeth purchased a notebook to serve as a common log among the different members of the personality system; Marie now found it very helpful to have a personal diary, but one that she had to read to know what was written!

This slow and painstaking process spanned approximately two years, with many setbacks and crises. Often, these crises were in the psychotherapy relationship itself. For example, a particular alter might get angry with Dr. Lu, and Marie would then find herself having missed a string of appointments, or learning that she had left a rageful, verbally abusive message on Dr. Lu's answering machine. Other times, setbacks would be prompted by real-life events. A particularly difficult stretch was when Marie's mother died (Marie had severed all contact with her family at the beginning of treatment). This led to a brief psychiatric hospitalization because "Tony" once again became extremely suicidal. Antidepressant and antianxiety medications helped her through the worst of this crisis. (In general, psychopharmacological treatment of DID can be quite complex, and requires great caution, because no medications currently treat the core problem of dissociation, and different alters may present markedly different or contradictory symptoms [Torem, 1996]).

Marie's general movement, however, was toward becoming more aware of her many alters, and regaining an ability to function in the world. Two and one-half years into treatment, she returned to her schedule of working part-time at the dance studio and doing freelance choreography. She continued to see Dr. Lu twice weekly and also participated in a psychotherapy group for women with dissociative disorders. Pablo had long since fully recovered from his heart attack. He had learned as much as possible about Marie's disorder, occasionally participated in psychotherapy sessions with her, and resumed his role as a primary source of support.

With increased internal communication and fewer dissociative episodes, Marie now experienced time as more linear and less fragmented or disjointed. She slowly felt somewhat more self-confident, as if "Marie" herself was beginning for the first time to have an identity. Yet this progress had a painful downside: It also brought to Marie's conscious awareness the dawning knowledge of the terrible childhood abuses she had suffered.

Previously, Marie's memory of her childhood, good and bad, had been a blank. These memories had been "held" by her alter personalities. For example, Pam, the terrified little girl, was suffused with the fears of her childhood but could only understand the facts as would a four- or five-year-old child. When she was present, there was a sense of immediate, timeless horror, as if the need to escape were as fresh as in the moment of the original trauma. Tony, the suicidal adolescent, also held many traumatic memories but with a painful, precisely detailed memory. Elizabeth had the best overall recall but only in an unemotional, detached way.

Treatment had by now segued into its second major phase—recovering and working through trauma memories (the "stages" of treatment, in actual practice, overlap and interweave with one another). For Marie, this was a gut-wrenching process. At times it even challenged her will to live, and suicide once again became a concern. However, by slowly "integrating" these previously unknown fragments of memory, sharing them with Dr. Lu as a witness to what she had endured, and grieving over the many abuses she had suffered, Marie began to feel more like a whole person. She told Dr. Lu that perhaps Tony and Pam (and a few other alters) had always needed to be heard and have their stories taken seriously, but they had been too scared to seek help. Now that was finally happening, allowing her to heal. Marie was able to start knowing and facing her past.

It is at this point that we leave Marie's therapy, almost four years into the process. She and Dr. Lu have begun working on the third phase of treatment—coming to terms with her past and reconnecting with the world around her. With Dr. Lu's encouragement, Marie is attempting to broaden her support system beyond Pablo and to develop friendships for the first time in her life. She has recommitted to attending NA meetings in order to prevent a relapse of her drug dependence. She

---

Multiaxial DSM-IV Diagnosis at This Point in Treatment

Axis I: Dissociative Identity Disorder
             CONDITION: STABLE
             Polysubstance Dependence, in Remission
Axis II: No diagnosis
Axis III: None
Axis IV: History of severe abuse in childhood
Axis V: *Onset of Treatment:* 20 (some danger of hurting self;
             gross impairments in judgment)
             Current Time: 65 (mild to moderate difficulties in functioning;
             limited social support)

---

faces hard choices about disclosing her history and diagnosis to others—whom she wants to tell, when, and how much. But now, Marie is aware that it is she who is making these choices. Her treatment is likely to continue for several more years.

DISCUSSION

Perhaps no current psychological disorder evokes more controversy, fascination, and wonder than DID. With other disorders, clinicians and researchers might disagree about matters such as presumed etiology or the best treatment; with DID, the controversy is whether *to believe in it or not.* This controversy arises from the dramatic symptomatology involved, and from the explosion of diagnosed cases since the early 1980s. Although current prevalence estimates are hard to come by, until recently, the disorder was considered an extremely rare phenomenon.

Skeptics contend that DID is either an exaggerated, self-induced display made by a lonely person to gain attention, or the artificial creation of misguided therapists. Some dismiss it as a disorder that can easily be "faked" and give it about as much credence as UFO spottings (Ross, 1989). But "believers" counter that a true diagnosis of DID is often overlooked by clinicians who have not been adequately trained, or who let their biases interfere with an accurate clinical assessment (Coons, 1998). They point to the fact that the vast majority of patients with DID consistently present stories of horrific, abusive childhoods, and that most cases are far less exotic than those that have been sensationalized in the media (Kluft, 1996; Putnam, 1989).

The issue of whether DID can be "faked" actually does little to settle the question of its validity. Some individuals may attempt to fake DID, just as some individuals may attempt to fake any number of psychiatric and medical disorders. But that does not indicate that DID does not exist, any more than the ability to feign a headache means that real headaches do not exist. In addition, when professional actors were given accurate clinical information and challenged to fake DID, clinicians familiar with the disorder were able to distinguish the fakers from the real DID patients (Putnam, 1989).

Some of the most extensive efforts to validate and understand DID have looked at physiological and behavioral differences between various "alter" personalities in the same person (Barkin, Braun & Kluft, 1986; Coons, 1988; Putnam et al., 1986; Zahn, Moraga & Ray, 1996). Such differences have been documented with a range of functions, including heart rate, blood pressure, respiration rate, medication reactions, allergies, responses to alcohol, reading ability, visual acuity, dominant handedness, and sensitivity to pain. The demonstrable differences in autonomic nervous system functioning have been explained in various ways, ranging from actual distinct physiological states to changes that are voluntarily controlled to normative distinctions between various emotions (North et al., 1993). As intriguing as these data are, most studies of this sort have involved small samples or single subjects, and more research is needed to clarify the extent and nature of these phenomena (Zahn et al., 1996).

Dissociation

All theories that attempt to explain DID begin with the concept of dissociation. On a "normal" basis, most people experience dissociation to at least some minimal, nondisruptive degree (such as driving a car on a familiar route, and later not recalling any details of the trip). But dissociation also is a response that may develop spontaneously in the midst of traumatic events—events that produce "intense fear, helplessness, loss of control, and threat of annihilation" (Andreasen, 1985, p. 918). These dissociative states may then be triggered by specific sensory stimuli associated with prior abuse or with the perpetrator, such as the smell of alcohol or cologne, a certain tone of voice, or the sound of one's bedroom door opening.

In cases of severe trauma, dissociation can involve profound alterations in consciousness—a blurring of the usual connections between mind and body, reality and fantasy, attention and oblivion. A sense of time becomes distorted. A person feels detached from her or his own body, perhaps numb or insensitive to pain. The capacity for voluntary initiative is temporarily surrendered. Dissociation serves to create a means of psychological escape between a victim and the terrifying events taking place when no physical escape is possible—a means that may be so vital for survival that political prisoners have been known to teach each other *how* to dissociate during torture (Herman, 1992).

However, there are no substantiated cases of adults spontaneously developing DID, even among victims of severe or unrelenting trauma. There seems to be a "developmental window" during which one has the potential to develop DID (Putnam, 1989). Most adults diagnosed with DID report the first separation of consciousness occurred between the ages of four and eight (Coons, Bowman & Milstein, 1988). After this developmental threshold is passed, it seems a person is unlikely to develop the unique features of DID.

Theoretically, DID develops when young children are subject to repeated, inescapable abuse. Like Marie, these children may develop the capacity to enter a dissociative, trance-like state prior to, early in, or during an abusive episode. By entering into these states often enough, entire other identities unknown to the child's "core" personality may be created, each with a separate life history and unique way of engaging in the world. This process is a gradual evolution, rather than a sudden or dramatic transformation in identity and consciousness.

Although it may seem fantastical and alarming, the ability to remove oneself from sadistic abuse by dissociation can be an adaptive means of self-protection—"one of nature's small mercies" (Herman, 1992, p. 43). Marie's capacity to dissociate protected her from full recognition of the horrors she endured.

A Typical Case?

In some ways, Marie is very representative of the average person with DID. Most diagnosed cases of DID are women (female-to-male ratios are estimated at 5:1) who spend an average of six to seven years in the mental health system prior to accurate diagnosis, accumulating a variety of diagnoses (Herman, 1992; Putnam, 1988). Accurate diagnosis typically occurs when a person is in her or his late twenties (Putnam & Post, 1988). The overwhelming majority of individuals with DID report a history of severe childhood trauma, with several studies placing the figure at well over 90% (Kluft, 1996; Putnam et al., 1986). Putnam (1989) also indicates that the childhood abuse reported by those who develop DID tends to be far more sadistic and bizarre than that suffered by most victims of incest.

Many aspects of Marie's symptom picture also are typical. Depressive symptoms are the most common presenting problem. Reports of mood swings, low self-esteem, suicidal or self-destructive ideation, a sense of being overwhelmed and powerless, and a generalized negative outlook on life also are common, as is a history of at least one suicide attempt and polysubstance abuse (Bliss, 1984; Coons, 1984; Putnam, 1989). Given this initial presentation, it is not surprising that many individuals with DID are diagnosed with major depression or bipolar disorder at some point in their diagnostic journey. The single most common dissociative feature in DID is "time loss" or amnesia, although this may not be brought to the attention of mental health practitioners for several months (Putnam et al., 1986). While in extreme cases a person may have more than 25 alters, the modal number of alters is three, and the median is between eight and ten (Kluft, 1996).

Unfortunately, Marie's ability to find her way out of the mental health system in her late twenties, and into a more functional and satisfying life, is *not* typical. Several factors likely helped her achieve this period of stable functioning: Her relationship with Pablo, her ability to overcome her polysubstance dependence, and her love of dance were all important. Marie's talent provided her with an occupational potential that suited her strengths and allowed her to channel her energy into a specific medium.

Marie is also unusual in that her history does not include explicit sexual abuse, and the sadistic horrors she suffered were at the hands of her mother. From the description, Marie's mother likely had a severe mental disorder, although we do not have enough information to determine its exact nature. Among women with DID, the most common abuses reported are incest, physical abuse, and torture perpetrated by the child's father (Putnam et al., 1986).

So, is DID "real"? One leading expert on the disorder offers an interesting perspective. Ross (1997) maintains that most skeptics—and even adherents—fail to grasp "the central paradox" of DID: that *it is real and not real at the same time* (Ross, 1997, p. 62). It is not real in that no individual can literally have more than one personality, at least as we currently conceptualize personality. But on the other hand, DID is real in that it has face validity and diagnostic validity: When properly treated, individuals with this disorder function better in their lives and, in measurable terms, make far less use of psychiatric services. Further, severe DID, such as in the case of Marie, can be thought of as one end of a continuum of identity "integration": Almost all of us can identify different "parts" of ourselves. So, rather than considering DID and the other dissociative disorders to be the stuff of science fiction, they can be seen as extreme examples of understandable human phenomena.

The Broader Issue of Trauma

Dissociative identity disorder not only evokes controversy as a psychiatric diagnosis but raises disturbing societal questions (some argue that it evokes such controversy *because* it raises these disturbing issues). Acknowledging that the kinds of atrocities that Marie (and others) have endured contradicts our most basic values about what society, and family life, should be. *How can things like this happen?* One answer to this question is to assume that things like this do not, in fact, happen—that many or most reported childhood traumatic events are, in fact, imagined fantasies.

For example, the False Memory Syndrome Foundation, created in 1992, is an organization comprised largely of members who maintain they have been falsely accused by their adult children of abuses that occurred in childhood. The organization argues that certain vulnerable individuals are susceptible to a "false memory syndrome," in which poorly trained and overzealous therapists intentionally or unwittingly encourage the fabrication of "memories" of abuse.

Few current social issues—or areas of psychological inquiry—cause such heated argument. Are innocent people being falsely accused of heinous acts, with devastating consequences such as imprisonment or social censure? Or are heinous acts too commonly perpetrated in the protected, secluded secrecy of individual families, with victims carrying the terrible added burden of being disbelieved? Active research into the nature of memory may help us to resolve this dilemma, but for now we have no clear-cut answers to these vexing questions.

For example, it has been demonstrated that "false" memories, in the right situation, can be implanted in children and adults (Loftus, 1993). But it has also been documented, through careful investigation of old hospital and social service records, that adults can indeed "repress" or forget, sometimes for periods of many years, traumatic events that are known to have occurred in their childhoods (Williams, 1994).

Hopefully, ongoing investigation will help us develop techniques with which to distinguish memories that are false from those that are real. Regardless, we still must come to terms with the knowledge that far more abuse occurs in our society than has been previously acknowledged, a finding supported by a vast amount of psychological research and clinical experience. Among adult crimes such as rape, perhaps only about 15% are reported—and for the sexual assault of children, the rate of reporting is estimated to be far lower, ranging from 2% to 6% (Kilpatrick & Best, 1992; Russell, 1986). And while the women's movement of the past 30 years has heightened public awareness regarding the frequency of sexual and domestic violence against women and children, during Marie's childhood, awareness of such issues was close to nonexistent. In this regard, it is worth noting that a society for the prevention of cruelty to animals came into existence before a society for the prevention of cruelty to children.

Recognizing how often interpersonally abusive events occur, and their powerful, long-lasting impact on victims, has profound implications. Acknowledging the reality of trauma—ranging from domestic violence to childhood sexual abuse to the torture that Marie endured—may transform not only our notions of psychopathology but also may threaten some basic assumptions about our social structure. As Albee (1980, p. 223) suggests: "If the 'evil' is inside the person, then we do not need to change anything except the person, and the damaging status quo is left intact." But if the "evil" is not in the person, what then?

PROGNOSIS

Having finally been properly diagnosed, Marie's prognosis can be regarded as cautiously optimistic. Marie has the financial resources that allow her to access this type of intensive treatment. She also has a skilled therapist who is familiar with the disorder and is attuned to the careful pacing necessary to avoid retraumatization during the process of recalling and "working through" memories. In addition, from the beginning of treatment, Marie was fairly willing to accept her diagnosis and establish a strong therapeutic alliance with Dr. Lu—indicators that bode well for recovery (Putnam, 1989; Wilbur, 1984).

Marie also exhibits a number of other good prognostic indicators. In childhood, Marie had some access to caring adults (mainly the domestic staff and her ballet teachers) and was able to sustain connections with them. This may be extremely important to her ultimate ability to recover, as these early relationships, like the occasional oasis in a barren desert, provide the foundation for building a basic sense of trust in other people (Braun, 1986; Herman, 1992). Marie's relationship with Pablo, her commitment to her students, and her love for ballet also provide her with a valuable sense of support and purpose.

To sustain her progress, Marie will need to expand her support network beyond Pablo. Her ability to remain abstinent from abusing substances also may prove crucial, given that ongoing or recurrent substance dependence is a poor prognostic indicator (Putnam, 1989).

Not all survivors of trauma fare so well. The advent of managed care, which emphasizes short-term models of treatment, may make psychotherapies such as Marie's rare and shift the focus away from addressing the underlying disorder to crisis intervention. Further, those who lack Marie's financial resources and her relatively stable adult environment often face stressors that only exacerbate their psychological difficulties—chronic unemployment or underemployment, unsafe housing, poor nutrition, and abusive or destructive relationships. For too many adults with dissociative identity disorder, and other disorders that result from childhood trauma, daily survival itself is an ongoing struggle, and recovery an unattainable luxury.

CRITICAL THINKING QUESTIONS

1. How might dissociation be an adaptive response for a person in a traumatic situation? How is it maladaptive?
2. One of Marie's earlier diagnoses was bipolar disorder. What about her functioning might have suggested this? How is Marie's psychological functioning different than that of a person with bipolar disorder?
3. Dissociative identity disorder is diagnosed far more commonly today than it was before the 1980s. What factors might be relevant to this?
4. How might you attempt to determine if Marie were 9faking9 dissociative identity disorder?
5. What would you estimate Marie's Axis IV and V ratings to be prior to Pablo's heart attack?

Bulimia Nervosa

J enny Landau was a 21-year-old junior at a large state university. A bright and talented young woman, she had distinguished herself in several spheres of campus life, repeating a pattern of outstanding accomplishment from high school and earlier. She was a chief resident advisor, the treasurer of the ski club, and a reporter for the school newspaper—all while maintaining an A- average. She hoped to attend a top law school and studied constantly to meet this end (*too* constantly, some friends chided—couldn't she ever relax or slow down?). Her smile and enthusiastic demeanor were easily recognizable on campus.

Yet, despite her outward success and popularity, Jenny believed her life to be a sham. Beneath her mask of social competence, she was plagued by overwhelming feelings of doubt, inadequacy, and failure. She feared that others would discover the "truth" about her—that deep down, she was a worthless, stupid, inept person. And, even worse, she harbored a terrible, shameful secret, one that had been haunting her for years.

Jenny was bulimic. Once, twice, sometimes five times a day, she retreated to the privacy of a bathroom in her dorm or in a secluded part of the library. She would wait until nobody was around, lock the door, take a few deep breaths, stick her finger down her throat, and force herself to regurgitate her most recent indulgence.

And nobody knew except her.

PSYCHOSOCIAL HISTORY

Jenny was the elder of two children, with a sister, Ellen, two years younger. She was raised in a suburb of a large East coast city, where her father worked as an accountant. After graduating from college, Jenny's mother spent several years working for an advertising agency. Mrs. Landau enjoyed her career and was disappointed to interrupt it, but after her first pregnancy she opted to leave work to stay home and raise the children.

Jenny was always an exceptional student. From elementary school on, teachers commended her intelligence, resourcefulness, and cooperativeness. She regularly received compliments from her parents, teachers, and other adults: What a "good girl" she was, what a delightful young lady! Jenny also received compliments for her looks. She was always pretty and, although never overweight, was extremely conscious of her body. She recalled even as a child being told by her mother to watch what she ate and she heard many comments about dieting and weight—she wouldn't want to lose her lovely slim figure and grow up to be fat, like this particular neighbor or that particular relative. She also frequently overheard her father's sarcastic comments about Mrs. Landau's increasing size.

In contrast to Jenny, Ellen had more difficulties in childhood. These worsened when the girls entered adolescence, and Ellen grew more rebellious. At first subtly and then explicitly, she was identified as "the problem" in the family. Mr. Landau often made direct comparisons between the two: Why couldn't she be more like Jenny? In private, Mrs. Landau would thank Jenny for not making her life difficult, like Ellen did.

Family dinners became the scene of fierce arguments. Mr. Landau insisted that they all sit and eat together "like a family." Typically, he would attempt some superficial banter, talking about his day, making corny jokes, purposely ignoring an unspoken tension they all felt. But after just a few moments, someone would slip in a barbed or nasty comment. Jenny might try to defuse the increasing tension by changing the subject. This strategy typically failed, with a hostile fight erupting.

At first these fights involved a lot of screaming but then Mr. Landau's verbal rage turned physical, and he would hit Ellen, sometimes severely. Mrs. Landau might try to mediate but more often gave up. She would start sobbing that "another meal is ruined," retreat to her room, and medicate herself with Xanax, an anti-anxiety prescription drug.

During those meals, Jenny felt a painful knot in her stomach and lost her appetite. She would brace herself for the inevitable explosion with a sense of helplessness, like a person witnessing an accident who can do nothing to stop it. After the fight had reached its violent peak, with the meal abandoned, Jenny would quietly clear away the half-eaten dishes, absent-mindedly pick at the scraps of food on the plates, clean the kitchen, and then attempt to comfort her mother.

Outside the Landau home, nobody knew how badly things had deteriorated. Jenny intuitively sensed that revealing these things would feel like betraying a family secret. And so she said nothing but instead worked harder at her studies, hobbies, and school involvements. What had been already rewarding and fun activities now also became a refuge, and she approached her activities with an increasing sense of drivenness and perfectionism.

Jenny discovered self-induced vomiting, or *purging*, in part by accident, in part by curiosity. One evening following a family fight, she ate a large box of cookies alone in her room. She started eating them because she was quite hungry, but also found it comforting. Afterward, she felt bloated and nauseous. She had heard of bulimia yet found the idea of self-induced vomiting repulsive. Why would somebody do something so disgusting, so "gross"? Yet at the same time, she felt queasy, and thought vomiting might make her feel better. Perhaps it was worth a try? Well, maybe . . . just this once.

Jenny made herself vomit by forcing her finger down the back of her throat. This relieved her physical discomfort, but it also felt repulsive, and she accomplished it only after much effort. Jenny remained puzzled about how some women could turn it into a habit. She even felt mildly relieved that vomiting held so little appeal for her.

Jenny did not repeat this behavior for the remainder of high school, although she episodically indulged excessively in sweets or desserts. However, the family situation worsened: Mr. Landau became involved in a relationship with another woman and filed for a divorce. Mrs. Landau grew increasingly dependent on Xanax and often sat around the house in her nightgown and bathrobe, chain-smoking cigarettes. Ellen was rarely home. Jenny herself continued to excel at school but felt a constant sense of depression, loneliness, and self-hatred.

During her freshman year at college, Jenny lost several pounds because of an intestinal virus. To her delight, others noticed the weight loss. Jenny was within the range of normal weight for her height, but she had been steadily gaining weight throughout the year and considered herself to be fat. Frequent attempts at dieting had always failed. What great news—this minor stomach bug had achieved what she could not do on her own!

In the weeks that followed, Jenny strived to maintain this weight loss but still could not stick to a diet. She promised herself, several times, *this* one would work— no more cheating or excuses. And she would need to stop ignoring the impact of her private late night "snacks," which had been escalating in size and frequency— maybe a box of cookies, a few bag of candies, a quart of ice cream, one or two dozen doughnuts.

It was after one of those "snacks" that Jenny again decided to make herself vomit. Recalling her experience from a few years earlier, she still was not thrilled with the idea—but now neither was she completely opposed to it. Perhaps here was a way to lose weight, look attractive, and still indulge in the soothing, secret pleasure of gorging herself on sweets. So, Jenny actually thought the idea of making herself vomit to be a "logical" choice. At the same time, however, she also had this vague, helpless sense that what she was doing was out of her control. She had already developed this sense of detachment with her nightly eating frenzies, as if she were not fully present while glutting herself.

As with the first time, Jenny's vomiting led to a sense of relief. But unlike her previous experience, she no longer dismissed the possibility of self-induced vomiting as an option. Instead, she made a pact with herself (as she tried to do with many things): She would sharply limit how frequently she allowed herself to vomit. No more than once every two weeks, she decided, "so it doesn't become a problem."

Jenny stuck with her plan for just a few months until several things interfered. Spring term finals loomed closer, and she was anxious about grades. She learned that Ellen had been expelled from high school because she was using drugs. And a close friend's parents were divorcing, with the friend leaning heavily on Jenny for support. Jenny felt burdened by the intensity of her friend's need but felt she could not say "no" to helping out.

As Jenny became more overwhelmed, she could no longer concentrate on her schoolwork. Instead, her thoughts focused increasingly on eating and purging, and her pact. She realized how much she was looking forward to the next scheduled date to binge and purge—it seemed so long away! She wished she had allowed herself to do it more often. But of course, she *could* do it more often. Why not break from the schedule, just this once. . . .

Slowly, what had once sounded disgusting came to be a soothing activity. Self-induced vomiting—the fact of it, the idea of it—brought a sense of relief. More and more frequently, she engaged in an orgiastic binge of sweets, then purged herself. Sometimes, she would induce vomiting after an ordinary meal or an insignificantly small snack. In classes, instead of focusing on the lecture, she would daydream about food, perhaps making lists of her caloric intake the previous day or planning little rituals of what "treat" to buy next, where to eat it, when to vomit.

By the middle of her sophomore year, bingeing and purging grew to be all-purpose solutions for any emotional distress. When Jenny felt a twinge of anxiety about an upcoming exam, she immediately contemplated purging to relieve the anxiety. If she felt at all criticized or humiliated, or believed others had seen her make a "mistake," she binged and purged to dispel the intolerable feelings of failure and shame that overwhelmed her.

Having heard often enough about bulimia from friends and the media, Jenny privately, and sadly, acknowledged that she had the disorder. She still managed to wear a positive mask for the outside world, but bingeing and purging were running her life. She had long ago abandoned any attempts at a pact with herself. She wore baggy clothes to disguise her fluctuating weight—what had once been a desirable thinness was now often a source of embarrassment and potentially awkward questions. She also worried about the money she spent on her increasingly expensive binges; she regularly lied to her parents about needing extra money for books, school materials, and other fictitious expenses.

By her junior year, Jenny had severed her friendships, fearing any close relationship would interfere with or expose her secret. She had not dated since high school. Her sense of shame and self-recrimination swelled out of control. She now added the label "sick" to the litany of criticisms she had long wielded against herself.

Jenny thought of contacting the University Counseling Service many times but felt too ashamed to call. Finally, she found the courage to make an appointment to speak with someone. At last, she had turned an important corner: she would admit to another person the "truth" about herself.

CONCEPTUALIZATION

Jenny Landau suffers from bulimia nervosa, an eating disorder defined by the following diagnostic criteria (APA, 1994, pp. 549–550):

A. Recurrent episodes of binge eating;
B. Recurrent misuse of inappropriate compensatory behaviors to avoid weight gain, such as self-induced vomiting, use of laxatives, diuretics, enemas or other medications, fasting, or excessive exercise;
C. Engaging in the behaviors of bingeing and inappropriate compensation, on average, at least twice a week for three months;
D. A self-evaluation that is unduly influenced by body shape and weight; and,
E. The disturbance does not occur exclusively during episodes of anorexia nervosa.

A *binge* has two main characteristics: 1) it is an episode when a large quantity of food is eaten in a discrete period of time, and 2) the person feels unable to control the eating until completely satiated. Exactly how much food constitutes a binge, or what the period of time is, can vary, with a loose guideline being that the quantity of food is far greater than what an average person would eat in the same amount of time.

The DSM-IV distinguishes between two types of bulimia nervosa. In *purging type*, the person engages in self-induced vomiting or misuses laxatives, diuretics, or enemas. In *nonpurging type*, the bulimic individual attempts to control her or his weight through inappropriate and extreme measures, such as fasting or excessive exercise, but not by purging behaviors. Jenny Landau suffers from bulimia nervosa, purging type.

Bulimia differs from the eating disorder *anorexia nervosa*, but symptoms of the two may coexist in the same person. Individuals (typically women) with anorexia greatly fear gaining weight and have markedly distorted notions of their true body size and shape. Anorexics accomplish their extreme weight loss either by "restricting" their food intake, engaging in the same binge/purge behaviors as bulimics, or both. The weight loss associated with anorexia can be quite dangerous, even lethal.

Like anorexia, individuals with bulimia also are greatly preoccupied with body weight and self-image and hold distorted views of their true size and shape. But a bulimic person's weight typically does not drop to perilously low levels. Body weight may remain in the normal range or it can vary greatly, in response to dramatic changes in eating patterns. Also unlike anorexia, bulimia is rarely fatal, although serious physical complications may result from the nutritional deficits and self-induced purges. For example, bulimic women who vomit regularly may permanently damage the dental enamel on their teeth because of the constant exposure to digestive acids; those who rely on laxatives risk serious damage to their gastrointestinal system.

The DSM-IV describes an additional eating disorder, *binge-eating disorder*, as a potential diagnostic category requiring more research to establish its reliability and validity. The essential feature of *binge-eating disorder* is engaging in binges *without* the compensatory weight-reducing measures associated with bulimia. It seems likely that binge-eating disorder will be recognized as a full disorder in the next DSM revision.

Jenny also meets diagnostic criteria for dysthymia, early onset, based on her chronically depressed mood and feelings of worthlessness. Although she has several symptoms of major depression, she does not have enough symptoms to warrant a full diagnosis.[1]

TREATMENT

Treatment for bulimia has been conceptualized from a wide array of theoretical perspectives. Jenny's treatment involved an *integrative* approach, including aspects of cognitive-behavioral, psychodynamic, and feminist theories. It also combined several different treatment modalities.

Before attending her first appointment, Jenny was uncertain if she would have the courage to reveal her real problem. She thought she might just talk more generally about how horrible things were and how badly she felt about herself. But she immediately felt comfortable with the clinical psychologist she met with, Anne Katz. Just a few minutes into their meeting, Jenny broke down in tears and shared the truth of her situation.

Dr. Katz listened empathically. She asked many questions to determine the severity of Jenny's eating disorder: How frequently was she bingeing and purging? Did she ever "restrict" her food intake as well, fasting or denying herself vital nutrition? Was her health in immediate danger because of her eating disorder? Did she have thoughts of suicide or hurting herself? Dr. Katz also inquired about any related difficulties Jenny might be having, such as depression, a substance abuse problem, or symptoms of an obsessive-compulsive disorder.

Toward the end of their meeting, Dr. Katz frankly discussed her concerns about the severity, and potential danger, of Jenny's bulimia. Although Jenny was somewhat alarmed to hear the depth of Dr. Katz's concerns, she felt relieved that she had finally revealed her secret and that her distress was being taken seriously. She agreed to meet again early the following week, and to contact a physician for a medical examination. In the meantime, Dr. Katz wanted Jenny to try something new: If she felt the need to binge or purge before their next meeting, she wanted her to make a note of it. Jenny need not fight these impulses—not yet—but she should simply write down the time of day, what she was thinking and feeling prior to the activity, and what she was thinking or feeling afterward.

At their next appointment, Jenny talked about her low self-esteem, including how "ugly," "fat," and "stupid" she felt. She had binged and purged four times since their first session. She had written down her thoughts and feelings for two of these episodes. She and Anne (they both agreed that using each others' first name felt more comfortable) decided that it would be helpful to continue doing this, examining the patterns that emerged.

---

[1]See Chapter 3 for a case presentation on dysthymia.

Also in that meeting, Anne asked Jenny questions about her childhood and family. Even though her voice sounded flat as she spoke, Jenny answered that they had been a "pretty happy" family, maybe with "a few problems" but "nothing out of the ordinary." On further questioning, she mentioned the divorce, the violence that characterized her adolescence, and Ellen and her mother's substance abuse problems. But she did so in a manner that seemed to shrug off any real difficulties. Toward the end of this session, Anne and Jenny negotiated a treatment contract. Anne recommended a three-pronged approach to treatment: individual psychotherapy, a psychiatric consultation for antidepressant medication, and an eating-disorders group. The group lasted 10 weeks and was offered twice a year by the university's counseling service. Jenny had missed the start of the current group but another would begin the next semester.

Jenny agreed to individual psychotherapy and to the group, but she was hesitant about taking medication. She thought doing so would made her feel even more like a "failure." Anne accepted this decision but encouraged Jenny to keep an open mind.

Because it seemed of primary importance for Jenny to gain some mastery over her symptoms, psychotherapy started with a cognitive-behavioral focus. They expanded the *mood monitoring* from the first session. In this technique, a person keeps a log to see how particular moods and thoughts may correspond with an unwanted behavior. Jenny developed the habit of keeping a little notebook with her. At specified times of the day, she would jot down what she was thinking and feeling, and how depressed or anxious she was, on a scale of 1 to 10. She also kept a log of her actual bingeing and purging episodes: when they happened, what she felt before and afterward, and what, if anything, she could have done instead.

Jenny began to see that her eating disorder followed certain patterns. For example, she purged regularly at certain times during the day, and at other times in response to certain feelings—most frequently anxiety, hopelessness, shame, and perceived criticism. Anne worked with her to develop alternate strategies to label and cope with these difficult feelings. She also encouraged Jenny to try delaying her need to purge—perhaps when she felt the impulse, she could wait ten minutes before acting. At first this was difficult for Jenny, but as she was able to do this, she began developing a small sense of control over her behavior. Sometimes, after ten minutes the urge had passed, and Jenny would not need to binge or purge.

Jenny also began to identify certain rituals and patterns that were part of her eating behavior. Using the technique of *stimulus control* (altering one's daily routine or environment to disrupt the stimuli that may lead to dysfunctional behaviors), she and Anne attempted to "throw a monkey wrench" into these harmful patterns. For example, Jenny regularly stopped at a particular sweet shop on her way home from class; could she find a different route that passed no sweet shop or convenience store? And when Jenny studied in the library, she always escaped to the same quiet bathroom to purge. Why not study in a different part of the library, where she could still work quietly but resist the lure of a nearby secluded bathroom?

Another topic they addressed was appropriate meal planning. It turned out that Jenny held erroneous ideas about the actual nutritional and caloric value of many foods; clearing up these misconceptions helped her to feel better about a healthy diet. She learned that she could eat more nutritiously and still allow herself occasional moderate indulgences.

In general, treatment seemed to be getting off to a good start—maybe too good? After her initial despair, Jenny usually arrived for sessions smiling, well dressed, her cognitive-behavioral assignments diligently completed. She steadily reported progress. If Anne tried to probe about any difficulties, Jenny seemed to deflect the question.

It was only after many weeks that Jenny again broke down in tears. She admitted that much of the time she was lying to Anne about how much she had binged and vomited. She often made up the "facts" in her mood monitoring charts. If anything, it seemed to her that she was getting worse. She felt ashamed, hopeless, and depressed. Lying to Anne only made her hate herself more than she already did.

This painful session actually became a positive turning point in treatment. Jenny feared that Anne would respond by criticizing her or by being disappointed. But Anne's reaction was the opposite: She commended Jenny on her courage in sharing the truth. She empathized with how helpless Jenny felt and how burdened she was by her disorder. Could Jenny allow herself to trust that in therapy she did not have to do anything to please Anne, but just to be herself?

After this session, Jenny steadily grew more comfortable presenting herself to Anne without a "mask"; if she was feeling miserable, she let herself be miserable. She stopped lying about her progress. She conceded how bad her bulimia still was and now agreed to try antidepressant medication. The psychiatrist at the Counseling Service prescribed Zoloft, one of the Selective Serotonin Reuptake Inhibitors (SSRIs). Although Jenny was at first not certain what effect the medication was having, it did seem to take away the intensity of her down moods and harsh self-criticism, and helped reduce the frequency of her purges.

As the time arrived to join the eating disorders group, Jenny felt as frightened as she did when first coming in to see Anne, or more so. The idea of talking to a professional was nerve-wracking enough, but she could not fathom exposing her most vulnerable secret to a group of other students. She went, however, and the most difficult moment happened immediately upon entering the room: Jenny recognized Joanne, an acquaintance from the school newspaper. The two seemed embarrassed to see each other, but then smiled, awkwardly, in acknowledgment of the secret bond they shared. Jenny relaxed as the meeting continued.

The group offered an opportunity for information and support. Each week, the group facilitator introduced a new topic related to eating disorders, such as dieting, thinness, body image, dating, learning how to deal with feelings such as anger or rejection. She encouraged the group members to think about, and work on, the particular issue of that week. The second half of each group was an unstructured discussion, where the eight members could talk about whatever was on their minds.

Jenny soon realized that some of the fears that plagued her—a sensitivity to criticism, the belief that others would find her to be a fraud—were not nearly as unique as she thought. Many of her misconceptions about food, body weight, and nutrition also were shared. Over time, deeper commonalities emerged among the women as well.

One of these was *secrecy*. On one level, each of the women had developed a secret life to hide her eating disorder. In addition, several also had grown up with a forced need to keep family life secret. They had experienced destructive family be-haviors—perhaps alcoholism, or physical or sexual abuse—that had created a se-cret conflict between their private family life and how they presented themselves in public.

Another prominent theme was *control*. Ironically, this issue cut both ways. On the one hand, most of the women lacked a sense of control over food and had diffi-culty mastering their symptoms. Yet looked at differently, most also felt that they lacked a sense of control in their own lives, and eating was the one thing they *could* exercise control over. They shared an underlying sense of powerlessness and their ability to exert control over what they ate, even though it was unhealthy and self-destructive, could temporarily relieve their sense of being powerless.

Outside the group, Jenny and Joanne got to know each other better and began to lean on each other for support. Jenny sometimes found it helpful to call Joanne when she felt the impulse to binge or purge—she could talk with her briefly, get sup-port, and no longer feel the intense impulse that had overwhelmed her just mo-ments before.

By the end of the spring semester in her junior year, with medication, the group, and her individual meetings with Anne, Jenny was making progress in reducing the frequency of her binges and purges. She also had learned a lot about bulimia, no longer felt so isolated or depressed, and had even gone a few stretches of several days without purging at all—quite an accomplishment, after bingeing and/or purging al-most daily for two years. Yet, she still binged and purged, on average, two or three times weekly and continued to feel hopeless about the future.

That summer Jenny opted to remain on campus, as she had the previous year. But she visited her family for two weeks after finals ended, and this visit was very upsetting. It was as if she were seeing for the first time how unhappy and disturbed her family was. The tensions with Ellen, her father's violence, her mother's passive withdrawal into a drug-induced apathy—oddly, she had never before really regis-tered these as so unusual or so painful. Now, Jenny began acknowledging the extent of her family's dysfunction and placing her eating disorder in this context. For one thing, mealtimes had been the family's chosen battleground. But Jenny also realized how frightened she had felt growing up and the helplessness she felt because of her inability to control any of the events around her. And she had a disturbing insight: She felt guilty about leaving home and even about being so successful (at least out-wardly). It was as if she had turned her back on her mother and Ellen, making her a "bad" sister and daughter.

Now for the second time since treatment started, Jenny's bulimic and depressive symptoms escalated significantly. She again began bingeing and purging at least once daily. She started ruminating about harming or killing herself and needed to telephone Anne frequently between their sessions for reassurance.

With these developments, psychotherapy shifted into a deeper exploration of family and interpersonal matters. Anne helped Jenny think about the ongoing im-pact of her childhood and adolescence: Did she still have to be a "good girl"? What would it mean if she rebelled, like Ellen? Was it okay to express angry feelings? Did she need to take care of other people, at her own expense? When appropriate, Anne used the therapy relationship itself to point out relevant dynamics. For example, she recalled Jenny's need earlier in treatment to please her, to be a "good patient," and connected this with her role in the family of being the good daughter.

Around this time, Jenny also started accepting Anne's recommendations of particular books and films, relating to eating disorders and general women's issues. Anne had suggested such things earlier; Jenny had always responded with a polite smile, but inwardly bristled—she did not consider herself to be a "feminist" and did not want material that was too "preachy." Now, she began to react more strongly at realizing how much day-to-day sexism she had previously taken for granted, such as the constant media bombardment of messages regarding thinness. How hard it was for women *not* to base their self-worth on physical attractiveness—and how frustrating that even becoming aware of it, and feeling angry about it, did not stop her from feeling influenced by it.

During her senior year, Jenny participated in the eating disorders group both semesters and continued with individual psychotherapy and medication. Although her progress was uneven, the general direction was gaining more control over her bulimic behaviors. Her bingeing and purging worsened during times of high stress, such as taking the law school entrance exams, filling out applications, and informing her mother about her decision to go to school across the country. Perhaps most difficult was dealing with rejections from several law schools, including her top choice.

Yet, these setbacks came more and more to feel like slips, not like a regular activity. Jenny often now went many days at a time without needing to binge or purge. In the spring, she was accepted to a law school she considered a reasonable alternative to her top choice. She felt pride in her accomplishment and a sense of excitement about moving on with her life.

Jenny and Anne spent several months saying goodbye during the *termination* phase of psychotherapy. They explored the progress Jenny had made over eighteen months of treatment and the potential pitfalls that lay ahead. Jenny had developed a warm and close relationship with Anne, and leaving therapy was among the most difficult aspects of moving across the country. But Anne encouraged her to make this important move and invited Jenny to contact her periodically if she felt the need to do so.

DISCUSSION

It is hard to imagine that until the mid 1980s few people had heard of bulimia nervosa, for today it is one of the most widely known and well-publicized of psychological disorders. Adolescent and young adult females are at highest risk, with an estimated 1% to 4% of high-school and college-aged women meeting diagnostic criteria for the disorder (Fairburn & Beglin, 1990; Katzman, Walchik, and Braver, 1984). It seems likely, however, that these percentages grossly underestimate how many women suffer from some sort of food or eating-related problem. Community samples estimate that for every woman who meets DSM-IV criteria for an eating disorder, at least two more meet at least partial criteria (Shisslak, Crago, & Estes, 1995). Because so many women experience some bulimic symptomatology, the DSM-IV threshold of bingeing and/or purging "twice a week for three months"

Multiaxial DSM-IV Diagnosis at Time of Termination

Axis I:	Bulimia Nervosa, Purging Type
	CONDITION: IMPROVED
	Dysthymia, Early Onset
	CONDITION: IMPROVED
Axis II:	No diagnosis
Axis III:	None
Axis IV:	History of family discord and violence
Axis V:	*Treatment Onset:* 55 (serious symptoms, moderate to serious impairment in social and academic functioning)
	Termination: 70 (some social impairment and mild symptoms, but generally functioning pretty well)

(APA, 1994, p. 549) has been challenged as being too restrictive (Sullivan, Bulik & Kendler, 1998).

Even among the age group at highest risk, bulimia is particularly prevalent among certain subpopulations. For example, ballet students, wrestlers, skaters, and gymnasts all demonstrate a higher rate of the disorder than do their peers because of the intense pressure for thinness or weight management in these groups (Garner & Rosen, 1991). And although bulimia is far more prevalent among women than men, the number of male bulimics has been on the rise (Andersen, 1990; Carlat & Camargo, 1991). Among males, athletes, gay men, and men with a childhood history of obesity or sexual abuse tend to be at highest risk (Carlat, Camargo & Herzog, 1997; Olivardia et al., 1995).

The symptomatology of bulimia nervosa is at once very simple yet enormously puzzling and dramatic. Eating is one of most basic of all human functions. What leads someone to develop such a pronounced dysfunction with this particular behavior? How can we explain the fact that bulimia and anorexia are most prevalent among young women from middle class or well-to-do families, where the availability of food is not a concern, and currently more common among whites than minority populations (Johnson, 1994)?

Some theorists believe that bulimia is a variant of depression (Pope et al., 1983). They point out that affective disorders are more prevalent in first degree relatives of bulimics than in the general population, and bulimia is often comorbid with major depression or another affective disorder. In addition, antidepressant medications, particularly those that affect serotonin functioning (such as Zoloft, the medication prescribed for Jenny), can be an extremely effective treatment component, at least in the short run (Freeman, 1998). However, not all bulimic women are depressed, and the vast majority of depressed individuals do not develop bulimia. To some extent, the role of depression in bulimia is like a "chicken and egg" question: Does depression cause bulimia, or does someone become depressed because of living with the unwanted and self-destructive bulimic symptoms?

Bulimia also has been conceptualized as an impulse control disorder, a variant of obsessive-compulsive disorder, and an addiction. In part, it is similar to each of these. Like Jenny, bulimic individuals often will describe their experience with language similar to that of addiction: "I want to stop but I can't . . . ." "It feels out of my control . . . ." "If I don't purge, I can't stop thinking about it." Substance abuse and poor impulse control are frequently associated with the disorder (Marcus & Katz, 1990; Lilenfeld et al., 1997). And biologists point out that the regulation of satiation, hunger, mood, and impulsivity all involve the same key neurotransmitters, particularly norepinephrine and serotonin.

Bulimia also has been examined in relation to personality disorders. Much evidence suggests that the majority of bulimics also meet DSM-IV criteria for a personality disorder. Borderline personality disorder may be the most common, although avoidant, obsessive compulsive, and histrionic personality disorders are also represented (Waller, 1993; Wonderlich et al., 1990).

The role of sexual abuse in the lives of bulimic women also has been explored. The matter is still somewhat controversial because of conflicting findings, but the preponderance of research and clinical data indicate that childhood sexual abuse, or adult victimization, are significant risk factors for bulimia, and a history of trauma is more common among females with bulimia than among women in the general population (Everill & Waller, 1995; Wooley, 1994).

Theoretical Perspectives

Historically, psychodynamic theories of eating disorders emphasized that the typical onset of bulimia and anorexia was during adolescence. As such, some theorists (Crisp, 1965; Ross, 1977) understood eating disorders as an attempt to forestall or reject the development of adult sexuality. Yet much more happens during adolescence than the budding of sexual identity, and more current psychodynamic perspectives (Bruch, 1978; Steiner-Adair, 1986) also emphasize the developmental tasks of individuation and separation that are central to this age. Bulimic symptoms may reflect a powerful underlying sense of inadequacy or deficiency stemming from disturbed family relationships, or an attempt to exert control in a situation that is perceived as uncontrollable.

According to this view, the pre-bulimic child is treated by her parents in a way that does not affirm or "mirror" her true identity. She learns to comply with parental expectations and be a "good girl," but only by sacrificing the development of a more complete and self-sufficient sense of self. In adolescence, these earlier failures to achieve a separate autonomous identity are reawakened.

In this regard, psychodynamic theorists overlap with family systems theorists, who also view family disturbance as crucial in eating disorders (Kog & Vandereycken, 1989). The families of bulimic women have been described as extremely chaotic, disorganized, overly rigid, or abusive (Kog & Vandereycken, 1989; Strober & Humphrey, 1987). Mood disorders and substance abuse disorders are more common in first-degree relatives of bulimics than in the general population, and this may give rise to the many potential family complications when a member has a substance abuse problem (Lilenfeld et al., 1997).

However, not all bulimic families are actively abusive or chaotic. In one family systems theory, families of eating-disordered patients are seen as *enmeshed* (Minuchin, Rosman & Baker, 1978). In such families, no one member can assert an identity independent of the others members. Arguments or conflict are avoided or poorly resolved, parents act overprotectively toward their children, interpersonal boundaries are not well established, and privacy may be discouraged. For example, a family norm may be that closing the door to one's room is wrong, or that when disagreements arise, expressing anger only makes matters worse.

Theoretically, in these families an adolescent's natural developmental push toward increasing independence is thwarted, in a manner that provides no satisfactory outcome. If she moves toward an autonomous identity, she violates the unspoken rules of the family; if she does not, she hampers her own development. In other words, she is caught in a no-win bind. The self-destructive behavior of the eating disorder is an attempt to overcome the helplessness of being caught in this situation by exerting control over a very private and basic function of life.

Biological theorists point out that bulimia may have a genetic component. In one study, the concordance rate for bulimia was significantly higher for monozygotic than dizygotic twins (Kendler et al., 1991). The effectiveness of the SSRIs in treating bulimia also clearly indicates that biology is involved and that certain neurotransmitters are crucial in regulating the binge–purge cycle. Yet of course, this does not necessarily indicate that a biochemical abnormality plays a *causal* role in the etiology of the disorder. For example, it may be that neurotransmitter imbalances themselves result from the compulsive cycle of bingeing and purging, or that bulimic behaviors and the neurotransmitters interact in a complex cause-and-effect manner.

Cognitive behaviorists, not surprisingly, look at the behaviors and cognitions related to the disordered eating. They focus on mistaken or distorted cognitions about food, body image, and weight, and specific strategies to change the eating behavior itself.

How do these ideas relate to Jenny's treatment? Jenny's background of family violence, the stark contrast between how Ellen was perceived as "bad" and Jenny "good," and the need to hide a shameful family secret, would all be emphasized from a family-systems perspective. Jenny may have been in a "no-win" familial situation, in which she faced two unsatisfactory options: always needing to be "good," or being treated with the abuse that Ellen received. And psychodynamic clinicians would extend the same material by adding how this affected Jenny's self-identity and unconscious functioning, with underlying issues such as low self-worth, unrealistic self-expectations and perfectionism, and a limited ability to express or cope with painful emotions.

Anne also incorporated a *feminist* perspective into her treatment with Jenny. More than a specific theory, feminist psychology offers a *stance* regarding the psychology of women. As such, it can be integrated with various other theoretical orientations. While specific definitions vary, a feminist perspective has at its core a few central beliefs: The psychology of women is unique and distinct from the psychology of men; individual psychopathology cannot be separated from the larger cultural context, which is often devaluing of and oppressive toward women; and a desirable goal of psychotherapy, research, and scholarship is social change toward a society that is less disempowering toward women (Fallon, Katzman & Wooley, 1994; Worell & Remer, 1992).

We can see these principles demonstrated in Jenny's treatment. For example, Anne recommended books and films in which Jenny could learn about—whether or not she agreed—the broader social context in which her bulimia occurred. She highlighted Jenny's struggles to juggle competing demands on women—her dilemma about leaving home to pursue her own independence and her guilt at how she felt this meant abandoning her mother. Even Anne's decision to use her first name, rather than "Dr. Katz," related to Anne's feminist ideals, in that it helped minimize the power differential that can sometimes characterize a psychotherapy relationship, where one person is the "doctor" and the other the "patient" or "client."

Is there a "best" treatment for bulimia? Current data suggest that both cognitive-behavioral and psychodynamic treatments can be effective in curtailing bulimic behavior (Fairburn et al., 1993). In one study, cognitive-behavioral therapy had a greater immediate impact in eliminating or reducing bingeing and purging, but at a twelve-month follow-up, neither treatment emerged as significantly better (Fairburn et al., 1993). Making comparisons between the wide array of treatment modalities can be difficult, however, because not all are equally well researched; cognitive-behavioral models have been studied the most (Wilson, 1995).

Sociocultural Factors

No psychological disorder can be viewed outside the context of sociocultural factors, and this may be especially evident with eating disorders. Our culture places an inordinate and unrealistic value on thinness, particularly for women. Messages touting the advantages of thinness pervade our society, and the pressure to conform to this abstract ideal can be immense.

This pressure has intensified over the past few decades—a fact that can be observed in some unusual, but telling, ways. For example, between 1960 and 1980, the average weight of the winner of the Miss America pageant steadily decreased. So did the typical measurements of *Playboy* centerfolds. At the same time, the diet industry has skyrocketed to become a multi-billion dollar business—all while the weight of the average American woman continues to rise (Garner et al., 1980). The pressure for thinness is so embedded in our culture that the very same behaviors typifying eating disorders often are regarded as normal or desirable and may even be highly praised. Societal norms may offer an imperceptible line between the pathological and the sought after—when does thin become too thin, or exercise unhealthy, or dieting a sickness?

Yet as important as these body weight issues are, even deeper sociocultural factors also may be relevant in eating disorders. Katzman and Lee (1997) note that that cross-culturally, eating disorders are now becoming more prevalent in developing nations. As in western cultures, this increase disproportionately affects females—but interestingly, in other cultures the pressure to conform to a thin body ideal is *not* the central feature. Instead, these authors suggest that underlying issues of oppression, disempowerment, and role transition in women's lives are the deeper, more universal factors in the etiology of eating disorders. Similarly, African-American women with eating disorders may not report a "drive for thinness" as being as salient a factor for them as it is for white women (Williamson, 1998). In other words, in our culture and others, women are in personal, familial, and societal situations that leave them without the power to exert control or make important life choices far more often than is the case for men. In Jenny's psychotherapy group, the discussions related to secrecy, control, and feelings of powerlessness suggest the relevance of these underlying issues, and Jenny's conflict regarding her "success" highlight the difficulty of being caught in contradictory roles.

It is also interesting not only to think of Jenny's situation from this perspective but Mrs. Landau's. Although she did not have an eating disorder, feminist psychologists might see her problems with substance dependence and depression as related to her disempowerment in the family, her loss of status after the divorce, and perhaps even to the difficult choice she was forced to make between her career and motherhood.

Along similar lines, one intriguing theory suggests that eating disorders are yet the newest manifestation of a long line of psychological ailments that have historically plagued women (Perlick & Silverstein, 1994). History is filled with disorders that primarily affect young women—from a phenomenon called *chlorosis* in the 17th and 18th centuries, which included anorectic-like symptoms, to the *hysterical neuroses* and nervous diseases such as *neurasthenia* prevalent in 19th-century Europe, which Freud described. Anorexia nervosa and bulimia may be the newest manifestations of a struggle that has waged for hundreds of years: how women can accept and embrace a healthy sense of self-esteem and identity but also succeed in a male-dominated culture.

PROGNOSIS

Jenny Landau made excellent use of her treatment. In her work with Anne, she developed skills to gain a sense of control over the bulimic behaviors that had come to dominate her life. In the group, she found a sense of support and camaraderie with other women struggling with similar issues. The antidepressant medication improved her mood and may have even directly reduced her compulsive need to binge and purge (Kramer, 1993). After eighteen months of psychotherapy, Jenny's bingeing and purging behavior had been reduced to an average of only once or twice a month, during particularly stressful times. This was still short of her hope that the behaviors would be completely eliminated, but Jenny also felt proud about regaining a sense of control that had long eluded her. There were other changes as well: She was less depressed, less perfectionistic, had developed greater self-esteem, and was and able to tolerate a wider range of emotions.

Jenny wrote to Anne one year after graduation. The move across the country and the start of law school had been stressful. For a period of several weeks, her eating disorder had escalated. However, Jenny was able to act before things got out of hand. She was disappointed to learn that her new school did not offer an eating disorders group, but they did recommend such a group at a nearby clinic. This group was of great help in providing an outlet for Jenny's anxieties and feelings of sadness, loneliness, and fear. She continued to take a reduced dose of antidepressant medication and hoped to be able to discontinue this within a year. Now, she had not binged or purged in six months. This was her longest period of "sobriety" yet; tough times remained, but she felt herself on the road to recovery.

Jenny's prognosis may be considered one of guarded optimism. The optimism stems from Jenny's mastery over the symptoms, her ability to develop adequate strategies to interfere with the binge–purge cycle, and her growing repertoire of coping skills to handle a range of emotional pressures that once overwhelmed her. The fact that Jenny had gone six months without purging—surmounting the stressful obstacles of leaving college, moving to a new city, and starting law school—was encouraging indeed.

However, Jenny's prognosis must still be considered "guarded," for much remains to be learned about the long-term course of bulimia. Although we know that treatment can be very helpful for many women and men in eliminating or reducing bulimic behaviors, we do not have enough research to make long-term prognoses with any degree of certainty. One review of the available longitudinal studies suggests that five to ten years following treatment, 50% of bulimic women have fully recovered, 20% still have the disorder, and 30% experience at least one full relapse, usually within the first four years of treatment (Keel & Mitchell, 1997). Yet, research into the long-term prognosis of bulimia is still in its infancy, and the specific factors associated with a positive recovery are yet to be fully understood. Amid an abundance of food, eating should be the most problem free of human functions. Why this basic process goes terribly awry, for so many people, remains a mystery that defies simple explanation.

CRITICAL THINKING QUESTIONS

1. How are Jenny's symptoms different than those of a person with anorexia nervosa? In what ways, if at all, do they overlap?
2. How might a psychotherapist with a psychodynamic orientation think about Jenny's treatment?
3. Eating disorders are far more common in females than males. What factors are relevant to this?
4. What are some reasons that group psychotherapy was helpful for Jenny?
5. Eating a low-fat diet and getting regular exercise are behaviors that promote health, but if taken to extreme, they also can cause physical and psychological harm. How would you determine when engaging in these behaviors stops being healthy and starts becoming unhealthy?

CASE 8

Narcissistic Personality Disorder

T wice before, Brian Hamilton had started psychotherapy. And twice before, he stopped it abruptly. The first time, Brian was a 21-year-old college senior. He contacted the counseling center at his school's health service because he felt depressed. Despite his insistence about his need for an "expert," the center would not heed his request to refer him to a psychotherapist in private practice. At the end of one session with a staff clinician (a well-qualified and highly regarded professional), he informed her that she "lacked the experience" to help him. He then sent an angry note to the counseling center director, citing the "lackluster quality" of the staff and complaining that "despite the fortune my father pays in tuition, I was not offered the treatment I needed and deserved."

In a second attempt at therapy several years later, Brian did meet with a therapist in private practice. This relationship lasted five sessions. Brian at first liked this psychologist, finding him to be a "good listener." However, he ended treatment abruptly after arriving 30 minutes late for his fifth appointment. Traffic that day had been unexpectedly heavy. Since being late "was clearly not my fault," Brian assumed that the therapist would reduce his fee or extend the session for the half-hour he had missed. (When asked how this last plan might affect clients with later appointments, Brian answered, "Well, that's not *my* problem, is it?"). The therapist stated he would neither reduce the fee nor extend the session. Brian responded that he would not return to therapy—"it's a matter of principle."

Now, however, at age 32, Brian had no choice but to return. Psychotherapy was court-ordered, part of a lenient sentencing arrangement to avoid serving time in prison.

Earlier that year, Brian had been bumped from a plane flight. When he arrived at the gate just minutes prior to the scheduled departure time, he was told that even though he had a valid ticket, the flight was fully booked, and he had neglected to check-in at least one-half hour early (as the ticket stipulated). His seat was no longer available. The airline could accommodate him on the next available flight, several hours later. Brian engaged the ticketing clerk, and then her supervisor, in a heated argument. He became increasingly belligerent. Finally, disbelieving that the flight was actually taking off without him, he announced that he had already checked his suitcase onto the plane, and it had a bomb in it.

The supervisor notified airport security. Brian immediately recanted his story and repeatedly apologized for it. The plane was delayed for hours to search through the luggage. With an understanding smile, the airport's chief of security accepted Brian's apology. And with the same smile, he arrested him for the felony of intentionally communicating a false bomb threat.

PSYCHOSOCIAL HISTORY

Brian Hamilton grew up in a middle-class home in Los Angeles. His parents divorced, acrimoniously, when he was four years old. After a difficult custody battle, Brian and his older brother continued to live with their mother and spend weekends and vacations with their father. Each parent openly disparaged the other, and in many ways (some subtle, some not) competed to be the "best loved" parent. During one particularly nasty spell, Mrs. Hamilton refused to let the boys see their father despite the custody arrangement, in retaliation for his delinquent alimony. This tense situation continued until Brian was nine, when his father moved to Europe and then had little to do (other than financially) with his ex-wife or sons. Brian's mother then remarried when he was 13 years old. Brian's relationship with his mother's new husband was distant but not overtly hostile. This marriage also ended in divorce when Brian was in college.

Throughout his childhood and adolescence, Brian and his brother had a close relationship, but they drifted apart in their early twenties. However, Brian always remained extremely devoted his mother. From an early age, she relied on him as her confidante and friend, "the one sure thing in my life." For his part, Brian was pleased to have such a special relationship with her. He saw his mother as a sophisticated and stylish woman and relished how tight they were. When Brian was young, she confided secrets to him that she said nobody else knew. However, when he displeased her, she often grew cold toward him, and said things such as, "You wouldn't behave this way if you really loved me."

Brian did well at school. He was a good student, but if worried about receiving a poor grade, he might act unscrupulously. For example, in college he sometimes paid other students to write papers for him in classes he found difficult or boring. In one course, he dated the teaching assistant, with the hidden aim of learning exam questions from her in advance. He lost interest in her when the course ended.

After college, Brian's first years were marked by financial and career success. He went to work as a salesman and quickly established an impressive sales record. His supervisors praised his determination to get ahead, but most of his peers were wary of him. His reputation was of someone who would "stab you in the back" to get ahead.

Not surprisingly, Brian's demeanor was usually one of cocky self-assuredness, even arrogance. Yet inwardly, his self-esteem was very shaky. Just as frequent as periods of feeling "superior" or "special" were times of depression and self-hate. Bouts of insecurity and loneliness had plagued him since adolescence, and it was because of those times that he had earlier sought psychotherapy.

Brian also was extremely sensitive to criticism. He could not tolerate any pointing out of what he saw as his "failings" or "imperfections." Sometimes when he was criticized he became enraged and acted contemptuously toward whomever voiced the criticism. But just as often, he would ruminate about the criticism endlessly, feeling devastated or humiliated, and lose sight of any positive feedback that also was directed his way.

Socially, Brian had an engaging way of relating to people. He had a superficial popularity, but deeper friendships and sustained romantic involvements eluded him. He had a strong need to be admired and ended friendships and dating relationships if he did not feel this admiration from the other person. As he got to know some people, he felt "superior" to them and grew uninterested in their company; with others, he was overcome with feelings of competition and envy if the other person achieved any accomplishment or success. Several girlfriends had broken up with him because they saw him as too self-absorbed, or felt that he treated them as inhuman objects. Brian publicly mocked these women to his male companions, but in his darker moments, he wondered if he would ever be able to sustain an ongoing commitment.

Prior to the incident that led to his arrest, nothing in Brian's life carried such major legal consequences. However, in smaller ways, Brian had already had a few problems with the law. These typically resulted from his belief that rules and laws for other people did not apply to him. For example, Brian once insulted a policeman for giving him an "undeserved" speeding ticket (yes, he was speeding, but with a valid reason—he was late for an appointment with an important client). When the policeman responded to Brian's insults by threatening to arrest him, Brian held his tongue (but then sped off in his car—and got another ticket). In another incident, Brian caused a scene in a hair salon. He was so dissatisfied with a haircut that he not only refused to pay but demanded the stylist pay *him* for damages! When he became increasingly rude, the owner of the shop threatened to telephone the police. Brian threw the proper payment down on the counter before he stormed out. He threatened to sue the owner but then forgot about it after he got caught up in yet another incident where he was "mistreated."

Since high school, Brian had used alcohol and recreational drugs on an occasional basis. However he did not overly indulge in these activities, and they did not pose a major problem.

CONCEPTUALIZATION

Brian Hamilton fits the diagnosis of narcissistic personality disorder (NPD), one of the personality disorders described in the DSM-IV (APA, 1994, p. 661). He meets the following diagnostic criteria:

A pervasive pattern of grandiosity (in fantasy or behavior), need for admiration, and lack of empathy, beginning by early adulthood and present in a variety of contexts, as indicated by five (or more) of the following:

1. has a grandiose sense of self-importance (e.g., exaggerates achievements and talents, expects to be recognized as superior without commensurate achievements)

2. is preoccupied with fantasies of unlimited success, power, brilliance, beauty, or ideal love

3. believes that he or she is "special" and unique and can only be understood by, or should associate with, other special or high-status people (or institutions)

4. requires excessive admiration

5. has a sense of entitlement (i.e., unreasonable expectations of especially favorable treatment or automatic compliance with his or her expectations)

6. is interpersonally exploitative (i.e., takes advantage of others to achieve his or her own ends)

7. lacks empathy: is unwilling to recognize or identify with the feelings and needs of others

8. is often envious of others or believes that others are envious of him or her

9. shows arrogant, haughty behaviors or attitudes

The DSM-IV organizes personality disorders into three separate clusters, each with a different unifying focus. NPD is grouped in one cluster with antisocial, borderline, and histrionic personality disorders, with the unifying theme being a significant disturbance in a person's sense of identity or self. Although each of the personality disorders in this cluster has distinct diagnostic criteria, they also overlap with one another. As such, reliable diagnosis can be complicated. In fact, the diagnostic reliability of personality disorders in general is worse than with most every other DSM-IV category, with NPD among the most difficult of disorders to diagnose reliably (Gorton & Ahktar, 1990; Livesley & Jackson, 1991; Morey & Jones, 1997). For example, Brian's NPD seems fairly clear cut, as he seems to meet all the diagnostic criteria. However, aspects of his character also overlap with *antisocial personality disorder,* particularly his lack of empathy and willingness to exploit other people for his own benefit.

In addition to narcissistic personality disorder, Brian also suffers from episodes of depression. Based on the information presented, these periods do not seem to warrant a diagnosis of major depressive episodes, or another mood disorder (such as dysthymia, cyclothymia, or bipolar II disorder). Still, their presence is important in gaining a fuller clinical picture of his functioning. Brian's occasional use of recreational drugs and alcohol also is important, but he does not misuse substances to the degree of a substance abuse disorder. However, such diagnoses are not uncommon among people with NPD: Perhaps as many as 50% of such individuals also suffer from dysthymia or major depression, and between 25% and 50% have a comorbid substance problem (Ronningstam, 1997).

TREATMENT

The most detailed advanced theories regarding the etiology and treatment of narcissistic personality disorder come from a psychoanalytic perspective. These treatments also are considered the most effective option, although this issue has not been extensively researched. As with any personality disorder, treatment for NPD is considered to be a long-term, intensive undertaking, perhaps involving meeting more than once weekly for several years.

Brian contacted a psychologist named Wilson Amory, recommended through a friend of his mother's. Dr. Amory's theoretical approach was shaped by *self psychology*, one of the newer branches of psychoanalytic thought. In comparison to more traditional psychoanalytic frameworks, self psychologists pay little (or no) attention to constructs such as the Oedipal complex or psychosexual stages of development. Instead, they focus on a person's earliest relationships and how these relationships are unconsciously internalized to form a sense of self. Self psychologists are particularly interested in the concept of *empathy,* the ability of one person to understand and meet the emotional needs of another. They believe that parents' empathic responsiveness to their children's needs, spoken and unspoken, is the foundation of healthy identity. If there are significant deficits in an infant or child's *empathic environment,* pathological adult narcissism may result.

So as psychoanalysts have done since the time of Freud, self psychologists explore links between the past and present. But rather than offering *interpretations*— statements that analyze unconscious fears and wishes—self psychologists instead attempt to repair the early *empathic failures* that they theorize have left long-lasting psychological damage (*empathic failures* occur when a caretaker repeatedly does not understand or acknowledge a child's emotional needs). The treatment emphasis is on the "here-and-now," especially in analyzing the therapeutic relationship itself. And in contrast with traditional psychoanalytic therapists who present themselves as a "blank screen," in self psychology the therapist's warmth and emotional engagement are considered to be key aspects of treatment.

As should be no surprise, given his situation, Brian was angry about his forced psychotherapy. In his first meeting, he told Dr. Amory that he was there against his will, all because "a stupid misunderstanding got blown way out of proportion." He spent the session fuming about the mess his life had become since the bomb threat—his arrest and trial; the guilty plea his lawyer encouraged him to offer; the media coverage of the incident; and his distress that family members, friends, and coworkers (and "probably everyone else on the goddamn planet") knew what had happened.

Brian angrily complained that the price he had already paid was "too high"—"I was hounded on the evening news. . . . I got hate mail. . . . I've been publicly humiliated. . . . I almost got fired. . . . *You* try going through that." His belief that he had been mistreated seemed endless—"Real criminals are getting away with murder, and the courts have nothing better to do than waste their time with me?"

This was not a typical beginning to psychotherapy! Brian barely acknowledged Dr. Amory's presence, other than to proclaim "I think all you guys are scumbags. You charge a zillion bucks just to sit there. . . . I could do your job in my spare time."

Dr. Amory listened to Brian's angry rantings and demeaning putdowns. He silently noted to himself that Brian gave no indication of seeing his actions as wrong; he instead perceived that *he* was being treated unfairly and made to suffer. But even as he observed these things, Dr. Amory chose not to bring them up. He felt to do so would only further alienate Brian, who already seemed ready to dismiss him as one more "scumbag" therapist. Instead, he focused on what Brian was doing to cope with such a difficult situation. He also acknowledged that starting treatment under such circumstances was far from ideal, especially since Brian's previous attempts at therapy (which he had described) left such a bitter taste in his mouth.

Although Dr. Amory recommended twice weekly meetings, Brian agreed to see him once weekly—this was what the court had mandated—for a period of at least two years. The next few sessions were no different than the first, with Brian always returning to his outrage at "the injustice" of his circumstances. Again, Dr. Amory endured these tirades. From his perspective, he understood Brian's arrogance, however unpleasant, as a defense against deeper fears of inadequacy and powerlessness. Beneath his bluster, Dr. Amory sensed that Brian was, in fact, quite frightened and ashamed about what had happened to him.

This nonconfrontational approach paid off. Brian came into his fifth session with his grandiose bravado gone, like the air deflated from a balloon. He talked instead about how insecure he was, what a "loser." His life was "a big pathetic joke." At one point his eyes teared up: "I hate myself, I'm nothing." He continued on in this manner, saying, "*this* is the real me—the rest is just pretend."

Dr. Amory empathized with how lonely it must be always having to wear a mask for other people. Perhaps Brian had "pretended" so often, and for so long, that he no longer knew who he really was, other than this tough, false front? Brian shrugged his shoulders and looked away: "I don't know who I am. I'm 32 years old and I don't even have a clue. That's how pathetic I am." Together, they discussed how this issue—finding out "who Brian really is"—could serve as one of the long-term goals of treatment.

This session seemed like it might pave the way for a more collaborative spirit in treatment (i.e., a stronger *treatment alliance*). But in the following weeks, Brian again returned to his more familiar style of interaction. There was no acknowledgement of the vulnerability he had displayed, nor any mention of the brief moments of empathic connection between Dr. Amory and himself. In fact, Dr. Amory once again felt that Brian treated him as if he were invisible. Rather than inviting discussion, Brian delivered monologues. When Dr. Amory managed to squeeze in relevant comments, Brian seemed to ignore them, or conveyed (through facial gestures or tone of voice) that they felt like an intrusion.

Brian began explicitly questioning whether Dr. Amory could help him. The venom of his earlier attacks subsided, but his tone was still demeaning. He conceded that perhaps Dr. Amory might be a good therapist for other people, but was he good enough for somebody as "complicated and intelligent" as himself? Dr. Amory reminded Brian that they were under no obligation to work together, and Brian was free to consult with another psychotherapist. But maybe the deeper issue was whether Brian could trust anyone to help him, or if he had felt let down or mistreated by other people so often that he needed always to keep his guard up, to protect himself?

After more sessions of this wrangling, Dr. Amory changed his tack. Although direct confrontation is not the typical style of a self psychologist, Dr. Amory suspected that Brian's grandiosity and self-centeredness would continue unabated unless he directly expressed his authority as a therapist. In a gentle but frank manner, he confronted Brian on the obstacles he continually threw in the way of engaging in treatment. Brian was "throwing his money away"—he had now spent three months harping on Dr. Amory's questionable competence and complaining about how the world mistreated and misunderstood him. Well, maybe Dr. Amory really *was* incompetent. Maybe the world *did* mistreat him. But whatever the case, by continually acting in a disrespectful and arrogant manner, Brian was not engaging in therapy and treatment was "wasting your money and both of our time."

Brian was a bit stunned by this blunt appraisal. He spat out a sharp-tongued response ("If I'm wasting my money, it's because you're not doing your job"), but then sat in a long silence. To his own surprise, he felt relieved by Dr. Amory's frankness; in fact, this session was a useful turning point. As he was able to express only much later, throughout his life Brian had always "run the show," with little accountability for his behavior. As a child, he easily manipulated his parents, using their divorce to his own gain (at least materially). The few times he was punished, he charmed or slithered his way out of it, with no repercussions. So even though Brian was insulted when Dr. Amory confronted him on his arrogance, he also felt he was being taken seriously, even respected.

Brian continued to question Dr. Amory's skills and the helpfulness of treatment, but bit by bit he grew more engaged in the therapy process. For his part, Dr. Amory rarely suggested that Brian talk about a particular topic, encouraging him to share whatever was on his mind. He occasionally reiterated his recommendation for meeting more than once weekly, but each time Brian refused to consider this option.

As their meetings continued, a few central themes emerged. One was Brian's childhood. At first, he denied that the chaos of his childhood had a major negative impact. Many friends grew up in similar families. It was "no big deal"—maybe his parents' nasty divorce even made him tougher, and "cooler." But as Brian began to engage less defensively in therapy, old memories came back to him. He recalled how horrible the aftermath of the divorce actually was. He had loved both his father and mother—but how they hated each other!

In recalling and describing long-forgotten memories, Brian came to the insight that as a child his mother acted betrayed and hurt whenever he expressed love for his father. He was not even sure if she *was* hurt or betrayed, or if he just sensed that she was. But either way, Dr. Amory validated his emotional reality that he had felt torn between his two parents and that he feared displeasing and hurting his mother.

Throughout his adulthood, Brian and his mother had remained close. She was the one person who was shielded from his arrogance; if anything, he held her up on a pedestal (as she did him). Being careful not to criticize, Dr. Amory helped Brian see the many ways during his childhood that *he* was actually parenting *her,* and not the other way around. And it should not be the role of a young child to take care of a parent—by so doing, important needs of Brian's were not being met.

As therapy continued, his mother's pedestal became more shaky. In fact, Brian developed a great deal of anger toward her. He eventually decided to confront her about many aspects of their relationship, past and present, that he now questioned. But this confrontation proved quite upsetting: When he expressed any negative feelings about her or their relationship, she responded either with silence or by pleading with him not to "attack" her—she could not "stand it" if he was angry with her.

Dr. Amory told Brian that if this pattern was longstanding—which he believed it was, based on all that Brian said—it must have created a terrible conflict for him as a child. As a young boy, he seemed to sense that in order to maintain his mother's love, he needed always to be a "good boy" in her eyes, at the cost of denying important parts of himself. Perhaps his mother's need to feel loved by Brian was more important to her—consciously or not—than her ability to respond empathically to him, especially when his needs or emotions were not to her pleasing.

As therapy continued and Brian focused more deeply on his relationship with his mother and his childhood in general, he grew increasingly depressed. What had previously been periodic bouts of self-hate and despair evolved into a nearly continuous sense of sadness. At first, Brian reacted by blaming Dr. Amory—shouldn't therapy make him feel better, not worse? Yet it made sense when Dr. Amory labeled this depression as an important aspect of treatment; Brian was beginning to acknowledge the losses and disappointments of his childhood, and he was going through a necessary, if delayed, process of coming to terms with these losses.

Another theme interwoven throughout therapy was Brian's interpersonal difficulties. One year into treatment, Brian began dating a woman whom he wanted to see more seriously, but she abruptly ended the relationship. Brian was hurt and enraged. In exploring these reactions, Dr. Amory empathized with how hard it is to experience such a rejection. But he also observed that Brian seemed to assume that if he liked or wanted something (or someone), it should automatically be his. Could Brian tolerate the disappointment of wanting something and not getting it?

From there, they looked at the many times "the shoe was on the other foot"— for example, times when Brian callously treated a woman who was interested in him or acted dishonestly with a coworker. In this manner, Brian gained some awareness of empathy. He had never really perceived that his actions could cause hurt to another person, mainly because in some ways, it never occurred to him that other people had feelings. But by experiencing feelings of hurt and rejection himself, without immediately defending against them with rage or arrogance, Brian slowly began to treat other people as if they had feelings, too.

Yet above and beyond all this, the central aspect of treatment was the deepening relationship that evolved between Brian and Dr. Amory. Over time, Brian began to think about Wilson (he called him by his first name now) often during the course of the day (perhaps noting to himself, "I wonder what Wilson will think about this"). He occasionally dreamed about him, and they discussed these dreams in therapy. In sessions, Brian sometimes talked about what he felt toward Wilson—often a mix of admiration and envy. Wilson shared very little information about his personal life, but Brian imagined it as an ideal existence, free from the interpersonal difficulties and inner turmoil that he faced.

Although he did nothing to encourage this idealization, Wilson also did nothing to discourage it. In many ways, this was the crux of treatment. Brian had never before had a reliable caretaker in his life with whom he could identify. He had idealized his mother, but she seemed more invested in taking care of her own emotional needs than his. By the time he was nine, his father had essentially abandoned him and his brother. Wilson saw these childhood events as related to Brian's adult narcissism. Hopefully, Brian could now use his feelings toward Wilson to re-experience some of these developmental needs in a safe, healing relationship, and by so doing repair this inner damage and develop healthier self-esteem.

Still, Brian's idealization of Wilson faded in and out, and the therapy relationship was often tempestuous. Brian often was enraged with Wilson or demeaning toward him. He boycotted therapy for several weeks when Wilson raised his fee one year into treatment. Wilson acknowledged Brian's displeasure at the change, but unless financial hardship was a factor (which it was not—Brian's income remained high), he would not make an exception for him. This remained a topic of discussion for a long while, particularly around Brian's longing to be treated as "special," and his disappointment and anger when that did not happen.

Brian also got very angry the times he felt that Wilson "missed the boat" in how he responded (or did not respond) to him. Wilson saw these as moments of *empathic failure* and likened them to opening scars on old injuries. He looked for unconscious connections with what Brian might have felt as an infant or child when he did not see his inner needs or wishes reflected (although not necessarily gratified) by those around him. In such situations, Brian perhaps felt a sense of shame, abandonment, or deep loneliness. But more important than discussing these early connections, Wilson empathized with the anger or hurt Brian felt *now*, in the current moment. Together, they looked at how easily Brian was prone to feeling misunderstood and how he reacted when this happened: with rage, or a defensive superiority, or self-hatred, or shame. Wilson encouraged Brian to work on applying the awarenesses he was developing in therapy to other, non-therapy relationships.

After two years, Brian's court-mandated psychotherapy ended. Although he vacillated for months before making a decision, Brian decided to continue with treatment. After doing so, therapy felt different: It was now something freely chosen, not imposed by the law. In fact, Brian's decision to continue in treatment seemed therapeutic in itself. He was accepting the fact that he wanted help and that Wilson might be able to help him. The very nature of that acknowledgment suggested that Brian's narcissistic grandiosity—and isolation—were amenable to ongoing change.

Multiaxial DSM-IV Diagnosis at This Point in Treatment

Axis I: Major Depressive Episode, Moderate
               CONDITION: SOMEWHAT IMPROVED
Axis II: Narcissistic Personality Disorder
               CONDITION: SOMEWHAT IMPROVED
Axis III: No diagnosis
Axis IV: Legal difficulties (arrest and probation)
Axis V: *Treatment Onset:* 55 (moderate to serious difficulty in social func-
               tioning, few meaningful interpersonal relationships)
               Current Time: 60 (moderate difficulty in social functioning and in-
               terpersonal relationships)

DISCUSSION

The tale of Narcissus—a handsome young man who scorned the love offered him by others—is one of the most oft-told myths from ancient Greece. The gods grew weary of Narcissus's unfeeling, selfish behavior and punished him with the onus of falling in love with the next face he saw—his own reflection, mirrored in a pond. Enamored only of himself, Narcissus eventually drowned, transfixed by his own gaze, longing to connect with his own reflected image.

Perhaps this myth's popularity endures because it conveys a message particularly resonant with modern culture. This tale may even be considered the central psychological myth of our era, much as Freud invoked the Greek tale of Oedipus as the foundation for his theory of the "Oedipus complex" (Betcher & Pollack, 1993).

Narcissistic personality disorder overlaps with many popular notions of "egoism." Acting in a self-centered manner, treating others coldly, believing oneself to be deserving of special privilege—these "egotistical" qualities are all aspects of the disorder. In other ways, however, NPD is more than simply being too full of oneself. As with Brian, the self-image of people with this disorder often vacillates between extremes of grandiosity and self-loathing. Periods of feeling superior give way to significant bouts of worthlessness. These repeated fluctuations have been referred to as a cycle of "depression and grandiosity" (Miller, 1981). In fact, one of the most reliable components of NPD is *low* self-confidence (Livesley & Schroeder, 1990).

As was the case with Brian's early failed attempts at psychotherapy, it can be these periods of depressive self-loathing (or a related concern, such as substance abuse) that lead a person with NPD to seek treatment. More often, however, interpersonal difficulties cause the most distress—but the distress, unfortunately, is often that of the other people who bear the brunt of the narcissist's exploitative or unempathic behavior. People with NPD are prone to seeing interpersonal difficulties as caused by other people, not themselves. As such, psychotherapy often starts under less than optimal circumstances—perhaps not the legal mandate Brian faced but under the threat of divorce or other end of a relationship.

A Brief History

Narcissism as a psychological disorder did not become a prominent concept until the past few decades, and NPD as a diagnostic entity was first introduced in the DSM-III in 1980. Still, the concept of narcissism has been a part of psychoanalytic theory since its inception. Early psychoanalysts did not necessarily emphasize narcissism as pathological; Freud described a period of "healthy narcissism," or self-love, during infancy. The concept of healthy narcissism is still relevant; it is when narcissistic traits become severe, limiting a person's capacity for empathy or leading to exploitative behaviors, that narcissism develops into a disorder.

To understand current ideas about narcissism and how they apply to Brian's treatment, we need an overview of how psychoanalytic theory has evolved since Freud first developed his then-revolutionary ideas one hundred years ago (Pine, 1990). At its inception, psychoanalysis was a *drive theory*. Freud theorized that all infants are born with two powerful, innate drives: sex and aggression. He believed that human functioning—intrapsychically and societally—was shaped by the need to harness, and find suitable outlets for, these drives.

While still recognizing the importance of drives, as psychoanalysis developed interest began to shift more to *ego psychology* (Adler, 1931; Hartmann, 1950; Horney, 1950). Along with the id and superego, the ego is one of three parts of personality postulated by Freud. It is responsible for negotiating the stresses, decisions, and necessities of daily life. Consciously or unconsciously, the ego provides *defense mechanisms* to cope with anxiety and painful emotion, and to keep our sexual and aggressive drives in check. (It is also the "ego" that is reading these pages, learning the information, and deciding whether or you agree or disagree with what you read.)

Another major psychoanalytic shift came with the introduction of *object relations theory* (Fairbairn, 1944; Klein, 1940, 1964; Winnicott, 1971). Instead of drives, this theory emphasizes the importance of early caretaking relationships in shaping psychological functioning.

According to object relationists, infants and young children develop complex internal representations of themselves in relation to others. These unconscious representations are shaped by actual parent–child interactions but also involve deeply buried wishes and fears. Psychological health is determined by the nature of these unconscious relationships. For example, in relating to other people, does a person see him or herself as loved and cared for, or as always in a victim–victimizer situation, or as always being "better than" or "less than"? Object relationists place such strong emphasis on early relationships that one theorist, D. W. Winnicott, is quoted as saying, "There is no such thing as an infant"—a startling yet profound statement, highlighting the fact that an infant can survive only in a caretaking relationship. No infant can exist on its own.

A still newer development in psychanalytic theory has been the emergence of *self psychology* (Kohut, 1971, 1977). Self psychologists believe that the outcome of healthy development is a cohesive and integrated sense of self. The "self" is an elusive concept, and many theorists have offered definitions for it over the past 100 years (Mead, 1934; Mischel, 1968). For self psychologists, a healthy "self" includes a capacity to relate to others openly and mutually, to feel whole by oneself and tolerate aloneness, and to have a general sense of well-being (Wolf, 1988). When an individual has a self that is too "fragmented," he or she may be unable to achieve these things and suffer from a *disorder of the self,* such as NPD.

Like object relationists, self psychologists believe that a healthy self grows out of early caretaking relationships that are able to satisfy some basic emotional needs. Central among these are a need for *mirroring* and a need to *idealize an important other.* In mirroring, a child's inner world is reflected, acknowledged, and admired by his or her caretakers. This includes not only a wide range of emotions but also the childhood belief in one's own omnipotence and grandiosity. Being adequately recognized for these inner states is regarded as the seed of good self-esteem and appropriate ambition. And through the process of idealization, a child learns to identify with another person. This identification allows children to feel they can share in an adult's strength, and then model themselves on it. This is the root for empathy and an internalized set of values.

To some degree, these needs continue throughout life. However, if the environment is not responsive enough to these needs in childhood, a "cohesive" self will not develop. Like Brian, adults who have an excessive need for admiration or recognition (mirroring), or who form relationships based on idealization and devaluation rather than mutuality, are still attempting to satisfy these early needs. In other words, NPD is more likely to develop in children who do not receive the genuine admiration they need than in children lavished with too much attention.

On first view, this self psychological position contrasts with other schools of thought, particularly behaviorism or a social learning perspective. The laws of reinforcement suggest that through operant conditioning, children who are overly indulged, and who are positively reinforced as being "special," will learn to carry similar expectations into adulthood. So whereas self psychology posits that NPD has its roots in a childhood where needs for admiration go unmet, social learning theory assumes that it develops when children are too easily gratified.

However, this contrast may not be so clear cut. Self psychologists argue that for healthy development, a child's *inner* experience needs to be mirrored and regarded as special. This can fail to occur even while a child is praised as being special, or overly indulged in other ways. Or, it occurs when children are valued more for who their parents want or need them to be than for who they are. This fits Brian's situation: As a young boy his mother had a "close" and "special" relationship with him, but this closeness seemed to depend on him behaving, or feeling, in certain ways. So theoretically, both social learning theory and self psychology can be relevant in the etiology of NPD.

Whatever the case, conducting empirical research on questions regarding the development of narcissistic personality disorder is no easy task, given the complex variables involved. Although it has been the focus of much psychoanalytic writing, few studies have scrutinized NPD empirically. While scales have been developed to measure narcissistic traits (Gunderson, Ronningstam & Bodkin, 1990), qualities such as "excessive need for admiration," feeling "special," and "grandiose sense of self-importance" are difficult to pin down. And for researchers and clinicians with a behavioral orientation, the broader concept of personality disorders raises problems in general, given that these disorders often involve intangible aspects of a person's character rather than specific behaviors.

Reflections on Brian's Treatment

We can see the relevance of self-psychological concepts in Brian's treatment. Dr. Amory theorized that Brian's personality disorder had its roots in his childhood and particularly in how his mother and father were not empathically attuned enough to his needs. The goal of treatment was to repair these early empathic failures, based on the assumption that this healing would then allow him to establish healthier relationships. By "repair," Dr. Amory did not choose wantonly to indulge Brian's belief that he deserved special treatment (other than in the first sessions, when this seemed necessary to establish a treatment alliance). Instead, he sought to mirror Brian's underlying emotional hurts, while still holding him responsible for his behaviors and actions, and to provide Brian with a stable, caring presence for Brian to identify with and idealize.

In keeping with his psychoanalytic principles, Dr. Amory looked for unconscious connections between Brian's past and present, encouraged him to verbalize whatever was on his mind, and used the therapist–patient relationship as a key factor of treatment. The overall theme of Brian's search for "who he was" can be seen as a process of developing a more cohesive self.

A Note on Divorce

The traumatic impact of Brian's parents' divorce played a specific role in how Dr. Amory conceptualized Brian's difficulties, although he paid more attention to the quality of the parenting Brian received than to the divorce itself. No strong relationship has been empirically demonstrated between divorce and any single type of subsequent psychopathology. It appears that some children from divorced families suffer a range of adverse, long-lasting psychological effects yet others respond with great resilience (Amato & Keith, 1991; Wallerstein, Corbin & Lewis, 1988). Gaining accurate data about the long-term impact of divorce on children has been difficult, again because so many complex factors are involved. These include pre- and post-divorce life events, economic changes, and a host of psychological variables related to the child, each parent, and parent–child relationships.

Still, even in the absence of hard data, certain theorists (Kernberg, 1997) believe that divorce increases a child's risk for NPD, given how children in this situation may be inappropriately cast in the role of a surrogate spouse, or be encouraged to adopt the same hostile feelings that the parents may feel for each other. Both of these factors are relevant in Brian's history.

Narcissism and Culture

Narcissistic personality disorder offers a prime example of the interplay between psychopathology and culture. In recent years, we have witnessed the "me" decade.

Our society has been labeled a "culture of narcissism" (Lasch, 1978). One telling indication of how linked this disorder is to western, and particularly American, culture is that it is not even represented in the ICD-10, the international diagnostic manual of the World Health Organization (WHO, 1992).

Yet, our culture's link to narcissism has not always been so pronounced: Recall that as a disorder narcissism is a relatively new concept. NPD may be as much an outgrowth of our modern culture as "hysteria" (now known as conversion disorder)[1] was of Victorian times—an era marked by much more sexual repression and more rigid social roles and expectations than today.

It is interesting to see that predominant modes of psychopathology change over the years. What has led to the rise of narcissism? Perhaps it arises from changes in childrearing practices, or more relaxed sexual mores, or the reconfiguring of family life. Does it reflect the "dark side" of how much emphasis we place on individualism and autonomy? What role do television and other media play in how they present such a dizzying array of possible options for how people live? Of course, no simple answer will explain this. But once again we see how culture cannot be separated from psychopathology. Psychological distress does not exist in a vacuum; it is shaped and guided by the society, and the time, in which we live.

PROGNOSIS

Several months after Brian agreed to continue in treatment, he accepted Wilson's recommendation to meet twice weekly. His treatment lasted approximately another 15 months, until it ended rather abruptly when Brian decided to relocate to another city for a job promotion.

At the time of his termination, Brian reported that he was dissatisfied with the progress he had made because his basic problems remained much the same. Still, he had made some changes: He was, at least at times, less arrogant in his interpersonal dealings and more empathic to the feelings of those around him. His self-esteem had improved and was more even, in that he was less grandiose but also less self-hating. He thought himself more "humble." Of most significance to him, he had gotten involved in a relationship with a woman that had lasted one year, his longest and most serious romantic involvement yet.

Because so little empirical research has been conducted with NPD, it remains uncertain what factors affect the long-term prognosis. Kernberg (1975), a prominent NPD theorist, suggests that the ability to tolerate depression and grief over childhood losses, such as Brian evinced, is a good prognostic indicator. But as a general rule, personality disorders are considered chronic conditions, not readily amenable to major improvement. With appropriate and successful treatment—most likely of an intensive or long-term nature—perhaps a good outcome is a reduction in the severity of impairment, not a dramatic change of personality. And unlike

---

[1]A modern case of conversion disorder is presented in Chapter 5.

other personality disorders, which may become less severe on their own over the decades of a person's life, NPD has been known to worsen as a person reaches middle age (Kernberg, 1980).

Perhaps Brian's treatment, then, will have been successful to the degree that he can more empathically relate to others, maintain good (but not overly inflated) self-esteem, and accept a fact that sounds simple, but for some people is among the hardest things imaginable—knowing that each of us is a human being just like everyone else, with human strengths and flaws.

CRITICAL THINKING QUESTIONS

1. Inter-rater reliability is lower when diagnosing personality disorders than with any other category of disorders. What are some of the difficulties with making such a diagnosis?
2. How might sociocultural factors affect the prevalence of narcissistic personality disorder?
3. If Brian had some of the same personality features as he does, but to a less prominent degree, would he still have a personality disorder? How would you determine this?
4. Do you think the judge in Brian's case was too lenient in sentencing him only to probation? Would there be a benefit to Brian serving time in prison?
5. Individuals with narcissistic personality disorder also frequently experience depression and difficulties with alcohol or substance abuse. Why might this be?

Borderline Personality Disorder

D r. Foley's pager went off at 3:00 AM. She roused herself from sleep. She recognized the electronic number on display, and somewhat anxiously called the County Hospital Emergency Room.

"Hello. This is Dr. Beth Foley. I was just paged to this number."

"Yes, Dr. Foley, thank you for responding so soon. This is Dr. Owings, on-call physician at County Emergency. I'm calling in regard to a psychotherapy patient of yours, Denise Gilmartin. She gave me written permission to talk with you."

"Is she alright?"

"She arrived about two hours ago with four self-inflicted incisions on her left forearm, moderately deep cuts which required stitching. She used an exact-o® knife. She also admits to having taken an overdose of 6 milligrams of Ativan.[1] That's enough to make her groggy, but it doesn't require medical intervention."

"I see. What is her mood and state of mind right now?"

"She says she feels angry and depressed, but denies any risk of further self-harm or suicide. Her thought processes seem clear and focused."

"Did she say why she's depressed and angry?" asked Dr. Foley.

"No. When I asked, she said, quote, it's none of your goddamn business, end quote. But she did say she would discuss it with you."

"That sounds like Denise. How can I be of help, Dr. Owings?"

"I called for your input as to whether Ms. Gilmartin needs to be hospitalized. There's no medical reason to keep her and she denies risk of suicide, but I wanted to hear if you think it's safe to discharge her. You know her better than we do."

---

[1]Ativan is a type of *anxiolytic*, or anti-anxiety medication.

Dr. Foley paused before answering. "Yes, I think it's alright. This has happened before. Denise can be quite self-destructive, but she's usually honest about her safety regarding any risk for suicide."

"Okay, I'm sending her back home then. Thanks for your help. And sorry to have woken you."

"Please tell her that we spoke and I'll see her tomorrow at our scheduled appointment."

"Good night."

"Yes, good night."

Denise Gilmartin was an intelligent, attractive, and stylish 26-year-old single woman. She had been in psychotherapy with Dr. Foley for nearly two years when this incident occurred. Dr. Foley suspected she knew the reason for this most recent bout of self-destructive behavior: Days earlier, another stormy romance had ended.

Such a scenario had indeed "happened before," many times. In the past several years, Denise had attempted suicide once and frequently engaged in *parasuicidal* behaviors, dangerous activities such as self-mutilation and taking small overdoses. These behaviors did not necessarily threaten her life but still caused her harm. They also, obviously, greatly distressed and alarmed people around her—a fact that was not lost on Denise. "Let's face it," she once told Dr. Foley. "No words ever grab someone's attention like an overdose can." Denise's body gave mute testimony to her self-destructiveness: Scars on her arms and legs spoke to years of cutting, scratching, and sometimes burning herself.

Denise lived in an urban downtown area, a section of the city known for its nightlife. She did not have roommates (the few times she tried it was "a disaster"). But she dreaded being by herself and rarely spent time alone. Denise described being alone as "terrifying—I feel so empty. It's like I don't exist." She relied on whatever she could to avoid solitude—many short-lived romances, going out to clubs, her job as a waitress.

Since college, Denise had a history of tempestuous, brief romances, friendships quickly gained and lost, and unsteady employment. She had done well in school and was regarded as a good student. But in the four years since graduation, she had not kept a job for more than a few months.

A business major, Denise hoped to work in marketing after graduation. A friend of her father's helped secure her a plum job with a market research firm. But interpersonal difficulties developed within a few weeks, and she soon resigned rather than risk being fired. She then decided she did not like marketing, anyway, and took a paralegal course. She found work as a paralegal, only to repeat the same situation as in marketing.

Denise then decided to "give up on the corporate world" and work as a waitress. She felt this suited her better—the easy camaraderie, the fast pace, the late-night schedule, the partying after work into the early hours of the morning. But even as a waitress, Denise hopped from one job to the next. Her enthusiasm about a new restaurant, and new co-workers, always soured into disappointment. She left one job because she found the other staff members "too catty." At another restaurant they were "too snobby" and at another "too dull." She was fired from one job after becoming so angry at a customer that she threw a drink at him.

It was not that Denise had difficulty starting friendships: People quickly responded to her charm and apparent happy-go-lucky manner. But she rarely sustained contact with people beyond a superficial level. Since high school, she had often formed quick, intense attachments with potential new friends. At those times she felt elated and described her new contacts with terms such as "wonderful," "incredibly special," "the best friend I've always wanted." But just as quickly as these friendships formed they would falter, and Denise then felt nothing but "contempt" and "loathing" where she once gushed with warmth and admiration.

Twice, Denise quit her job after becoming sexually involved with a co-worker. Each time the relationship started as the "casual fling" she explicitly said she wanted. But soon the man treated it *too* casually, she felt. He did not pay her enough attention or make enough of a commitment. She then felt enraged, used, and devastated that "the jerk" did not take it more seriously.

Denise's one serious suicide attempt followed the break-up of a ten-month romance. This was the longest relationship Denise had maintained, and the one she was sure, from the first moment, "would be it." Several times, Donald had discussed breaking up with her, but each time Denise pleaded with him not to. Donald described her as "clingy," and she saw how he might be right, but she felt she could not help herself—and couldn't he please give her one more try? Finally, Donald began seeing somebody else and told Denise it was over.

A few days after Donald left, Denise could no longer tolerate her intense emotions about his "vicious betrayal." She impulsively took an overdose of whatever pills and liquor she found in her apartment. She telephoned Donald and left a teary message on his answering machine, her voice slurred: "Don't worry. It's not really your fault. But how could you do this to me? You bastard." Donald heard the message a few hours later; when he telephoned Denise and received no answer, he became worried and contacted the police, who went to Denise's apartment. They found her unconscious and brought her to the hospital.

And so now yet another brief relationship had ended, and Denise was back again at the emergency room. Before she went back to sleep, Dr. Foley ironically noted to herself that she was relieved that Denise's current destructiveness had not been more severe than it was, given her proven potential for self-harm.

PSYCHOSOCIAL HISTORY

Denise Gilmartin grew up in a suburb of Boston, Massachusetts. She was the third of four children, and the only girl. Her two older brothers were three and six years her senior, and her other brother was two years younger. Her father's family background was Irish, her mother's Polish. Denise was raised Catholic, and she attended parochial school until the 9th grade. Denise's father was a lawyer and prominent in local town affairs. Her mother was an elementary school teacher.

The Gilmartins were quite conscious of social appearances. To their neighbors, many acquaintances, and the outside world in general, they presented the picture of a loving and close family. But that image contrasted sharply with the details of their private family life.

In fact, Denise's childhood was marked by loneliness, neglect, and cruelty. Her mother spent little time with her. When Mrs. Gilmartin was home—which was not all that often—she was preoccupied with preparing classes, grading papers, or some other work. Most of her free time, though, she was out doing something: school meetings, a church group, one of multiple volunteer responsibilities. In addition, every school year she had a few favorite students. At home she talked about these children frequently, and always in glowing terms. Denise felt the not-so-hidden criticism in how Mrs. Gilmartin spoke of these children—neither she nor her brothers ever received such praise or seemed to match up.

Denise adored, but feared, her powerful father. His rule was law in the house—and tyrannical rule it was. When she read *Dr. Jekyll and Mr. Hyde* in 8th grade, she thought this described him exactly. At times he was loving and playful; other times, he unexpectedly exploded into rage or brutality.

For example, Denise recalled the following incident as typical of her childhood. When she was 10 years old, she absentmindedly forgot her table manners one evening and sat at dinner with her elbows on the table (and how many times had he reminded her not to do that?). To punish her—or, as he said, to "teach" her—Mr. Gilmartin tied her hands to the sides of her chair and made her sit silent, and hungry, while the rest of the family continued with their meal. She was left tied to the chair for an hour after everyone else had left the table, with the other family members instructed not to talk to her.

Another time, a Saturday afternoon perhaps a year later, Mr. Gilmartin got angry at Denise for playing her stereo too loudly. He had dozed off watching television and the noise woke him up. He did not yell at or hit her, as she feared he might. Instead, he quietly asked her to join him in his study. He then took down a valentine card she had made for him years earlier, which was framed and hanging on his wall. Silently, looking at her with an unwavering stare, he cut the valentine into little pieces and threw it in the trash. Denise sat there crying, until he nodded his head slightly to dismiss her.

Invariably, a few hours after such incidents, Mr. Gilmartin came to find Denise. His tone would be somewhat apologetic. He would try joking with her, and then say, "Daddy needs to know you love him. Can you say, 'I love you, Daddy?' Tell Daddy you love him." If she did not say it, he would look hurt, and then ignore her for several days. When she would respond by saying she loved him, he answered, "And I love you too, baby. You know you're my special little angel." It was only a matter of time, however, before another incident occurred.

Mr. Gilmartin's cruel and arbitrary rule was only part of Denise's private childhood torment. Beginning when she eight years old, her oldest brother Andrew (then 14 years old) began coercing her into sexual activity. It started under the guise of a game all the kids played, "I dare you . . . ." But it soon stopped being a game. Whenever the two of them were alone in the house, Andrew coaxed, cajoled, or forced Denise into unwanted sexual contact. He did not force Denise to engage in sexual intercourse with him, but he pressured her into several other sexual activities.

In front of the rest of the family, Andrew acted quite fondly toward her. He sometimes buffered her from their father's sporadic rage, drawing Mr. Gilmartin's anger toward himself so as to protect her. But in private, that protectiveness disappeared. He threatened Denise, "If you ever tell anyone what's going on, my buddies will have you killed." The threat was empty, Denise came to realize years later. But as a child it seemed real enough to keep her awake at nights in fear.

Denise wondered if her mother and father knew about what Andrew was doing; she recalled that one afternoon Mrs. Gilmartin came home unexpectedly and caught him hurriedly leaving her room. Mrs. Gilmartin questioned why he was there, seemed to pause for a moment, but then let the matter go and never brought it up again.

The sexual abuse occurred intermittently for four years, until Andrew went away to college. When he returned from school on vacations, he treated Denise distantly. He seemed ill at ease around her. She also ignored him. The few times it seemed likely that the two of them would be alone in the house, Denise found an excuse to leave.

By the time she was 16, Denise had grown accustomed to feeling like Dr. Jekyll and Mr. Hyde herself: She looked and acted fine at school, where she earned good grades and participated in student life. But inside she felt despair, self-hatred, and emptiness. She thought about suicide frequently. It was about that time that she first took a razor blade and intentionally cut herself on the arm. She felt ashamed by what she had done and kept it secret. Cutting herself brought a strange relief from the intolerable despair and rage she felt. Since then, self-destructiveness—with pills, with a sharp knife, sometimes with a lit cigarette—had become a regular ritual. As the years continued, the self-destructiveness frequently remained a private activity. But not always: Denise sometimes divulged what she had done, so that she could let someone know "what you drove me to."

Through her college years and into her twenties, Denise was severely depressed much of the time, even though she tried to hide it publicly. Yet her mood also varied tremendously; at times her depression suddenly lifted, and she felt driven with energy or filled with rage. She also engaged in risky, impulsive behaviors, including shoplifting and heavy binge drinking.

Her current relationship with her parents was strained. Many of their interactions revolved around money. Denise had a habit of impulsively buying expensive, luxurious treats, and then asking her parents to bail her out of debt. A pattern had been long established: Denise would beseech them for money, which angered them ("Why did you do this again—can't you be more responsible?"). Denise would then experience a deluge of strong emotions in response to their anger—rage at them, self-hate at her own irresponsibility, fear that they would not help out. Her rage would then give way to depression and then to despair and thoughts of suicide. Her mother would become worried: "We hate to see you like this. What can we do to help?"

In the end, a little extra money always seemed the least they could do.

CONCEPTUALIZATION

Denise Gilmartin demonstrates a pattern of severe and long-standing difficulties that affect several facets of her life—interpersonal relationships, occupational functioning, and her own inner experience. Because these "personality traits are inflexible and maladaptive and cause significant functional impairment or subjective distress" (APA, 1994, p. 630), they are best understood as a personality disorder.

Of the ten personality disorders detailed in DSM-IV, Denise best fits the criteria for borderline personality disorder (BPD). This personality disorder is defined by "an instability of interpersonal relationships, self-image, and affects, and marked impulsivity that begins by early adulthood and is present in a variety of contexts" (APA, 1994, p. 650). Nine criteria are listed:

A. frantic efforts to avoid real or imagined abandonment
B. a pattern of unstable and intense interpersonal relationships characterized by alternating between extremes of idealization and devaluation
C. identity disturbance: markedly and persistently unstable self-image or sense of self
D. impulsivity in at least two areas that are potentially self-damaging (e.g., spending, sex, substance abuse, reckless driving, binge eating)
E. recurrent suicidal behavior, gestures, or threats, or self-mutilating behavior
F. affective instability due to a marked reactivity of mood (e.g., intense episodic dysphoria, irritability, or anxiety usually lasting a few hours and only rarely more than a few days)
G. chronic feelings of emptiness
H. inappropriate, intense anger or difficulty controlling anger (e.g., frequent displays of temper, constant anger, recurrent physical fights)
I. transient, stress-related paranoid ideation or severe dissociative symptoms

Five of these traits are necessary to make the diagnosis of BPD. Denise amply meets these criteria: with the possible exception of the last criterion, it seems likely that she meets them all.

Denise also meets diagnostic criteria for major depression, given her chronic feelings of self-hatred, suicidal ideation, and depressed mood. She also engages in binge drinking, which, depending on its extent, may indicate an additional problem with alcohol abuse.

Had Denise's shoplifting occurred by itself, and she engaged in the behavior in a repetitive, compulsive manner, this would warrant the diagnosis of an impulse control disorder not-otherwise-specified. However, because this impulsivity occurs in the context of the broader impairment of a personality disorder, this additional diagnosis is not necessary.

TREATMENT

Regardless of theoretical orientation, treatment for all personality disorders is considered to be a challenging and long-term endeavor. By definition, the problematic personality traits are deeply ingrained and inflexible, so they are not easily amenable to change.

One key theoretical debate in the treatment of BPD is how directive or confrontational the therapist should be regarding the patient's maladaptive patterns (Gunderson, 1994). At the risk of oversimplifying a complex issue, some argue that these individuals' potential for manipulative behavior, and their rapid and sudden shifts between extremes of idealizing and devaluing others (a defense mechanism known as *splitting*), need to be directly confronted (Kernberg, 1984). Others advocate a more supportive approach: If these behaviors are seen not as manipulation, but as a genuine (if misguided) attempt to communicate an inner desperation, then the underlying pain needs to be the focus (Adler, 1993).

Regardless, psychotherapy for BPD can be exceptionally demanding for a psychotherapist because the treatment relationship often becomes the focus for the underlying rages, longings, and fears of abandonment. As such, successful therapy for BPD almost always involves reducing "acting out" behaviors, such as provocative suicidal threats or gestures, that can undermine or destroy the treatment (Allen, 1997; Linehan, 1993).

Before Denise began psychotherapy with Dr. Foley, she had had a series of brief attempts at treatment with several therapists, some psychodynamically oriented and others cognitive-behavioral. Not surprisingly, given her interpersonal style, none of these had gone well. Denise sometimes quit after one session. Other times, she recreated the pattern that characterized her friendships, idealizing the therapist at first, but then becoming enraged when her expectations were not met.

Denise's therapist immediately prior to Dr. Foley ended treatment following her serious suicide attempt. He told her that he questioned his helpfulness to her, given the severity of what had happened. But Denise also sensed that he was relieved to rid himself of her; she later read in her treatment file that he described her with words such as "rude . . . manipulative . . . conniving."

Dr. Foley was the first psychologist with whom Denise had maintained a steady relationship. For the past two years, they had met twice weekly for forty-five minute psychotherapy sessions. In addition to these meetings, Denise also saw a psychiatrist, who prescribed her anti-anxiety and antidepressant medications.

Over the course of this comprehensive treatment, Denise had made progress. She had reduced the frequency and severity of her self-destructive activity, her extravagant spending, and her shoplifting. And by maintaining, for the first time, a steady psychotherapy relationship, she had begun to trust she could share herself openly and honestly with another person without being greeted by the "contempt" and "disgust" she assumed others felt about her.

Yet treatment was far more of a roller coaster than a steady ride. All too often her progress evaporated, and she fell back to her more disturbed style of functioning. These *regressions* often occurred in response to events and interruptions in therapy, such as Dr. Foley's vacations, or when Dr. Foley did not respond quickly enough when Denise paged her during a "crisis" (just what constituted a crisis differed for Dr. Foley and Denise, and this was a subject of much discussion). She also regressed when life events became too stressful, as was the case with her current episode of cutting and overdosing.

Dr. Foley was trained psychodynamically. From her experience with patients such as Denise, however—most of whom were women in their twenties and early thirties—she knew that traditional treatment approaches had not proven effective. Instead, with these women Dr. Foley used an *integrative* treatment approach.

She kept a psychodynamic framework, in particular paying attention to what are referred to as *treatment frame* issues: using psychotherapy to provide an anchoring sense of stability, consistency, and limit-setting. Dr. Foley created this environment by paying attention to the "frame" around therapy. For example, she insisted that Denise attend all her regularly scheduled appointments, arrive promptly, and pay her bills on time. Their discussions regarding out-of-session contact related to maintaining the treatment frame.

Dr. Foley also negotiated an explicit *treatment contract* with Denise at the beginning of their work together. This contract specified Denise's goals for psychotherapy, which included developing strategies to reduce self-destructive behaviors and learning ways to act less impulsively. The treatment contract also laid out what Denise needed to do in order to remain in treatment with Dr. Foley. Among other things, this included honoring her commitment to the treatment frame, and letting Dr. Foley know if she were ever at risk for acting on a suicidal urge.

Dr. Foley also integrated aspects of *dialectical behavior therapy*, a relatively new treatment designed specifically for BPD (Linehan, 1993). This treatment merges aspects of standard cognitive-behavioral therapy along with an emphasis on validation and acceptance of a person's emotions. Dialectical behavior therapy also emphasizes *mindfulness*, a concept derived from Zen Buddhism. Mindfulness involves becoming aware of, and accepting, reality as it is in the current moment, regardless of how good or bad it is. Accepting this reality does not mean that a person has to approve of it. But instead of pretending that things are different than they are, acceptance is seen as the first step in changing one's situation, or changing one's own response to it. The *dialectic* (or tension between the contradictory opposites) is between acceptance of how things currently are and the simultaneous need for change.

For example, Dr. Foley challenged some of Denise's habitual cognitive distortions, which are common among people with BPD. These include *black and white thinking* (seeing things only in absolute and extreme terms) and *catastrophizing* (assuming that horrendous outcomes are unavoidable). But at the same time, she validated and empathized with whatever Denise was feeling in the present moment. If Denise were thinking in a catastrophic manner, it was understandable because she *had* experienced catastrophic events in the past—and emotionally, it might seem as if a catastrophe could still occur at any moment. Could she become more self-aware of what led her to fear catastrophe in the current moment, accept her reaction without self-judgment, yet also try to balance her terrifying emotions and thoughts with more moderate ones?

Perhaps surprisingly, Denise's history of sexual and emotional abuse was not (or not yet) a significant focus of treatment. Early in therapy, Dr. Foley listened as Denise talked about her childhood, including her father's cruelty, her mother's emotional unavailability, and her brother Andrew's sexual abuse. Both she and Denise saw these childhood events as crucial in understanding Denise's current difficulties, and both believed that a time would come in therapy when it would be important to focus on these traumas directly. (Denise had never confronted her parents about what had happened between Andrew and her or how much they knew. Andrew now lived across the country and barely kept in contact with the family; Denise had not spoken with him for several years).

But Dr. Foley convinced Denise that as important and terrible as these experiences were, the time was not yet appropriate to dig into them. The priority must be Denise's current safety and ability to take care of herself. What would be gained by dredging up the past, until she had learned to protect and care for herself in the present? And so after acknowledging that a long-term goal of therapy was to overcome the effects of Denise's abusive childhood, the two first set out on a path of strengthening Denise's current functioning.

These principles are demonstrated in the psychotherapy sessions that followed Denise's visit to the emergency room. That next morning, Denise arrived on time for her appointment but sat silently for a long time. She then looked at Dr. Foley accusingly, and finally said, "Well, are you satisfied?" Dr. Foley responding by asking Denise what she meant. As they continued to talk, Denise revealed that she assumed that Dr. Foley, "like everyone else," was just waiting for her to "screw up," because "I always do—why should this time be any different?" She then began sobbing.

When Dr. Foley asked what she was crying about, Denise answered that she felt miserable. The break-up with her boyfriend hurt so much, and how did she end up in the same stupid situation again? She hated him and she hated herself. She was a complete failure. She had believed that over the past few months she had made real progress in reducing her self-mutilative behaviors, but now "it was all ruined."

Dr. Foley questioned Denise's belief that "all was ruined" and suggested that this might be an incidence of black and white thinking. This was a setback, but it could be overcome. She also acknowledged how devastated Denise was feeling and pursued the theme of her self-hatred. Denise then revealed she felt "ashamed" because she had acted so impulsively the night before. After discussing this for a moment, Dr. Foley connected this feeling of shame with her accusatory tone earlier in the session. Perhaps by assuming Dr. Foley felt "satisfied" that she had hurt herself, was Denise trying to avoid the shame and disappointment she felt in herself?

Dr. Foley had intended this as a helpful comment, but Denise did not take it that way. The atmosphere in the room suddenly changed. After a silence, Denise responded coldly, "You don't get it, do you?"

Dr. Foley answered, "I'd like to try to understand what you're feeling right now. What is it that you think I don't get?"

"I almost kill myself because I'm in so much pain that I can't stand it, and all you offer is some goddamn therapy analysis of how ashamed I am."

Another long silence followed, and then Denise said, "I hate how insensitive you are. You sound just like a textbook."

Dr. Foley said that it was not her intention to dismiss or minimize what Denise was feeling, but acknowledged that Denise heard it that way. Another long silence followed. From many similar previous encounters, Dr. Foley sensed that re-establishing rapport with Denise would be difficult that session. It was not her perception that what she had said was insensitive, although she did allow for the possibility: Sometimes in the past, Denise's actions or words had so angered or upset her that she did not know how to respond without expressing her sense of being hurt or angry. But rather than engaging Denise in a confrontation about this, she instead validated what she assumed to be Denise's immediate experience: how painful and enraging it must be to feel so misunderstood, especially by someone Denise relied on for support.

That afternoon, Denise left a hostile message on Dr. Foley's answering machine "reminding" her of what a bad therapist she was. But as she arrived for her next session three days later, she felt not anger, but more self-hatred over how she had lost her temper. She was depressed. Her rage had not disappeared; now it was all aimed again at her ex-boyfriend (and herself).

Now that the therapy relationship felt somewhat settled down, Dr. Foley brought up their tense interchange from the previous session. Denise at first bristled but after some discussion was able to see that she may have been blaming Dr. Foley as a way to avoid her own feelings. They then discussed the impact that such reactions had on her ability to sustain relationships outside of therapy. This led to Denise expressing her hopelessness about ever changing. Using the therapy relationship as an example, Dr. Foley pointed out that despite intense emotions, relationships need not "hang by a thread." Together, they had already weathered many instances of Denise's feeling so enraged or misunderstood by Dr. Foley that she was convinced the relationship could not continue—but it had.

By the end of that session, Denise's attitude had changed from one of despair and "utter failure" to something a bit more measured. She still felt devastated by the recent break-up, but she was also able to acknowledge that the world had not ended, Dr. Foley had not berated or abandoned her, and perhaps she could get through this newest bout of misery without any firther self harm.

DISCUSSION

Most mental health professionals are familiar with individuals who fit Denise's pattern of self-destructiveness, mood instability, and chaotic interpersonal relationships. Such individuals comprise an estimated 10% of the population of outpatient mental health clinics and represent 15% to 20% of all inpatient psychiatric hospital admissions (Kroll et al., 1982; Widiger & Trull, 1993). Among the general population, prevalence estimates for BPD range from between .2% to 4% (Institute of Medicine, 1985; Widiger & Trull, 1993).

It is not only mental health professionals who are familiar with this disorder—so are moviegoers. Such individuals seem to grip the public imagination. In recent

---

Multiaxial DSM-IV Diagnosis at This Point in Treatment

Axis I:	Major Depressive Disorder, Recurrent, Moderate CONDITION: VARIABLE
Axis II:	Borderline Personality Disorder CONDITION: SOMEWHAT IMPROVED
Axis III:	None
Axis IV:	History of sexual, physical, and emotional abuse in childhood
Axis V:	*Treatment Onset:* 15 (severe danger of hurting self or others) *Current Time:* 45 (serious symptoms, potential for self-harm, major impairment in social functioning)

years, compelling female villains in films such as *Fatal Attraction, Mommy Dearest,* and *Single White Female* would all be diagnosed with BPD. (Careful observers might note that in *Fatal Attraction,* the disturbed main character wore only black and white clothes—a clever comment on the black and white thinking typical of the disorder.)

Few other current psychological diagnoses generate as much controversy. This controversy is not about the validity or existence of the disorder, as is the case with dissociative identity disorder[1] but more about related questions: What causes it? How can it be accurately defined, how best treated? Why is it three to four times more frequently diagnosed in women than men (Stiver, 1988; Widiger & Trull, 1993)?

One possible explanation for the male–female differential is gender bias in diagnosis (Kass, Spitzer & Williams, 1983). Perhaps the label "borderline" is more frequently applied to women than men, even when men meet the required diagnostic criteria. Men may instead be more commonly diagnosed with another personality disorder, such as antisocial or narcissistic personality disorder, whereas women who present with the same characteristics are more likely to be diagnosed as having BPD (Pollack, 1988). Several key symptoms of BPD overlap with both antisocial personality disorder and narcissistic personality disorder, and this can lead to diagnostic confusion (Morey & Jones, 1997; Paris, 1997; Zanarini & Gunderson, 1997). It may also be that the DSM-IV criteria emphasize behaviors that are considered more pathological in women than men.

In contrast, a second view suggests that the gender difference is real: More women than men meet the actual diagnostic criteria for BPD (Bardenstein & Mc-Glashan, 1988; Gibson, 1990; Gunderson, 1994). According to this view, diagnostic biases may occur but not to an extent that adequately explains the difference between male and female prevalences.

Difficulties with Definition

In its present form, borderline personality disorder entered our diagnostic nomenclature with DSM-III in 1980, but the concept goes back several decades earlier (Knight, 1953; Stern, 1938). It is an old concept and has long been a confusing one; even though the term has been used for decades, its meaning often has been imprecise and unclear. Does "borderline" refer to a person who is on the border of a psychotic disorder such as schizophrenia, or the border of normal, or someplace between the two? Part of the confusion also arises because "borderline" is now often identified as a catch-all diagnosis for patients (primarily women) who do not fit easily into other categories, who are difficult to treat, and who have an angry and volatile emotional style (Herman, 1992).

Even among leading theorists, not everyone agrees on what BPD is. For example, Kernberg (1984) believes that instead of conceptualizing this as a distinct personality disorder, it is more accurately conceptualized as a *level of personality organization*. From this view, at the core of identity, all people have an underly-

---

[1]See Chapter 6 for a presentation of dissociative identity disorder.

ing structure that shapes their personality, in the same way that the foundation of a house determines the shape, and strength, of the building above. Kernberg (1984) proposes that personality can be organized at three distinct levels: psychotic, borderline, or neurotic.[2] A borderline personality organization describes individuals with reality testing that is usually intact (i.e., they are not psychotic), but who experience profound disturbances in self-identity and interpersonal relationships.

Adding still more complexity, BPD seldom occurs without at least one comorbid disorder. Prominent among these are uni- and bipolar mood disorders, posttraumatic stress disorder, eating disorders, and substance abuse (Widiger & Trull, 1993). The overlap of BPD with other personality disorders also is large and confusing, although self-destructive behaviors and intense/unstable interpersonal difficulties seem to best distinguish this disorder from all others (Widiger & Frances, 1988; Zanarini et al., 1990).

Theoretical Perspectives

Not surprisingly, theorists and clinicians also have a wide range of opinions about what might be considered the main disturbance, or central underlying problem, in BPD. For example, Linehan (1993), the pioneer of dialectical behavior therapy, regards the central problem as *affective dysregulation*, or the inability to experience and express emotions in a measured, non-destructive way. Linehan takes a *biosocial* approach, assuming that BPD arises from the interaction between an invalidating or unresponsive environment in childhood and a biological vulnerability to strong emotionality. She theorizes that the variety of symptoms that characterize BPD all have their root in this pervasive underlying difficulty with emotional modulation.

From a feminist perspective, *self-in-relation theory* (Jordan et al., 1991) posits that womens' core sense of identity is *relational*, or based in relating to others. From this perspective, women with BPD lack the skills necessary to maintain relationships in a mature, reciprocal manner but still need, as all people do, to stay connected with other people. As such, behaviors such as manipulativeness, clinginess, and frantic efforts to avoid abandonment reflect this basic need to relate. This failure to create or sustain nurturing, stable relationships is assumed to result from destructive, unhealthy, or inadequate caretaking relationships in childhood.

Biological theorists point out that like many other psychiatric disorders, BPD is not evenly distributed among the population: It clusters in families. A diagnosis of BPD is five times more common among first degree biological relatives of individuals with the disorder than in the general population (Loranger, Oldham & Tulis, 1982). One intriguing biological theory has been that BPD is in fact a variant of mood disorders (Akiskal, 1981; Stone, 1980). As may be evident in the description

---

[2]The terms *neurotic* and *neurosis* are not used in the language of DSM-IV but are traditional psychoanalytic concepts. Neuroses are intrapsychic conflicts that lead to maladaptive or self-defeating behaviors. However, from this school of thought, *all* people have intrapsychic conflicts, and conflicts of a neurotic nature are less severe than those that are borderline or psychotic.

of Denise, many people with BPD suffer from major depression and experience intense mood swings that can look very similar to bipolar II disorder.

However, the weight of evidence now suggests that BPD is distinct from mood disorders, even though they are often comorbid (Gunderson, 1994). And the fact that the disorder clusters in families may be environmental rather than genetic, with certain parenting and familial styles perpetuating a cycle of psychopathology, affecting generation after generation. One family systems theorist has labeled this phenomenon the "multigenerational transmission process" of dysfunctional or maladaptive behavior (Bowen, 1978).

Psychoanalytic theorists have had various ideas about BPD. Some regard the central disturbance as a terror of *aloneness* (Adler, 1993; Adler & Buie, 1979). According to this view, individuals with BPD lack a capacity called *evocative memory*. Theoretically, most people have an unconscious ability to evoke a soothing memory of being lovingly held and cared for by one's mother in infancy. As such, even when we are alone, unconsciously we are not alone: We remain connected to someone else. However, people with BPD can easily lose the ability to evoke any soothing memory of human connection, especially when flooded with extreme emotion. In such moments, all memories of feeling cared for by another person—mother, therapist, partner—vanish, and the person thus engages in desperate efforts to avoid being alone.

Other psychoanalytic theorists also see the roots of the disorder in infancy and how infants and mothers negotiate a developmental process called *individuation and separation*. This is a series of stages by which an infant learns that he or she is an independent human being, separate from, but capable of relating to, others in her or his world (Mahler, Pine & Bergman, 1975).

Problems at resolving this stage of development have been theorized as basic in the etiology of BPD. Individuals with BPD have extreme difficulty striking a balance between independence and dependence. They often seem to be stuck between two equally unacceptable options—if they act too independently they fear abandonment, but if they act too dependently they are enraged at how their natural desires for autonomy are stifled. This bind was succinctly captured in the title of a popular book on BPD: *I Hate You: Don't Leave Me* (Kreisman & Straus, 1989).

Is this, then, where development goes awry and the seeds of BPD are planted—when an infant fails to establish an appropriately separate identity, and as such is left vulnerable to deep fears of abandonment and a terror of aloneness (Gunderson, 1994; Masterson, 1976)?

The Role of Trauma

It may be that early difficulties with separation and individuation do play a role in BPD, but we now know that this is not the entire picture. A series of important studies since the mid 1980s have provided crucial additional information: Most adults diagnosed with BPD report ongoing and sometimes severe physical, emotional, or sexual abuse in childhood (Herman, Perry & van der Kolk, 1989; Zanarini et al., 1989). In situations where overt abuse was not present, family life was apt to be chaotic, unstable, or neglectful (Zanarini et al., 1997). In other words, childhood traumatic events of some sort play a key role in the development of BPD.

So given this, an intriguing theoretical question arises: Should BPD be considered a personality disorder, or even a mental disorder, at all? Distinct from whether it is a *reliable* diagnosis (i.e., the diagnostic criteria are clear and internally consistent), is it *valid* to think of this constellation of symptoms as a personality disorder?

Maybe not, according to several authors, particularly from a feminist perspective (Herman, 1992; Jordan et al., 1991). These theorists argue that if the roots of BPD are embedded in childhood trauma, then it is more sensible to think of the disorder as a variant of posttraumatic stress disorder (PTSD). This change has more than semantic repercussions, given that the diagnostic label "borderline" often has pejorative and demeaning connotations. Labeling women who have survived childhood abuse with a pathological personality disorder can be seen as another way of wrongly blaming them for their traumatic past (Herman, 1992).

To address these concerns, Herman (1992) contends that a new diagnostic category is needed to augment our current conceptualization of PTSD, representing the experience of individuals who have experienced chronic and/or inescapable abuse. She proposes a disorder called "complex posttraumatic stress disorder." Such a disorder would include many of the current diagnostic criteria of BPD but would emphasize the roots of the disorder as stemming from a traumatic environment. Whether this concept becomes part of our diagnostic vocabulary will remain a matter of debate in the next several years.

Regardless, the controversy surrounding the diagnosis highlights a crucial development in the field of clinical psychology over the past two decades: our increased awareness of the pervasiveness, and long-lasting damage, of childhood trauma. Childhood abuse and/or neglect of various forms is now understood to play a key role in the development of several types of severe psychopathology, with the link particularly well established in BPD (Zanarini et al., 1997).

This knowledge of trauma's terrible potential legacy has led to a dramatic shift in our understanding of many types of psychopathology. One way to measure the fundamental importance of this change is to read abnormal psychology textbooks from the 1970s and earlier. Scanning these texts, you would find only minor references to childhood sexual abuse, and little or no explanation of the role of childhood trauma in adult personality functioning. For example, one well-regarded textbook from the mid 1970s devoted only three paragraphs to *pedophilia*, or sexual contact with children (Rimm & Somervill, 1977). Regarding incest (sexual abuse that occurs within a family), it said that this type of abuse was exceedingly rare, "prohibited in almost all cultures," and its severest impact on children was limited to "disturbed sexual functioning" in adulthood (Rimm & Somervill, 1977, p. 364–365).

We now know this not to be true: Incest and other forms of childhood abuse are far more common than had previously been assumed, with potentially devastating consequences into adulthood (Russell, 1986). Childhood trauma has been particularly implicated in the etiology of PTSD, dissociative identity disorder, eating disorders, and borderline personality disorder—diagnoses that many regard as conceptually related because of this common root (Sabo, 1997). Interestingly, these are also the current disorders that generate the most social and professional controversy.

The dramatic change in our understanding of psychopathology over the past 15 years raises an important reminder for us all: Which of the "facts" we now regard as true will seem naive and misguided a decade or two from now?

PROGNOSIS

While her life is still chaotic, her moods labile, and her self-image unstable, Denise is making gains in her treatment. She is learning strategies to delay acting on dangerous and self-harming impulses. Her self-esteem is improving slowly, as she has come to trust and appreciate Dr. Foley's consistent and respectful manner of dealing with her. She is beginning to negotiate, and survive, periods of anger, distrust, and disappointment in treatment. With occasional success, she is working on translating this perseverance into her unsteady world of tempestuous romance and short-lived friendships.

Denise's long-term prognosis is guardedly optimistic. In one typical course of BPD, mood instability and risk of self-harm or suicide are greatest in early adulthood, with symptoms abating over time and often curtailed by middle age (Stone, Hurt & Stone, 1987). Assuming that Denise continues to gain mastery over her self-destructive patterns, she has the possibility of leading a less chaotic, more productive life. Still, a substantial minority of individuals with BPD, especially those with severe symptoatology or a comorbid personality disorder, remained impaired on a long-term or chronic course (Links, Heslegrave, & van Reekum, 1998).

Regardless, Denise will likely need to stay in treatment for a long time. The bulk of research and clinical experience suggests that outcome is best when individuals remain in treatment for many years—decades, perhaps (McGlashen, 1986). And the next few years will be crucial for Denise: the suicide rate for individuals with BPD is distressingly high, with estimates as high as 9%, with most of these suicides occurring before the age of 30 (Stone, Hurt & Stone, 1987).

On a more optimistic note, dialectical behavior therapy has thus far seemed impressive in its ability to reduce parasuicidal behaviors and increase social functioning in people with BPD, and to do so more effectively and quickly than traditional treatments (Shearin & Linehan, 1994). And some researchers suggest that the prognosis for BPD is often seen as more grim than it should be (Najavits & Gunderson, 1995).

Denise fortunately has the familial financial resources to pay for long-term therapy. But with the expansion of managed-care models in psychotherapy, treatment of this sort is becoming less common, and far less affordable, to most people. The current shift in health care toward time-limited psychotherapy raises concerns about the future treatment options for individuals with this disorder, or any personality disorder, given the intensive involvement needed to bring about personality change. And given what we now know about the prevalence of childhood abuse and neglect, and their role in adult psychopathology, this is not a problem that will soon disappear. In coming years the conceptualization or naming of this disorder may change, but without addressing the underlying societal and familial issues that now seem so relevant to its etiology, BPD will remain a tragic and disabling presence in far too many lives.

CRITICAL THINKING QUESTIONS

1. How might a psychotherapist with a behavioral orientation treat Denise?
2. If Denise began to consider confronting her brother Andrew about the sexual abuse, what are some factors to consider before making this decision?
3. Many other psychological disorders are associated with borderline personality disorder, including major depression, substance abuse disorders, and eating disorders. What factors are relevant in the comorbidity of BPD and these disorders?
4. What makes borderline personality disorder a controversial diagnosis?
5. Many individuals with borderline personalty disorder engage in self-mutilative behaviors, such as self-inflicted cutting or burning. How are some ways you might explain this behavior?
6. Borderline personality disorder is diagnosed almost three times more frequently in females than males. What factors do you consider most relevant in explaining this?

Heroin (Opioid) Dependence

M atthew Fabrizi looked older than his 32 years. His body was in good shape: He went to the gym regularly and felt proud of his large muscular physique. But his face was already somewhat weathered and craggy-looking, the circles around his eyes dark, his mouth tense. Life was not easy for him.

In fact, life had never been easy for Matthew. His childhood was marked by difficulties at home and school. Repeated attempts to accept adult responsibilities and privileges (such as consistent or gainful employment, education, or even a steady dating relationship) had all failed. But since he started using heroin, life had become much harder.

When Matthew first began using heroin at age 26, he thought he found in his "drug of choice" a remedy for chronic feelings of emptiness, anxiety, loneliness, and poor self-esteem. And he usually did find this relief—in small snatches that faded far too quickly. In the first few euphoric moments after getting high, Matthew typically felt calm and powerful. Heroin provided a sense of contented well-being that was absent from the rest of his life.

But with sad irony, relying on heroin as a solution to his troubles quickly became a much more serious problem than any he was trying to escape. What first seemed like entering a dream soured into a nightmare. Twice, Matthew had come close to death from heroin overdoses. Numerous times he had been hospitalized for *detoxification* (or "detox"), the medically supervised process of safe withdrawal from a dangerous amount of heroin or other substance. Matthew also had been assaulted and robbed several times in his attempts to procure drugs.

Even outside the drama of these life-threatening situations, Matthew's life was in a shambles. His existence revolved around getting high and finding the cash to maintain his habit—money sometimes gotten through work or theft, other times by conning, threatening, or pleading with his mother. He drifted from one job to another, usually getting fired or quitting within weeks or months because of behaviors related to his drug use, such as not showing up or calling in sick too often. Rather than achieving his desired goals of increased self-esteem and decreased anxiety, Matthew's ongoing heroin use only made him feel worse about himself and more unhappy with his life.

Matthew had reached this conclusion himself several years back. But sadly, this awareness was not enough to help break his habit. Now Matthew was back in an in-patient substance abuse treatment unit, following yet another detox, another lost job, and another bout of despair and shame over his inability to overcome his drug use and keep his life on track.

PSYCHOSOCIAL HISTORY

Matthew Fabrizi was the oldest of four children (two girls and two boys), raised in a Roman Catholic family in a working-class Philadelphia neighborhood. Although he had been close with his sisters in his youth, in the past few years each took the difficult step of severing contact with him because of his addiction. Matthew's brother had a serious problem with alcohol abuse. His brother's drinking had led to spending time in treatment programs, halfway houses, and prison.

During Matthew's childhood, his father held a steady job as a dispatcher for a trucking company. Family life, however, veered from crisis to crisis. Mr. Fabrizi was a compulsive gambler, and the family faced frequent financial emergencies. Matthew recalled his father as an angry man, critical of all the family members. He was also alcoholic—a binge drinker who would episodically become violent when drunk. In looking back on his childhood and adolescence, Matthew never felt loved or praised by his father, or remembered even having a conversation with him for more than ten minutes. Matthew described his mother, who worked for the telephone company, as constantly worried about her husband's alcoholism and financial irre-sponsibility. She often threatened to end the marriage, but never took action.

As a child, Matthew had difficulty in school. In grade school, he was placed in a special class for children with learning difficulties. He responded well to the indi-vidualized care he received from the special education teachers, and his school per-formance improved. He had a harder time, however, when he began high school and was mainstreamed into classes with other students. Outwardly, he developed a tough "bully" exterior and socialized with a rough crowd. Inwardly, he felt certain he was the "stupid jackass" his father constantly accused him of being.

Matthew experimented with drugs and alcohol in his early teens, but his more serious drug use began the summer after his sophomore year in high school. A one-year relationship with his first girlfriend ended. This relationship had meant a great deal to him—in addition to having fun together, she was the only person he con-fided in about his insecurities and family troubles. He was devastated when she un-expectedly broke up with him and started dating someone else.

Matthew responded to the break-up by using alcohol or marijuana daily. Within the next year, this drug use broadened to include hallucinogens such as LSD and psilocybin (hallucinogenic mushrooms). In part, these drugs offered a common social activity with friends. But more often than not, Matthew chose to drink or smoke pot by himself. His grades, poor to begin with, plummeted. His performance in school deteriorated to the extent that he needed to repeat his junior year, and he barely managed to graduate when he was 19.

Matthew joined the marines after graduation. However, the demands of boot camp proved too rigorous, and he was discharged after three months. He then trained and worked as a machinist for five years. Despite ongoing regular use of alcohol and other substances, this was a long, productive stretch of stable, steady employment for him. A couple of brief dating relationships also started in that period, but none lasted more than a few months.

In addition to his other difficulties, Matthew was often anxious. He was a constant worrier and typically felt "keyed up," his body tense. This anxiety worsened when he was 25, after his father died unexpectedly. Matthew then developed strong fears that something terrible would happen to his mother. He ruminated incessantly about her safety: Perhaps she, too, would die suddenly, or be mugged or killed, or have a serious car accident? His constant worries led to a belief that she was unsafe if out of his protective oversight. Even though he continued to live at home and saw her nightly, he started telephoning her many times every day at work to make sure she was all right.

It was around this time that Matthew began using heroin. What a relief it seemed! When he was high on heroin, he stopped ruminating about his mother's safety. His insecurities and loneliness dwindled and were replaced by a wave of self-confidence. The initial "rush" of the drug provided an intense euphoric sensation unlike any other he had experienced. Once he discovered heroin, he stopped using all other drugs he had relied on or experimented with in the past, including cocaine, marijuana, benzodiazapenes, hallucinogens, and alcohol.

At first, Matthew used heroin only intermittently. He did not want to indulge too frequently, knowing the drug's addictive potential. He said to himself things such as, "I'm in control of this . . . no drug is going to get the better of me . . . it's okay if I treat myself every now and then." But this ability to modulate his use quickly faded. He often found himself daydreaming about heroin, and when the urge to get high struck him (which it did with increasing frequency), he would quickly dismiss any internal reservations or concerns.

Six months after his first use, Matthew switched from snorting the drug to injecting it intravenously. This heightened the intensity of the rush that he felt from the drug and led to even more frequent use. Now, during the past six years, despite frequent attempts to stop, Matthew had never gone longer than four months without giving in to what he described as his "craving" for heroin. Despite his long history of drug and alcohol use, for most of that time he denied, to himself and others, that he had a substance abuse problem.

In a typical week, Matthew used heroin four or five times. Each episode usually involved two or three bags of heroin (a common unit by which heroin is bought on the street). After his second near-fatal overdose at age 30, and because of his fears about contracting HIV from sharing needles, he ceased using injection needles and returned to his earlier habit of snorting. Although this was far short of abstaining from the drug, he saw this as at least a small victory in his attempt to control his addiction.

Matthew lived with his mother in the house where he grew up. In addition to his fears that something terrible would happen to her, the relationship with his mother troubled him in other ways. On the one hand, he was extremely overprotective of her; since his father's death, he tried to be "the man of the house." Yet, he also was unusually dependent on her and was unable to make a major life decision without her input. He could not break away from her, but because he hated the thought of being a "momma's boy" he would often treat her in a hostile, sarcastic manner.

Further complicating their relationship, Matthew frequently stole money and jewelry from his mother to pay for his addiction. At other times, instead of stealing, he sobbed to her that he was "desperate": He couldn't help himself. He wanted so much to change, but for now, if she did not give him money for drugs, he would "be forced" to commit crimes. More often than not, reluctant, depressed, and too weary to argue, she turned her head away, sighed, and gave him the cash he wanted.

CONCEPTUALIZATION

Heroin is an opioid, one of eleven categories of substances that can lead to inappropriate use and the diagnosis of a DSM-IV substance disorder (alcohol, amphetamines, caffeine, cannabis, hallucinogens, inhalants, nicotine, opioids, phencyclidine, sedatives, and hypnotics, or anxiolytics). Matthew Fabrizi meets diagnostic criteria for opioid dependence. Like many other individuals with addiction problems, he has a history of *polysubstance* abuse, or the misuse of multiple substances.

With almost all substances that can result in misuse or addiction, the DSM-IV distinguishes between *abuse* of the substance and *dependence* on it. The essential feature of substance *abuse* is the harmful repeated misuse of a drug (including alcohol). One or more of the following criteria must be met (APA, 1994, pp. 182–183):

A. recurrent substance use resulting in a failure to fulfill major role obligations at work, school, or home (e.g., repeated absences or poor work performance related to substance use; substance-related absences, suspensions, or expulsions from school; neglect of children or household)

B. recurrent substance use in situations in which it is physically hazardous (e.g., driving an automobile or operating a machine when impaired by substance use)

C. recurrent substance-related legal problems (e.g., arrests for substance-related disorderly conduct)

D. continued substance use despite having persistent or recurrent social or interpersonal problems caused or exacerbated by the effects of the substance (e.g., arguments with spouse about consequences of intoxication, physical fights).

Substance *dependence* represents a more severe or chronic problem than abuse. In substance dependence, a person develops a physical *tolerance* for the substance and experiences *withdrawal* when the substance is discontinued or unavailable. *Tolerance* means that a person needs more of the substance to produce the same desired high. *Withdrawal* is the body's physiological reaction to the absence of the drug.

Withdrawal reactions range from mild to severe, depending on the substance, the amount taken, and the degree of tolerance that the person has established. A diagnosis of substance dependence also can be made when drug-taking behavior becomes compulsive and significantly interferes with a person's life, even without the presence of tolerance or withdrawal.

In addition to his heroin dependence, Matthew also suffers from generalized anxiety disorder. The primary feature of this anxiety disorder is excessive, uncontrollable worry, along with somatic symptoms such as feeling tense, edgy, restless, irritable, and/or easily fatiguable (APA, 1994). Additional symptoms of generalized anxiety disorder include difficulty concentrating and/or sleeping.

Matthew has several personality features that merit clinical attention but do not warrant the diagnosis of a personality disorder. Among these are his *antisocial* traits, such as his thievery and conning his mother into giving him money, and *dependent* traits, primarily his unusually strong attachment to his mother. It also is quite possible that he had some sort of undiagnosed learning disorder or emotional disorder in childhood, given the early problems he had in school.

The fact that Matthew has psychological difficulties other than his substance dependence is not unusual; many people with a substance abuse problem also meet criteria for other disorders. The co-existence of a mood, anxiety, or personality disorder is typical (Craig, 1993; Seivewright & Daly, 1997). Individuals with severe mental illnesses (such as schizophrenia or other psychotic disorders) also are at increased risk for a substance disorder.

TREATMENT

Given the likely presence of a comorbid disorder, the physiological or psychological cravings produced by the substance, and a host of additional personal and environmental factors, treatment for substance dependence presents enormous challenges. Treatments have been designed from many different theoretical perspectives and modalities. With any approach, perhaps three over-arching goals are central in promoting recovery: 1) addressing general issues of physical and mental health, in addition to the addiction; 2) educating drug users and their families about the nature of addiction; and 3) helping the addicted person restructure a life based in abstinence, including developing a drug-free peer group and learning new ways to spend free time (Schuckit, 1995).

Matthew's Prior Treatment History

In the six years of his heroin addiction, Matthew had attempted treatment several times, mostly unsuccessfully.

Twice, Matthew left home to participate in a *therapeutic community*. This involved residing in a *halfway house* with other men and women attempting to recover from substance addiction, along with a small support staff of substance abuse counselors. (Halfway houses are residential facilities for people with substance abuse problems or major psychiatric disorders who need treatment and support but who do not require the restrictions of an inpatient hospital.) Matthew also attended several treatment groups daily. Group members, as well as other residents of the halfway house, provided mutual support yet also confronted each other about the impact and dangers of addiction.

Through his stays there, along with various inpatient detoxifications and hospitalizations and participation in Narcotics Anonymous (NA) meetings, Matthew had learned a great deal about addiction. For example, he came to accept that he used heroin as a form of "self-medication"—an attempt to find relief from his chronic anxiety, ruminative thoughts, disturbing emotions, and low self-esteem. Similarly, he acknowledged that several important psychological issues related to his addiction. These included the negative impact of his childhood, with his father's criticism, violence, and gambling; his dependent and ambivalent relationship with his mother; and fears about dating women.

Matthew's two longest periods of sobriety occurred during his involvements with the therapeutic community. He felt proud, each time, of his progress and sobriety. But even with such comprehensive support, he was unable to sustain the gains he made. Despite his earnest desire to stop, his cravings for heroin always got the better of him. He then had to leave the therapeutic community because of his drug use.

Matthew had also attempted *methadone treatment*. Like heroin, methadone is an opiate but it is longer-acting, less dangerous, and without any euphoric high. Because of their chemical similarity, taking methadone alleviates the harsh symptoms of heroin withdrawal. The aim of methadone treatment is to curb a person's cravings for heroin with controlled doses of methadone, dispensed at a medical clinic under careful supervision, and administered orally rather than by injection. Ideally, the person can then gain enough stability to address the debilitating problems that go hand-in-hand with addiction, such as job, family, health, and economic stress, underlying psychological issues, and the general trappings of the "drug lifestyle." Unfortunately, Matthew fared no better with methadone treatment than with abstinence.

Matthew's anxiety disorder also had been a focus of treatment. He could no longer find a physician to prescribe him anti-anxiety medications, because these drugs (*benzodiazapenes*) have high addictive potential, and Matthew had abused them in the past. He had learned progressive muscle relaxation and other cognitive-behavioral techniques to help reduce anxiety but gave up quickly on them because he was impatient, and they did not work quickly enough for him.

Current Treatment Plan

Matthew was now back on an inpatient substance abuse treatment unit. In designing a treatment plan for his discharge, his treatment team took into account his psychological strengths as well as his prior difficulties sticking with treatment. Among his assets, Matthew had a strong desire to quit his drug use, even though his previous attempts have failed. Another asset was the education and self-awareness he had gained from prior treatments. Still, Matthew knew that he could not fully examine any underlying psychological concerns until addressing the more immediate problem of his heroin use. And self-knowledge and earnest intentions had not helped in the past; what would make the difference now?

Matthew's team strongly recommended that he attempt another stay in a therapeutic community and move to a halfway house, rather than return home with his mother. Against their advice he rejected the idea, saying that if he "failed" at this a third time, he would be left without hope. He instead agreed to a treatment plan that included four components: 1) medication; 2) attendance at Narcotics Anonymous (NA) meetings; 3) individual and group psychotherapy; and 4) family meetings with his mother.

Medication   Matthew was put on Naltrexone, a medication that has gained popularity in the past few years in the treatment of severe alcohol and opioid dependence. Naltrexone is an opiate *antagonist*. Opiate antagonists work by occupying the same receptor sites in the brain as do opiates but without stimulating the neurons in the same euphoria-producing manner. As such, they block an opioid's desired effects. So even if a person on Naltrexone continues to use heroin, he or she does not experience the customary high. Ideally, the person realizes that the desired high will not be attainable, and can begin to cope with the emotions or anxiety that led to the urge to use.

Despite Naltrexone's effectiveness and relative safety, it often can fail in the treatment of heroin addiction. This is because complying with it is voluntary, and a person can easily stop taking it. Matthew, however, was enthusiastic about Naltrexone. He hoped that it would provide him the extra support he needed to break his addiction, given the great difficulty he had staying "clean" in the past.

Matthew also was prescribed Prozac for his anxiety. Although Prozac is an antidepressant, it also is sometimes used as an anxiolytic (anti-anxiety medication). This has become a common practice when treating anxiety disorders in people who abuse substances because Prozac and the other SSRI's do not have any addictive potential.

One particular concern with Naltrexone is the risk for liver damage. Because of this, individuals on this medication need to have their liver functioning monitored on a regular basis.

Narcotics Anonymous (NA)   Narcotics Anonymous is a "12-step" program that follows in the footsteps of Alcoholics Anonymous (AA), the widely popular, non-professional support group conceived in the 1930s to help alcoholics achieve and maintain sobriety. Matthew had attended NA meetings previously but only sporadically. He never continued with the program for very long. Whenever he used heroin after a few days or weeks of sobriety, he saw this as a failure and chose not to return to an NA meeting.

According to the philosophy of AA and NA, alcoholism or drug dependence is a disease. Until an addicted person acknowledges this truth—and also admits his or her powerlessness in combatting the disease without outside help—sobriety will remain an elusive goal. Recovery from addiction can occur only in the context of a spiritual awakening, which involves asking for and accepting help from a "higher power," however a person conceives of this. The goal for people in AA and NA is complete abstinence, because any use of the substance is seen to further the disease's course.

The great popularity of programs such as AA and NA suggests that they succeed in helping many people curtail their addictive behaviors. However, because of the confidential, peer nature of these programs, little is actually known about their success rates. Although anecdotal evidence certainly supports their potential benefit, it also seems the case that many people attend meetings but then quickly discontinue with the program, as did Matthew (Chappel, 1993).

As part of his current treatment, Matthew agreed to attend at least four NA meetings weekly. He also agreed to find a "sponsor" in the NA program—another participant who attended meetings and who had successfully used NA's philosophy to achieve a recovery from substance use for an extended period of time. By providing advice, support, and encouragement, a sponsor can be a key figure in somebody's ongoing struggle to remain sober.

Individual and Group Psychotherapy   Matthew also joined a weekly substance abuse group with other recovering addicts. The group was an opportunity for mutual support, to share strategies and problems in staying abstinent, and to learn more about the physiological and psychological experience of addiction. The group leaders also focused on the treatment strategy of *relapse prevention* (Rawson et al., 1993).

One goal of relapse prevention is to help addicted individuals recognize their personal early warning signs of potential relapse in order to monitor or change these risky behaviors before the problem grows too severe. In part, this overlaps with the behavioral technique of *stimulus control,* where a person alters his or her environment to decrease the likelihood of an unwanted behavior occurring. For example, Matthew was especially likely to use heroin on days when he received his paycheck, because he had ample funds available. To reduce the likelihood of this happening, he agreed to arrange for his salary to be deposited directly into his bank account, rather than receiving the paycheck himself (he had found a factory job one month after his most recent hospitalization). This precaution added one more obstacle to overcome before indulging his impulsive eagerness to get high.

Relapse prevention also focuses on what happens if a relapse does occur. If the relapse can be understood as an isolated event, with identifiable causes and triggers, then a person may be able to analyze it, learn from it, and step back more quickly into sobriety. If, however, the relapse is seen as the inevitable start of a downhill slide, this may become a self-fulfilling prophecy, snowballing into larger trouble.

Matthew's individual counseling involved a weekly session with a counselor trained in substance abuse issues. The focus of these sessions was to help him learn to cope with his emotions. In particular, following the idea that Matthew used heroin as self-medication, counseling was structured to help him develop more adaptive ways to tolerate and express feelings and anxieties he was trying to escape. The counselor emphasized that his worries would not go away so easily, but Matthew might gain some mastery in facing them, and so not need to flee them as readily as he did.

Matthew also used individual counseling sessions to address his low self-esteem and his ever-present sense of failure. Despite an occasional outward bluster that using heroin made him "cool," Matthew was ashamed of his addiction. His counselor talked with him about the stigma of drug addiction and helped him look at ways that he might enhance his self-esteem, such as taking care of himself physically and pursuing enjoyable, non-drug–related social activities.

Matthew also talked about his fears of AIDS. He had twice taken the HIV-antibody test and tested negative. But since his last test he had shared needles with other intravenous (IV) drug users at least twice. Sharing needles is an extremely risky activity for the transmission of HIV because of the possibility of direct blood to blood contact. Together, he and his counselor talked about Matthew's anxieties and worked out a plan for Matthew to take a new HIV antibody test.

Family Meetings   Finally, treatment involved counseling with Matthew and his mother together. With most substance abuse issues (including alcoholism), treatment is considered most likely to succeed when family members or other key people in the addicted person's life are included in strategies to help maintain sobriety (Schuckit, 1995). In Matthew's situation, the central issue for family therapy was to address the role that his mother (or their relationship) might play in maintaining his addiction.

From her vantage point, Mrs. Fabrizi felt constantly worried about Matthew, sometimes very angry with him, and worn down by his years of addiction. However, in her concern, she also acted in ways that perpetuated, rather than halted, his heroin use. In the language of Alcoholics Anonymous and other 12-step programs, this is known as "enabling," or being "co-dependent" with the substance abuser.

For example, many times Mrs. Fabrizi stepped in to protect Matthew from some of the grimmer realities of heroin addiction. They had many nasty arguments about his use of heroin, but she became frightened when he turned to thievery or other crime, and often gave him money to purchase drugs, rather than have him risk arrest by stealing. Further, she repeatedly threatened to kick him out of the house if he continued to use drugs but never followed through on her word.

In family meetings, the counselor helped Matthew and Mrs. Fabrizi see how protecting Matthew from harsh consequences perpetuated his drug use. In the course of a few meetings, the counselor helped Matthew and his mother negotiate the following contract:

1. Until such time that Matthew felt he could safely take responsibility for his own abstinence, Mrs. Fabrizi would hold Matthew's bankcard, credit card, and car keys (they shared one car). In this way, Matthew would be unable to purchase heroin impulsively or drive to the familiar neighborhoods where he routinely found dealers. She also agreed not to give him any spending money he could not account for.
2. They would use family sessions to discuss difficult emotional issues between them. These included Matthew's sense that his mother "nagged" him and did not trust him, his fears that something would happen to her, and his strong dependence on her. Mrs. Fabrizi had additional issues to address, including her anger and resentment about the huge impact Matthew's addiction had on her life.
3. Mrs. Fabrizi agreed that if Matthew continued to use heroin, she would follow through on the difficult step of evicting him. She feared what might happen to him if this came to pass, but also had reached a point where "enough is enough." And despite her concerns about taking such a step, in

family sessions she came to see how *not* taking action had not been helpful, in that it had not resulted in Matthew breaking his habit.

Mrs. Fabrizi was also referred to Nar-Anon, a self-help group for families of substance abusers. There she learned from other relatives of substance abusers what she could do to "detach" herself from Matthew's addiction and how to help him to be more responsible for his own behavior.

Treatment Outcome

Treatment went well for several months. Matthew took his Naltrexone and Prozac as prescribed. He attended NA meetings and connected with a sponsor, an old high-school friend. He was performing well at his new job, and his self-esteem was starting to grow.

But after this period of optimism and sobriety, several factors conspired to provide obstacles larger than he could manage. Perhaps central among these, Matthew needed to discontinue Naltrexone because he developed potentially severe liver abnormalities. These difficulties most likely arose because his liver had already been damaged from his prior heroin and alcohol use.

Matthew was upset and demoralized by needing to give up Naltrexone. In his perception, this was the key component of his sobriety. He had taken great comfort in believing Naltrexone had "forced" him not to use heroin, and he did not think he could rely on himself to maintain sobriety. Once Matthew was told he could no longer use Naltrexone, he also stopped taking Prozac. His attendance at NA meetings then grew erratic, and Matthew stopped contacting his sponsor.

A few weeks after discontinuing Naltrexone, Matthew missed several counseling appointments in a row. He did not respond to repeated telephone calls and letters from his counselor. Soon thereafter, Mrs. Fabrizi telephoned to say that Matthew had begun using heroin again and in fact had been hospitalized in a medical emergency following another serious overdose. In keeping with the treatment contract, this time she refused his request to return home after discharge from the hospital. He was living at a Salvation Army shelter, where he was on a waiting list for a bed in a therapeutic community. She said she would pass along to Matthew the counselor's interest in speaking with him. She may have done so, but the counselor did not hear from Matthew again.

DISCUSSION

The misuse of substances—ranging from alcohol to prescription medications to heroin and other drugs—certainly ranks near the top of the list of modern social problems. No other category of psychological disorders has such pervasive impact: Current estimates suggest that in the United States, thirty-five percent of all men and eighteen percent of women will meet diagnostic criteria for a substance abuse disorder at some point in their lifetime, with alcohol dependence being the most common (Kessler et al., 1994). Yet, by no means is the situation modern; ingesting substances for emotion- and mind-altering experiences is seemingly as old as humanity.

> ## Multiaxial DSM-IV Diagnosis at Time of Termination
>
> Axis I: Opioid Dependence with Physiological Dependence
> CONDITION: UNCHANGED
> History of polysubstance dependence
> Generalized Anxiety Disorder
> CONDITION: UNCHANGED
>
> Axis II: No diagnosis; note antisocial and dependent traits
>
> Axis III: None
>
> Axis IV: Marginal employment, social isolation
>
> Axis V: *Treatment Onset:* 40 (major impairments
> in several areas of functioning)
> *Present Time:* Unknown

As often occurs in science, the creation of heroin was at first heralded as an exciting medical breakthrough. Manufactured in a German research laboratory in the late 19th century, it seemed a desirable alternative to *morphine,* a natural derivative of the opium poppy flower. At that time, physicians regularly prescribed morphine as a powerful analgesic (pain reliever) but also were concerned about its debilitating addictive qualities. In the United States, morphine addiction had been common among soldiers in the Civil War and patients who were exposed to it through medical treatment. Because it was legally and easily obtained, morphine also became a substance of abuse for other populations, most notably American and European women from middle class and well-to-do backgrounds. (Such is the situation harrowingly portrayed in Eugene O'Neill's autobiographical drama, *Long Day's Journey into Night.*)

The initial hope was that heroin, a synthetic compound also derived from the opium poppy, could equal morphine's analgesic properties without the same risk of addiction. Of course, that was not to be. The creation of heroin merely added technology—and alas, mass availability—to the world of addictive agents available.

Opioids were legal in the United States until the early 20th century. In the first half of this century, and particularly following the Second World War, heroin use grew to be an increasing problem among poor, minority men in urban inner cities. However, with the increasing availability of the drug since the 1960s, heroin (and more recently even stronger synthetic drugs, such as crack cocaine) has once again become a wider problem, devastating poor urban communities but increasingly common among middle class individuals. Its popularity in the 1990s is growing among young adults across a range of socioeconomic borders, echoing shades of morphine abuse ninety years ago (Hartnoll, 1994).

Heroin can be used in a variety of ways. It can be injected, either through *skin popping* (injecting it subcutaneously) or *mainlining* it directly into the bloodstream. It also can be smoked, eaten, and inhaled or "snorted" through the nose. Although many, if not most, heroin users progress to intravenous injection, most begin by snorting it only (Casriel, Rockwell & Stepherson, 1988).

One component of heroin's addictiveness is the desire to avoid withdrawal symptoms. These typically start soon after cessation of the drug, perhaps eight to twelve hours after it is metabolized. Symptoms of opioid withdrawal are similar to those of severe flu: chills, physical weakness, sweating, running nose, abdominal pain, gastrointestinal upset, insomnia, and "gooseflesh" or "goosebumps" (this last symptom leading to the phrase "cold turkey," now often applied to quitting any substance abruptly). Yet, many individuals withdrawing from opioids experience the emotional aspects of withdrawal—feelings of despair, hopelessness, and extreme dysphoria—as the worst aspect of the process. As unpleasant as these symptoms may be, they are not usually life-threatening. As was the case with Matthew, heroin's greater dangers lie in the potential for toxic overdose, HIV transmission, and the cumulative damage of long-term use.

In the past two decades, scientists have unlocked some of the biochemical mysteries that underlie the powerful addictive allure of opiates. It is now known that the body produces natural opiates (called *endorphins*, or *enkaphalins*), used in the regulation of pain and perhaps even in the maintenance of daily moods (Schuckit, 1995). When emitted, these neurotransmitters produce pleasurable sensations. It seems likely that opioids such as heroin mimic the body's natural opiate system, occupying the same receptor sites in the brain and thus producing feelings of euphoric contentment.

Of course, unraveling the biochemistry of addiction (to opiates, to alcohol, to stimulants such as cocaine) is of great benefit, particularly in how such knowledge may lead to developing more effective treatments. Ongoing research also is attempting to shed light on the potential contribution of genetic factors in addiction (Matthew's father and brother also misused substances, but whether this was due to a common biological vulnerability, a shared environment, or both is uncertain). Converging evidence strongly suggests that genetics influence the development of certain types of alcoholism (Cloninger, 1988), but it remains unclear what role genetics might play in other types of substance abuse, including opioid addiction (Schilling, Schenke & El-Bassel, 1993).

Regardless of the biological components of addiction, it is equally important to look at the broader societal context in which addiction occurs. This includes factors such as hopelessness, peer group pressures, social disconnection, poverty, and the easy availability of drugs in many communities, rich and poor. In fact, the *economics* of heroin use deserves special scrutiny. Heroin is big business: The profit to be made in its synthesis and distribution is enormous. Worldwide, the underground heroin economy may yield profits in the vicinity of 750 billion dollars annually (Booth, 1998). For individuals who have amassed fortunes through heroin's illegal production and sale, there is a great financial incentive to create a demand, and then maintain a supply, for this lucrative drug.

Heroin Use and AIDS

Heroin always has been dangerous, but its use became markedly more perilous in the 1980s, with the widespread dissemination of the human immunodeficiency virus

(HIV), the causal agent of AIDS. In the United States, more new cases of HIV infection now arise annually from intravenous drug use than from sexual contact (Centers for Disease Control, 1998). Not only are individuals who share hypodermic needles at high risk for contracting HIV but so are the sexual partners of these individuals, who may have no knowledge of their partners' HIV status or drug use.

To combat the spread of HIV (and other blood-borne diseases, such as hepatitis) among IV drug users, several advocacy organizations have attempted to institute "needle exchange" programs in urban areas heavily burdened with the dual dilemmas of drug addiction and AIDS. These programs provide clean needles to people who inject drugs, not as an endorsement of addiction but to help curtail the spread of the epidemic. Most research on needle exchange indicates that these programs are successful in reducing HIV transmission, especially in the context of a comprehensive approach including AIDS education, confidential HIV counseling, and community outreach (Kaplan, Khoshnood & Heimer, 1994; Schoenbaum, Hartel & Gourevitch, 1996; Watters, 1996). However, translating such programs into social policy has been an uphill battle. Critics argue that providing clean needles to IV drug users only promotes addiction. The evidence seems to weigh against them (Goskin, 1997), but advocates of needle exchange programs have been unable to combat the fear, stigma, and misinformation that shapes discussion of this emotionally-laden topic.

Treatment Issues

Most treatment options for opioid addiction rely on cognitive-behavioral strategies, relapse prevention, psychopharmacology, or AA-type spiritually-based, self-help programs. Treatment occurs in many settings, ranging from inpatient hospital units and residential centers to outpatient clinics and peer-led groups. Despite the plethora of options available, it is difficult to determine what the most effective treatment will be for any particular individual (Office of National Drug Control Policy, 1996).

The use of methadone, as described in Matthew's treatment, is one commonly used intervention in heroin addiction. But this, too, is not without controversy. Proponents argue that by acknowledging the reality of physiological craving, providing methadone is the most humane and holistic approach to treatment. Critics challenge the basic principle of such treatment—substituting one addictive opiate (methadone) for another (heroin). They contend that this does not address the fundamental problem of addiction.

The relatively small amount of controlled research data are inconclusive, but tilt in the direction that methadone maintenance is successful, at least for some people. Still, even advocates admit that although methadone maintenance can work, the dropout or failure rate from methadone programs remains high (Moolchan & Hoffman, 1994). It may be that methadone maintenance works best when part of a more comprehensive, psychosocial-based treatment program (McLellan, Arndt et al., 1993). Long-term methadone maintenance appears to be more effective than time-limited treatment because when a person is tapered off methadone, he or she experiences the unpleasant symptoms of opioid withdrawal (Ward, Mattick & Hall, 1994).

Acupuncture also may be beneficial in the treatment of opioid dependence (Riet, Kleijnen, & Knipschild, 1990). Acupuncture appears to stimulate the body's natural production of endorphins. Many clinicians who use acupuncture in this context report it to be a valuable tool; however, few controlled studies have carefully examined its efficacy, and the limited research available questions its usefulness, compared to more established treatments (McLellan, Grossman et al., 1993). Still, acupuncture may offer a promising treatment option and is the source of ongoing research.

Whatever strategy is employed, treatment outcome is less impressive for addictions than for many other psychological difficulties. This speaks to how deeply entrenched addictive behaviors may be and the many interwoven factors involved (including different issues for male and female IV drug users [Powis et al., 1996]). It also seems that only a minority of addicted individuals conquer their difficulties in the first go-around of treatment.

Taking this into account, Prochaska, DiClemente, and Norcross (1992) propose a transtheoretical model of how people break a cycle of addiction over time. They theorize that changing an addictive behavior includes five distinct stages: 1) *precontemplation*, in which a person does not believe he or she has a problem; 2) *contemplation*, in which a person recognizes the problem, but is not yet ready to change it; 3) *preparation*, which involves planning necessary steps to make a change; 4) *action*, or putting the plan for change in place; and 5) *maintenance*, or restructuring one's life to support the changes that have been made.

Prochaska et al. (1992) liken these stages to a spiral. Each time an addicted person goes through a successful cycle of change but then relapses, he or she starts the entire process again—but hopefully with the benefit of learning from prior mistakes, so that after several attempts, the desired changes can take root.

PROGNOSIS

In time, Matthew Fabrizi may achieve his desire for long-lasting abstinence, but his prognosis must be considered poor—as it is for many other individuals in his situation. Even after intensive treatment, the relapse rate for opioid addiction is high. A majority of opiate users return to drugs within six months of their first treatment intervention (Schuckit, 1995), perhaps falling back to "stage one" of the model proposed by Prochaska et al. (1992). Matthew's situation is particularly worrisome: He exhibits many characteristics associated with a poor prognosis, including employment problems, a long history of substance abuse, and several previous unsuccessful treatment attempts (Brewer et al., 1998).

One typical pattern of addiction over the course of a lifetime is to cycle between bouts of intensified use and periods of abstinence. For those who are unable to achieve sobriety, the results can be tragic. In one study that followed a large cohort of addicts in California longitudinally over 24 years (Hser, Anglin & Powers, 1993), fourteen percent of the original cohort were dead within ten years, and more than 25% had died within twenty years. Most of these deaths were attributed to homicide, suicide, accident, or a direct effect of drug use, such as overdose. Because these data were collected in the mid 1980s, they do not reflect the even greater mortality risk added by AIDS.

However, this pessimistic state of affairs is balanced by more hopeful data. Despite the high relapse or failure rate in treatment programs, it also is true that many substance-addicted individuals do succeed in their efforts to achieve abstinence from the habit—*with or without* therapy or other professional intervention (Hser et al., 1993; Sobell et al., 1993). It appears that the more stable the environment surrounding the addicted individual—in terms of pre-addiction job history, economic stability, physical health, and family situation—the greater the likelihood of achieving abstinence, with a wide range of substances including alcohol and heroin (Schuckit, 1995). In addition, psychopharmacological advances over the past several years have generated excitement about new detoxification and maintenance treatments for opioids (Best, Oliveto & Kosten, 1996). For example, buprenorphine, an opioid similar to methadone, seems to be an effective agent for maintenance therapy, with far less severe withdrawal symptoms than either heroin or methadone (Bickel & Amass, 1995).

Not all individuals experience difficulties with treatment to the extent that Matthew Fabrizi did. Yet even with his poor prognosis, the case is not closed on him. Statistics speak only to group trends, not specific lives; even against great odds and dire predictions, people sometimes find ways to recover from problems that can seem insurmountable or hopeless. Repeated disappointments and failures notwithstanding, Matthew may need to spiral through his cycle at least once again, and perhaps several more times, before succeeding in the goal of breaking his addiction.

CRITICAL THINKING QUESTIONS

1. Methadone treatment for heroin dependence is sometimes criticized because it substitutes one addictive substance for another. What are the pros and cons of this approach to treatment?
2. Although the weight of evidence supports the use of needle exchange programs to reduce the transmission of HIV among individuals who inject drugs, many urban communities have not instituted such programs. What are your opinions on this issue?
3. What are some additional ways Matthew's family could participate in his treatment?
4. Do you think Matthew has a personality disorder? Which one? How would you determine this?
5. The three most frequently used substances in our society are alcohol, tobacco, and caffeine. All of these are legal substances. Based on what criteria do you think some substances should be legal and others illegal?

Transvestic Fetishism

arry Atkins sat uncomfortably in the waiting room of a psychotherapist, whose name he had found in the phone book. He had never spoken to a counselor before, and he could not recall ever feeling so nervous. He was 31 years old and had been married for seven years. Throughout his life, he had often thought he was "sick" and needed help, but now he was here in less than optimal circumstances: His wife Cheryl had threatened to divorce him if he did not speak to a therapist immediately.

Two evenings before, Cheryl returned home several hours earlier than expected from a night out with a friend. When she walked in, she was dumbfounded by what she saw. At first she thought that an intruder had broken into the house—a female intruder. But the deeper shock came a moment later, when she realized that the strange woman she saw in her living room was in fact Harry, wearing a wig, make-up, dress, stockings, and high heels.

Harry mumbled some feeble excuse for his attire, but his story made no sense at all. He then began sobbing and told Cheryl, "I can't help myself." He revealed that he had been secretly dressing as a woman for years, whenever he had the opportunity to do so without her knowledge. He said he hated himself for doing it but was unable to stop.

Nothing about Harry's everyday appearance was out of the ordinary. He was a pleasant-looking, rather unassuming man, neither remarkably masculine nor effeminate. He worked as an accountant in a midsized corporation, where he maintained friendly, if distant, relationships with most of his coworkers. He did not have any close friends. Most people who knew him, through work or the church he and Cheryl regularly attended, thought him "one of the guys," even though he rarely socialized beyond the minimum requirements of his work and church responsibilities.

When Harry entered the therapist's office, his anxiety was immediately apparent, even in a brief exchange of pleasantries. Within moments Harry was shaking and crying, telling the therapist "my world is collapsing around me," and "I feel like killing myself." It was only after he had calmed down that he could reveal to the therapist the details of what had brought him to psychotherapy and tell some of his life story.

PSYCHOSOCIAL HISTORY

Harry grew up in a small midwestern town, the only child in a middle-class family. He was somewhat shy as a child and young adolescent but maintained a few friendships. He was well-behaved in social situations and a reasonably good student. Harry's parents married relatively late in life. His mother was the more dominant presence in the household; Harry recalled his father as a soft-spoken, passive man who usually acceded to his mother's desires.

Even as a very young child, Harry was fascinated with female clothing. He used to love playing "dress-up." He enjoyed going through his mother's dresser and closet, riffling through her clothes, touching all the different fabrics, enchanted by the textures, colors, and patterns. He would play for hours by himself, putting on his mother's shoes, jewelry, scarves, and hats, sometimes her blouses or skirts. His parents tolerated these whims, despite their discomfort. They hoped it was a phase he would "grow out of."

When Harry was five years old, his paternal grandparents visited from out of state. Harry barely knew Grandma and Grandpa Atkins, and they had never seen (or been told about) Harry's pleasure in female clothing. During the visit, Harry innocently walked into the living room where the adults were talking. Smiling and laughing, a pair of his mother's clip-on earrings dangled from his ears and his feet were lost in a pair of her high-heeled pumps. He was greeted with an awkward silence, and then his startled grandmother angrily scolded him. She yelled that he looked "disgusting" and "perverted." It was "a sin" for a boy to dress like a girl— what was his name, Harry or Harriet? Later, she continued to express her displeasure to Harry's parents—how could they tolerate such behavior? She counseled them to act aggressively in stamping out these (and any other) "perverted" behaviors—"for his own good."

Harry's mother did not approve of her mother-in-law's sharp-tongued criticism, but she did decide that perhaps it would be in Harry's best interest to try to curtail his cross-dressing behaviors. From that time on, she began expressing frank displeasure when Harry engaged in his dress-up play. However, this did not stop him, so she threatened to punish him if he continued to indulge in this behavior. Several weeks later, when she found him again wearing her clothing, she lost her temper and gave him a painful, prolonged spanking.

After this punishment, Harry ceased his cross-dressing activity, and it did not re-emerge for several years. The topic was never discussed in the family. Shortly after going through puberty, however, Harry again became preoccupied with this secret fantasy. Occasionally, acting now with great caution, he would "borrow" one of his mother's brassieres and put it on while he masturbated, which greatly heightened his sexual arousal. Yet, Harry also felt deeply ashamed about these fantasies.

After several months, he again forced himself to stop any hint of cross-dressing activity and even attempted to banish the fantasies from his mind. He maintained this abstinence for several years, throwing himself into school life and extracurricular activity. He was an average but conscientious student, participated on the school's track team, and took a leadership position in his church's youth organization. He left home to go to college, where he began dating one of his classmates, Cheryl.

One night at school, he and Cheryl went to see a student theater production that happened to include several "female" characters who were, in fact, men dressed as women. The show was an innocent comedy, but Harry watched uncomfortably with a private sense of panic and recognition. The old feelings of forbidden pleasure came back to him with a jolt. In daydreams, sexual fantasies, and even a few dreams at night, he began imagining himself cross-dressing. These fantasies were tinged with a mixture of dread, pleasure, self-disgust, and sexual arousal.

Harry fought off these desires for a few months but one day impulsively stole a tube of lipstick and some rouge from Cheryl's medicine cabinet. That evening, with his roommate out of town, Harry nervously locked the door to his dorm room, went into the bathroom, and applied the lipstick and rouge. He stared at himself in the mirror for several minutes—fascinated, repulsed, and aroused by what he saw. He then masturbated.

Cheryl and Harry got married the year following college. Although a few times he came close to confessing his secret to her, he was always too ashamed to mention it (to Cheryl or anyone else). Over time, his cross-dressing forays became more elaborate: Bit by bit he acquired cosmetics, several articles of clothing, shoes, lingerie, and a wig. He kept these items carefully hidden in a locked cabinet in his workroom. Cheryl seemed to have no idea, and Harry always timed his activities to make sure he had ample time to indulge without her finding out.

During the day, Harry developed the habit of privately carrying with him an inconspicuous feminine item, most often a small handkerchief. He thought of this as a kind of "security blanket" because it often made him less anxious knowing it was there. But he continued to feel ashamed by his desires and periodically swore to himself that he would stop. In church, he prayed that God would take away his "sickness." A few times he punished himself, punching his thighs repeatedly until he was black and blue.

Occasionally, he did stop cross-dressing for months at a time. Twice he threw out all the paraphernalia he had collected, only to have the desires (and his wardrobe) build up again. Harry hated his "weakness" at not fighting off his urges but inevitably resigned himself to the belief, "It's out of my control—I can't help it." Dressed as a woman, he felt a pleasurable sense of relaxation; only afterwards did he feel intense guilt and self-hate. When he made love to Cheryl—which happened less and less frequently as the marriage continued—he was able to perform sexually only by fantasizing that he was wearing female lingerie or make-up.

By the time Cheryl came home unexpectedly and surprised him in full female regalia, he had to admit that he was partly relieved at being caught. He did not know how much longer he could carry the burden of his secret.

CONCEPTUALIZATION

Harry Atkins fits the description of transvestic fetishism, one of the *paraphilias* described in the DSM-IV's section on sexual and gender identity disorders. The word *paraphilia* roughly translates into "deviation [*para*] of love [*philia*]." Formerly called *perversions*, paraphilias are "recurrent, intense sexually arousing fantasies, sexual urges, or behaviors generally involving 1) nonhuman objects, 2) the suffering or humiliation of oneself or one's partner, or 3) children or other nonconsenting persons" (APA, 1994, pp. 522–523). Transvestic fetishism has two criteria:

A. Over a period of at least 6 months, in a heterosexual male, recurrent, intense, sexually arousing fantasies, sexual urges, or behaviors involving cross-dressing; and
B. The fantasies, sexual urges, or behaviors cause clinically significant distress or impairment in social, occupational, or other important areas of functioning.

Paraphilias are diagnosed to a far greater extent in males than females, although this gap appears to be narrowing some in recent years (Masters, Johnson & Kolodny, 1994). In some cases, the paraphiliac object or activity is necessary to achieve erotic pleasure; in others cases, the paraphilia is instead episodic or occasional. Most paraphiliacs meet diagnostic criteria for more than one paraphilia (Abel et al., 1988; Abel & Osborn, 1992). This may be less true for transvestites, although when a second paraphilia is present, it is most often *sexual masochism*, or finding erotic pleasure in being "humiliated, beaten, bound, or otherwise made to suffer" (APA, 1994, p. 529; Zucker & Blanchard, 1997).

Because engaging in certain paraphilias can infringe upon other people's rights or cause serious harm, they carry serious legal consequences. For example, *exhibitionism* (deriving sexual pleasure from exposing one's genitals to unsuspecting others), *voyeurism* (deriving sexual pleasure from watching an unsuspecting person undress or perform a sexual act), and *pedophilia* (adult sexual activity that involves children) are all illegal activities. As such, most people who are in treatment for these paraphilias are court-ordered.

However, not all paraphilias are illegal. For example, transvestic fetishism, practiced as it was by Harry in the privacy of his home, did not infringe upon anyone else's rights. It caused him significant distress and interfered with his marriage, but engaging in his erotic activities did not breach another person's safety or rights.

In addition to transvestic fetishism, Harry also meets diagnostic criteria for adjustment disorder with mixed anxiety and depressed mood. A person is diagnosed with an adjustment disorder if he or she experiences "clinically significant emotional or behavioral symptoms in response to an identifiable stressor or stressors" (APA, 1994, p. 623). Adjustment disorders are specified by the particular nature of the person's reaction, such as "with anxiety," "with depressed mood," or "with disturbance of conduct." These symptoms are expected to remit within six months. If they continue beyond that time, the diagnosis is changed from adjustment disorder to whatever most accurately reflects the clinical situation (e.g., major depression, panic disorder, etc.).

It is important to note that Harry's being diagnosed with an adjustment disorder is not due directly to his cross-dressing. Instead, he is so diagnosed because of his severe anxiety and depression in response to Cheryl's discovery of his secret.

TREATMENT

Basic Considerations

Treatment for a non-harmful paraphilia such as Harry's—one which is neither dangerous nor interpersonally exploitative—can be approached from one of two directions. The first direction attempts to change or eradicate the behavior. For example, several behavioral techniques, collectively called *aversion therapies*, attempt to pair an unwanted behavior with a noxious consequence, and then positively reinforce a more socially desirable response. However, in the treatment of paraphilias, the success of these techniques over the long-term is questionable (Stermac, 1990). Further, aversive techniques raise significant ethical questions about the appropriate role of psychological treatment—if something is socially undesirable yet non-harmful, should psychologists use their knowledge of aversive techniques to change it?

The second direction assumes that the behavior, even if unwanted, may not easily be eradicated. This often is the case with behaviors related to sexual arousal, desire, and object choice. If something cannot be altered, perhaps offering a false hope of change may cause someone more damage in the long run. Further, the fact that a person sees his or her behavior as "unwanted" may primarily reflect social disapproval. In those situations, some psychologists argue that the goal of treatment should lean more toward helping people tolerate being "different" in society's eyes, rather than trying to conform to a role that does not fit.

In other words, instead of overtly attempting to change the paraphilia, the second path emphasizes the distressing emotional, practical, and interpersonal issues that often go hand-in-hand with it. With transvestism, these include emotional issues such as shame, loneliness, depression, and anxiety; practical considerations of how to incorporate the behavior into one's life in a safe and non-disruptive manner; and interpersonal issues of marital and familial difficulties that may arise because of the desire to cross-dress.

Harry's Treatment

Harry's treatment eventually followed this latter path. However, in his first meeting with the therapist, Harry stated that he hated his cross-dressing. It was the bane of his life and a cause of great misery—couldn't therapy just stamp it out altogether? The therapist acknowledged Harry's distress but also explained that a behavior as pronounced and long-standing as Harry's cross-dressing could not be changed overnight—if at all. The immediate challenge was to address the emotional crisis of having been found out. How serious was Harry about suicide? Was Cheryl about to leave him? Did Harry have any emotional supports to fall back on?

By the end of the session, Harry admitted that he did not really want to kill himself, but he was deeply ashamed that Cheryl now knew. He did not know if she would divorce him but was frightened she might. He also feared that Cheryl would reveal his secret to other people.

The therapist referred Harry to a colleague of his, Dr. Craig Andrews, a psychologist with expertise in paraphilias and gender identity disorders. When Dr. Andrews spoke to Harry to arrange for a meeting, he requested that both Harry and Cheryl come in together so that they could discuss the impact of Harry's cross-dressing on the marriage. Cheryl was skeptical—she saw the problem as Harry's, not hers—but agreed to the meeting.

In that session, Harry told both Dr. Andrews and Cheryl about his life-long involvement with cross-dressing. He expressed his fears that Cheryl would divorce him and that she would tell his secret to other people. For her part, Cheryl expressed anger and discomfort with the situation. She was as angry at having been excluded from a key part of Harry's life as at the fact of his cross-dressing itself; she felt betrayed. She did not yet know if she wanted to divorce Harry, but something had changed significantly in her ability to trust him. She felt confused about whether to stay in the marriage but agreed not to take precipitous action. And no, she would not tell anyone—frankly, she thought this was as embarrassing for her as for him.

Cheryl also directly asked a question she had been fearing: Did Harry want to be a woman, was he planning on having a sex change operation? Harry answered that he could not quite understand it himself, or explain how he felt, but no, he did not actually want to be a woman. Even though he greatly enjoyed cross-dressing, he basically felt comfortable about being a man.

At the end of that first session, the following treatment plan was arranged: Harry would continue to see Dr. Andrews on a weekly basis for individual psychotherapy. Cheryl agreed to join them once monthly, to continue exploring how Harry's cross-dressing affected the marriage. Dr. Andrews also recommended that Cheryl speak to a counselor herself, to help her cope with how this revelation affected her, but she said she was not interested in doing so.

The first stage of Harry's individual treatment involved providing emotional support and psychoeducation about transvestism. The worst moments of the crisis with Cheryl had passed, but life was still far from what it had been. Harry expressed much bitterness and sadness about his situation. He doubted he would ever be able to accept it. He was not sure he even wanted to, given how "sick" he thought it was. Wouldn't he really be better off trying to rid himself of it?

Dr. Andrews continued to remind Harry, gently, that eradicating his desire to cross-dress was unlikely, or at least extremely difficult. But at the same time, Dr. Andrews did not express a strong position about what Harry should do: Ethically, he saw this as Harry's decision. He did say, however, that if Harry decided to pursue the option of trying to "cure" himself of his transvestism, he would refer him to another clinician, as he did not believe himself to be adequately trained in that type of treatment. After several weeks of these discussions, Harry concluded that despite his deep wish to change, he was not sure he could. He had had so little success in his previous attempts to stop and felt so driven to indulge his behaviors that perhaps the best option was to work toward self-acceptance.

Harry also had a hard time letting go of a question that had hounded him for years: "Why am I like this?" Dr. Andrews responded that despite many theories, nobody knew the answer to that question. And rather than focus on "why?," perhaps it made more sense to focus on the current realities of his life. What could Harry do to live with his need to cross-dress? How could he counteract his powerful sense of shame? What were the lingering effects of his memories of his mother's and grandmother's criticism and punishment?

Harry found some comfort in Dr. Andrews' assurances that he was not alone. Other heterosexual men, many of whom were married and had children, led lives similar to his. In fact, a nearby city had a local support group for cross-dressers. They offered a telephone support line, published a newsletter (called *Bloomers*), and held monthly social gatherings. Dr. Andrews showed Harry a copy of the newsletter, which included articles and advertisements of interest to men who cross-dress—information ranging from the pros and cons of undergoing female hormone treatments, to advertisements for electrolysis (a technique to remove body hair), to where to shop discreetly for female shoes and clothes.

Harry did not want to contact the organization, but he took their phone number. He could not imagine revealing his secret to anyone else, even to other men with similar interests. However, what proved of significant benefit was purchasing a home computer. Harry began to search the Internet for topics related to transvestism. He found a lot of information and located the web page of the support and advocacy organization Dr. Andrews had mentioned. Much of what he learned was relevant to his life. It was heartening to read positive stories of other "t.v.'s" (transvestites) who described their experiences, and who felt more comfortable with themselves than he did. Thankful for the confidentiality the Internet offered, Harry also began chatting with other cross-dressing men.

In addition to his cross-dressing and marital issues, psychotherapy focused on Harry's symptoms of depression and anxiety, which were less acute but still prominent. Since Cheryl had discovered his secret, Harry was dealing with feelings about his transvestism that he had never faced before (he had never even said out loud to anyone that he wore women's clothes). It seemed that Harry had long lived with a chronic, low-level depression related to his transvestism. He had few friends, lacked emotional or sexual closeness with his wife, and felt a sense of shame that often escalated into self-loathing. This depression had many traits of dysthymia but did not seem to warrant a full diagnosis.[1]

To address these issues, Dr. Andrews intensified his efforts to counteract Harry's life-long assumption that he was "sick." Using techniques of cognitive therapy, he helped Harry dispel some irrational beliefs that impeded his ability to think accurately about his situation. For example, Harry's thinking was characterized by several distortions, some of them rather marked. He believed that if he told just one person about his cross-dressing, then everyone would somehow magically know. He sometimes thought that people who looked at him guessed his secret, even though

---

[1]See Chapter 3 for a case vignette of dysthymic disorder.

nothing in his demeanor communicated a sense of femininity. Dr. Andrews helped Harry question the soundness of these beliefs, and to gain more of a sense of control over any eventual decision to tell other people or to start dressing in public.

Start dressing in public? The idea seemed terrifying! From *Bloomers* and the Internet, Harry knew that some men were relatively open about their cross-dressing—going shopping, attending concerts, or participating in other social activities as women. Harry did not want to do any of this and worried (again, irrationally) that if he were to meet other t.v.'s face-to-face, they would pressure him to go to public places with them cross-dressed. Dr. Andrews assured Harry that he could move at his own pace and need not take any steps that he did not want until he was ready or interested in doing so.

As the couple's sessions continued, it became clear that Cheryl had grown somewhat resigned to Harry's behavior but remained unhappy about it. She had tried to understand his desires and agreed to consider his request to include his cross-dressing in their lovemaking. Ultimately, she was too uncomfortable with the idea. She said she did not ever want to see Harry cross-dressed and would not participate in any activity, sexual or nonsexual, that involved his transvestism. Harry agreed to this but became more assertive in stating his desire—or need—to indulge his behavior. In a difficult session with Dr. Andrews, they negotiated an agreement in which one night weekly, Cheryl went out and provided Harry privacy at home to do as he wished. For his part, Harry came to the conclusion that cross-dressing might always be part of his life. He told Cheryl that he hoped they could remain married, but he was not promising that he could change—or, anymore, that he even wanted to.

Eight months after beginning treatment, Cheryl asked Harry for a divorce. She said that despite her desire to work things out and her love for him, she could not bring herself to accept his behavior. Further, she wanted to have children and felt too uneasy contemplating raising children together.

This precipitated another crisis for Harry, who again felt that his "world was falling apart." After months of having made gains in improving his self-esteem and reducing his shame, he again hated himself. He blamed himself for the divorce. He became steadily more depressed, to the point that he was having trouble sleeping, concentrating, and meeting the demands of his job. His distress grew to the extent that he lapsed into a major depressive episode, although Dr. Andrews still considered this an adjustment disorder because it was so clearly a reaction to the divorce.

To halt a further decline in his functioning, psychotherapy was supplemented with the antidepressant medication Zoloft. This helped Harry get through the worst of the crisis and cope with the sudden changes he now faced—finding a new place to live, being alone, and telling others about the divorce (both he and Cheryl agreed simply to say that they had "grown apart").

Prompted by the divorce and his strong feelings of isolation, Harry finally worked up the nerve to move beyond the computer in making contact with other people. He had developed an on-line friendship with one man in particular, someone who had gone through a similar situation several years earlier and now felt much better about himself. They agreed to meet. This proved to be of great benefit, providing a relieving sense of support and camaraderie. With this friend's encouragement, Harry then contacted the support organization.

> ## Multiaxial DSM-IV Diagnosis at This Point in Treatment
>
> Axis I: Transvestic Fetishism
> CONDITION: UNCHANGED
> Adjustment Disorder with Mixed Anxiety and Depressed Mood
> CONDITION: RESOLVED
>
> Axis II: No diagnosis
>
> Axis III: None
>
> Axis IV: Revelation of cross-dressing behavior, marital discord, divorce
>
> Axis V: *Treatment Onset:* 45 (serious symptoms, including suicidal ideation)
> *Current Time:* 70 (mild symptoms, generally functioning pretty well)

Now that he lived alone and no longer worried about being caught, Harry be-gan cross-dressing more frequently. As he did so, he became aware of a curious change: His transvestic behaviors felt less and less sexual. What had started out as an erotic activity became more of a way for Harry to feel relaxed or calm. Within six months after separating from Cheryl, Harry spent most evenings at home alone, usually doing nothing more exciting than putting on female clothes, cooking din-ner, and reading a magazine or watching television.

Harry continued meeting with Dr. Andrews but after 18 months began schedul-ing appointments less frequently. Psychotherapy continued to provide support and focus on how to integrate cross-dressing, and Harry's "feminine side," into his life in a reasonable, non-destructive manner. As he continued to meet other t.v.'s through the support organization, Harry's acute sense of shame lifted and his self-hatred abated. He missed Cheryl, who had been not only his wife but his only close com-panion. But with new friends with whom he felt at ease, in time he actually felt less isolated or freakish than he did during his marriage.

DISCUSSION

No one knows the prevalence of transvestic fetishism. On the one hand, it is thought to be a relatively uncommon phenomenon, encountered less frequently in clinical settings than many of the other paraphilias. However, given the social taboo that surrounds this usually secret practice, actual estimates of prevalence are hard to come by. Still, no matter how rare or common, transvestism raises fascinat-ing questions about some of our most basic and fundamental psychological con-cepts, including gender, sexuality, and identity. To explore these, some definitions are first in order.

The term *transvestism* was coined by Magnus Hirschfeld, a pioneering early-20th-century sex researcher. He used the term to describe anyone who derived sex-ual pleasure from dressing like the opposite gender, whether the person was male or female, heterosexual or homosexual. Over time, the term has come to refer more narrowly to heterosexual men who cross-dress. (In gay male culture, men who cross-dress on a regular basis, and who do not do so for sexual arousal, are popularly referred to as "drag queens.") Some men who cross-dress limit the activity to a particular item of clothing—lingerie perhaps, or other undergarments, or female shoes. Others enjoy undergoing a complete fashion transformation, dressing in female clothing from head-to-toe, and perhaps adopting a female name for themselves.

Transvestism can be distinguished from *transsexuality*, or gender identity disorder, as it is referred to in the DSM-IV. Transsexuals are people who believe themselves to be, or profoundly wish to be, a member of the opposite gender. Adult transsexuals often will seek medical intervention to assist in their deep desire to live as what they internally feel is their "true" gender. This may involve taking female or male hormones, or undergoing *sex reassignment surgery* to alter their bodies anatomically. For female-to-male transsexuals, the surgical process may include removal of the breasts and internal reproductive organs and *phalloplasty*, or the artificial creation of a penis and scrotum. For male-to-female transsexuals, the operation involves removal of the penis and *vaginoplasty*, or the creation of a simulated vagina. Not all transsexuals elect to undergo surgery or are considered appropriate candidates for this major transformation, based on other aspects of physical and mental health and life circumstance (Dickey & Steiner, 1990).

Both transvestism and transsexuality are distinct from *sexual orientation*. This term refers to whether a person is sexually attracted to members of the opposite gender (heterosexual), the same gender (homosexual), or both genders (bisexual). Most adults, regardless of whether they are gay, straight, or bisexual, have a basic sense of maleness or femaleness that matches their biological gender. In other words, sexual orientation is not the same as *core gender identity* (Stoller, 1968), the internal sense of being male or female.

Yet, even though core gender identity, sexual orientation, transvestism, and transsexuality are all distinct phenomena, the differences between them may not always be so clear cut. They sometimes interact in ways that remain poorly understood.

For example, adult heterosexual transvestites often begin cross-dressing in childhood or adolescence. But as boys, other than their attraction to female clothing, they are not typically effeminate or otherwise out-of-the-ordinary in their gender-related activities (Blanchard, 1990). However, many boys who *are* effeminate, or who prefer childhood female sex-typed activities over male sex-typed activities, grow up to develop a homosexual orientation in adulthood (Green, 1987); but with an adult core gender identity of being male. In other words, most adult gay men, including those who preferred stereotypically female activities in childhood, neither think of themselves as female nor engage in cross-dressing activity.

Among adult heterosexual men with transvestic desires, the interaction of sex, gender, and identity can be even more confusing. For one thing, the exact relationship between transvestism and transsexuality is unclear. Most transvestites are not transsexual: They may enjoy the fantasy of being a woman while cross-dressed, but, like Harry, do not harbor a deep sense of themselves as female (Blanchard, 1990). However, a minority of men who engage in transvestic behavior develop a transsexual orientation over time, becoming more interested in actually becoming a woman than dressing as one (Bradley et al., 1991; Schmidt, 1995). Because of this, some theorists see transvestism and transsexuality as related to each other on a continuum of gender identity, with transsexuality representing a more pronounced degree of cross-gender identification (Benjamin, 1966).

Further, the role of sexual arousal in transvestism often changes over time. What may begin as an overtly sexual activity or fantasy fades into a nonsexual means for relaxation or contentment. This is what occurred with Harry: Over time, cross-dressing became a way for him to feel calm and relaxed rather than sexually aroused. It is unclear exactly how to conceptualize this interaction of sexual drive and identity, but it highlights the powerful—and often mysterious—interconnections of sexuality, gender, and self-identity.

Theoretical Perspectives

Behavioral and cognitive-behavioral theorists assume that transvestic fetishism develops through the traditional channels of classical and operant conditioning. Intentionally or not, a boy's dressing as a female may be positively reinforced during early childhood by an important person in the child's life. Other adult men who cross-dress report childhood experiences of "petticoat punishment," or being forced by their parents or other caretakers to wear girls' clothing as a form of humiliating punishment. The cross-dressing becomes connected with sexual pleasure, and the bond between sexuality and transvestic behavior, once established through the powerful reinforcement of sexual arousal, becomes very hard to break.

In regard to Harry, we know that he did not have to endure "petticoat punishment." And it seems quite unlikely that he was positively reinforced for his desires. However, it is hard to know for sure that his early childhood cross-dressing was not subtly, inadvertently reinforced, perhaps by the increased attention he received (even if negative) for his behaviors.

Psychodynamic theorists offer a variety of explanations for transvestism. From a "classical" (Freudian) perspective, with its emphasis on psychosexual stages of development, transvestism is thought to relate to *castration anxiety*, or a male's unconscious fear that powerful others (either male or female) have the power to castrate him (Fenichel, 1945). From this perspective, transvestites are unconsciously afraid of women, who they view as more powerful than men. The wish to cross-dress provides a means to identify with women and thus gain a sense of control and mastery over these fears. This process involves a defense mechanism called *identification with the aggressor*—if a person identifies with that which he or she is frightened of, the threat is reduced. Along similar lines, transvestism also has been theorized as a way to defensively neutralize a sense of rage or hatred toward women (Stoller, 1968).

Speculatively, these ideas also may relate to Harry. In his family, his mother and possibly his paternal grandmother were the dominant family figures. Perhaps unconsciously, Harry's cross-dressing was a way to identify with his mother—the powerful "aggressor" in the family—or, conversely, to counteract his own frightening sense of rage toward her for being so powerful.

Not surprisingly, most theorists from a biological perspective reject the importance of these psychological explanations and emphasize instead genetic, biochemical, and hormonal functions related to gender. Although it seems unlikely that people carry a specific gene that directly influences the clothing we choose to wear, the issues of core gender identity and sexual orientation may well be influenced by genetic factors (Burr, 1996). From this perspective, the early childhood development of transvestism, and the typically spontaneous pleasure some children find in cross-dressing, is determined more by biological factors than psychological or familial ones.

This, too, may apply to Harry. Perhaps his cross-dressing was neither inadvertently reinforced, nor an unconscious expression of hostility or fear, but instead a result of biological factors related to gender. From this view, the intensity of his need to cross-dress may be "hard-wired." It is (or was) perhaps influenced by psychological or familial factors, but it has its roots in biology.

And even without understanding the exact biological mechanisms involved, medication is sometimes effective in the treatment of transvestism. No controlled studies have examined the effect of medication on cross-dressing behavior. However, medications ranging from lithium (which is most commonly used in the treatment of bipolar disorder) to the newer SSRI (selective serotonin reuptake inhibitor) antidepressants, such as Fluoxetine (Prozac) and Sertraline (Zoloft), have sometimes been successful in halting cross-dressing behavior (Kafka, 1994). This may have to do with the effectiveness of these medications in treating compulsive behaviors of many sorts. In addition, as was the case with Harry, antidepressant or anti-anxiety medications also can help address issues of depression or anxiety related to the cross-dressing.

Each of these perspectives—psychoanalytic, behavioral, and biological—provides a sliver of insight into transvestism. Still, none offers a full explanation for why some men find sexual gratification, or a sense of relaxation, from dressing as women.

Sociocultural Comparisons with Homosexuality

From a cultural standpoint, thinking about transvestism has some overlaps with thinking about homosexuality. Like males and females who are sexually attracted to members of their own gender, transvestites grow up against a cultural backdrop of condemnation and disapproval. The internal sense of shame that develops from being different then becomes difficult to separate out from the impulse to cross-dress itself. This certainly applied to Harry. In therapy, Dr. Andrews helped Harry reduce his shame by framing it in the context of always having felt immense social and familial animosity for his desires.

In a broader way, the decision whether to use psychological treatment to help a person change transvestic behavior, or instead accept it, also parallels psychology's history of dealing with homosexuality. With homosexuality, the general focus has shifted over the past few decades from attempts to alter sexual orientation (through psychoanalysis, medication, behaviorism, and even more dangerous and drastic techniques such as aversive conditioning and psychosurgery) to helping gay people live more fulfilling lives in the context of their sexual orientation.

In fact, the question arises: Should transvestism be considered a disorder at all? Despite occasional sensationalized media depictions of cross-dressers who are serial rapists or murderers, most men with transvestic interests do not behave in a harmful or interpersonally exploitative manner. In the few studies available that look at the psychological health of men who cross-dress, standard personality measures indicate that, as a group, these men are indistinguishable from their noncross-dressing peers (Brown et al., 1996; Meyer & Deitsch, 1996).

Further, while for some men (such as Harry) transvestism is *ego-dystonic*—an unwanted and unacceptable part of the self—for others it is *ego-syntonic*, or an accepted and comfortable part of the self. One reason mental health professionals long held distorted views about homosexuality was because they assumed that the gay individuals they saw in treatment were representative of the larger gay population, even though this was a distorted and skewed sample. Similarly, we cannot make assumptions about transvestism in general based on a clinical population, because this does not take into account transvestic men not in treatment, for whom transvestism may be ego-syntonic.

Perhaps transvestism still is considered a mental disorder, whereas homosexuality is not, for two primary reasons. First, transvestism is rarer, more secretive, and more shameful than homosexuality, at least in today's culture. Most men who cross-dress likely feel great fear about publicly identifying themselves. This fear may be well-grounded: A person easily risks scorn, isolation, physical attack, or the loss of his employment or social standing by revealing his transvestism. Many homosexuals face similar risks—however, groups of gay men and lesbians who were willing to be open about their orientation played a key role in declassifying homosexuality as a mental illness in the early 1970s, even picketing and disrupting the conventions of the American Psychiatric Association and American Psychological Association to advocate for gay rights (Bayer, 1981). This type of political and social activism regarding transgender issues has become more prominent in recent years. However, it seems likley most such individuals prefer a life where privacy is a paramount goal and so have not banded together to advocate for tolerance and social change.

Second, transvestism still may be considered a disorder, whereas homosexuality no longer is, for reasons related to sexism, and particularly to society's deep discomfort with men who choose to act like women. For example, a brief look at how fashion has evolved over the past several decades shows that many of the "unisex" clothes that men and women wear are, in fact, traditionally male clothes. Women today who wear pants, or masculine shoes, or no make-up, don this "male" garb matter-of-factly. But imagine the reverse: a man wearing a dress or a blouse, or lipstick, or high-heels? It is interesting to note that in everyday circumstances adopting male attire is considered "normal," but adopting female attire is considered pathological.

Critics of this position argue that transvestic fetishism indicates a much deeper disturbance than is seen in the whims of fashion, or than is reflected in sexual orientation. From this vantage point, transvestic fetishism is a psychological disorder because it represents an abnormality in a person's core sense of gender—one of the most fundamental starting points in how we build a sense of identity.

PROGNOSIS

Two years after his divorce and three years after starting treatment, Harry Atkins had little contact with Cheryl, who had remarried and moved to another city. He had received a promotion at work. He had made a few friends with other men who cross-dressed. Twice a month, these men got together at someone's home to dress, exchange support and make-up tips, and play bridge. He said he felt "more myself" than ever before. Other than at these private gatherings, Harry had not gone out publicly dressed as a female; he was not sure he ever wanted to.

In general, paraphilias are considered chronic, lifelong disorders that are difficult to treat. With the passing of time, the fantasies or behaviors may become less urgent or driven. The desire to engage in the paraphilia sometimes recedes for years but then episodically re-emerges, after long periods of relative quiescence, especially in times of stress. In rare conditions, a paraphilia begins later in life, in a person with no previous history of engaging in the behaviors. In such situations, the behavior may have an organic basis, such as dementia (Travin & Protter, 1993).

The fact that Harry and Cheryl divorced is not unusual, but this is not the only possible outcome for couples in this situation. Some learn to integrate the cross-dressing behavior into their lives, with varying degrees of comfort, acceptance, and shared participation (social or sexual) in the activity. Among women who remain married to cross-dressing men, a higher degree of acceptance is associated with having known about the cross-dressing behavior before marriage and finding the activity at least potentially erotic (Brown, 1994).

Many men who cross-dress also follow a path similar to Harry's, in that what starts as an intense sexual urge gradually gives way to a self-state more akin to soothing or relaxation. Harry still sometimes wished that transvestism was not, nor had ever been, part of his life. He doubted that he would ever date or marry again, mainly out of fear about revealing his transvestism to a potential partner, and this caused him great sadness. He thought that all things considered, his life would have been easier without cross-dressing.

But in other ways, Harry felt less lonely or depressed than at any time previously. He had made friends with whom he could share his secret and saw little value in dwelling negatively on what he saw as unchangeable. Life now had some bright moments he had previously not thought possible.

Was Harry's outcome a "good" one? He was happier than he had been but still looked to the future with an expectation of loneliness. He had gained a stronger sense of his own identity but lost the most intimate relationship of his life. Perhaps in some cases, finding the appropriate measure for treatment "success" is an elusive, intangible goal.

CRITICAL THINKING QUESTIONS

1. What are some differences between transvestism and transsexuality? Some similarities? Do you think they are distinct or related phenomena?
2. How are the concepts of gender identity and sexual orientation different?
3. Do you think Harry's interest in dressing in women's clothing should be considered a psychological disorder? Why or why not?
4. Do you consider Harry's treatment "successful"? Why or why not?
5. How would you think about this case differently if it were not about a man interested in wearing women's clothes but a woman interested in wearing men's clothes?

Male Erectile Disorder

F|ive years into their marriage, Brenda and Joel Mahoney knew their relationship was in trouble. They argued often. When not fighting, they spent much of their time in wary silence. Both still felt they loved each other, but they no longer took pleasure in each other's company. They had stopped hugging, kissing, or sharing any physical contact at all.

This stood in sharp contrast to how things had been earlier. For the first few years, the Mahoneys's marriage had been a good one. They saw themselves as living proof of the motto "opposites attract." Brenda tended to be extroverted, emotional, and rather colorful (colleagues and friends knew her by her curly raven hair and flamboyant, stylish clothes). Joel, on the other hand, was reserved, soft-spoken, and had a gentle disposition. They enjoyed doing things together and spent hours talking about everything. Brenda felt she had never met a man she trusted more than Joel, and Joel valued how much this lively and energetic woman relied on him for emotional support.

Now, the Mahoneys's frequent arguments followed a familiar pattern. Brenda, who by far had the quicker temper and sharper tongue, would lash out with words she later regretted, knowing how much they hurt Joel: What kind of husband was he? Why didn't he go for help? Since it was *his* problem that was making such a mess of things, why didn't he do something about it? Joel would respond to Brenda's angry accusations by listening patiently and silently but cringing inwardly. He fought by withdrawing. Did they need to go through this again? Even if Brenda was right (which he believed she was), what good was it to have his "problem" thrown in his face?

The "problem" threatening to destroy their marriage was Joel's inability to maintain an erection during sexual intercourse. Earlier in their relationship this had been only an occasional experience, and they both dismissed it as not a serious concern. But now they had not made love for over two years.

At different times, in different ways, the Mahoneys had worked together to try and fix the situation. They altered the pattern and time of their lovemaking. They sought moments when they both felt relaxed. But despite these efforts, Joel's inability to maintain an erection grew more constant, and Brenda became steadily angrier and more frustrated. For one thing, she felt deprived of the pleasure she received from sexual activity. For another, she was 38 years old and was panicked that her childbearing years were passing quickly. Nor did she see Joel (who was 35) doing anything to address the situation.

A few years back, at Brenda's urging, Joel confided his erectile difficulties to his physician. The physician referred him to a urologist, who conducted a wide range of tests to assess Joel's hormonal, nerve, and circulatory functioning, all of which may lead to erection failures. The urologist determined the problem did not have a physiological cause and recommended that Joel contact a colleague of his, a sex therapist, Dr. Neesa Donnelly.[1]

Brenda had suggested often that Joel see Dr. Donnelly or that they go together. Time and again Joel agreed but then stopped short of taking action. He once went so far as to dial Dr. Donnelly's telephone number but then hung up on the answering machine. When it came right down to it, he felt too embarrassed to reveal his problem to a stranger. Inwardly, he worried that anyone who heard about his difficulties, even a therapist (male or female), would laugh at him behind his back.

What eventually led Joel to take action was the birth of a nephew, the first son of his older brother. Joel's brother asked him to be the baby's godfather. At the christening, Joel and Brenda spent a lot of time holding their newborn nephew and carrying him around. To their joint discomfort, several family members eagerly asked when it would be *their* turn. Joel and Brenda smiled politely at these comments, but Joel also felt the burden of Brenda's private, sharp glances. And the fact was, as they stood there as a couple cradling this baby, each imagined what it would be like if he were theirs. They both felt a sadness and yearning for a child of their own.

Driving home from the christening, Joel told Brenda that he would "bite the bullet" and seek help. He started to cry, and acknowledged how much their marriage had suffered. Brenda responded with silence—for a change, she was the quiet one. But she smiled, moved closer to Joel, and put her hand gently on his thigh.

PSYCHOSOCIAL HISTORIES

Joel Mahoney

Joel Mahoney was the youngest of five children (three boys and two girls), with a span of ten years between him and his oldest brother. His grandparents all emigrated from Ireland. His father was a high school math teacher; his mother stayed

---

[1]Joel's difficulties occurred prior to the availability of Viagra (Sildenafil), a medication for male erectile difficulty. This issue is addressed in more detail in the "Discussion" section.)

home to raise the children. In running the household, Mrs. Mahoney was strongly opinionated and a strict disciplinarian, but she also encouraged her children to succeed in academic endeavors. Mr. Mahoney was a rather quiet man, with whom Joel enjoyed a warm relationship. The family were devoutly Catholic and attended mass regularly. All the Mahoney children began their education at a Catholic elementary school.

Throughout his childhood, Joel's older siblings and parents doted on him. He was the "baby" of the family. Perhaps because of this, his mother tended to treat him as younger than he was. For example, until he reached puberty she frequently encouraged him to sit on her lap. Although he disliked this and was embarrassed by it, he continued to do so because his mother said how much it pleased her. He was generally perceived as mother's "favorite."

Joel's family was not one in which emotions were openly shared or important topics discussed. For example, after Joel was born, his parents moved into separate twin beds. The reasons for this move (or even the fact of it) were never talked about. This lack of open discussion extended to all matters of sexuality. In the Mahoney household, sex was a taboo subject, unmentionable except for Mrs. Mahoney's frequent pronouncements that people who had sex before marriage "would go to hell."

Joel was an excellent student and well liked by his peers, who saw him as friendly, if rather quiet. After graduating college with honors, he got a job teaching science in a local school. He lived at his parents' home until his late twenties, when he moved to a nearby city and enrolled in graduate school in theoretical physics. He continued to do well academically, and his scholastic achievements became a great source of pride.

In regard to sexual development, Joel grew up feeling uncomfortable with his own sexuality. Throughout his adolescent years, he never masturbated and felt ashamed of his frequent *nocturnal emissions* (orgasm and ejaculation that occur during sleep). He dated two girls casually and nonsexually during high school. Joel began to masturbate when he was in college (perhaps because for the first time he had his own bedroom). He also experimented with noncoital sex with a girlfriend (*noncoital* sexual activity does not include intercourse). Despite the pleasure these new activities brought, they also left him feeling anxious and guilty.

In graduate school, Joel had his first experience with sexual intercourse, and it was not pleasant. He and a female acquaintance were drinking heavily. They decided to have sex, but Joel's erection failed. The woman responded by teasing and insulting Joel. The humiliation of that evening plagued him—what was wrong with him? Would he ever have sex? Although Joel was able to engage in intercourse with a different woman one year later, that relationship ended quickly, and Joel's fears about his sexual capacity were not quelled.

When Joel met Brenda, he immediately had the sense that she "felt right" for him. They dated for several months before deciding to have sex. When they did have intercourse, Brenda was very responsive. In truth, Joel did not feel particularly aroused, but he took great pride in satisfying her. Joel was attracted not only by

Brenda's looks but also by her strong personality and confidence. When they decided to get married, he remembered that day as the high point of his life.

Brenda Mahoney

Brenda Orsini Mahoney was born into a second-generation Italian-American family. She was the eldest of three daughters, each born two years apart. Brenda's parents had professional careers. Her mother worked part-time as a clinical social worker; her father was a physician with a busy practice.

Mrs. Orsini was a thin, attractive woman for whom it was important to dress well and "look good." Despite a buoyant social presentation, she often suffered from depression, particularly after the birth of Brenda's youngest sister. Starting around that time, Mrs. Orsini began losing interest in running the household, and by the age of 9, Brenda had taken over many of these chores. In her early years, Brenda "adored" her father, who spent little time at home. She remembered him as kind and gentle, mostly, but also with a marked tendency to criticize her and the other family members. Her father's criticisms exacerbated Brenda's already shaky self-esteem, which centered, since her early youth, on her belief that she was overweight and unattractive.

Brenda was popular throughout high school, known especially for her vivacity. Still, in private she was unhappy; she saw herself as "fat and ugly with no boyfriend" (Brenda was plump, but not exceedingly overweight). At home, her relationship with her parents and sisters deteriorated. She fought often with her mother and father. She was jealous of her younger sisters, both of whom were thinner and prettier. At 18, she welcomed the opportunity to move away and attend university.

This move improved Brenda's relationship with her family, perhaps because the increased distance made for less friction. At the same time, Brenda's mother began taking medication for her longstanding depression. This led to a significant improvement in Mrs. Orsini's mood and energy level, and she made a special effort to reach out to her oldest daughter. Their relationship became much warmer.

Brenda's college years were a mixed experience. She socialized quite a bit, formed a few deep friendships with other women, and excelled in several leadership positions. But she continued to feel lonely, disliking herself, and hating her appearance because she was overweight. She went through college without ever having a boyfriend and envied her classmates who were more successful at dating. After graduating, Brenda chose to pursue clinical social work, like her mother.

While Brenda was growing up, the Orsini family handled sexual matters quite differently than the Mahoneys. Brenda's parents were openly affectionate and sometimes playful with one another. Mrs. Orsini was active in a local group supporting women's reproductive rights, and she talked explicitly and frequently about matters of sexuality and contraception. As children, the Orsini girls had candid discussions with their parents about sex. And even though she had never had a boyfriend, Brenda grew up enjoying her sexuality. She took pleasure in masturbation. She indulged a recurrent fantasy that she was a beautifully dressed woman, with whom men were eager to make passionate love.

By her mid twenties, Brenda was desperate to have her first relationship. She was relieved when another student at social-work school, Bennett, expressed interest in her. Bennett was several years older. They began dating, and Brenda lost her virginity with him. She relished this opportunity to explore her sexuality with another person but was disappointed that neither her family nor her friends expressed enthusiasm about the relationship. Brenda felt that she was "lucky" to be involved with Bennett—much less to have found anyone at all.

Brenda and Bennett stayed together for three years. The relationship ended calamitously after Brenda learned that Bennett had been sexually involved with several other women throughout their time together. This betrayal sent her into a depression that lasted almost two years. A few years later, Brenda had two other short-lived relationships. Then she met Joel.

Brenda was attracted by Joel's kindness and mild disposition, even his shyness about sex. She recalled telling a close friend, "this is not a man who will play around." She felt safe with him. During their sexual play, she did not mind the occasional times that Joel lost his erection; in some ways, it even made him more "human" and desirable. When they married, Brenda expressed her joy at having found this man with so many wonderful qualities, a man she thought would make such a devoted husband and, eventually, father.

CONCEPTUALIZATION

Joel Mahoney suffers from male erectile disorder, a sexual dysfunction described in DSM-IV by the following criteria (APA, 1994, p. 504):

A. Persistent or recurrent inability to attain, or to maintain until completion of the sexual activity, an adequate erection.
B. The disturbance causes marked distress or interpersonal difficulty.
C. The erectile dysfunction is not better accounted for by another Axis I disorder (other than a sexual dysfunction) and is not due exclusively to the direct physiological effects of a substance (e.g., a drug of abuse, a medication) or a general medical condition.

The diagnosis of male erectile disorder requires three additional specifiers: lifelong or acquired; generalized or situational; and due to psychological factors or due to combined (psychological and physiological) factors. Joel's erectile difficulties are *acquired* (he has demonstrated a prior ability to maintain an erection through the duration of sexual activity); *situational* (present in certain circumstances, but not in all sexual activity), and *due to psychological factors* (his urological exam ruled out the contribution of a physiological cause, or any role played by substance abuse, prescription medication, or general illness).

Male erectile disorder follows different patterns. Some men experience an adequate erection at the onset of sexual activity but lose it prior to, or during, intercourse (this was the case for Joel). Others report an inability to attain an erection at any time throughout sexual activity with a partner. And although some men experience erectile difficulties to the extent that they cannot attain an erection even for masturbation, this is a rarer occurrence, particularly when the difficulty is psychological and not physiological.

Note that Criterion A stipulates the erectile difficulty must be "persistent." Although "persistence" is not determined in specific numbers, the requirement is meant to emphasize that occasional erectile difficulty is an expectable part of male sexuality and not a sexual dysfunction.

TREATMENT

When male erectile disorder occurs in the context of an ongoing relationship, as is the case with Joel and Brenda, the recommended treatment is couple's therapy. As we will see, Dr. Neesa Donnelly treated sexual dysfunctions by using a comprehensive integration of techniques from behavioral, cognitive, psychodynamic, and systems' theories. The Mahoneys's treatment spanned a period of eight months, with weekly sessions giving way to sessions every other week. Interspersed with these couples meetings were six individual sessions for Brenda. Treatment began with an extended assessment.

In their first moments together, Dr. Donnelly saw the tension of the Mahoneys's relationship mirrored in their physical presence: Joel sat hunched over, avoiding eye contact, staring blankly in Brenda's direction. Brenda had placed herself on the far end of the couch, her body turned away from Joel, her eyes focused on the therapist. And even before knowing the full details of their situation (Brenda had given a brief summary on the telephone), Dr. Donnelly had several goals for this initial meeting: to normalize Joel's problem; to create hope about changing it; and to have both members of the couple share responsibility for it.

Dr. Donnelly asked many questions about the Mahoneys's relationship, backgrounds, and each partner's perspectives on the problem. Joel squirmed around quite a bit, but when he spoke about his work, his whole demeanor brightened. When Brenda described her view of the problem, she spoke loudly and critically of Joel but became teary when Dr. Donnelly empathized with how hard this must be for her and how strongly she wanted a child.

Dr. Donnelly complimented the couple on their earlier attempts to face their sexual difficulties and picked up on their recognition that relaxation was a factor in the solution. Even though this had not been effective before, they had been on the right track. That would be an excellent place to start again! By the time the Mahoneys answered Dr. Donnelly's later questions about their courtship, Brenda and Joel were exchanging warm glances with each other, and Brenda had turned her body toward Joel.

At this point, Dr. Donnelly told them she would be glad to help them work on *their* problem. The problem was not only Joel's and did not exist in a vacuum; she believed that other difficulties they had as a couple contributed to it.

Dr. Donnelly then explained a principle that she called the "90/10 rule." By this she meant that couples were usually 90% on the side of wanting an undesirable symptom to change but were also 10% on the side of *not* wanting it to change—and this 10% was usually out of conscious awareness. The symptom might provide some positive function, like protecting them from an even worse problem. She asked them each to think about fears related to Joel's overcoming his erectile difficulties. Brenda playfully said, "He might cheat on me!," and both she and Joel laughed. Dr. Donnelly said to keep that in mind, and asked Joel to think of his fears as well. If later they got stuck, they would come back to this. At the session's end, Dr. Donnelly recommended a book on male sexuality and suggested each read what appealed to them. This was their first homework assignment. She then requested to meet with each of them individually before coming back together as a couple.

Dr. Donnelly used these individual sessions to gather detailed sexual histories. In the confidentiality of these private meetings, she questioned Brenda and Joel about many issues—sexual experiences growing up, their physical attraction toward each other, their view of the partner's lovemaking skills. Was homosexuality or bisexuality an issue? Had either had an affair? What would they do regarding the marriage if the problem was not resolved? Dr. Donnelly also asked about any variation from "the norm" of sexual experiences or preferences and questioned them about any possible sexual abuse. She tried to ease Joel's shame about his erectile difficulties. Joel and Brenda each reported that they felt a deep attraction toward the other. They were not hiding anything from each other or considering ending the marriage if treatment did not work out, at least for the current time.

After this assessment, the first goal of therapy was helping Joel and Brenda learn to relax. Dr. Donnelly explained that relaxation would lessen their anxieties in intercourse and enhance their awareness of sexual sensations. She chose specific relaxation exercises that involved them as a "team." She taught them to coach each other in a series of exercises: first deep breathing, then progressive relaxation of different body parts, and finally, monitoring each others' reactions to determine how relaxed they had become. The Mahoneys arranged a time to do these exercises in the evenings. Dr. Donnelly cautioned them that the benefits of these exercises might take some time. This proved to be true for Joel, but Brenda noticed an immediate reduction in her general "uptightness."

These relaxation exercises were then expanded to include erotic touch. Dr. Donnelly taught the Mahoneys a gentle sensual massage technique, *sensate focus* (Kaplan, 1974). Sensate focus is designed to heighten a couple's physical intimacy and to illuminate, by their reactions, sensitive or problematic aspects of sensual physical contact. Dr. Donnelly explained that the Mahoneys needed to return to erotic rather than sexual pleasure, and to experiment with touching each other without the pressure or anxiety of intercourse.

Dr. Donnelly described in detail the nature of the touching and emphasized the importance of communicating to each other, verbally and nonverbally, what they liked. This communication—reactions, feelings, even sharing memories—was as important to the exercise as the touch itself. She predicted that these exercises might feel awkward at first but asked them to persevere with them: "There is no such thing as failure here. . . . Whatever goes on is valuable information for us all to learn. . . . Don't look to be aroused, but if arousal is there, fine . . . ." She explicitly stated that the sensate focus exercises should *not* lead to intercourse and asked

Brenda and Joel to refrain from touching breasts or genitals as part of their explorations—at least for now.

When the Mahoneys returned for their next appointment, they were holding hands. They spent two sessions discussing how the sensate focus was progressing. Joel found it easier to give pleasure than to receive it: He enjoyed touching Brenda, but when she touched him, he had a hard time letting her know about his reactions. Brenda found it frustrating that Joel would not say what he liked, until Joel admitted that he did not really *know* what he liked.

Joel realized that in general, not only with sex, he rarely paid attention to what felt good to him. After discussing this topic for a while, Dr. Donnelly connected it with his role in his family, which was to make other people, and particularly his mother, feel good. Maybe he tried to do that with Brenda as well? In fact, Joel saw that his pleasure in sex was derived mostly from pleasing her rather than himself.

The next step of treatment was to include touching breasts and genitals in their sensual massage—not to focus on them, but to learn what was enjoyable. Joel's task was to try identifying what felt good to him and to share this with Brenda. The next session, Joel smiled and said he had felt very aroused and gotten a firm erection. He was even ready to attempt intercourse, but Brenda had reminded him of the prohibition against this. Echoing what Dr. Donnelly had said, Brenda told Joel that when he got aroused maybe he could just relax, enjoy it, and not rush to *do* something about it. Joel grinned and said, "I might just get the hang of this!"

After this progress in treatment, Joel and Brenda had a setback. One evening during their relaxation time, Brenda left the room to answer the telephone. Joel waited thirty minutes before she came back. He then said nothing but could no longer enjoy or concentrate on their exercises. Brenda lost her patience and yelled at him. This was their old familiar pattern.

In therapy, the Mahoneys talked about how each had experienced this event. It dawned on Joel that he was angry that Brenda was away for so long, but as usual, rather than expressing what he saw as a "negative feeling," he withdrew. For Brenda, the incident highlighted her difficulty expressing her fears in calm words, rather than yelling.

Dr. Donnelly suggested that these reactions were relevant to their sexual difficulties. Did Joel's discomfort with feeling or expressing anger leave him with a sense of powerlessness—in a way, impotent? Could Brenda allow herself to be more vulnerable, instead of combative, in the moments she was upset or angry?

Brenda then revealed that beneath her anger, she feared that Joel did not desire her sexually. This took Joel by surprise—he had no idea she felt that way. He responded by taking her hand. He told her how attractive she was and how he never seemed to find the words to express that. As this discussion continued, Brenda realized that it also would be helpful for her to explore further one of her individual issues—poor body image.

To meet this end, Dr. Donnelly and Brenda agreed to meet for a few individual sessions. In these sessions, Dr. Donnelly encouraged Brenda to realize that she had the power to change her own attitude about her body. She presented Brenda a technique called the *mirror exercise* (Heiman & Lo Piccolo, 1988), in which a person identifies negative reactions to certain parts of her or his naked body in the mirror, and then sends "healing messages" to those parts. At home Brenda did this exercise with positive self-affirmations, or conciliatory statements like, "Okay, in spite of the cellulite, I can accept my body. I am moving to a healthier self image." Dr. Donnelly also encouraged Brenda to make lifestyle behavioral changes, such as monitoring food intake and doing more physical exercise.

Brenda also gained insight into the extent to which her poor body image had been influenced by early experiences, and particularly her painful childhood awareness that she did not fit her mother's standard of beauty. How envious she had been of her thin mother and sisters, and how excluded and rejected she felt! Realizing this, Brenda felt more compassion toward herself, and grew less burdened by feelings of anger and resentment—many of which had been directed at Joel.

Beginning around this time, Dr. Donnelly also integrated a cognitive focus into treatment, teaching Joel and Brenda to recognize various forms of "distorted thinking." For example, Joel frequently told himself he "never" had good erections (when for much of his life he had); Brenda often fretted that there was "no chance" they would have a child (this conclusion seemed quite premature). Joel's negative thoughts such as, "I can't have erections. . . . I'm a failure as a man," were substituted by affirmations like, "I am a sexually healthy man, who is enjoying making love with the woman I love." He was encouraged not only to say this to himself often but to imagine it visually. Brenda recalled her earlier adolescent fantasy about being desirable. She consciously and frequently resurrected it.

Dr. Donnelly then returned to a behavioral focus, introducing a series of genital stimulation exercises. Joel was instructed to do these alone first and then with Brenda. These exercises were designed to increase his awareness of arousal. One exercise, called the *stop–start* technique (Kaplan, 1974), had the added benefit of giving him a sense of control over getting an erection, losing it, and then getting it back again. The stop-start technique involves stimulating the penis until it is erect, stopping the stimulation until the erection subsides, and then repeating this sequence.

More than any previous aspect of therapy, these masturbation exercises elicited Joel's strong anxieties about sex. He became aware of how awkward and guilty he felt about sexuality, and the negative impact of the childhood messages he had received. Growing up, he had learned that sex was worse than bad—it was a sin. To address these damaging old beliefs, Dr. Donnelly suggested he meet with a Catholic priest who was trained in human sexuality counseling. Joel agreed, and the priest helped Joel see how he had misapplied religious restrictions on premarital sex to sex in any context. In essence, the priest gave Joel his blessing around expressing and receiving sexual pleasure with Brenda.

Of equal help, Brenda gave him her blessing, too—but of a different sort. To his surprise, she encouraged him to indulge in fantasies during their sexual activity—about her, or other women, or images of women from men's magazines. Dr. Donnelly highlighted such a use of fantasy as important for many people's sexual arousal. Joel had always feared Brenda would be angry if he did this. Having her explicit permission to engage in fantasies, he felt freer and less constricted. They then progressed to partner exercises.

Soon after this, Joel and Brenda came to therapy grinning sheepishly. They announced that they "broke training" twice during sensate focus and enjoyed exciting intercourse. Dr. Donnelly smiled but cautioned them only to have intercourse if both were ready and Joel felt relaxed, fully aroused, and confident of an erection.

Dr. Donnelly also encouraged the Mahoneys to practice erotic activities when Joel did not have an erection, so they could learn what to do together to continue to have a good time. They could continue to make love in other ways, do sensual massage, talk, go for a walk, or take a bubble bath. The aim was to achieve a "sexual attitude" beyond the perception that intercourse was essential to lovemaking. They no longer needed to relegate noncoital sex, which they both enjoyed, to secondary status. And if moments arose when Joel felt concerns about failing Brenda or himself, could he verbally express them?

Based on their progress to date, the Mahoneys were now ready to reintroduce intercourse into their regular sexual activity. Soon after doing so they returned to therapy exclaiming their success but then experienced another setback. They had not been following Dr. Donnelly's recommendations over the past several weeks, were not spending any time together in noncoital erotic activity, and Joel's erections had failed the last three times they had sex. In spite of having learned how to respond to inevitable lapses in erections, Joel had reverted to old ways of reacting, immediately withdrawing from Brenda. She had managed to refrain from yelling at him, but rather than talk calmly she would quickly get up and leave the room.

Dr. Donnelly then reminded them of the "90/10 rule." Perhaps this was now an obstacle to improvement? Brenda readily remembered her fear that Joel might be unfaithful if he were able to perform sexually. Dr. Donnelly speculated that Joel might still worry that being sexual was "bad"— Brenda, like his mother, had always loved him for being "good." What now? She mused that maybe both of them were afraid they would lose the other if change continued—perhaps there was reason for them to be stuck!

The couple left thoughtful but not cheered up. But the next week they were happily back on track. They had decided that the 90/10 rule did not apply to them, or at least it was not a problem: They were no longer afraid of losing each other.

As part of the termination phase of treatment, the Mahoneys used a few more sessions to discuss the "right conditions" each needed for enjoyable sex. Joel spoke of how he liked being a good lover for Brenda but that too often he had been "over-concerned" about her, to his own detriment. He also learned that he needed her to be there for *him*, as a safe friend and an attentive lover who could provide the kind of stimulation he liked. He recalled the incident of his first attempt at intercourse in his twenties and realized how poor the conditions were—he barely knew the woman, and they were both drunk. "I thought men were supposed to be like sex machines. I'm glad that's all behind me." Brenda squeezed his arm.

In their final meeting, Brenda shared the gleeful news that she was pregnant. They told Dr. Donnelly they would be back to see her when their baby was born. Dr. Donnelly expressed her delight at this and invited them back for occasional "tune-ups," if needed.

DISCUSSION

Accurate data about the incidence of male erectile disorder are difficult to find. Estimates typically suggest a prevalence of between 4% and 9% in community samples,

Multiaxial DSM-IV Diagnosis at Time of Termination

Joel Mahoney

Axis I: Male Erectile Disorder, Acquired, Situational, Due to Psychological Factors
               CONDITION: RESOLVED

Axis II: No diagnosis

Axis III: None

Axis IV: Marital stress (prior to treatment)

Axis V: *Onset of Treatment:* 65 (generally functioning pretty well, but significant impairment in marital functioning)
               Termination: 90 (minimal symptoms, generally satisfied with everyday life)

Brenda Mahoney

Axis I: Partner Relational Problem[2]

Axis II: No diagnosis

Axis III: None

Axis IV: Marital stress (prior to treatment)

Axis V: *Onset of Treatment:* 65 (generally functioning pretty well, but significant impairment in marital functioning)
               Termination: 90 (minimal symptoms, generally satisfied with everyday life)

---

[2]Partner relational problem is one example of a problem that may be the focus of psychological treatment, even though it is not considered to be a disorder. Some other examples of this are bereavement, religious or spiritual problem, and phase of life problem. These topics often are referred to as "V codes" because in the DSM-IV, all such items begin with the letter "V" in the numerical coding system for disorders.

although it has also been estimated as high as 34% (Rosen & Leiblum, 1992; Spector & Carey, 1990). The incidence seems to rise among middle-aged and older men, and although this is likely influenced by various physiological changes, the precise mechanisms are not well understood. Among men who seek sex therapy, approximately half cite erectile dysfunction as the main problem (Rosen & Leiblum, 1992).

Over the course of the past century, theories about erectile difficulty (including what causes it and what to do about it) have evolved into what is now a sophisticated, well-integrated treatment approach—but it took a while to get here. In the Victorian era, "moral degeneracy," caused by childhood masturbation, was seen as the culprit. To prevent children from masturbating, methods as drastic as the use of metal mittens were recommended. For grown men with erectile difficulties, bland diets were prescribed to avoid stimulation of the senses (Kraft-Ebing, 1902).

Freud and other early psychoanalysts led the focus away from immorality into the realm of unconscious conflict. They saw the root of the difficulty as a man's failure to resolve the Oedipus complex, a developmental period in which a young boy (theoretically) desires his mother sexually and feels threatened in rivalry with his father. Unresolved anxiety regarding this taboo desire is then transferred into adult sexuality, and the symptom of impaired erection helps fend off this anxiety. Psychoanalytic treatment aimed at gaining insight about these repressed desires, with the assumption that this insight would then lead to relief from the anxiety causing the problem.

Although this Freudian approach is no longer used in sex therapy, more recent psychoanalytic theories are used. For example, object relations theory and self psychology emphasize not unconscious sexual fantasy but the quality of child–parent relationships in infancy and childhood. These relationships are seen to promote or arrest the development of a healthy self, which then in turn affects an adult ability to achieve sexual and emotional intimacy.

For early behaviorists, *performance anxiety* was seen as the major cause of erectile failure. As such, emphasis was placed on eliminating this anxiety through various means of *counterconditioning*, such as relaxation. Behavioral treatments grew more sophisticated with the work of Masters and Johnson (1970), who pioneered new treatment techniques, such as sensate focus. Masters and Johnson approached sex as a "learned skill." As such, they assigned genital exercises as part of treatment and encouraged couples to learn new sexual techniques.

In an important move forward, Kaplan (1974) united these new behavioral techniques with a psychodynamic understanding of early relationships, seeing both as important in the treatment of sexual disorders. From this perspective, it was necessary to identify the immediate stresses *and* the (usually unconscious) childhood factors that contributed to the impairment. She also emphasized that sexual difficulties did not exist in a vacuum but were likely connected to a couple's conflicts regarding issues such as intimacy, power, control, and trust. She expanded Masters and Johnson's technique of sensate focus to include communication about the touch, which might illuminate these relational issues.

From this position, it was a natural evolution to expand treatment by including aspects of cognitive therapy. Perhaps more so than with any other aspect of human behavior, sexuality is an area of functioning particularly susceptible to cognitive distortions. Many people hold mistaken beliefs about their own body, or how to gratify their partner, or what adequate sexual performance involves. These distorted cognitions can negatively affect sexual functioning, and identifying and correcting them can be a crucial aspect of treating erectile difficulties and other sexual dysfunctions.

Most current psychological treatments for erectile disorder follow this integrative approach, along with a *systems perspective* (Lo Piccolo, 1992). With its roots in family therapy, a systems perspective regards the couple, not the individuals, as the primary focus. Imagine two people on a see-saw together—neither can make a move without affecting the other. From this perspective, any particular symptom in one person (in this case, Joel's erectile disorder) not only affects that person but also the system as a whole, and may reflect or mask broader difficulties in the couple. And paradoxically, the symptom may even serve the hidden purpose of keeping the system in balance, or to keep the people from teetering off the see-saw.

We can see the influence of each of these theories in the Mahoneys's treatment. Dr. Donnelly was interested not only in the mechanics of the sexual difficulties but also the childhood and early familial dynamics of Joel and Brenda. She included behavioral techniques like sensate focus and encouraged the communication that arose from these exercises. She emphasized patterns in the Mahoneys's relationship that provided the context for Joel's erectile difficulties.

Dr. Donnelly's "90/10" rule—the suggestion that Joel's erectile difficulty might have had a hidden benefit—is a good example of a systems perspective at work. Perhaps each feared losing the other—Joel losing Brenda because of his "badness" (sexuality), Brenda losing Joel to another woman if he were more potent. In this way, the symptom kept them in balance. Therapy aimed to replace the symptom with more positive ways to stay together, such as deepened communication and intimacy, and a new confidence in their ability to solve problems together.

Since the 1980s, treatments for erectile disorder also have followed a markedly different course: the increasing prominence of medical, rather than psychological, intervention. These treatments have been spurred on by scientific advances that suggest, in contrast with earlier beliefs, that perhaps as many as two-thirds of erectile disorders involve at least some degree of physiological impairment (Mohr & Beutler, 1990; Morgentaler, 1993).

A broad array of medical interventions have been developed in the last 20 years, running the gamut from the relatively benign use of medications (particularly vasodilators, which increase blood flow), to various types of surgery (including the implantation of penile prostheses), to the injection of hormones or drugs directly into the penis or scrotum (Linet & Ogrinc, 1996). These medical treatments can be effective, although most also run the risk of potentially harmful or painful side effects. They also tend to ignore completely relevant psychological and interpersonal factors. For example, penile implant surgeries often are performed when there appears to be only minimal physiological impairment and the erectile difficulty can be treated successfully with sex therapy (Lo Piccolo, 1992).

Viagra and Erectile Disorder

With the mass market introduction of Viagra (sildenafil citrate) in 1998, treatment for male erectile disorder has taken a markedly different turn. Viagra (Sildenafil) is an oral medication that temporarily increases blood flow into the penis, allowing for erection to occur. Few (if any) medications in recent history have been greeted with so much public enthusiasm so quickly.

Assuming that they can work effectively without any unwanted side effects, Viagra, and other similar medications that may soon be available, have the potential to revolutionize the treatment of erectile disorder. But does this mean that psychological treatment will become a thing of the past? Likely not. For one thing, Viagra does not work for everyone, and some men are unable to take it because of specific side effects or other physiological factors (the same also will be true for any newer medications). Of equal importance, no medication, by itself, can address the communication and relational issues that may be related to the erectile difficulties.

For a couple struggling with erectile difficulties, having the problem suddenly and fully healed may be a welcome blessing. But if, from a systems perspective, the problem is part of a couple's delicate interpersonal balance, then having a sexual dysfunction disappear may lead to other difficulties—perhaps the threat of infidelity, or problems about *both* partners' mutual desire in each other, or other relational dynamics regarding power, trust, and intimacy that were masked by the erectile problem. And in situations where a couple focuses only on "fixing" the sexual performance, Viagra may underscore other sexual difficulties, related to connection, desire, and enjoyment of the sexual experience. So, perhaps where the field is next heading is a multidisciplinary approach involving combined sex therapy and medical intervention, to assess and treat more fully the subtle multiple causes, effects, and meanings of erectile difficulties (Gregoire, 1992).

It seems quite reasonable to assume that had it been available, Joel Mahoney would have tried Viagra prior to, or instead of, psychotherapy (the Mahoneys's treatment occurred prior to its creation). Although such speculation can only be hypothetical, it is interesting to wonder how Joel and Brenda's lives might have been different, for better and worse, without the treatment they had with Dr. Donnelly.

Sociocultural Factors

In addition to these psychological and medical perspectives, it also is crucial to look at sociocultural factors in erectile difficulties. Our society places unrealistic expectations on men, emotionally and sexually. Traditionally, boys and men have been taught to be strong, performance-driven, and to value self-reliance over emotion and relatedness. Yet, a competing contemporary ideal is for men to develop and express their sensitive side, especially with a partner. Taken individually or together, these contradictory expectations—being in touch with one's feelings, while also remaining driven to succeed in the external world—can create tremendous pressures on male performance, including sexuality.

Zilbergeld (1992) catalogues several erroneous, destructive myths about male sexuality that foster unrealistic expectations for men and women in their sexual relationships. Some of these myths are that "real men" do not talk about tender feelings and need not listen to what their partner desires sexually; that all physical touch (other than contact sports) is always sexual; that only a huge, rock-hard penis will satisfy a woman; that men are biologically hard-wired to be ready for intercourse at any time; and it is unmanly or shameful to admit having sexual problems. Cultural changes heralded by the women's movement over the past three decades have chipped away at some of these false beliefs. Yet ironically, some new myths have also cropped up, such as a belief that men's emotional and interpersonal needs should not be as connected with sexuality as women's.

Perhaps as our culture continues to change and men accommodate to the shifting definitions and demands of masculinity (much as women have done with femininity over the past few decades), a new generation of young men will experience more freedom to explore and act on their sexuality without the pressure of these false beliefs.

PROGNOSIS

Joel and Brenda visited Dr. Donnelly again five months after their last meeting. Joel was acting more assertively, they were communicating well, and their sex had been "great," even on the few occasions when Joel did not have an erection. However, they were worried about another setback because Brenda's temper had once again started flaring up. In the session, Brenda was able to voice her worries about how pregnancy and delivery would affect the shape of her body. But with Joel's support, she remembered the progress she had made until recently around this old fear. She even acknowledged that she enjoyed buying maternity clothes and liked the way her pregnant body looked. So maybe there also were other reasons to worry now?

Dr. Donnelly suggested that the birth of a baby often was a developmental crisis in a couple's life, and some reversion to old fears and ways of handling them was to be expected. Perhaps that was why the positive changes they had accomplished were harder to maintain in that moment. Several months later, the Mahoneys visited Dr. Donnelly again—to show off their son Matthew and to report that things were going fine.

The outcome of the Mahoneys's therapy was a good one and the prognosis, considering their intention to keep working on the relationship, is hopeful. Is such an outcome typical? Unfortunately, it is hard to know; data on the outcome of sex therapy cases are surprisingly scant, and as of now there is not enough information to reach broad conclusions. In one study (Hawton, Catalan & Fagg, 1992), seventy percent of couples who underwent sex therapy achieved "complete resolution" or "marked improvement" of an erectile disorder. At a three month follow-up, the number had dropped to fifty-six percent, and longer-term prognoses were uncertain. Regardless, considering the various treatment approaches currently available, the introduction of Viagra, and the likelihood of even newer behavioral, medical, and pharmacological interventions to come, this is an exciting time in treating erectile difficulties, and couples have good reason to be optimistic.

CRITICAL THINKING QUESTIONS

1. What are some factors that make it difficult for a person experiencing a sexual dysfunction to seek professional help?
2. How would you think about this case differently if you learned Joel was having a secret sexual relationship with another woman?
3. How would you determine if, in addition to erectile difficulties, Joel has hypoactive sexual desire disorder, characterized by a minimal interest in sexual activity?
4. Why is couple's treatment considered to be the treatment of choice for sexual dysfunctions?
5. With current scientific breakthroughs, Joel could have chosen to correct his erectile difficulties with prescription medication or a surgical implant. What do you think of these options?

Schizophrenia, Paranoid Type

E|ileen Larkin was at her wits' end and terrified all over again. Once again, her 25-year-old son Roger was acting in a strange and violent way. Once again, she needed to summon the police to their suburban home for assistance. Once again, the same familiar and wrenching scene was about to unfold: a tense scuffle, physical restraints, frightened screaming from Roger about "Satanic forces" closing in on him, and another involuntary commitment to a psychiatric hospital.

Mrs. Larkin watched this current exacerbation of Roger's symptoms with a weary sense of *deja vu*. The same scenario had been replayed often in the past few years, with minor variations. This time, Roger brandished a large hunting knife and was poised to stab anyone who neared his bedroom. The time before, he had punched out all the windows on the upper floor of the house. And the time before (or was it the time before that?), he threatened to strangle his mother to punish her for masterminding a plot to hide "millions of dollars" from him.

Mrs. Larkin had anticipated this current escalation of Roger's symptoms. She had recognized the usual warning signs building over the past several days. Roger had become more agitated, withdrawn, and odd. He had stopped shaving and washing, yet seemed oblivious to his rumpled, smelly clothes and his disheveled appearance.

He paced around the house endlessly. Eileen overheard him muttering cryptic phrases to himself—"They'd better give it to me," "He's going to punish all of you," "Elusive victory will be ours." He also occasionally interrupted his pacing to scrawl down notes, feverishly, in a little book he carried with him. Sometimes, he would suddenly stand or sit absolutely still. His attention would become intensely focused, his face taut with concentration and fear, as if he were a person home alone convinced that an intruder had entered the house.

From experience, Eileen realized in those moments that Roger was hearing voices. She surmised that the voices were becoming stronger and more insistent—she had seen it before, leading to his ruptures of violence. Roger was becoming more acutely *psychotic*, losing ever greater touch with reality. He was falling deeper and deeper into his own frightening—and potentially dangerous—world of unreal beliefs and perceptions.

Roger had been diagnosed with schizophrenia when he was twenty. His primary symptoms were the voices he heard, or *auditory hallucinations*, and *delusions*, or firmly held beliefs that contradict reality but which cannot be shaken despite any logic or contrary evidence.

Among these delusions, Roger insisted that his father, who had died of pancreatic cancer ten years earlier, was actually murdered as part of a far-reaching conspiracy. Many individuals and governmental agencies were involved in the conspiracy: the CIA, NASA, his mother and brother, an orderly who worked in the hospital where his father died, the Secretary General of the United Nations, and several media personalities, including Geraldo Rivera and Kurt Cobain. With strained logic, Roger took the news of Kurt Cobain's suicide in 1994 as "proof" of his role as a co-conspirator in his father's murder.

Roger also "knew" that contrary to outward appearances, his father (a middle-class man who owned a hardware store) was in fact a sought-after nuclear physicist and multi-millionaire, with a fortune derived from top-secret research he conducted for the State Department. His mother spearheaded a plot to keep Roger's large inheritance hidden from him. Roger was so convinced of this that several times, he hired lawyers to sue his mother for his inheritance and enlisted private detectives to track down the money. He also had repeatedly telephoned NASA, the FBI, and the CIA "to collect what is rightfully mine" and to warn them, "I know what's going on."

Roger also had other delusions. He believed that certain people, including those involved in the conspiracy, could read his thoughts whenever they chose to, because years ago a physician involved in the conspiracy "planted a descrambling and transmitting device in my brain." At times, he insisted that his mother and brother were not in fact his mother and brother but instead were sophisticated robotic replicas planted in his home "to spy" on him and report his whereabouts to the others.

Roger heard several different hallucinated voices. One was his father's, who would tell him to avenge his death and bring honor to the family name. He also heard voices whom he referred to as "the Satans." These voices taunted him, belittling and mocking him with cruel and derogatory comments. The Satans would hiss that Roger "belonged in Hell" for all his "sins," that he was a "piece of manure" who "should never have been born," that he was a "coward" and a "pansy." And sometimes, Roger heard the voice of God, who told him—no, commanded him—to "do your manly duty" and fight for what is his, no matter what it takes.

In addition to these *positive* symptoms of schizophrenia (so called because they represent excesses or additions to usual functioning), Roger also had *negative* symptoms of schizophrenia, or deficits from usual functioning. These included social aloofness, a limited range of emotional expression, and difficulties with motivation.

PSYCHOSOCIAL HISTORY

On first appearance, Roger Larkin looked and sounded like an average 25 year old—perhaps a bit anxious and awkward, but nothing too out of the ordinary. He was of slight build and normal height and usually maintained adequate personal hygiene and grooming. However, after only a brief interaction, one would be struck by the dramatic and severe oddities of his functioning.

Eileen Larkin met Roger's biological father when she was 18 years old and married him when she became pregnant a few months later. Six months into the pregnancy, Roger's father left abruptly, moving away with no forwarding address. Mrs. Larkin never heard from him again. She recalled him mentioning, in passing, that his mother (whom she had never met) had spent many years in a psychiatric institution, as had one of his cousins.

Mrs. Larkin carried Roger for a full-term pregnancy. His birth was complicated by *anoxia*, a period of time during birth where the neonate suffers from a lack of sufficient oxygen. Still, she remembered him as basically a healthy and "normal" baby. His infancy was uneventful, and he met important developmental milestones, such as learning to crawl, walk, and talk, on time. He was fussy in that he did not care to be held very much, but in most other regards he seemed no different from other infants.

When Roger was fifteen months old, Eileen married Ed Larkin. Mr. Larkin was quite fond of the toddler, and within a short time came to see himself as Roger's father. He adopted Roger a few months after the marriage. The Larkins had another son a few years later.

As a boy, Roger was considered by his parents and teachers to be somewhat odd and isolative. He often had a "spacey" quality about him, tending to daydream in class and drift off into his own world. He kept to himself most of the time. Still, he was a capable student and seemed to be liked well enough by his peers, even though he did not develop close friendships.

Ed Larkin died when Roger was 14 years old. This was a great loss for him: Roger idolized his father and felt closer to him than to anyone else. After his death, Roger became steadily more withdrawn. He maintained adequate grades at school but participated less and less in any kind of social activity. He spent a great deal of time by himself. He began keeping an elaborate notebook, filling it with writings, drawings, and poems.

Roger graduated from high school and enrolled in classes at a nearby community college. He continued to live at home with his mother and younger brother. At the suggestion of his mother, after his freshman year he decided to transfer to the state university several hours away. Mrs. Larkin felt that Roger could get a better education there. She also hoped that moving away from home might help break Roger out of his solitary shell—she fretted about his increasing isolation, his lack of communicativeness, and the generally sad, fearful expression he wore most of the time. He seemed far less social or engaged in life than the typical 19 year old.

At the university, Roger moved into a dorm room with two other students. Immediately, he started having difficulties. His coursework was more challenging than at the community college, and he struggled to keep up with his classes. More stressful than the work, however, was having to live amid so many people and share his living quarters with two strangers.

At first, Roger's roommates attempted to be friendly, including him in various social activities. His continual refusals, however, along with his reclusive and odd manner, quickly led to him being left out of their plans. By November, Roger had made no friends and was helplessly behind in his schoolwork. He felt increasingly ill at ease. He began to ruminate about whether his roommates were poking fun at him behind his back (which perhaps they were)—several times, he thought he caught them exchanging glances and smirks when they assumed he was not looking. He began sleeping less and letting his hygiene slip. He kept as his sole companion his notebook, writing for hours at a time, late into the night.

In early December, Roger's roommates returned from an evening out to find all the mattresses and bedding in the dorm room slashed apart, the contents of their dressers emptied and strewn about. Roger was sitting huddled in a corner, in the dark, talking about "the Satans" and how "no one can harm us now." One of the roommates contacted Campus Security, who escorted Roger to the student health facility. He was transferred to a nearby psychiatric hospital, where he was treated with *neuroleptics*, or *antipsychotic medication*. He stayed in the hospital for two months and then returned home to his mother.

Roger's life then slid downhill. He was unable to return to school, he could not hold a job for more than a few weeks, and he did not develop any friendships or romantic relationships. A few brief stretches of improved functioning offered hope that he might be able to get back on his feet, but each of these periods eventually culminated in another psychotic "break."

Roger's psychotic symptoms often escalated following a stressful event but sometimes got worse with no known precipitant. He would become increasingly engrossed in the delusions that distorted his thinking—the plot against his father, his presumed danger because of the conspiracy, and his mother's purposely hiding his inheritance. He would then stop taking his medication, for how could he be sure that the pills were not part of the conspiracy? After that, it was only a matter of days until the voices became insistent, frightening, and dangerous. And then Roger would land back in the hospital (this had happened seven times now), with the same grim cycle ready to start yet all over again.

CONCEPTUALIZATION

Roger is one of an estimated 2,500,000 to 3,000,000 adult Americans with schizophrenia. He meets sufficient DSM-IV criteria to make this diagnosis (APA, 1994, pp. 285–286):

   A. *Characteristic Symptoms:* Two (or more) of the following, each present for a significant portion of time during a 1-month period (or less if successfully treated):
   1. delusions
   2. hallucinations
   3. disorganized speech (e.g., frequent derailment or incoherence)

4. grossly disorganized or catatonic behavior

5. negative symptoms (i.e., affective flattening, alogia, or avolition)

B. *Social/Occupational Dysfunction:* For a significant portion of time since the onset of the disturbance, one or more major areas of functioning such as work, interpersonal relations, or self-care are markedly below the level achieved prior to the onset (or when onset is in childhood or adolescence, failure to achieve expected level of interpersonal, academic, or occupational achievement).

C. *Duration:* Continuous signs of the disturbance persist for at least 6 months.

Roger suffers from delusions, hears auditory hallucinations, and demonstrates evidence of negative symptoms. Additionally, his functioning is markedly impaired because of his psychological difficulties, and his symptoms have persisted for well beyond six months.

Of the various subtypes of schizophrenia—disorganized type, catatonic type, paranoid type, undifferentiated type, and residual type—Roger best fits the criteria for the paranoid subtype. The most essential component of schizophrenia, paranoid type is a network of related delusions or auditory hallucinations, usually in the context of relatively intact emotional and intellectual functioning. Although Roger also demonstrates more pervasive emotional difficulties, his disorder centers on his delusions about his father's death, and conspiratorial plots against both his father and him. His delusions include themes of *persecution* and *grandiosity*—persecution in that others are out to get him, and grandiosity in the fame and stature of those he believes to be his tormentors. Roger's negative symptoms, although present, are not as prominent as his delusions; this is another characteristic of the paranoid subtype of schizophrenia.

Roger's schizophrenia is additionally specified with the descriptor *episodic with interepisode residual symptoms*. This indicates that between periods of *florid* psychosis, or times of acutely symptomatic behavior, he continues to experience at least some symptomatic impairment to a reduced degree.

TREATMENT

After the police responded to Mrs. Larkin's urgent phone call, the scene unfolded much as it had in previous situations. Roger was taken by ambulance to the psychiatric unit of a local hospital where he had been admitted several times before. He was interviewed by a psychiatrist who committed Roger involuntarily to the psychiatric unit for observation. The psychiatrist made this determination based on Roger's immediate potential to inflict harm on himself or someone else because of his behavior with the hunting knife and his inability to distinguish between reality and his delusions.

Since this was an involuntary hospitalization, Roger had no choice but to remain in the hospital for at least 10 days, the maximum period of time for an involuntary commitment in the state where he lived (the length of an involuntary commitment changes from state to state). The hospital would then need to file a court petition for a longer commitment if they determined Roger was still mentally unstable and dangerous. As it turned out, that was not necessary.

As in the past, Roger grumbled for a few days about his confinement and refused to take medication. But then with the staff's gentle coaxing, he relented. Within several days, his acute psychotic symptoms subsided: His voices diminished, his delusions lessened in intensity (although they did not disappear), and he returned to his characteristic withdrawn, anxious, and guarded style.

But this was Roger's seventh psychiatric hospitalization in six years. The same grim pattern had already repeated itself over and over—in and out of the hospital, on and off his medication, his life going nowhere. If anything, he seemed to be on a deteriorating course, with shorter periods of stability between episodes. What would be different this time?

Two important developments occurred. Taken together, they offered a ray of hope that this downward spiral might be halted.

First, Eileen Larkin had had enough. She loved her son and was committed to helping him. But she was exhausted by Roger's repeated threats of violence and episodes of florid psychosis. Eileen had always believed that she could be of most assistance to Roger by being kind and supportive, by sticking by him—but had this really helped?

For the past several years, whenever Roger was hospitalized, the hospital staff had strongly recommended that he attend a community-based day treatment program after his discharge. Eileen had always thought this a good idea, but Roger had always refused to go. Each time she gave in to him, despite her better judgment. Now, Eileen made a difficult decision: She told Roger that in order for him to continue living at home, he must meet two non-negotiable expectations. First, he must attend the day treatment program recommended by the hospital staff. Second, he must continue to take his medication. If he did not agree to these rules, she would not allow him to live at home any longer. She warned him, reluctantly but with determination, that if he did not take responsibility for his proper treatment, she would throw him out of the house.

And second, Roger's psychiatrist recommended that he try a new antipsychotic medication. Clozaril, introduced in the United States in the late 1980s, had proven successful with many schizophrenic patients who had not responded well to other medications. Roger had always been treated with more traditional antipsychotic medications; it was time for a change.

Roger started taking Clozaril. Because the medication had the side effect of making him lethargic, he took his prescription in the evening, before going to sleep. In addition, Roger began having his white blood cell count monitored weekly because one rare but serious side effect of Clozaril is a potentially fatal blood disease, agranulocytosis.

Within a few weeks, the beneficial impact of Clozaril became apparent to Roger and those around him. He referred to his delusions less frequently. He reported that he no longer heard voices, or heard them in a manner that did not so easily threaten to overwhelm him. And he became more willing to interact with other people. These interpersonal behavioral changes were small but significant: He would end conversations less abruptly, attempt occasional pleasantries with his mother, and spend less time in his isolative private world.

Roger also began attending a neighborhood aftercare program called "Liberty House." Located about 20 minutes away from where he lived, Liberty House had two primary components to it: a *halfway house*, for people who needed the support of a structured living community but not the confines of a psychiatric hospital, and a *day program*, for those who lived independently or with family but still needed the daily help of regular and intensive treatment. Roger attended the day program, living at home as long as he kept his agreement with his mother.

Most of Roger's treatment at Liberty House took the form of small groups sessions. Each group consisted of several clients and was led by one or two of the program's counselors. The groups each had a particular focus, most frequently of a practical nature. With schizophrenic individuals, psychotherapy of this type (individual or group) is more effective than psychotherapy designed to achieve insight into the potential meaning of the symptoms or the illness (Penn & Mueser, 1996; Scott & Dixon, 1995).

For example, once a week Roger attended a *symptom management* group. In this group, Roger and other clients discussed the specific symptoms that hampered their functioning. For many people with schizophrenia, symptoms never completely go away, even with medication: Some disturbance may always be present, like a radio with volume that goes way down but never completely shuts off. And so one important focus of treatment is helping people with schizophrenia learn to recognize, label, and manage these symptoms.

Roger learned to identify some of the warning signs that had led to his relapses in the past—feeling anxious or overwhelmed, becoming more isolative. He also began to trust others when they reminded him that his hallucinated voices were imaginary and not real. This was difficult: When Roger heard the voices, they sounded as believable as anything he had "really" experienced. But he was beginning to accept that his voices were not, in fact, real, nor were they special communications to him. They were symptoms of an underlying psychiatric disorder. With this understanding, he became better able to manage their influence on his life.

Another group focused on *social skills* and met twice weekly. Because people with schizophrenia often exhibit marked deficits or oddities in how they interact with other people, another key focus of treatment is developing more appropriate ways to socialize. In the social skills group, Roger and the other clients learned new and more effective ways to interact with other people. This group included some role playing of different social situations, learning about nonverbal communication such as eye contact and body posture, and practicing some basics of social interaction.

Other weekly groups addressed family issues, current events, medication issues, work/school issues, and dual-diagnosis. *Dual-diagnosis* is the term used for individuals with a major mental illness and a substance or alcohol abuse problem. Although substance abuse was not a problem for Roger, it is for many people with schizophrenia. Perhaps as many as 50% of people with schizophrenia abuse substances at some point in the course of their illness (Buckley, 1998).

In addition to these specific groups, Liberty House adapted a *milieu therapy* approach to treatment. Created in the 1950s as a more humane model for inpatient psychiatric treatment, milieu therapies regard the entire physical setting of a treatment environment as relevant to the treatment. For Roger and the other clients of

Liberty House, this meant that program staff were often available to observe and participate in the informal, non-scheduled group interactions that happened in the program's living room, where people congregated to chat, watch television, and pass time between scheduled groups. Additionally, twice weekly the entire program—all staff and clients—met together for a community meeting, to talk about whatever issues were of current relevance to the treatment community.

Roger attended Liberty House five days a week, for several hours each day. Despite his initial reluctance, he soon began to go to the program each morning on his own initiative, without pressure from his mother. Other than during his hospital stays, this was his first opportunity to meet and talk with other people whose life experiences were similar to his. He also enjoyed his weekly meetings with Federico, one of the program's counselors with whom he felt particularly comfortable. Further, Eileen joined Roger at Liberty House twice a month for a family meeting, to discuss emotional and practical issues related to their home life. To say that Roger formed close relationships at Liberty House would be overstating the case, but he did connect with other people to a greater extent than at any time previously.

In addition to Roger's treatment at Liberty House, another important event developed after Roger left the hospital: Eileen began to seek help for herself. At the recommendation of a psychologist she spoke with during Roger's last hospitalization, Eileen contacted an advocacy group, the National Alliance for the Mentally Ill (NAMI). Eileen had heard of this organization before but never attempted to contact them. She did not consider herself a "joiner" of groups. And besides, what could they offer *her?* The problem was with Roger, not herself; she thought she could cope fine on her own.

A NAMI volunteer told Eileen about a local support group for family members of people with mental illnesses. Once she began attending their meetings, Eileen found the help invaluable. She realized that many other people also needed to cope with the emotional and financial hardships of having a psychotic family member. She appreciated the opportunity to share practical advice with the others, learn about new medication developments, and stay abreast of the laws, policies, and regulations that affected the treatment of mental illness. But perhaps most importantly, Eileen was able to reduce the sense of stigma and shame she felt regarding Roger's illness.

Eileen knew that Roger's illness was not her fault. She had educated herself enough about schizophrenia to realize she was not to blame, that families are not to blame. She did not really believe that Roger was schizophrenic because of anything she had done—*but still*. What if she had raised him differently? Should she have been tougher or more lenient? If she had sought help for him earlier on—in childhood perhaps, or after Ed died—would that have made a difference? Was it a dreadful mistake to encourage him to attend a school away from home?

Even more disturbing to her than these "what ifs . . . ," Eileen had to admit to herself that she felt embarrassed by Roger's illness. She loved Roger, but what did her quiet suburban neighbors think about having a crazy person next door? Despite their polite smiles, what did her friends and co-workers think—did they pity her, or hold her responsible? Why was she so ashamed to tell people she had a schizophrenic son, so worried about what would they would assume about her, about him?

> ## Multiaxial DSM-IV Diagnosis at This Point in Treatment
>
> Axis I: Schizophrenia, Paranoid Subtype, Episodic with Interepisode
>   Residual Symptoms
>   CONDITION: STABLE
> Axis II: No diagnosis
> Axis III: History of anoxia at birth
> Axis IV: Chronic mental illness
> Axis V: *Treatment Onset:* 25 (danger of hurting self or others, behavior
>   considerably influenced by delusions and hallucinations)
>   *Current Time:* 45 (serious global impairments in functioning)

Through her involvement with the NAMI support group, Eileen came to re-alize just how deeply the stigma of mental illness had affected her. And by realiz-ing this, she was able to reduce some of the shame she felt. She acknowledged, rather sadly, that this sense of shame did not go away completely, even though she wished it would just vanish. But it grew much less pronounced. She also came to realize how greatly this stigma affected Roger's perception of himself, and understanding this, she came to treat him in a more respectful and caring way.

DISCUSSION

Perhaps no other mental disorder has been subject to as much intensive scrutiny as schizophrenia. Researchers and clinicians have learned a great deal about this fasci-nating but terrible disease, hoping to alleviate its devastating impact. Yet funda-mental questions remain: What causes schizophrenia? Is it the result of one underly-ing etiological process, or do many different routes lead to it—in other words, does it make more sense to think in terms of *schizophrenias?* Are we currently using the most appropriate diagnostic criteria—for example, does the DSM-IV pay too much attention to the positive symptoms of the disease at the expense of negative symp-toms, thereby ignoring many individuals who may in fact be quietly schizophrenic but who do not experience delusions or hallucinations?

Questions also remain regarding how old schizophrenia might be. Although many accounts suggest that schizophrenia has been around as long as humankind, at least one noted schizophrenia researcher is not so sure. Gottesman (1991) offers the intriguing possibility that schizophrenia entered into the sphere of human function-ing at a specific point in history, perhaps by viral or bacterial transmission, in the 17th or 18th century. He notes that prior to that time, no accurate medical descrip-tions of a schizophrenic syndrome exist, and the 19th century witnessed a dramatic increase in documenting this type of mental illness. Gottesman looks at human immunodeficiency virus (HIV), the viral agent responsible for AIDS, to offer an analogy for how a pathogen may appear on the human scene suddenly and with mammoth impact.

Regardless of whether it is considered one entity or many, a recent phenomenon or as old as human history, almost all current perspectives assume that schizophrenia results from a complicated interaction of biological, environmental, and psychological factors. This *biopsychosocial* approach to thinking about schizophrenia suggests that biology plays an enormous role in the etiology of the disorder, but no single factor will be responsible for causing schizophrenia in a person's life (Carpenter & Buchanan, 1994; Zubin & Spring, 1977). Instead, certain individuals may be born with an inherited *vulnerability*. A multitude of life events, ranging from peri- and neonatal maturation, to early family interactions to childhood psychosocial development, to adult life stress, can tilt the balance in favor or away from mental illness.

How might a biopsychosocial model apply to Roger Larkin's life? At several points in his history, we can speculate about how such a perspective may be employed to understand Roger's schizophrenia.

First is the question of a genetic vulnerability. Eileen Larkin knew of no schizophrenic relatives in her family, but this may not have been the case for Roger's biological father. We can not know for sure, based on Eileen's sketchy information. But her recollection that Roger's paternal grandmother and at least one other relative had been in a psychiatric institution raises the possibility that schizophrenia was present in the family, and so there may be a genetic basis to Roger's illness.

We also know that Roger's birth was complicated by anoxia, which may be another contributing factor. Schizophrenic adults are more likely than nonschizophrenic adults to have a history of perinatal, neonatal, or birth complications, and neuromotor difficulties in infancy are thought to indicate a vulnerability to the development of schizophrenia in adulthood (Kagan & Zentner, 1996; Zornberg, 1998).

How about psychosocial factors—what role might these have? Roger was isolative as a child; did his withdrawal from social contact exacerbate a maladaptive tendency to get lost in his own thoughts? Or even earlier: What was his first year of infancy like—was Eileen, depressed and fearful over her husband's sudden abandonment, unresponsive to Roger's basic needs? Or perhaps the timing of Ed Larkin's death, at the onset of Roger's adolescence, was a psychological loss of great significance. And despite his isolation and oddity, Roger did not become psychotic until leaving home to attend university. Was this separation too much for him?

Could we say with any certainty that if Ed Larkin had not died, Roger would have been spared from the ravages of mental illness? Or if his birth had not been complicated by anoxia, or if Eileen had not raised him by herself during his first year of life, or if he had not been encouraged to move away from home perhaps before he was ready to do so? No, of course not. Yet it is worth speculating about how each of these events—or others—may have contributed to Roger's schizophrenia. Assuming Roger was born with a biological vulnerability for schizophrenia, a biopsychosocial approach theorizes that the particular stresses of his life may have accrued to be more than he could tolerate.

A Typical Case?

In several regards, Roger is typical of individuals with schizophrenia. His possible genetic predisposition, the timing and circumstances of his first psychotic episode, and the tenuous nature of his *premorbid functioning* (his psychosocial adjustment prior to the development of any symptoms) are all typical. Although the onset of schizophrenia can occur at any time, the most frequent age of onset, especially for males, is late adolescence or early adulthood (Lewine, 1981; Dworkin, 1990).

Roger's symptoms also are typical. For example, his belief that others can read his thoughts because of "a descrambling and transmitting device in my brain" is a phenomenon known as *thought broadcasting,* or the idea that one's thoughts are somehow magically broadcast to others. Thought broadcasting is considered to be one of the primary indicators, or "first-rank symptoms," of schizophrenia (Schneider, 1959). Two additional types of thought disorder, which Roger does not demonstrate, also are considered "first-rank symptoms": *thought insertion,* in which a person believes his or her thoughts have been implanted by an external force, and *thought removal,* in which a person believes his or her thoughts have been removed by an external force.

One significant difference between Roger and most individuals with schizophrenia is his potential for violence. Contrary to erroneous societal views and misleading media depictions, the vast majority of people with schizophrenia are not prone to act in a violent or criminal manner. Yet, people with schizophrenia may be more likely than others to be the *victims* of crime or violence. This may relate to various aspects of the disorder—impaired judgment, poor social skills, stigmatized status in society, homelessness, and the lack of social or economic support that individuals with schizophrenia often face.

Among the minority of people with schizophrenia who may act violently, most are of the paranoid subtype, like Roger. This is largely because such people are more apt to experience *command hallucinations*—auditory hallucinations that instruct them to act in potentially harmful or self-destructive ways.

Antipsychotic Medications

Like many important scientific advances, the discovery of medications to treat schizophrenia happened by chance. French chemists in the 1930s and 1940s created a powerful new class of medications called *phenothiazines.* These drugs grew out of a broader experimentation to develop antihistamines, and soon found value as anesthesia for surgical patients.

By the 1950s, newer and more sophisticated anesthetics had come along, but the psychiatric value of these drugs began receiving attention. Discovered first by chance and then with systematic observation, researchers realized that phenothiazines could dramatically reduce the presence of positive psychotic symptoms, such as auditory hallucinations and delusions. Their use in this regard then spread rapidly, revolutionizing the care and treatment of schizophrenia.

These medications were not (and are not) in any way a cure for schizophrenia, much as insulin is not a cure for diabetes. Further, early enthusiasm for their use was soon tempered with the discovery that they could lead to potentially serious side effects, most significantly *tardive dyskinesia*, an irreversible neuromuscular condition that causes tremors and involuntary motor difficulties affecting the face, hands, and feet. Still, phenothiazines quickly became the standard of care in treating schizophrenia because they lessened the severity of symptoms, and that was a feat that psychotherapy, except in isolated instances, had been unable to accomplish.

From the 1950s through the 1980s, many new antipsychotic medications were developed, but almost exclusively in the class of phenothiazines. It was not until the late 1980s that another breakthrough occurred with the creation of Clozaril. Clozaril (the trade name for clozapine) was much more effective than the older medications in reducing the positive symptoms of schizophrenia (Frankenburg, 1994). In some cases, people whose illness had been *treatment-refractory* (meaning that prior medications did not alleviate their psychotic symptoms) experienced unprecedented, life-changing gains. Clozapine ushered in a new, more optimistic era in the treatment of schizophrenia, and in the 1990s this progress has continued with the introduction of equally impressive medications, such as risperidone, olanzapine, and serquel. The next few years promise even more sophisticated medications, with greater potency and fewer side effects.

For some people, these "new generation antipsychotics" not only reduce the positive symptoms of schizophrenia but also attenuate negative symptoms, such as flat affect and lack of volition (Tran et al., 1997). They also can be effective in curbing violence and reducing alcohol, cocaine, and nicotine use (Buckley, 1998; Glazer & Dickson, 1998). In addition, it seems that medication compliance may be stronger with these newer medications because they have fewer side effects than the phenothiazines, and result in a greater subjective sense of well being (Marder, 1998).

Clozaril and these other new medications, called *atypical antipsychotics*, have fundamentally different biochemical properties than the earlier antipsychotic medications. Because of this, they have also reshaped the development of theories about schizophrenia. Until recently, the leading biochemical theory of schizophrenia was the *dopamine hypothesis*. This hypothesis stated that schizophrenia was due to the excessive transmission, or faulty inhibition, of the neurotransmitter dopamine. This theory came about from the observation that phenothiazines work mainly by inhibiting dopamine production. But Clozaril's superior ability to ameliorate schizophrenic symptoms unseated the dopamine hypothesis because Clozaril inhibits the production of two other transmitters, serotonin and noradrenaline, in addition to dopamine. And so a new theory, the *interaction hypothesis*, has replaced the dopamine hypothesis as a leading explanation for the biochemical underpinnings of schizophrenia. The interaction hypothesis assumes that schizophrenic symptoms result from the complex interaction and regulation of various neurotransmitters, not just dopamine.

Only time and careful research will tell if this new hypothesis can be supported. Yet, regardless of its validity, it is a good example of the circular route by which scientific theory is sometimes generated: A theory may be derived from the fortuitous discovery of why something works. Such can be the nature of theory-building in matters that remain largely unknown and mysterious.

Many other theories also have come and gone regarding the causes of schizophrenia. For example, family interaction theories generated interest for many years.

Yet, such research has dwindled because there has been little support that deviant family interactions cause schizophrenia, and these theories led to a great deal of misdirected blaming of family members (Carpenter & Buchanan, 1994).

While family theories have fallen out of favor in looking at the *causes* of schizophrenia, certain familial styles of communication do seem to influence the rate of relapse and rehospitalization (Nuechterlein et al., 1992; Vaughn & Leff, 1976). In particular, a variable identified as *expressed emotion (EE)* has proved useful in predicting relapse. In families with a "high EE" communication style, overt criticism, hostility, overinvolvement, and overprotectiveness are more frequently expressed than in "low EE" families. Many studies support that schizophrenic relapse is significantly more frequent in high EE families (Butzlaff & Hooley, 1998). And even as most researchers now minimize the potential role of family deviance in causing the disorder, some question whether the field has gone too far in ignoring the possible causal contributions of an unhealthy family environment (Gottesman, 1991; Schoenewolf, 1996).

Deinstitutionalization and Shorter Hospital Stays

Until quite recently, Roger might have spent long periods of time—months perhaps, or years, or even his entire adult life—in the confines of a psychiatric hospital. Beginning in the 1960s, however, a trend started that continues to gain momentum through the present day: Inpatient hospital stays have become briefer and briefer, even for people with severe mental illnesses. This change began well before managed care models of delivering health services ascended to prominence in the 1980s.

What prompted this change in the care of the severely mentally ill? Economic concerns were one factor. Schizophrenia is an enormously expensive disease, both in terms of treatment and in lost work productivity. In 1990, the estimated direct and indirect costs of the disease were $33 billion in the United States (Rupp & Keith, 1993). For decades, private insurance companies and the government (which subsidizes treatment for indigent and psychiatrically disabled individuals) bore the brunt of paying for lengthy hospital stays, and sought to minimize their costs.

In addition to economics, civil rights was a second major factor leading to shorter hospital stays. Until recently, many of the rights that most of us take for granted were denied to the mentally ill. This began changing in the 1960s and 1970s. At that time, a community mental health movement in the United States raised social awareness of mental health issues, and a series of landmark court decisions established that mental illness, by itself, was insufficient reason to deprive a person of his or her constitutional freedoms. The courts determined that mentally ill people have a right to treatment, a right to refuse treatment, a right to live free from custodial care, a right to live in communities, and a right to receive treatment in what is termed the *least restrictive environment*—a treatment setting that allows for the greatest degree of individual freedom without compromising the safety of the individual or the community. These decisions paved the way for unprecedented changes in the treatment of mentally ill individuals—changes perhaps no less profound than what occurred 200 years ago in the 1790s, when a radical health reformer named Philippe Pinel made the bold decision to unchain the mad inmates of Paris's asylums.

This movement came to be known as *deinstitutionalization*. By the mid 1980s, state mental hospitals housed less than 115,000 individuals—down from more than three times that number in 1970, and dramatically below the peak of over 550,000 people in 1955 (Morrissey, 1989). The intention of deinstitutionalization was to minimize hospitalizations and create less expensive, and more accessible, community-based treatment facilities.

Sadly, deinstitutionalization did not live up to its potential: Only half of its humane promise was kept. On the positive side, many individuals who had spent years in psychiatric hospitals were (and still are) granted an unprecedented ability to live freely. But vital community supports to assist them—the necessary other half of the equation—have not always materialized. Economic concerns, stigma, and fear continue to conspire against the provision of adequate outpatient and residential care. Because of this, many people with schizophrenia receive insufficient help and cycle in and out of psychiatric institutions, creating a "revolving door" phenomenon. Managed care, which seeks to contain costs by limiting treatment, has intensified the situation even more.

And so the pendulum has swung far away from where it once was. Whereas until recently individuals with major mental illness may have been institutionalized far longer than necessary—perhaps for a lifetime—today adequate treatment may be hard to find, and hospitals rarely keep patients beyond the time needed to curtail the acute florid symptoms of psychosis. Often, people are discharged back into situations without good aftercare. Interestingly, the civil rights issue also cuts both ways: While many people with mental illness now have legal protections against inhumane treatment, the strict guidelines for involuntary commitment often prevent concerned family members from obtaining care for a psychotic and potentially dangerous person who refuses treatment. Ironically, all these changes have occurred in the absence of data supporting them as sound fiscal or clinical policy; in the long run, more comprehensive treatment, including lengthier hospital or residential stays, may better help prevent relapse and reduce costs (Glazer, 1996).

PROGNOSIS

Roger participated in the day program of Liberty House for fifteen months. At no point in that time did his symptoms become so severe as to necessitate an inpatient hospitalization—a marked departure from his "revolving door" style of hospital admissions over the previous years. Through the combination of Clozaril, the skills and psychoeducational benefits of day treatment, and his mother's caring but firm insistence on medication compliance (along with the benefits of *her* supportive treatment), Roger was beginning to gain a sense of confidence that he could move forward in his life.

With the encouragement of his counselor Federico, Roger decided to taper the amount of his treatment in the day program. He cut back to two days per week and filled the additional time by re-enrolling at the community college where he had begun college almost a decade earlier. His plan was to start slowly, with one or two courses per semester.

Two years later, Roger has remained out of the hospital. He continues to take two college courses per semester and has developed several friendships with individuals he met at Liberty House. No longer involved in day treatment, his therapy now consists of two meetings weekly. One is an individual session with a psychologist, who sees her role as helping support Roger cope with whatever stressful events are currently affecting him. The second is a group therapy session with other individuals in his situation—people with schizophrenia who are stabilized on medication and seeking to improve the quality of their life. He has not moved out of the house with his mother, although is considering possibly moving into an apartment with a friend in the not too distant future.

It is as this point that we leave Roger. His future must be regarded as uncertain. On the one hand, the prognosis is better for paranoid schizophrenia than for the other schizophrenia subtypes. Yet, the course of schizophrenia is extremely variable, with some individuals displaying intermittent exacerbations and remissions, others maintaining long periods of stability, and still others sliding into a chronic, ever-worsening illness (Carpenter & Buchanan, 1994; Davidson & McGlashen, 1997). A better prognosis is associated with the presence of affective symptoms along with the schizophrenic symptoms, a later and acute onset, good responsiveness to biological treatments, and early, sustained treatment with medication (Davidson & McGlashen, 1997; Wyatt & Henter, 1998).

Roger is fortunate in that his mother has stood by him. Despite some harrowing episodes of bizarre and dangerous behavior, and the emotional and financial toll of coping with his illness, she has not abandoned him.

Like Roger, many people with schizophrenia have the benefit of caring families who have learned to tolerate the emotional and financial hardships that typically go hand-in-hand with this disease. But not all are so lucky. Many other people with schizophrenia—poor, unable to work, lacking adequate social skills and bereft of any family or interpersonal support—drift into a bleak world of homelessness and isolation. Although estimates vary, many studies suggest that a large proportion of homeless individuals suffer from mental illness (Koegel, Burnam & Farr, 1990; Rossi, 1990), with schizophrenia being one of the most representative diagnoses (Fischer & Breakey, 1991; Torrey, 1997). The suicide rate also is high among people with schizophrenia, with schizophrenia being one of the mental disorders that carries the greatest risk of suicide (Reid 1998).

With antipsychotic medication's, proper support, and adequate psychological treatment, life for people with schizophrenia can carry more hope today than at any time previously. Yet, too often this hope goes unrealized, and the ongoing human toll of schizophrenia remains incalculable.

CRITICAL THINKING QUESTIONS

1. How does the paranoid subtype of schizophrenia differ from other subtypes—disorganized type, catatonic type, and undifferentiated type?

2. If Roger were to suffer from paranoid (delusional) disorder instead of schizophrenia, how would we expect his functioning to be different?
3. What impact has the process of deinstitutionalization had on society? On individuals with severe mental illness?
4. If Roger had the same symptoms, but demonstrated them only after abusing substances, would you still consider this to be schizophrenia? Why or why not? What other diagnoses would you consider?
5. What converging strands of evidence suggest that genetic factors are important in the etiology of schizophrenia?

Dementia of the Alzheimer's Type

W ith a melancholy clarity that emerges only in hindsight, Gertie Sapperstein's two grown daughters now understood their mother's puzzling behaviors over the past several years. They had watched this once intelligent woman gradually become more forgetful and disorganized. Despite their resolve to treat her with gentle patience, they often snapped at her in irritation—she sometimes telephoned twenty times a day, repeatedly asking the same irrelevant questions. And they had more than once been embarrassed by her markedly rude and inappropriate behavior in public, such as the time she caused a scene in a restaurant, demanding to know why the "insolent, disgusting" waiter "will not stop staring at my breasts."

Gertie's family, and others close to her, at first tried to minimize or shrug off these oddities. Her daughters discussed their concerns with each other. Yes, she was becoming forgetful—but don't *all* old people get that way? Yes, she was becoming much more dependent and bothersome—but "imagine how lonely she must be since Dad died." And her behavior in the restaurant certainly crossed the boundaries of socially appropriate behavior—but after all, her vision *was* somewhat impaired, and she had forgotten her bifocals that evening. Perhaps she spoke a private thought a bit too loudly, or perhaps the waiter did look suggestively at her. Or maybe she was just having a "bad day" that would quickly pass.

After a certain point, however, Gertie's odd behaviors and worsening memory became too extreme to rationalize away as "bad days." For Gertie's younger daughter Eleanor, the realization that something was terribly amiss came one evening after her mother telephoned, her voiced filled with terror and panic.

"Eleanor, something awful has happened. You must come immediately [Eleanor lived in another state, several thousand miles away].

"What is it, mother?"

"I can't tell you—he may be listening! I know he's listening."

"What's going on, mother? Tell me . . . ."

"You must get here right away! It's so awful . . . ."

Alarmed, but unable to elicit specific information, Eleanor hung up and called one of her mother's neighbors. The friend volunteered to visit Gertie and found her cowering in a corner of the kitchen. The friend telephoned Eleanor later that evening to explain the crisis. Gertie had returned home from food shopping to discover that somebody had stolen her "prized living room furniture" and replaced it with a "cheap" sofa and chairs. The thief also had taken the family piano! And Gertie was convinced who the thief must be—her brother, "who's always been jealous of me." Afraid to be alone, Gertie agreed to spend the night at the friend's home.

Eleanor could no longer pretend nothing was wrong, or that the changes in her mother over the past few years were simply part of a normal aging process. Gertie Sapperstein had sold the "prized" living room set a decade earlier. Five years before that, she had given the piano to her grandson. And most distressing of all, the accused thief—Eleanor's uncle, Gertie's only brother—had been dead for over forty years.

PSYCHOSOCIAL HISTORY

At the time of the above incident, Gertie Sapperstein was 76 years old and lived by herself in a retirement community in Arizona. She had been a widow for six years, after nearly fifty years of marriage to her husband, Albert. Her two grown daughters (one of whom was married, the other divorced), and five young-adult grandchildren, all lived in other states.

Gertie grew up in New York City's Lower East Side, the child of Russian Jewish immigrants. She had three younger sisters and one younger brother. The family was poor, particularly during the Great Depression in the early 1930s. Gertie met Albert soon after she graduated high school; they married a short time later. They gave birth to their two daughters, Annette and Eleanor, in the years following Albert's return home from World War II.

Through most of her life, Gertie had been a bright, energetic, hard-working woman. When her daughters entered elementary school, she began taking classes at a local university. In her early forties, she earned her bachelor's degree and became an elementary school teacher. She then pursued a master's degree, and within a few years became a school administrator. She worked full-time until her retirement at age 65, when she and Albert relocated to Arizona.

In the past decade, Gertie had experienced many losses. Albert died of a sudden, unexpected heart attack five years after their retirement. One of Gertie's three sisters died months later. Of her two remaining sisters, one had been long estranged from the family, and the other lived overseas. Gertie's best friend of many years, who still lived in the northern community where they had been neighbors, was in poor health.

Still, at first Gertie seemed to have weathered these losses and transitions well enough. She established a new circle of friends in the retirement community. She found many activities to structure her days, including a book club, tennis, and weekly volunteer work at a children's literacy program. Her physical health seemed stable, and she had enough money to live in adequate comfort. She traveled to see each of her daughters' families twice a year, and they also visited her regularly. Gertie said that her attitude toward life had always been to make the most of what you are faced with; to her daughters and other observers, she seemed to live, happily and productively, by this maxim.

It was only in the last two or three years that cognitive changes started affecting Gertie's functioning. At first these changes seemed quite small and hard to recognize as anything out of the ordinary. For example, Gertie started misplacing small items such as housekeys or her purse. She would forget to purchase certain items at the grocery store. Familiar, everyday words slipped from her vocabulary. Often, she would walk into a room to do some chore, then forget what the chore was. She laughed these changes off—who *doesn't* experience such things? But privately, such incidents also worried her: She was not as sharp as she used to be.

Gertie's sense of direction and orientation then started becoming confused. Driving to run errands one day she made a wrong turn and became hopelessly lost, driving for several hours only a few blocks from where she lived, on streets she had traveled many times. A few weeks later, while grocery shopping, she angrily scolded the manager of the store: "Why did you rearrange the shopping aisles? What possessed you to do such a stupid thing?" The manager insisted that no such changes had occurred. It was only after a few moments of tense and confusing conversation that Gertie realized, with great embarrassment, that she was describing a different grocery store, several miles down the road.

Gertie's concentration also became impaired. She could no longer read books, or even newspaper or magazine articles, without losing the thread of the discussion. She stopped attending her book club, then discontinued her volunteer work. She did not let her daughters or friends know the real reason for letting these once-valued activities slip away.

Gertie's emotional stability, which helped see her through her sudden widowhood and other difficult life events, also started fading. She lost her characteristic optimism, her vitality ebbed, and she now often had fits of feeling extremely depressed, or ragefully angry. She became suspicious that others were attempting to humiliate or harass her, like the waiter that evening in the restaurant. She started telephoning her daughters incessantly, forgetting when she had last called or what they discussed. She complained that she missed Albert more than in the first years after he died. Sometimes she completely forgot that he had died and fretted that something must be wrong—why he would stay away from home for so long?

Yet these changes, so dramatic when taken together, happened slowly, bit by bit—allowing those who knew her, and Gertie herself, to convince themselves that nothing major was wrong. This belief was bolstered by the fact that some days she was fine—not quite her old self but able to function without any unusual incident or impairment. Still, the evidence had been slowly but undeniably accruing, over the past several years, that Gertie was suffering from dementia.

CONCEPTUALIZATION

Gertie Sapperstein has Alzheimer's Disease, officially called *dementia of the Alzheimer's type* (DAT) in the DSM-IV (APA, 1994). She meets the key DSM-IV criteria for the disorder (APA, 1994, pp. 142-143):

A. The development of multiple cognitive deficits manifested by both
  1. memory impairment (impaired ability to learn new information or to recall previously learned information)
  2. one (or more) of the following cognitive disturbances:
     a. aphasia (language disturbance)
     b. apraxia (impaired ability to carry out motor activities despite intact motor function)
     c. agnosia (failure to recognize or identify objects despite intact sensory function)
     d. disturbance in executive functioning (i.e., planning, organizing, sequencing, abstracting)
B. The[se] cognitive deficits . . . each cause significant impairment in social or occupational functioning and represent a significant decline from a previous level of functioning.
C. The course is characterized by gradual onset and continuing cognitive decline.

Gertie demonstrates memory failure and disturbances in executive functioning; her deficits cause significant impairment, and the course of her decline appears to be gradual but continual.

DAT is one of several dementias presented in DSM-IV. *Dementia* is a progressive, generalized deterioration of brain functioning that affects multiple cognitive capacities, including communication, memory, judgment, information processing, and motor functioning. Dementia may arise through various causes. It may have its root in medical illness (as is the case, for example, with dementia due to HIV disease or Parkinson's disease), substance abuse (as with substance-induced persisting dementia), repeated CVAs (cerebral vascular accidents, or strokes: vascular dementia), or a combination of factors (dementia due to multiple etiologies).

Gertie's DAT was *late onset* because it developed after the age of 65 (prior to this is *early onset*). A diagnosis of dementia may be further specified based on the predominant presence of *delirium* (an extreme, acute state of cognitive and sensory disorganization), delusions, or depressed mood. If none of these predominate, the dementia is referred to as *uncomplicated*.

It is important to distinguish between Alzheimer's disease, a medical condition, and dementia of the Alzheimer's type, a psychological disorder. It appears that certain individuals may experience the physiological effects of Alzheimer's disease without the grossly debilitating psychological and cognitive impairments of dementia (Snowdon et al., 1997).

TREATMENT

Assessment

The accurate diagnosis of Alzheimer's disease is not an easy task. No definitive test (medical or psychological) can identify with certainty this irreversible dementing illness, short of a post-mortem examination of the brain. And so diagnosing Alzheimer's disease most often involves careful observation over the course of time, along with corollary data from comprehensive medical and psychological evaluations and family history.

Further complicating the diagnostic picture, in its very early stages Alzheimer's disease can be hard to distinguish from the minor, less severe cognitive and memory slippages that sometimes accompany normal aging. And later on, it can be difficult to distinguish from other medical and psychological conditions that can grossly affect cognitive and behavioral functioning, such as major depression, delirium, or dementias caused by another source. Distinguishing among these possibilities is important because they can lead to different paths of treatment.

For example, in older individuals, depression often centers on symptoms of cognitive impairment—memory loss, difficulties with attention, decreased intellectual functioning. These same symptoms may lead observers to think that the depressed person is suffering from Alzheimer's disease or another dementia. In fact, this cluster of symptoms in major depression in the elderly is referred to as *pseudodementia* because it can look very much like dementia. Yet, accurate diagnosis is crucial because if the symptoms represent depression rather than dementia, the person often can find relief with appropriate psychological and psychopharmacological treatment.

An evaluation to determine Gertie's diagnosis was initiated after Eleanor and Annette consulted with their mother's physician. She recommended comprehensive diagnostic testing, including a neurological exam; an EEG (or electroencephalogram), which measures electrical activity in the brain; various laboratory tests; and a CT (or computerized tomography) scan of the brain, which is akin to a sophisticated x-ray that can show areas of damage to brain tissue. Gertie also was referred for neuropsychological testing. This testing can be useful to help provide the differential diagnosis between dementia and depression, and to pinpoint specific areas of cognitive strength and disturbance (such as memory impairment, visual-spatial relations, reasoning, expressive and receptive language use, and coordination). Even though neuropsychological testing cannot offer a definitive diagnosis, even a very brief battery of tests can indicate the presence of dementia (Solomon et al., 1998).

Gertie's physician also asked about the medical history of Gertie's extended family—had anyone else suffered from dementia? Although both Gertie's parents had died years before of coronary illness, in their old age two of her maternal uncles had become "senile" (the global term formerly used for dementias among the elderly). Although this offered no proof of Gertie's diagnosis, it could shed some additional light, as evidence points in the direction of a genetic component to Alzheimer's disease (Breitner et al., 1993).

Based on the results of these tests, along with the description of Gertie's gradual deterioration over the past few years, Gertie's physician arrived at a provisional diagnosis of Alzheimer's disease. A diagnosis is considered *provisional* if it cannot be determined with absolute certainty, due to insufficient evidence.

Course of Illness

At present there is no known treatment to halt or reverse the progressive deterioration of Alzheimer's disease. Still, through a combination of behavioral strategies, common-sense planning, and occasional use of medications to target specific symptoms (including antidepressant, anti-anxiety, and antipsychotic medications), disruption to normal life can be reduced or managed, at least in the earlier stages of the disease. Depending on the extent of a person's decompensation, a variety of possible interventions will make the most sense over the span of the illness. Yet even at best, the course of the illness often poses agonizing choices to the affected person and his or her loved ones.

The first of these decisions, shouldered by Gertie's daughters, was whether they should inform their mother of the diagnosis. After a brief deliberation, Eleanor and Annette agreed with the physician's advice that Gertie be told. Gertie always had valued autonomy. Despite the increasing frequency and severity of her impaired functioning, she was still competent enough to participate in her care and help plan for the difficult decisions that lay ahead. She should know.

Gertie took the news with a steadier emotional reaction than they had anticipated. She admitted that she, like her daughters, had long feared that she might have Alzheimer's disease and had hoped this was not the case. But unlike some other situations in which having accurate knowledge can make coping easier, learning the explanation for her puzzling behaviors brought scant solace. They all knew that the prognosis was grim and the road ahead of them would only grow more difficult.

The next major decision was whether Gertie could continue to live at home unassisted. She certainly did not seem to need—at least not yet—a level of care such as that offered by a nursing home, or other residential facility. But was she safe on her own? Should she continue to drive? What if an emergency arose? Would it be better if she were to live with one of them?

Gertie was at first adamant about not moving from her apartment. She did not want to give up her independence. She did not want to burden her daughters or interfere with their families' lives. And she did not want to admit that she needed so much help.

Reluctantly, Annette and Eleanor acceded to Gertie's wishes to stay home alone. Gertie agreed to stop driving—her now numerous experiences of getting lost, and the deep fear she felt when this occurred, convinced her that venturing out on her own, in her car or perhaps even by foot, was no longer a good idea. She also admitted that the time would inevitably come, perhaps sooner, perhaps later, when she needed additional support, but she was not yet ready to uproot her life.

Gertie hired a young woman (not a trained mental health or medical professional) to come to her home for a few hours, several days a week, to help with chores and errands. With the assistance of a social worker referred by the physician, they devised many household strategies to bolster Gertie's functioning. These included: 1) making a daily list of activities and chores and marking them off after completion; 2) keeping a "log book" by the telephone, so Gertie could write down the times she called her daughters or other people, and make a brief mention of what they spoke about; and 3) setting an alarm clock so Gertie could remember to take the medications she was on for various medical conditions. Because Gertie sometimes awoke in the middle of the night feeling disoriented and frightened, they equipped her apartment with several nightlights, so she would not awaken in complete darkness.

Gertie also began a trial of Tacrine (Cognex), a medication introduced in the mid 1990s for the treatment of dementia. Tacrine improves cognitive functioning in some, but not all, people with DAT (Rabins, 1996). However, it also can cause severe liver difficulties, and individuals on the medication must have their liver functioning monitored on a regular basis. Shortly after beginning Tacrine, Gertie's liver tests indicated that key enzymes were elevated, indicating a risk of serious harm. The medication was immediately discontinued.

Other than her inability to withstand Tacrine, Gertie's treatment plan worked well, at least for ten months or so. But soon one, and then another, hired assistant quit because of Gertie's erratic behavior. The first woman left after Gertie repeatedly accused her (falsely) of stealing old family photos and jewelry. The second left after Gertie strayed away from her in a department store—she had gone to report to the store manager, in a desperate, frightened voice, that the woman with her was plotting to kidnap her. Even more troublesome, however, was that Gertie one day wandered away from home on her own and got lost; an alarmed and angry neighbor called the police when she looked out her living room window and saw this strange older woman eating the flowers in her backyard.

Eleanor and Annette then decided that Gertie could no longer live on her own and convinced Gertie a major change was needed. One possibility was to arrange for live-in help, or at least full daily coverage. However, these options proved too expensive, and Gertie did not like the idea of a stranger moving in with her. After much deliberation, they decided the best option was for her to come live with one of them.

This caused much tension between the daughters: Both wanted to help out and felt committed to taking care of their mother but also worried about the intrusion and difficulty this would represent into their families' lives. Annette worked and Eleanor did not. Annette was divorced and still had children at home; Eleanor was married to Hal, and all but one child had left for college. Neither thought it fair that the other should have to shoulder greater responsibility for their mother.

Still, based on a variety of considerations—each daughter's lifestyle, economic situation, family dynamics, and, pragmatically, room in their houses (Eleanor had a spare room available, Annette did not) the decision was made, with Gertie shrugging her agreement, that she should move to Eleanor's.

This transition was very upsetting for Gertie. Eleanor's family took great care to make her feel wanted and at home. They set up her room with many of her favorite keepsakes and furniture from her home in Arizona. Still, Gertie felt sad, disoriented, and confused in her new surroundings. She did not want to interfere in the family's routines or be seen as a burden, but because she was so lonely and frightened, she also needed a lot of verbal reassurance that she was indeed wanted. It took her a long time to acclimate to her new household. It was painful to need so much help, but she was also aware—too aware—of how her mind was slipping.

The transition also was difficult on Eleanor's family. Despite everyone's best intentions, Gertie's arrival led to a significant strain on Eleanor's marriage and the entire family's life. Eleanor and Hal disagreed about how best to take care of Gertie; they began arguing frequently. Eleanor did not realize the extent to which she would need to alter her own schedule to take care of her mother.

Of great help, however, was Eleanor's contact with the local branch of ADRDA—the Alzheimer's Disease and Related Disorders Association. They offered a support group, a pile of written information and references, a telephone "chat-line," and a list of helpful professional referrals. In addition, Eleanor's teenaged son made use of the Internet to connect with other individuals in similar circumstances, and to keep up-to-date with medical and support information on the ADRDA web page. These attempts to reach out for support helped normalize what Gertie was going through in adjusting to living with her daughter's family and eased the path, at least somewhat, for all involved.

One thing they learned from others with similar experiences was that Gertie might feel most comfortable if she was included in family life in a way that made her feel valued but did not place unreasonable expectations on her. For example, she was given simple specific chores to do, to combat the sense that she was useless or invalid. Gertie enjoyed doing the laundry—in fact, this had become a problem because in her growing dementia she often attempted to launder the same clean clothes over and over, to the frustration of Eleanor. Keeping to a schedule of once daily, Gertie was given the responsibility of doing the family's laundry and was able to do this well.

Over the next two years, Gertie's functioning continued to deteriorate. Her memory got worse. She often forgot where she was. She regularly accused Eleanor, Hal, or their son of rearranging the furniture to taunt her, and even of moving around the clothing in her bureau drawers, even though the family paid great attention to keeping any big changes to an absolute minimum. She then developed the habit of sneaking into the kitchen at night and taking food from the refrigerator or pantry, hiding it in shoeboxes in the bottom of her closet.

As best they could, the family members tried not to react angrily to these events, realizing they arose from fear and confusion, not from malice. And when new behavioral problems came up (which was becoming a daily occurrence), they attempted to find pragmatic, straightforward solutions.

For example, Eleanor wrote out big labels for Gertie's bureau drawers: "Socks," "Undergarments," etc., to help Gertie remember what belonged where. She then put a lock on the doors of the refrigerator and pantry but kept unlocked a cabinet of canned goods, so that Gertie could harmlessly remove and hoard these if she so desired. In general, they attempted to keep family routine as consistent and unchanging as possible. And in case Gertie wandered away from home alone—a behavior that had ceased for a while but was again becoming worrisome—they had a metal medical identification tag made for her wrist, engraved with Gertie's name, Eleanor's address, phone number, and the words "memory impaired."

An important change occurred when a social worker helped the family enroll Gertie in a day program for individuals with dementing illnesses. Four days a week, several hours per day, Gertie could attend a program at a local care facility for the elderly. This provided some structure to her days and gave Eleanor and the rest of the family a much needed break.

The day program offered simple structured activities, mostly in a group format. It did not involve psychotherapy or rehabilitation per se because skills training and other similar behavioral interventions are not of great benefit with people suffering from dementia. However, the program did offer stability, a pleasant environment, and the opportunity for socializing.

Gertie's memory was now quite impaired. After several months of attending the program she was familiar with the surroundings and "vaguely" recognized a few of the staff and other clients, but did not know any of their names. Nor did she believe she was participating in a day program: She insisted that she was attending a professional convention, and spent much of her time asking other clients about their school districts. Her favorite activities at the program were twice-weekly music sessions, when a music therapist came in to play the piano and lead the group in singing old songs. Interestingly, despite Gertie (and the others') memory impairments, most were able to remember the words to songs popular in their childhood, or at least recall the melodies and hum along.

Throughout this time, Gertie's language skills were also slipping. As part of her dementia, she suffered from *aphasia*, or impairment in a person's capacity to use language to communicate. Aphasia can take many forms; with Gertie, it involved forgetting the words for many ordinary objects, and making up words in their place. For example, she began calling her wristwatch a "ticky-winder," her shoes "laceys," her purse a "clamp-it." Further, in a manner similar to how an infant first learns language, she began to overgeneralize certain words, such as calling all types of animals "doggy" and all food "soup."

As this situation steadily worsened, communicating with her became more and more difficult. Those nearest her tried to remain patient. They learned to ask, gently, what she might be trying to communicate—"Do you mean you can't find your wristwatch?" or "Are you trying to tell me your shoes hurt?" Gertie could usually then answer these yes or no questions correctly. Still, talking with her became increasingly vexing, and Gertie, in the moments she seemed aware of her own impairments, would look agitated and despairing. However, such moments of awareness occurred less and less regularly; most of the time, Gertie seemed lost in a world that was impenetrable to others, and likely no more comprehensible to herself.

Gertie's worsening dementia also affected her basic abilities to care for herself. Her ADLs (for "activities of daily living"), such as appropriate bathing and grooming, dressing, and attending to personal hygiene, deteriorated and became increasingly problematic. She looked disheveled and poorly groomed. She no longer wanted to shower and got in tense, angry stand-offs with Eleanor around the need to bathe.

Eventually, taking care of her at home was too much of a burden. Gertie was more and more uncommunicative. She was disoriented much of the time. She developed problems with urinary and bowel incontinence and often soiled herself.

> ## Multiaxial DSM-IV Diagnosis at Current Time
>
> Axis I: Dementia of the Alzheimer's Type, Late Onset, Uncomplicated
>   CONDITION: DETERIORATING
> Axis II: No diagnosis
> Axis III: Alzheimer's Disease
> Axis IV: Multiple stressors secondary to dementia
> Axis V: *Time of Assessment:* 40 (some impairment in reality testing, major
>   global impairments)
>   *Current Time:* 10 (persistent inability to maintain personal hygiene
>   or care for self)

She was becoming medically sick more often, running fevers, losing her balance and falling, growing more frail.

Again with the guidance and assistance of a social worker, Eleanor and Hal arranged for Gertie to move into a residential care facility. All the family members felt a mixture of grief, guilt, and relief at this inevitable turn of events. Eleanor believed that the past few years had been the most difficult of her life—she wondered how she endured the constant stress.

Yet for Gertie herself, this transition seemed far less disruptive than the move to Eleanor and Hal's home several years earlier. The residential facility was clean, homey, and built with the needs of an impaired person in mind. Within a few weeks, to the surprise of others, Gertie seemed to settle relatively comfortably into a simple daily routine.

Gertie's children and grandchildren visited regularly, but their visits tapered off in time. Some members of the family felt it too painful to see her so changed; others thought it unimportant to visit—why bother, since she no longer seemed to recognize them or know their names? Gertie no longer recalled any of her grandchildren. She mistook Eleanor's husband Hal for Albert and chided him for staying away from home for so long. She continued to remember and recognize her daughters but displayed dissatisfaction when she saw them, because they wore make-up ("teenaged girls shouldn't do that!").

It is at this point that we leave Gertie—80 years old, still alive, but psychologically and cognitively unrecognizable as the woman she once was.

DISCUSSION

Alzheimer's Disease is the most common form of dementia among the elderly—and an increasingly prominent, sorrowful presence in our culture. Although estimates vary widely, some researchers speculate that 10 percent of Americans over the age of 65 develop this currently incurable illness (Evans et al., 1989), with the figure perhaps rising to nearly 50 percent for those 85 and older (Fisher and Carstensen, 1990). The impact of the disease is tremendous—personally, socially, and economically, for those affected and those who care for them.

In the absence of a cure, new treatments, or adequate prevention, the future is even more worrisome. Given the continual increase in life expectancies and science's steady progress in vanquishing many other previously fatal infirmities, the prominence of this dementia will likely only increase in the years ahead. Alzheimer's disease has emerged as one of the great medical challenges of the late 20th century.

Alois Alzheimer was a German neuropsychiatrist who excelled at the cutting-edge medical research of his day—high-resolution microscopic study of bodily cells and tissue. With this technology, he was able to link the various clinical syndromes he saw in asylums and hospitals with distinctive patterns of abnormality in brain tissue. In 1907 he correctly identified, in a post-mortem examination, a unique pattern of deterioration from the brain of a woman who had died from dementia. This was the first firm evidence that distinguished dementia from other psychological disorders. The syndrome was named "Alzheimer's" disease in 1910 by Emil Kraepelin—Alzheimer's mentor, and one of the great pioneering schizophrenia researchers (Nuland, 1994).

What Alzheimer discovered in his post-mortem microscopic examination were abnormal patches of dense, darkly-colored brain matter, which came to be known as *senile plaques*. It is now known that these patches are akin to small trash repositories, composed of the wrecked remains of once healthy neurons. In essence, these plaques result from the massive destruction of neurons throughout the brain. The causes of this rampant destruction are still poorly understood, but most likely involve the gradual depletion of the neurotransmitter acetylcholine, along with the buildup of a protein called beta amyloid. This degeneration appears throughout the brain and thus affects a wide array of functions, ranging from complex abilities such as reasoning and social interaction, to language abilities, to memory, and ultimately to the most basic infantile skills of self-care such as bladder and bowel control.

Recent data raise the possibility that this disease process only becomes destructive if a person also experiences cerebral vascular accidents, even very small ones (Snowdon et al., 1997). These "ministrokes" may be so minor that they go unnoticed at the time; however, their far-reaching impact may determine whether or not a person develops confusion, extreme memory loss, and the other manifestations of dementia.

A Typical Course

The specific details of DAT vary from person to person, but a characteristic pattern remains the same. It begins slowly—perhaps with forgetfulness, absentmindedness, a general sense of lethargy, or an unobtrusive withdrawal from social contact. As we saw with Gertie, the person who is affected, as well as close family members or friends, may question whether anything is actually wrong. These symptoms may be difficult to distinguish from changes that sometimes, but not always, accompany typical aging. (In fact, contrary to many popular notions, "normal" aging often proceeds with no significant disruption to cognitive or psychological functioning.)

As the disease progresses, however, it becomes much clearer that something is, indeed, wrong. Again, Gertie's situation is illustrative. Unusual, uncharacteristic, and (frequently) bizarre behaviors and cognitions develop. These often include restless motor activity, such as pacing, wandering, or getting lost; hiding or hoarding food or other items; a marked suspiciousness or distrust of others; and significant memory impairments.

What inevitably follows is a gradual, irreversible downward course. Verbal communication abilities become grossly impaired, both expressively and receptively. Strong emotional responses seem to lose their connection with discernible life events and so lack an understandable rhyme or reason. Control over bodily functions and motor skill diminishes. Losses and lapses of memory become extreme—a person may forget the names or faces of those dearest in the world, including spouses, children, or siblings. The past often blurs with the present, with the person becoming lost in a confusing, timeless world in which memories of different years jangle together.

Eventually, a person succumbs to a withdrawn, near vegetative state. By the time Alzheimer's disease reaches its grim conclusion, a person has typically lost most or all capacity to function intellectually, interpersonally, or with any degree of mastery over his or her body or environment.

Occasionally, people with Alzheimer's become combative or violent, either due to changes in the brain region regulating aggressive behavior, or in helpless response to the unimaginable terror one feels when even small routines in life suddenly become unmanageable and incomprehensible. Yet, even when extreme changes of behavior are not present, at the very least a person undergoes a marked deterioration in socially appropriate behavior, and previous character traits may become much more prominent. An already shy person, for example, may become painfully timid, or a gregarious person inappropriately loud and boisterous. Others experience marked changes of personality, becoming strangers to those who had long been acquainted with them.

Impact on Caregivers

Alzheimer's Disease and other dementing illnesses often have a tremendous impact on caregivers—the spouses, children, grandchildren, and other family members who care for the demented person. Most Alzheimer's patients are cared for at home, for reasons involving both economics and family loyalty (Fisher & Carstensen, 1990; Mace & Rabins, 1991). But providing such care can be extremely difficult. As was the case with Eleanor, Hal, and their son (and to a lesser extent Annette, who continued to help out to the degree she could but shouldered less of the day-to-day burden), caregivers need to adapt to the changing demands of a person who may be argumentative, terrified, oblivious, sexually inappropriate, or increasingly bizarre and uncommunicative. The stress of the situation is often compounded by grief, as the beloved mate or parent gradually ceases to be the person he or she was. Not surprisingly, caregivers are at unusually high risk for depression and often feel that their life has been taking over by caring for the ill person (Cohen & Eisendorfer, 1988; Loos & Bowd, 1997).

Because of the extreme demands placed on family members, participating in some support group or network may be vital in effectively coping with the exhausting responsibility of providing good care (Hebert et al., 1994). Some families are able to arrange for respite care—brief periods when the Alzheimer's patient can be looked after in a residential facility or other environment, to seek some relief from the constant toll of caretaking. For many families, whether or not to institutionalize an ailing elderly member is one of the most stressful life decisions to be faced (Cohen et al., 1993).

Several studies suggest that the negative impact of dementia on family caregivers differs between ethnic groups (Connell & Gibson, 1997; Haley et al., 1996). In particular, caregivers in African-American and Latino families tend to report lower levels of depression and general stress than do white caregivers. These differences seem primarily related to cultural and ethnic factors, including a greater reliance on religion, faith, and prayer in the nonwhite communities and differing assumptions about expectations for family life. It also has been observed that for adolescents in caregiving families, the experience of caring for the demented family member may contain beneficial components along with the stresses, including an increased empathy for older individuals and stronger parent–child relationships (Beach, 1997).

PROGNOSIS

The prognosis for Gertie Sapperstein, as well as for that of other individuals with Alzheimer's disease, is grim. For now, Alzheimer's is a progressive, irreversible, terminal disease.

Typically, the disease works its slow destructive path over the course of approximately eight to ten years. Alzheimer's disease itself is not usually fatal, but it so devastates a person's mind and body that affected individuals usually die by some other illness or infection such as pneumonia, against which they can no longer muster any resistance.

At a one year follow-up after moving to the residential institution, Gertie's physical and mental health had continued to deteriorate. Yet, she sometimes surprised those around her with moments of lucidity and sustained, albeit brief, conversation. For Eleanor and Hal, life had returned somewhat to normal. Their daily routine had gotten much easier, but the sadness of Gertie's condition always seemed to be with them.

Despite the bleak picture, all is not without hope. In the past few years, several medications have been developed to combat the effects of Alzheimer's disease. Currently, among the most promising of these are Tacrine and Donepezil (Aracep). These medications work by increasing the supply of acetylcholine to the brain—yielding further indirect evidence that the depletion of this neurotransmitter plays a key role in Alzheimer's destructive course. At their best, these medications not only improve memory and cognitive functioning but also may reduce many of the emotional, personality, and behavioral abnormalities seen in Alzheimer's patients.

Alas, for now, these medications appear to help only a minority of people with Alzheimer's disease, and Tacrine must be prescribed cautiously because of its potential danger to the liver. And even when these drugs do work, they are only useful during the early stages of the disease, losing their efficacy as the neural deterioration inexorably continues. Still, their recent development is tangible evidence of progress. Many additional medications currently are being investigated, some designed to prevent or delay the onset of dementia in individuals at high-risk, others to stem the course of the disease once it has started (Kumar & Cantillon, 1996). Although much about Alzheimer's disease remains enshrouded in mystery, there also is reason to hope that improved treatments or a cure can soon be found to subdue this increasingly prominent killer.

CRITICAL THINKING QUESTIONS

1. What are some of the factors that complicate making a diagnosis of dementia of the Alzheimer's type?
2. How can Gertie's impairments be distinguished from normative aging processes?
3. Do you think psychotherapy would be of benefit to Gertie? Why or why not? What type of psychotherapy would you recommend?
4. Dementia of the Alzheimer's type can have a tremendous impact on families. What are some ways to address the impact?
5. Can you think of additional creative, practical ways to help Gertie function in daily life?

Attention-Deficit Hyperactivity Disorder

With some trepidation, Michael and Karen Howard scheduled an after-school appointment with Emily Jackson, their daughter Sally's second grade teacher. The week before, they had received the following note:

"Dear Mr. and Mrs. Howard: I'd like to find a time when we can meet to discuss Sally's behavior and academic problems. I believe an evaluation by the school psychologist would be helpful, but first I'd like to hear your views. I hope we can meet soon."

Michael and Karen were dismayed but not altogether surprised by Mrs. Jackson's note. Academic problems, so soon in the school year? It was only October! But they also had received similar reports from Sally's pre-school, kindergarten, and first-grade teachers—reports peppered with words like "flighty," "energetic," "distractible," "active," even "overbearing." Michael uneasily recalled Sally's preschool teacher's end-of-the-year summation: "Sally often gets disorganized at transition times during the day, like snack, circle time, or nap. She has trouble settling down. She's unable to stay seated, and she races from one activity to another. If she can have some one-to-one attention during these moments, she can usually be redirected. Sally also needs help learning to take turns."

The first time Michael read that note, he dismissed the implied concern. Didn't *all* four year olds have trouble taking turns, or settling down? What kind of expectation was that, for a young child to stay seated?

But that was only one problem, among many, that had become worse with age. Sally was not an easy child, not by anyone's definition. Her fidgetiness, stubborn streak, temper, and disobedience had all steadily become more of a problem. What Karen and Michael continually hoped was only "a phase" never seemed to end. Tantrums had long become a daily occurrence. The Howards had grown reluctant to take Sally to the grocery store, or to restaurants, or even to visit good friends.

Still, both Karen and Michael (particularly Michael) were hesitant to admit that anything was seriously wrong. Perhaps Sally was just bored at school, and boredom had bred mischief. Sally was clearly bright, and the Howards hoped that with the right amount of support and challenge, she could learn to settle down and flourish at home and in school.

Mrs. Jackson's note was further evidence that this had not happened. And events at home the day they received the note convinced Michael and Karen that maybe it was time to take action—events that unfortunately seemed run of the mill.

Michael had returned home from work to find Sally and a neighborhood friend riding bicycles in the driveway. Sally greeted him energetically and leaped into his arms. Then she was quickly off, running in circles around the driveway and yelling at her friend to get off her bike NOW! Thirty minutes later the Howards heard a screaming match and watched Sally's friend storm off in a huff.

Before they could react, Sally charged into the kitchen where Karen and Michael were talking. "Hi Mommy! Hi Daddy!" She climbed onto a counter, knocking things askew, and then sent a pile of papers to the floor with her as she tumbled down. "Can I have chocolate milk with dinner?"

After a tense quick look between Karen and Michael, Karen answered with a firm "No." She had set a rule of no chocolate in the evening because she thought it made Sally "too hyper." But what followed, starting halfway through the dinner (even after Michael tried to appease Sally by pouring a glass of chocolate milk) was yet another of Sally's temper tantrums—screaming, crying, fists pounding, and sharp words between Michael and Karen about how best to handle the situation. Hours later, after Sally finally fell asleep, Karen and Michael sat together on their stained and battered living room couch, exhausted, arguing yet again about whether Michael was undermining Karen's authority.

As they met together, Emily Jackson described more of Sally's problematic behavior to the Howards: "She jumps up out of her seat and runs to the window to look at anything that catches her eye . . . she blurts out answers for other children or before she hears the whole question . . . she's frequently talking when she should be working and that just disrupts the entire class . . . she acts very bossy with other children . . . ." The list seemed endless.

Yet, when Mrs. Jackson turned to the topic of a psychological evaluation, Michael expressed misgivings. "I just don't see it as a psychological problem. I mean, I was overly active as a kid, too, and I grew out of it. Plus, if Sally were a boy, would we even be having this conversation? Wouldn't we call it normal?"

Karen started to object, but Mrs. Jackson tactfully interrupted. "She may very well grow out of it, Mr. Howard. But in the meantime, what we have is a bright child who is experiencing both academic and social failures. This can't be good for her self-esteem. It could lead to long-term problems. What we need—what I need—is to figure out what's going on and to develop appropriate strategies to help us help her. That's part of the job of the school psychologist, and that's why I'd like to place the referral."

Both Michael and Karen had read many news stories about attention-deficit/hyperactivity disorder, or ADHD. In prior conversations, Michael had dismissed the diagnosis, telling Karen he saw it as "too trendy—what will they think of next?" But Karen thought it might fit for Sally and asked Mrs. Jackson what she thought.

Mrs. Jackson answered that she did not feel qualified to assess that on her own, but Dr. Winkler, the psychologist, could help determine how best to help Sally. The Howards agreed to a psychological evaluation.

"And just to be clear," Mrs. Jackson added as they were saying goodbye, "I've also seen boys with similar problems—in fact, far more boys than girls—and yes, I refer them to the psychologist, too."

PSYCHOSOCIAL HISTORY

Sally Howard, an only child, was born when her parents were in their late thirties. Michael Howard was a lawyer and Karen worked in sales for a software company. Sally was born after a long but normal labor, but as Karen often joked to friends, "She came out with an attitude." As an infant, Sally was easily distressed and difficult to soothe. For the first few months, she cried for hours almost every evening. She did not seem to enjoy being held, and both Karen and Michael felt their efforts to comfort her were in vain. Sally's crankiness and fussiness soon became a way of life.

Throughout Sally's toddler and pre-school years, Michael and Karen noticed that many of their friends had a much easier time disciplining their children. In playgroups or during family get-togethers, other children generally responded to a firm voice or to mild reprimands, while the Howards often had to take more extreme measures, such as removing Sally from the room in order to prevent a tantrum. Although Karen and Michael could sometimes identify what led to a tantrum, just as often one seemed to come out of the blue. Sally also regularly broke things and could not resist touching items designated as "off-limits." Michael and Karen had to watch her carefully because she often tripped or hurt herself, as if she could not judge her own limitations.

Yet in other ways, Sally was a quick learner. She knew how to count, recite the alphabet, and even read before most of her peers. Her parents valued her intellectual curiosity and enjoyed teaching her new words and concepts. So at least until she started kindergarten, Michael and Karen tried to overlook her unruly behavior and focus instead on her inquisitiveness and enthusiasm. Michael called her "spunky," and Karen (at least outwardly) praised Sally's gumption and animation, even while she complained about the "terrible twos" and the "trying threes."

Medically, Sally had regular physical exams and had no hearing or visual impairments. She had no history of persistent illnesses other than allergies and asthma in preschool. She had previously been on medication for her asthma, but only for one year.

Although Michael was less likely than Karen to express concerns that Sally's behavior was "not normal," he, too, harbored suspicions that her problems ran deeper than simple boisterousness. In many ways, she reminded him of himself. His mother had regarded him as a difficult child. In kinder moments, she referred to him as "prankish." When he felt at his wits' end with Sally, he recalled constant struggles with his parents regarding his behavior, dating back as far as he could remember (such as the time he scribbled red lipstick all over the living room sofa). In school, he had been the class clown. His grades were variable, but his conduct was inevitably rated as poor. Like Sally, he was easily frustrated, often bored in class, accident-prone, and abuzz with energy.

Michael made it through high school with the attentive help of a basketball coach who took a special interest in him. He attended college on a basketball scholarship, and he found he could avoid struggles and failures by loading up on courses which peaked his interest and captivated his otherwise wandering mind. This strategy also served him well in law school. But he never lost his sense of fidgetiness. As an adult he abhorred inactivity and continued to struggle with impatience, forgetfulness, disorganization, and procrastination. He continually frustrated Karen (and his colleagues) with his constant last-minute approach to writing briefs or preparing for trial. All too often, the sheer magnitude of projects overwhelmed him to the point of distraction.

ASSESSMENT

Dr. Winkler, the school psychologist, began his assessment of Sally by meeting with Karen and Michael. He explained that difficulties with disruptive, overly active behavior and poor attentional skills could be symptomatic of various underlying problems. This was why he intended to take a *multimodal* approach to the evaluation. This involved gathering information from several sources, looking at Sally's behavior in different settings, and using several measures to reach a conclusion. Only by such a comprehensive assessment could he discern whether Sally's problems were psychologically based (as in depression or anxiety disorders), indicative of problems with learning or with intellectual functioning, physiological in nature (such as poor vision or hearing), or symptoms of ADHD.

Dr. Winkler asked Karen, Michael, and Mrs. Jackson to complete the Conners Rating Scales (Conners, 1989). These measures are commonly used to rate various problematic behaviors both at home and at school (one rating scale is written specifically for parents and another one for teachers). Because these scales are based on actual observation and scored in comparison to established behavioral norms, they are useful in determining the extent to which a child's behaviors diverge from the average. Dr. Winkler also observed Sally's behavior in the classroom and in individual meetings in his office. He administered to Sally a battery of psychological tests, including the Wechsler Intelligence Scale for Children, 3rd Edition (Wechsler, 1991), to measure IQ and intellectual strengths and weaknesses; achievement tests to measure skills in the areas of reading, spelling, and arithmetic; and projective tests to assess Sally's emotional and psychological functioning.

Dr. Winkler also asked for the Howard's permission to contact Michael's parents by telephone, as they often babysat for Sally in their nearby home. He wanted to obtain *collateral information* from them regarding Sally's behavior in their presence. Lastly, he obtained written permission to speak with Sally's pediatrician, to learn about Sally's medical history and to include her, if necessary, in future treatment decisions.

CONCEPTUALIZATION

Based on the information he gathered during his assessment, Dr. Winkler concluded that Sally did in fact meet criteria for attention-deficit/hyperactivity disorder, combined type. He reached this diagnosis by taking into account three convergent strands of information.

First were classroom observations, where he was particularly struck by Sally's easy distractibility. By itself, this could signify other problems—perhaps cognitive dysfunction, a physical ailment, or another underlying emotional disorder such as anxiety or depression. But second, Sally's intellectual and psychological testing also pointed to ADHD, along with a marked difficulty with mathematics. And third, Sally's psychosocial history indicated that her hyperactive-impulsive and inattentive symptoms emerged some years before and were consistent across many contexts. They were not explained by moments of transition or by external stressors.

The DSM-IV (APA, 1994, pp. 83–85) specifies the following criteria for attention-deficit/hyperactivity disorder (ADHD):

A. Either (1) or (2):

  1. six (or more) of the following symptoms of *inattention* have persisted for at least 6 months to a degree that is maladaptive and inconsistent with developmental level:

Inattention

  a. often fails to give close attention to details or makes careless mistakes in schoolwork, work, or other activities
  b. often has difficulty sustaining attention in tasks or play activities
  c. often does not seem to listen when spoken to directly
  d. often does not follow through on instructions and fails to finish schoolwork, chores, or duties in the workplace (not due to oppositional behavior or failure to understand instructions)
  e. often has difficulty organizing tasks and activities
  f. often avoids, dislikes, or is reluctant to engage in tasks that require sustained mental effort (such as schoolwork or homework)
  g. often loses things necessary for tasks or activities (e.g., toys, school assignments, pencils, books, or tools)
  h. is often easily distracted by extraneous stimuli
  i. is often forgetful in daily activities

  2. six (or more) of the following symptoms of *hyperactivity-impulsivity* have persisted for at least 6 months to a degree that is maladaptive and inconsistent with developmental level:

Hyperactivity

  a. often fidgets with hands or feet or squirms in seat

    b. often leaves seat in classroom or in other situations in which remaining seated is expected

    c. often runs about or climbs excessively in situations in which it is inappropriate (in adolescents or adults, may be limited to subjective feelings of restlessness)

    d. often has difficulty playing or engaging in leisure activities quietly

    e. is often "on the go" or often acts as if "driven by a motor"

    f. often talks excessively

Impulsivity

    a. often blurts out answers before questions have been completed

    b. often has difficulty awaiting turn

    c. often interrupts or intrudes on others (e.g., butts into conversations or games)

B. Some hyperactive-impulsive or inattentive symptoms that caused the impairment were present before age 7 years.

C. Some impairment from the symptoms is present in two or more settings (e.g., at school [or work] and at home).

As usual, the DSM-IV also states that these symptoms must result in clinically significant impairment in social, academic, or occupational functioning.

DSM-IV specifies three subtypes of ADHD, each based on the predominant symptom pattern for the preceding six months. In *ADHD, combined type* (which is the most common among children and adolescents diagnosed with this disorder), six or more symptoms of inattention, and six or more symptoms of hyperactivity-impulsivity, have persisted for at least six months. In *ADHD, predominantly inattentive type*, six or more symptoms of inattention, but fewer than six symptoms of hyperactivity-impulsivity, are present. Conversely, *ADHD, predominantly hyperactive-impulsive type* is diagnosed when there are six or more symptoms of hyperactivity-impulsivity, but fewer than six of inattention.

From his assessment, Dr. Winkler also determined that Sally suffered from mathematics disorder, one of the learning disorders detailed in the DSM-IV. Mathematics disorder has the following criteria (APA, 1994, p. 51):

A. Mathematical ability, as measured by individually administered standardized tests, is substantially below that expected given the person's chronological age, measured intelligence, and age-appropriate education.

B. The disturbance in Criterion A significantly interferes with academic achievement or activities of daily living that require mathematical ability.

When Dr. Winkler shared his findings with the Howards, he also took them by surprise by expressing his strong hunch that Michael, too, had long struggled with ADHD symptoms. Michael at first disagreed, but then realized that his childhood problems with sustained attention, his poor organization skills, distractibility, and forgetfulness had indeed reverberated throughout his adult life.

TREATMENT

Dr. Winkler proposed a *multidisciplinary* approach to Sally's treatment, designed to address comprehensively not only those problems directly related to her ADHD (such as impulsivity and inattention) but also her academic and social problems. He explained that such a treatment approach required a team of treaters, including himself and other mental health professionals, Sally's pediatrician, her teachers, and Karen and Michael themselves.

Sally's treatment included four components: (1) medication, prescribed by her pediatrician; (2) classroom-based interventions, designed by Dr. Winkler and implemented by Mrs. Jackson; (3) remedial education in the area of math; and (4) parent training sessions, offered at a nearby mental health clinic.

Medication

Initially, Michael and Karen balked at the idea of using medication to help Sally. They were aware that the drugs most frequently used to treat ADHD are psychostimulants. The idea seemed counterintuitive and worrisome—weren't stimulants known to cut appetite, interfere with sleep, and potentially lead to drug dependence?

Dr. Winkler was not surprised by the Howards's reservations; these were common parental concerns. He explained that medications such as Ritalin (methylphenidate) and Dexedrine (dextroamphetamine) did in fact stimulate brain functions, but in correct dosage they acted in helpful ways, such as increasing attention and regulating motor control. In effect, by stimulating the brain, many children with ADHD are better able to focus attention and gain control over their activity. These drugs did not cure ADHD, but they could decrease some symptoms and thus increase opportunities for success and accomplishment.

Dr. Winkler informed the Howards that the most common side effects of psychostimulants, appetite suppression and trouble falling asleep, typically decreased quickly over time or could be alleviated by decreasing the dose or adjusting times of administration. And regarding drug dependence, Dr. Winkler assured the Howards that Ritalin was not addictive and that children treated with stimulants seemed no more likely to develop substance abuse problems than children not treated with stimulants (Goldman et al., 1998; Weiss & Hechtman, 1993).

Sally's pediatrician supported the use of Ritalin for Sally after conferring with Dr. Winkler, and Michael and Karen decided to give it a trial run. However, the initial results were not impressive: After one month, Sally's inattentive and impulsive behaviors were essentially unchanged. Although the Howards's first impulse was to discontinue the medication, they agreed instead to try a slightly higher dosage.

With this increase, the Howards and Mrs. Jackson noticed improvements. Sally was less impulsive and distractible in the classroom, more cooperative in her interactions with peers, and more attentive for longer stretches of time. These changes led to more opportunities for pleasant and rewarding moments at school and home. These positive changes did not get past Sally; she told her parents that it was easier to do homework, concentrate, and even play soccer when she took her medicine.

She began asking for her Ritalin on Saturday mornings when she had a soccer game, to help her feel more prepared.

Yet even with these benefits, Sally remained prone to temper tantrums and restlessness in the evenings. Rather than further increasing her medication, Sally's pediatrician, Dr. Winkler, and Michael and Karen agreed that it made sense to focus on the behavioral components of the treatment plan.

Classroom-Based Interventions

Mrs. Jackson worked closely with Dr. Winkler to develop specific behavior management strategies for Sally. She started with some simple classroom changes. She moved Sally's desk near her own and farther away from the distractions of the hallway and windows. On a large bulletin board, using simple words and colorful symbols, she posted the daily schedule and classroom rules and reviewed them carefully with Sally each day. She gave directions in clear and specific language, and she often asked Sally to repeat them afterwards. She found that by dividing more complicated assignments into smaller tasks, Sally's attention was less likely to wander and she was more likely to work to completion. She helped Sally prepare for transition times, like recess or lunch, with gentle warnings and by stating explicitly what tasks needed to be completed. She gave Sally responsibilities, such as handing out assignments and feeding the fish, all with an eye toward improving her sense of productivity, self-worth, and accomplishment.

Additionally, Dr. Winkler emphasized that it was important to provide Sally with direct and immediate feedback about her behavior. He wanted to reduce specific disruptive behaviors, and to reward prosocial behaviors. He and Mrs. Jackson identified two problematic *target behaviors* to change: jumping out of her seat and talking out of turn. Mrs. Jackson began to record the number of times these behaviors occurred each day over the course of one week, and found that Sally was out of her seat without permission an average of 13 times a day and talked out of turn an average of 11 times a day. Dr. Winkler suspected that these frequent interactions between Sally and her teacher inadvertently provided positive reinforcement for Sally's disruptive behavior—in other words, Sally enjoyed Mrs. Jackson's attention, and relied on it to manage her impulsivity.

Dr. Winkler thought it important not only to decrease these frequent disruptions but also to facilitate Sally's capacity for self-monitoring. To reach these goals, Dr. Winkler proposed a *contingency management approach* to treat Sally's targeted classroom behaviors. Contingency management programs are behavior modification strategies implemented in specific settings, such as home or school, and usually monitored by a professional. The aim is to increase desired behaviors and decrease unwanted ones with principles of operant conditioning. This may include token or reward systems for increasing prosocial and academic behavior and *response-cost* programs for reducing disruptive behaviors. In response cost programs, an individual loses a designated reward or privilege for engaging in an unwanted behavior.

The plan was simple in design. Each morning, Sally started off the day with 25 tiddlywinks, to be used as tokens. Any single incident of the two target behaviors cost her one token. At the end of the day, Sally could "buy" items such as special pencils, notebooks, or snacks from the school store with the remaining tokens. Additionally, her parents agreed that a total of 20 tokens bought Sally dinner at her favorite fast-food restaurant.

For three days each week, Mrs. Jackson carefully recorded the target behaviors. She found that after six weeks of the program, the average number of times Sally left her seat dropped to four. The average number of times she talked out of turn decreased to three. Eventually, as these beneficial changes became more routine, the program was expanded to target additional problem areas, such as the completion of assignments. The reward system also grew more complex, with Sally able to save her tokens for bigger rewards, such as a new toy. Moving to weekly rewards and longer-term reinforcers helped to sustain Sally's motivation over longer periods of time.

Remedial Education

Sally's learning disorder in mathematics made her eligible for remedial classes. Three times each week she and a small group of students met with a special education teacher to receive intensive instruction on basic math skills. Some of these other students also had mathematics learning disorders or ADHD; others just needed more help in math than could be offered in a typical classroom.

This remedial instruction helped Sally progress to grade level by year's end. However, she continued to find the concepts difficult to grasp. Treatment of her ADHD symptoms made it easier for Sally to concentrate but did not ameliorate the separate problem of her mathematics learning disorder. Arithmetic homework continued to feel like a chore, as did tests, and she resisted both.

Parent Training

A parent training group at the mental health center provided Michael and Karen with twelve weeks of intensive education about the nature of ADHD, and recommended strategies for managing such problems as Sally's temper tantrums, noncompliance with rules and limits, and aggression toward playmates.

Armed with the knowledge that even without a cure the course of ADHD can be modified, the Howards first made some general changes at home. These changes emphasized the principles of consistency and predictability. The Howards set up consistent routines for waking, bedtime, meals, and homework. In simple language, on a bulletin board by the kitchen table, they posted household rules such as "eat food in the kitchen" and "no jumping on the stairs." They learned to give instructions and commands simply, briefly, and calmly, without distracting wordiness or unnecessary stimulation. They also began to decrease the overall level of stimulation in the house on any given day, such as keeping the TV off except during approved hours, enforcing rules about putting toys and games away, and allowing only one playmate over at a time.

Michael and Karen also learned to look for opportunities to praise Sally, whether for wiping her feet before coming inside or for getting to bed on time. In their efforts to move away from criticizing her, they learned the skill of framing statements in the positive rather than the negative (e.g., saying, "Sally, please *walk* on the stairs" instead of "Stop jumping!").

The parent education group also provided training in the use of behavior modification techniques, similar to what Dr. Winkler and Mrs. Jackson initiated at school. Sally was rewarded at home with tokens for engaging in desirable behaviors and lost tokens for engaging in negative behaviors. For example, Sally received five tokens every time she was able to get through an evening without a tantrum. Well-mannered playdates with friends were also rewarded with five tokens, as was expressing anger or frustration appropriately (i.e., without screaming, hitting, or throwing things, and by using words like "I'm really mad" instead of actions).

Eventually, once the system of rewards and accompanying positive interactions were well established, a response-cost system was introduced so that Sally also was penalized for unwanted behaviors. Michael and Karen chose two particularly disruptive behaviors, Sally's temper tantrums and aggression toward friends, as the behaviors they most strongly wanted to reduce or eliminate. Although Michael and Karen had concerns about acting too harshly, their group leader supported them in taking a firm line on these behaviors. She emphasized the importance of appropriate use of punishment, citing research that suggests that misbehavior may worsen with hyperactive children when there is no immediate consequence for negative behavior (Pfiffner & O'Leary, 1993). Accordingly, the Howards discovered that the loss of tokens went a long way in managing Sally's outbursts.

Taken together, these home-based interventions gave the entire family a greater sense of orderliness in their daily lives. Not only did Sally's behavior improve, but so did the Howards's confidence in their parenting skills. With Sally's hyperactivity no longer defining the family's interactions, all three began experiencing greater pleasure in each others' company.

Karen and Michael also found the group helpful in reducing their own sense of guilt and inadequacy. Listening to others describe similar frustrations with setting limits and containing tantrums eased their fears that they were incapable parents, responsible for Sally's difficulties. But at the same time, they saw how certain behaviors of theirs could exacerbate problems, such as how frequently they offered inconsistent messages (as with the chocolate milk).

Michael found an added relief in the group by talking about his own history of ADHD. Two other parents described a similar experience. Although he chose not to pursue medication for himself, he began reading books on the topic, and devised new strategies to help organize his hectic life.

After the 12-week group ended, the group leader recommended that Michael and Karen continue to attend workshops for parents of children with ADHD and join the local chapter of CH.A.D.D. (Children and Adults with Attention-Deficit Disorder), a national nonprofit organization offering support and access to the latest developments in research and treatment.

DISCUSSION

With what appears to be continually escalating momentum, attention-deficit/hyperactivity disorder has generated an enormous amount of research, public interest, and controversy over the past few decades. Popular books on the topic line the

Multiaxial DSM-IV Diagnosis at This Point in Time

Axis I: Attention-Deficit/Hyperactivity Disorder, Combined Type
              CONDITION: IMPROVED
              Mathematics Disorder
              CONDITION: SOMEWHAT IMPROVED
Axis II: No diagnosis
Axis III: No diagnosis
Axis IV: None
Axis V: *Treatment Onset:* 55 (moderate difficulties in academic and social
              functioning)
              Current Time: 75 (some difficulty in academic and social function-
              ing, but generally functioning pretty well)

shelves of many bookstores. Given the assumed prevalence of the disorder, this level of interest and scholarly activity is not surprising. Estimates vary, but one comprehensive study indicated a prevalence rate of 9% for elementary school-age boys and 3% for girls (Szatmari, Offord & Boyle, 1989).

In many regards, Sally Howard is typical of children with ADHD. Her extreme restlessness, difficulties with concentration, and impulsivity are hallmarks of the disorder. The fact that she had a learning disorder (in her case, mathematics disorder) is also not unusual. Although estimates vary greatly, many children with ADHD also meet criteria for one of the learning disorders (Biederman, Newcorn & Sprich, 1991). There also is substantial comorbidity between ADHD and *conduct disorder,* a childhood and adolescent disorder marked by aggressive or violent behavior and a disregard for societal norms, as well as *oppositional defiant disorder,* a disorder marked by a pattern of defiance, hostility, and oppositionality toward authority (Goldman et al., 1998).

However, Sally is not typical of children with ADHD in one significant way: her gender. Here, too, estimates vary, but most studies suggest the disorder is 3 to 4 times more common among boys than girls.

Theories of Etiology

Theories about the etiology of ADHD fall into two broad categories: biological and environmental. Genetics may be involved, in that first-degree relatives share an elevated risk for the disorder. In one study, 26 of 31 adults with ADHD (84%) had at least one child with ADHD, and 48 out of the 84 children in the study sample (57%) had the disorder (Biederman et al., 1995). Of course, as always in such situations, it can be hard to disentangle the biological from the environmental. However, also supporting a biological influence is the fact that the disorder has a substantially higher concordance rate among monozygotic twins than dizygotic twins (Goodman & Stevenson, 1989; Gillis et al., 1992).

Biological researchers have long speculated that the disorder is caused by structural abnormalities in the central nervous system. The 1960s term *minimal brain dysfunction,* no longer in frequent usage, was invoked to explain the symptoms of the disorder. More recent research suggests that deficits or abnormalities in frontal lobe functioning are associated with ADHD (Lorys-Vernon et al., 1993; Zametkin et al., 1990).

Also in a biological vein, a possible link between diet and hyperactivity has generated a lot of interest. Like Karen Howard, many parents are convinced that chocolate and other sugary foods are the culprits behind delayed bedtimes and a surge of frenetic activity in their children. However, current evidence lends little credence to this hypothesis (Weiss & Hechtman, 1993). This may be an example of an *illusory correlation*, in which two factors appear to be associated or related to each other when they are not. It may also be that in certain situations, associated or contextual factors are the cause of unruliness or commotion, not the sweets themselves. Many childhood social activities involve not just sugar and chocolate but enthusiastic anticipation, disruption in normal routine, and an infectious group or family excitement that can be hard to quell.

But even as current researchers and theorists generally accept a biological basis for ADHD, environmental and familial factors also are understood to influence its development. Parent–child interaction studies have shown that parents are often more controlling, less responsive, and more negative in their interactions with their ADHD sons or daughters than with their other children (Mash & Johnston, 1983; Tallmadge & Barkley, 1983). Even when these children are compliant and cooperative, the parents may have trouble responding positively. It appears that this parenting style is at least in part a consequence of the child's behavior rather than a comment on the parents' personalities, but it can still have an adverse effect (Weiss & Hechtman, 1993). Other researchers have demonstrated improvements in mother–child interactions, and in overall family functioning, once a hyperactive child is treated with Ritalin (Schachar et al., 1987). Yet, even these interactions remain less positive overall than those between these same mothers and their other, non-ADHD children.

Treatment Issues

Contemporary multimodal approaches of treating ADHD reflect the prevailing view that the etiology and course of this disorder are influenced by biological and psychosocial factors. For those children whose problems are limited to attentional deficits, psychostimulant medication by itself may be all that is needed. But for most children with ADHD, a combined approach appears to be more effective than either psychostimulants or behavior therapy alone (Carlson et al., 1992; Gittleman et al., 1980; Pelham & Murphy, 1986; Pelham, 1993). In one study, most children's dose of Ritalin could be reduced by half when a contingency management system was employed in the classroom (Carlson et al., 1992). These same researchers also found that while the medication benefited academic performance, behavior modification was more effective in changing disruptive behavior.

Multimodal treatments also may include more than behavioral interventions and medication. As we saw with Sally, including parents in the treatment can be of great value, as behavior management strategies are most effective when continued outside of the classroom or the therapist's office. Individual therapy for the child also is often useful to address low self-esteem and feelings of inadequacy that frequently accompany ADHD. In clinical practice, the components of multimodal treatment may vary greatly from child to child, or even over time for the same child.

ADHD Beyond Childhood

In the 1970s and 1980s, several studies dispelled the then common assumption that hyperactive children outgrow their symptoms. ADHD is now known not just to be limited to children, but to affect adolescents and adults as well (Barkley et al., 1990; Weiss & Hechtman, 1993).

The outdated notion of "outgrowing" ADHD appears to have been based on the fact that with age, certain symptoms attenuate and so may render the disorder less conspicuous. Further, the symptoms also may be masked by other factors. For example, adolescent problems such as poor school performance, discordant relationships with peers and adults, low self-esteem, or potentially severe discipline problems can take center stage (Mendelson, Johnson & Stewart, 1971; Weiss et al., 1971; Minde, Weiss & Mendelson, 1972). And beyond adolescence and into adulthood, environmental changes can work in a person's favor: Many behaviors required in childhood, such as sitting still, taking turns, and being quiet at someone else's behest, are far less relevant in most adult situations. However, the core features of restlessness, attentional difficulties, and impulsivity often persist beyond childhood, even if diminished in severity.

By adulthood, approximately one-third of children with ADHD are thought to be free of symptoms (Weiss & Hechtman, 1993). An estimated 50% to 66% continued to struggle with at least one disruptive symptom, such as inattention, lack of inhibition, or disorganization. Like Michael Howard, many adults with continuing symptoms of ADHD report chronic feelings of internal restlessness or difficulty with any activities that require sustained mental attention. Weiss and Hechtman (1993) report that as many as 75% or more of children with ADHD continue to experience social adjustment difficulties in adulthood, including impaired peer and family relationships and poor work performance. And severe symptoms persist in a significant subset of adults (perhaps 20%), most often when ADHD interacts with comorbid problems such as antisocial personality disorder, substance abuse disorders, depression, and anxiety disorders, poor coping skills, low self-esteem, or poor family functioning.

Still, the notion of ADHD as an adult disorder is not without controversy, in part due to the dramatic increase in diagnosis over the past few years. For this to be a valid diagnosis in a particular person, there must be clear evidence that he or she suffered from the disorder in childhood (Culbertson & Krull, 1996). But unfortunately, documentation of such evidence rarely exists, and so adult diagnosis is complicated by the need to rely mainly on self-reported retrospective data or the subjective memories of others, both of which are easily subject to unintentional distortion or bias.

The Controversy over Psychostimulant Therapy

An even greater and more widely publicized controversy regarding ADHD is treatment with psychostimulants, especially in childhood. On the one hand, a wealth of studies has indicated that many children with ADHD treated with Ritalin show clear benefit, including improvements in school performance, peer and family relationships, impulse control, motor coordination, and social judgement (Abikoff & Gittelman, 1985; Gittleman-Klein, 1987; Goldman et al., 1998; Rapport et al., 1988; Whalen, 1989; Whalen, Henker & Granger, 1990). Through careful monitoring and dosage adjustments, side effects can be minimized, as was true for Sally.

However, like any medication, Ritalin use is not without risks. One significant side effect is the potential for growth retardation, and data on this topic are somewhat contradictory and inconclusive (Klein & Mannuzza, 1988; Goldman et al., 1998; Satterfield et al., 1979). Because of this concern, prescribing physicians typically closely monitor the growth of children taking Ritalin, particularly those who are on relatively high doses or who have taken the medication for several consecutive years. In such cases, these children are often given "drug holidays." By temporarily going off the medication during summer months, when sustained and focused attention is less crucial, or during the times of adolescent growth spurts, effects on growth can be minimized.

Still, even with controllable side effects and proven efficacy, psychostimulant treatment remains controversial. For one thing, there is widespread concern about overuse. In one study in the late 1980s, six percent of public school elementary children in Baltimore County were being treated with stimulant therapy (Safer & Krager, 1988). Some estimates suggest that 1.3 million children in the United States between the ages of 5 and 14 were regularly taking Ritalin in 1995, with this number having more than doubled since the beginning of the decade (Safer, Zito, & Fine, 1996).

Perhaps Ritalin has been mistakenly perceived by teachers and parents as a panacea for a host of childhood difficulties, ranging from boisterousness to poor grades to unruliness (which may be irritating, but to some degree is developmentally ordinary). In fact, the more relevant issue may not be overprescribing of Ritalin but overdiagnosing ADHD. Since fidgetiness, impulsivity, and inattention can signal a range of underlying problems—as well as reflecting aspects of normal childhood—careful and comprehensive assessment is essential to rule out competing diagnoses, to diagnose any comorbid problems, and to develop problem-specific treatment plans.

It is worth noting that unlike several other controversial diagnoses, disagreements regarding ADHD and psychostimulant treatment are far more pronounced amid the general public than among professionals. ADHD has been (and continues to be) very well researched, and most experts concur that when properly assessed it is a valid and reliable diagnosis, with psychostimulant treatment a demonstrably effective intervention (Goldman et al., 1998)

Still, the Ritalin controversy continues and is but one part of a broader societal issue, with important philosophical and ethical ramifications: To what extent do we want to encourage the treatment of psychological difficulties with medications, even in childhood? Ritalin is not the only psychiatric medication now commonly applied to childhood problems: Prozac and the other SSRIs are increasingly prescribed for children, most often in the context of depression.

In recent years, we have witnessed extraordinary advances in psychopharmacology. This progress seems likely to continue, and we are very possibly entering an era where medications will be available not only to treat psychological disorders but to address unwanted traits or behaviors, enhance moods, and improve a subjective sense of well-being in children and adults (Kramer, 1993; Schwartz, 1991). Already, at least one of the SSRIs, Paxil (or Paroxetine), has been demonstrated to reduce hostile affect and increase sociability in people *with no psychiatric diagnosis* (Knutson et al., 1998). The cultural and ethical implications of these medication breakthroughs may well be enormous: Are we facing a future, not far away, when people with no "disorder" will take some daily pill to give them an increased sense of confidence or productivity at work, at school, in relationships, at sports?

PROGNOSIS

Within a few months of starting treatment, Sally Howard had improved in her functioning at home and at school. Dr. Winkler was optimistic that Michael and Karen could expect these improvements to continue and to fuel further progress.

Sally's prognosis may be regarded as favorable, influenced by several factors. Although she met criteria for a learning disorder in math, she did not have another comorbid condition such as conduct disorder, depression, or an anxiety disorder, all of which may negatively affect prognosis (Culbertson & Krull, 1996). Her aggressive behavior was limited in scope and apparently related to her impulsivity and low tolerance for frustration. She responded well to the treatment plan of medication combined with behavioral interventions. And as her capacity for sustained attention improved, she developed more opportunities for positive social interactions, further enhancing her sense of self-confidence and self-esteem.

Sally's ability to improve was further aided by the participation of key people in her life—her parents, teachers, her pediatrician, and Dr. Winkler. In general, a favorable prognosis is related to strong family support and involvement, as well as the inclusion of school personnel in the treatment plan (Culbertson & Krull, 1996). However, not all teachers have the perseverance and patience of Mrs. Jackson, and not all school districts can provide the helpful resources, such as manageable class sizes, comprehensive assessment, and adequate remedial help, that were available to Sally. In her treatment, these factors made an enormous difference; without them, or Karen and Michael's participation, it is hard to say if Ritalin alone would have made a significant difference.

It may be that Sally will gradually be tapered off her medication within a few years, especially if behavior management plans sustain her improved functioning. However, she also may remain on Ritalin treatment on an ongoing basis, most likely with periodic drug holidays. Whatever the case, Sally, Karen, and Michael will continually need to re-devise effective behavioral strategies to keep pace with her changing developmental needs as she matures. Her symptoms can be expected to ebb and flow over time in intensity and frequency. Sally's ADHD will not simply go away—certainly not for a while, at least. But with appropriate care, it need not run, or ruin, the Howards's lives.

CRITICAL THINKING QUESTIONS

1. In what ways is Sally similar to the "typical" child with ADHD? How is she different?
2. What do you think of the Howards's decision to use Ritalin in Sally's treatment? What are the pros and cons?
3. If Sally behaved appropriately in all situations except school, would you still consider her to have ADHD? What other possible explanations might account for her behavior?
4. What cultural factors, if any, do you think contribute to ADHD?
5. As with Michael Howard, ADHD is now increasingly diagnosed in adults. This has created some controversy, as some psychologists wonder if ADHD is becoming overdiagnosed. What are some benefits or concerns in applying this diagnostic concept to adults?

References

Abel, G. G., Becker, J. V., Cunningham-Rathner, J., Mittleman, M., and Roleau, J. L. 1988. Multiple paraphiliac diagnoses among sex offenders. *Bulletin of the American Academy of Psychiatry and Law, 16, (2)* 153–168.

Abel, G. G., and Osborn, C. 1992. The paraphilias: The extent and nature of sexually deviant and criminal behavior. *Psychiatric Clinics of North America, 15,* 675–687.

Abikoff, H., and Gittleman, R. 1985. The normalizing effects of methylphenidate on the classroom behavior of ADHD children. *Journal of Abnormal Child Psychology, 13(1),* 33–44.

Abraham, K. 1911. Notes on the psychoanalytic investigation and treatment of manic-depressive insanity and allied conditions. In *Selected papers on psycho-analysis* (pp. 137–156). London: Hogarth Press.

Adler, A. 1931/1958. *What life should mean to you* (A. Porter, Ed.). New York: Capricorn.

Adler, G. 1993. The psychotherapy of core borderline psychopathology. *American Journal of Psychotherapy, 47, 2,* 194–205.

Adler, G., and Buie, D. 1979. The misuse of confrontation with borderline patients. *International Journal of Psychoanalytic Psychotherapy, 1,* 109–120.

Akiskal, H. S. 1981. Sub-affective disorders, dysthymic, cyclothymic, and bipolar II disorders in the "borderline" realm. *Psychiatric Clinics of North America, 4, (1)* 25–46.

———. 1989. Validating affective personality types. In L. N. Robins and J. E. Barrett (Eds.), *The validity of psychiatric diagnosis.* New York: Raven Press.

Albee, G. 1980. A competency model must replace the defect model. In L. Bond and J. Rosen (Eds.), *Competence and coping during adulthood.* New York: Harper & Row.

Allen, D. M. 1997. Techniques for reducing therapy-interfering behavior in patients with borderline personalty disorder: Similarities in four diverse treatment paradigms. *Journal of Psychotherapy Practice and Research, 6, 1,* 25–35.

Amato, P. R., and Keith, B. 1991. Parental divorce and the well-being of children: A meta-analysis. *Psychological Bulletin, 110, (1)* 26–46.

American Association for the Advancement of Science. 1998. *Losing ground: Science and engineering graduate education of Black and Hispanic Americans.* Washington, DC: Author.

American Psychiatric Association 1952. *Diagnostic and statistical manual of mental disorders*. Washington, DC: Author.

———. 1968. *Diagnostic and statistical manual of mental disorders* (2nd ed.). Washington, DC: Author.

———. 1980. *Diagnostic and statistical manual of mental disorders* (3rd ed.). Washington, DC: Author.

———. 1994. *Diagnostic and statistical manual of mental disorders* (4th ed.). Washington, DC: Author.

———. 1996. Expert consensus treatment guidelines for bipolar disorder: A guide for patients and families. *Journal of Clinical Psychiatry, 57*, 81–88.

Andersen, A. E. 1990. *Males with eating disorders*. (Eating Disorders Monographs: No. 4) New York: Brunner/Mazel.

Andreasen, N. C. 1985. Posttraumatic stress disorder. In H. I. Kaplan and B. J. Saddock, (Eds.), *Comprehensive textbook of psychiatry* (4th ed.). Baltimore: Williams and Wilkins, pp. 918–924.

Andreoli, A., Gressot, G., Aapro, N., Tricot, L., and Gognalons, M. Y. 1989. Personality disorders as a predictor of outcome. *Journal of Personality Disorders, 3*, 307–320.

Auden, W. H. 1947. *The age of anxiety: A baroque eclogue*. New York: Random House.

Bandura, A. 1986. *Social foundations of thought and action: A social cognitive theory*. Englewood Cliffs, NJ: Prentice-Hall.

Bardenstein, K. K., and McGlashan, T. H. 1988. The natural history of a residentially treated borderline sample: Gender differences. *Journal of Personality Disorders, 2(1)*, 69–83.

Barkin, R. Braun, B. G., and Kluft, R. P. 1986. The dilemma of drug therapy for multiple personality disorder. In B. G. Braun (Ed.), *The treatment of multiple personality disorder*. Washington, DC: American Psychiatric Press, pp. 107–132.

Barkley, R. A., Fischer, M., Edelbrock, C. S., and Smallish, L. 1990. The adolescent outcome of hyperactive children diagnosed by research criteria: I. An 8-year prospective follow-up. *Journal of the American Academy of Child and Adolescent Psychiatry, 29(4)*, 546–557.

Barlow, D. H. 1997. Cognitive-behavior therapy for panic disorder: Current status. *Journal of Clinical Psychiatry, 58 (Suppl. 2)*, 32–37.

Baruch, G. 1997. The manic defense in analysis: The creation of a false narrative. *International Journal of Psychoanalysis, 78 (3)*, 549–559.

Bayer, R. 1981. *Homosexuality and American psychiatry: The politics of diagnosis*. New York: Basic Books.

Beach, D. L. 1997. Family caregiving: The positive impact on adolescent relationships. *Gerontologist, 37(2)*, 233–238.

Beck, A. 1976. *Cognitive therapy and the emotional disorders*. New York: International Universities Press.

Beck, A. T., Rush, J. A., Shaw, B. F., and Emery, G. 1979. *Cognitive therapy of depression*. New York: Guilford.

Bemporad, J. R. 1985. Long-term analytic treatment of depression. In E. E. Beckham and W. R. Leber (Eds.), *Handbook of depression: Treatment, assessment, and research*. Homewood, IL: Dorsey Press , pp. 82–99.

Benjamin, H. 1966. *The transsexual phenomenon*. New York: Julian.

Berrill, K. T. 1992. Anti-gay violence and victimization in the United States: An overview. In G. M. Herek and K. T. Berrill (Eds.), *Hate crimes: Confronting violence against lesbians and gay men*. Newbury Park, CA: Sage.

Best, S. E., Oliveto, A. H., and Kosten, T. R. 1996. Opioid addiction: Recent advances in detoxification and maintenance therapy. *CNS Drugs, 6, 4*, 301–314.

Betcher, R. W., and Pollack, W. S. 1993. *In a time of fallen heroes: The re-creation of masculinity*. New York: Athenaeum.

Beutler, L. E., Machado, P. P. P., and Neufelt, S. A. 1994. Therapist variables. In A. E. Bergin and S. L. Garfield (Eds.), *Handbook of psychotherapy and behavior change* (4th ed). New York: Wiley & Sons, pp. 229–269.

Bickel, W. K., and Amass, L. 1995. Buprenorphine treatment of opioid dependence: A review. *Experimental and Clinical Psychopharmacology, 3, 4,* 477–489.

Biederman, J., Faraone, S. V., Mick, E., Spencer, T., Wilens, T., Kiely, K., Guite, J., Ablon, J. S., Reed, E., and Warburton, R. 1995. High risk for attention deficit hyperactivity disorder among children of parents with childhood onset of the disorder: A pilot study. *The American Journal of Psychiatry, 152(3),* 431–435.

Biederman, J., Newcorn, J., and Sprich, S. 1991. Comorbidity of attention deficit hyperactivity disorder with conduct, depressive, anxiety, and other disorders. *American Journal of Psychiatry, 148(5),* 564–577.

Blanchard, R. 1990. Gender identity disorders in adult men. In R. Blanchard and B. W. Steiner (Eds.), *Clinical management of gender identity disorders in children and adults.* (Clinical Practice, No. 14) 1st Ed. Washington, DC: American Psychiatric Press.

Bliss, E. L. 1984. A symptom profile of patients with multiple personalities, including MMPI. *Journal of Nervous and Mental Disorders, 172(4),* 197–202.

Booth, M. 1998. *Opium: A history*. New York: St. Martin's Press.

Bowen, M. 1978. *Family therapy in clinical practice*. New York: J. Aronson.

Bowlby, J. 1980. *Attachment and loss: Volume II: Loss: Sadness and depression*. New York: Basic Books.

Bradley, S. J., Blanchard, R., Coates, S., Green, R., Levine, S. B., Meyer-Bahlburg, H. F. L., Pauly, I. B., and Zucker, K. J. 1991. Interim report of the DSM-IV subcommittee on gender identity disorders. *Archives of Sexual Behavior, 20(4),* 333–343.

Braun, B. G. 1986. Issues in the psychotherapy of multiple personality. In B.G. Braun (Ed.), *The treatment of multiple personality disorder*. Washington, DC, American Psychiatric Press.

Breitner, J. C. S., Gatz, M., Bergem, A. L. M., Christian, J. C., Mortimer, J. A., McClearn, G. E., Heston, L. L., Welsh, K. A., Anthony, J. C., Folstein, M. F., and Radebaugh, T. S. 1993. Use of twin cohorts for research in Alzheimer's disease. *Neurology, 43(2),* 261–267.

Brewer, D. D., Catalano, R. F., Haggerty, K., Gainey, R. R., and Fleming, C. B. 1998. A meta-analysis of predictors of continued drug use during and after treatment for opiate addiction. *Addiction, 93, 1,* 73–92.

Brom, D., Kleber, R. J., and Defares, P. B. 1989. Brief psychotherapy for posttraumatic stress disorders. *Journal of Consulting and Clinical Psychology, 57, (5)* 607–612.

Brown, D. P., and Fromm, E. 1987. *Hypnosis and behavioral medicine*. Hillsdale, NJ: Lawrence Erlbaum.

Brown, G. R. 1994. Women in relationships with cross-dressing men: A descriptive study from a nonclinical setting. *Archives of Sexual Behavior, 23(5),* 515–530.

Brown, G. R., Wise, T. M., Costa, P. T., Herbst, J. H., Fagan, P. J., and Schmidt, C. W. 1996. Personality characteristics and sexual functioning of 188 cross-dressing men. *Journal of Nervous and Mental Disease, 184(5),* 265–273.

Bruch, H. 1978. *The golden cage: The enigma of anorexia nervosa*. Cambridge, MA: Harvard University Press.

Buckley, P. F. 1998. Substance abuse in schizophrenia: A review. *Journal of Clinical Psychiatry, 59(Suppl. 3),* 26–30.

Burgess, A. W., and Holmstrom, L. L. 1974. Rape trauma syndrome. *American Journal of Psychiatry, 131, (9)* 981–986.

Burr, C. 1996. *A separate creation: The search for the biological origins of sexual orientation*. New York: Hyperion.

Butzlaff, R. L., and Hooley, J M. 1998. Expressed emotion and psychiatric relapse. *Archives of General Psychiatry, 55(6)*, 547–552.

Canino, I. A., and Canino, G. J. 1993. Psychiatric care of Puerto Ricans. In A. C. Gaw, (Ed.), *Culture, ethnicity, and mental illness* Washington, DC: American Psychiatric Press, pp. 467–499.

Carlat, D. J., and Camargo, C. A. Jr., 1991. Review of bulimia nervosa in males. *American Journal of Psychiatry, 148, (7)* 831–843.

Carlat, D. J., Camargo, C. A. Jr., and Herzog, D. B. 1997. Eating disorders in males: A report on 135 patients. *American Journal of Psychiatry, 154, 8,* 1127–1132.

Carlson, C. L., Pelham, W. E. Jr., Milich, R., and Dixon, J. 1992. Single and combined effects of methylphenidate and behavior therapy on the classroom performance of children with attention-deficit hyperactivity disorder. *Journal of Abnormal Child Psychology, 20, (20)* 213–232.

Carpenter, W. T. Jr., and Buchanan, R. W. 1994. Schizophrenia. *New England Journal of Medicine, 330, 10,* 681–690.

Casriel, C., Rockwell, R., and Stepherson, B. 1988. Heroin sniffers: Between two worlds. *Journal of Psychoactive Drugs, 20, (4)* 437–440.

Chappel, J. N. 1993. Long-term recovery from alcoholism. *Psychiatric Clinics of North America, 16, (1)* 177–187.

Clark, D. M. 1986. A cognitive approach to panic. *Behavior Research and Therapy, 24, 4,* 461–470.

Clark, D. M., Salkovskis, P. M., Gelder, M. G. 1988. Tests of a cognitive theory of panic. In I. Hand and H. U. Wittchen (Eds.), *Panic and phobias II*. New York: Springer-Verlag.

Clark, D. M., Salkovskis, P. M., Hackmann, A., Middleton, H., Anastasiades, P., and Gelder, M. 1994. A comparison of cognitive therapy, applied relaxation, and imipramine in the treatment of panic disorder. *British Journal of Psychiatry, 164, (6)* 759–769.

Cloninger, C. R. 1988. Etiologic factors in substance abuse: An adoption study perspective. In R. W. Pickens and D. S. Svikis (Eds.), *Biological vulnerability to drug abuse* (Research monograph No. 89). Rockville, MD: National Institute on Drug Abuse.

Cohen, C. A., Gold, D. P., Shulman, K. I., Wortley, J. T., McDonald, G., and Wargon, M. 1993. Factors determining the decision to institutionalize dementing individuals: A prospective study. *Gerontologist, 33, 6,* 714–720.

Cohen, D., and Eisendorfer, C. 1988. Depression in family members caring for a relative with Alzheimer's Disease. *Journal of the American Geriatric Society, 36, (10)* 885–889.

Cohen, L. S., Friedman, J. M., Jefferson, J. W., Johnson, E. M., and Weiner, M. L. 1994. A reevaluation of risk of in utero exposure to lithium. *Journal of American Medical Association, 271, (2)* 146–150.

Cohen, L. S., Sichel, D. A., Robertson, L. M., Heckscher, E., and Rosenbaum, J. F. 1995. Postpartum prophylaxis for women with bipolar disorder. *American Journal of Psychiatry, 152, (11)* 1641–1645.

Colom, F., Vieta, E., Martinez, A., Jorquera, A., and Gasto, C. 1998. What is the role of psychotherapy in the treatment of bipolar disorder? *Psychotherapy and Psychosomatics, 67(1),* 3–9.

Comas-Diaz, L. 1992. The future of psychotherapy with ethnic minorities. *Psychotherapy, 29, (1)* 88–94.

Connell, C. M., and Gibson, G. D. 1997. Racial, ethnic, and cultural differences in dementia caregiving: Review and analysis. *Gerontologist, 37(3),* 355–364.

Conners, C. K. 1989. *Manual for Conners rating scales (Conners Teacher Rating Scales, Conners Parent Rating Scales)*. North Tonawanda, NY: Multi-Health Systems.

Coons, P. M. 1998. The dissoviative disorders: Rarely considered and underdiagnosed. *Psychiatric Clinics of North America, 21(3)*, 637–648.

———. 1984. The differential diagnosis of multiple personality: A comprehensive review. *Psychiatric Clinics of North America, 7, (1)* 51–67.

———. 1988. Psychophysiologic aspects of multiple personality disorder: A review. *Dissociation, 1*, 47–53.

Coons, P. M., Bowman, E. S., and Milstein, V. 1988 Multiple personality disorder: A clinical investigation of 50 cases. *Journal of Nervous and Mental Disorder, 176, (9)* 519–527.

Couprie, W., Wijdicks, E. F. M., Rooijmans, H. G. M., and van Gijn, J. 1995. Outcome in conversion disorder: A follow-up study. *Journal of Neurology, Neurosurgery and Psychiatry, 58(6)*, 750–752.

Craig, R. 1993. Contemporary trends in substance abuse. *Professional Psychology, 24*, 182–189.

Craske, M. G., and Barlow, D. H. 1993. Panic disorder and agoraphobia. In D. H. Barlow (Ed.), *Clinical handbook of psychological disorders: A step-by-step treatment manual, 2nd edition*. New York: Guilford, pp. 1–47.

Crisp, A. H. 1965. Clinical and therapeutic aspects of anorexia nervosa: Study of 30 cases. *Journal of Psychosomatic Research, 9, (1)* 67–78.

Crowe, R. R., Noyes, R., Pauls, D. L., and Slymen, D. J. 1983. A family study of panic disorder. *Archives of General Psychiatry, 40, (10)* 1065–1069.

Culbertson, F. M. 1997. Depression and gender: An international review. *American Psychologist, 52, 1*, 25–31.

Culbertson, J. L., and Krull, K. R. 1996. Attention deficit hyperactivity disorder. In R. D. Adams, O. A. Parson, J. L. Culbertson, and S. J. Nixon (Eds.), *Neuropsychology for clinical practice: Etiology, assessment, and treatment of common neurological disorders*. 1st Ed. Washington, DC: American Psychological Association Press.

Davidson, L., and McGlashen, T. H. 1997. The varied outcomes of schizophrenia. *Canadian Journal of Psychiatry, 42, 1*, 34–43.

Dean, C., Williams, R. J., and Brockington, I. F. 1989. Is puerperal psychosis the same as bipolar manic-depressive disorder? A family study. *Psychological Medicine, 19, (3)* 637–647.

Dickey, R., and Steiner, B. W. 1990. Hormone treatment and surgery. In R. Blanchard and B. W. Steiner (Eds.), *Clinical management of gender identity disorders in children and adults*. Washington, DC: American Psychiatric Press.

Dworkin, R. H. 1990. Patterns of sex differences in negative symptoms and social functioning consistent with separate dimensions of schizophrenic psychopathology. *American Journal of Psychiatry, 147, (3)* 347–349.

Elkin, I., Shea, M. T., Watkins, J. T., Imber, S. D., Sotsky, S. M., Collins, J. F., Glass, D. R., Pilkonis, P. A., Leber, W. R., Docherty, J. P., Fiester, S. J., and Parloff, M. B. 1989. National Institute of Mental Health treatment of depression collaborative research program: General effectiveness of treatments. *Archives of General Psychiatry, 46, (11)* 971–983.

Evans, D. A., Funkerstein, H. H., Albert, M. S., Scherr, P. A., Cook, N. R., Chown, M. J., Hebert, L. E., Hennekens, C. H., and Taylor, J. O. 1989. Prevalence of Alzheimer's disease in a community of older persons: Higher than previously reported. *Journal of American Medical Association, 262, (18)* 2551–2556.

Everill, J. T., and Waller, G. 1995. Reported sexual abuse and eating psychopathology: A review of the evidence for a causal link. *International Journal of Eating Disorders, 18, 1*, 1–11.

Fairbairn, W. R. D. 1944/1952. Endopsychic structure considered in terms of object-relationships. In, *An object-relations theory of personality*. New York: Basic Books.

Fairburn, C. G., and Beglin, S. J. 1990. Studies of the epidemiology of bulimia nervosa. *American Journal of Psychiatry, 147, (4)* 401–408.

Fairburn, C. G., Jones, R., Peveler, R. C., Hope, R. A., and O'Connor, M. 1993. Psychotherapy and bulimia nervosa: Longer-term effects of interpersonal psychotherapy, behavior therapy, and cognitive behavior therapy. *Archives of General Psychiatry, 50, (6)* 419–428.

Fallon, P., Katzman, M. A., and Wooley, S. C. (Eds.). 1994. *Feminist perspectives on eating disorders*. New York: Guilford.

Fenichel, O. 1945. *The psychoanalytic theory of neuroses*. New York: Norton.

Fischer, P. J., and Breakey, W. R. 1991. The epidemiology of alcohol, drug, and mental disorders among homeless persons. *American Psychologist, 46, (11)* 1115–1128.

Fisher, J. E., and Carstensen, L. L. 1990. Behavior management for the dementias. *Clinical Psychology Review, 10,* 611–630.

Foa, E. B. 1997. Psychological processes related to recovery from a trauma and an effective treatment for PTSD. In Yehuda, R., McFarlane, A. C. et al. (Eds.), *Psychobiology of posttraumatic stress disorder*. New York: New York Academy of Sciences, pp. 410–424.

Foa, E. B., and Steketee, G. 1989. Behavioral/cognitive conceptualization of post-trauatic stress disorder. *Behavior Therapy, 20, (2)* 155–176.

Folks, D. G., Ford, C. V., and Regan, W. M. 1984. Conversion symptoms in a general hospital. *Psychosomatics, 25, (4)* 285–295.

Frankenburg, F. R. 1994. History of the development of antipsychotic medication. *Psychiatric Clinics of North America, 17(3),* 531–40.

Frankl, V. 1959/1946. *Man's search for meaning*. Boston: Beacon Press.

Freeman, C. 1998. Drug treatment for bulimia nervosa. *Neuropsychobiology, 37(2),* 72–79.

Freeman, T. 1971. Observations on mania. *International Journal of Psychoanalysis, 52,* 479–486.

Freud, S. 1917/1957. Mourning and melancholia. *Standard Edition* (Vol. 14, pp. 243–258). London: Hogarth Press.

Garfield, S. L., and Bergin, A. E. 1994. Introduction and historical overview. In A. E. Bergin and S. L. Garfield (Eds.), *Handbook of psychotherapy and behavior change* (4th ed). New York: Wiley & Sons, pp. 3–18.

Garner, D. M., Garfinkel, P. E., Schwartz, D. M., and Thompson, M. M. 1980. Cultural expectations of thinness in women. *Psychological Reports, 47, (2)* 483–491.

Garner, D. M., and Rosen, L. W. 1991. Eating disorders in athletes: Research and recommendations. *Journal of Applied Sports Research, 5,* 100–107.

Garrison, V. 1977. The "Puerto Rican syndrome" in psychiatry and *espiritismo*. In V. Crapanzano and V. Garrison (Eds.) *Case studies in spirit possession*. New York: Wiley, pp. 383–449.

Gershon, E. S. 1990. Genetics. In F. K. Goodwin and K. R. Jamison (Eds.), *Manic-depressive illness*. New York: Oxford University Press.

Gibson, D. 1990. Borderline personality disorder issues of etiology and gender. *Occupational Therapy in Mental Health, 10, 4,* 63–77.

Gillis, J. J., Gilger, J. W., Pennington, B. F., and DeFries, J. C. 1992. Attention deficit disorder in reading-disabled twins: Evidence for a genetic etiology. *Journal of Abnormal Child Psychology, 20, (3)* 303–315.

Gittelman, R., Abikoff, H., Pollack, E., Klein, D., Katz, F., and Mattes, J. 1980. A controlled trial of behavior modification and methylphenidate in hyperactive children. In C. Whalen and B. Henker (Eds.), *Hyperactive children: The social ecology of identification and treatment*. New York: Academic Press.

Gittelman-Klein, R., and Klein, D. F. 1973. School phobia: Diagnostic considerations in the light of imipramine effects. *Journal of Nervous and Mental Disease, 156, (3)* 199–215.

Gittelman-Klein, R. 1987. Pharmacotherapy of childhood hyperactivity: An update. In H. Y. Meltzer (Ed.), *Psychopharmacology: The third generation of progress*. New York: Raven Press.

Klein, R. G., and Mannuzza, S. 1988. Hyperactive boys almost grown up: III. Methylphenidate effects on ultimate height. *Archives of General Psychiatry, 45, (12)* 1131–1134.

Glazer, W. M. 1996. The impact of managed care systems on relapse prevention and quality of life for patients with schizophrenia. *European Neuropsychopharmacology, 6 (Suppl. 2)*, S35–39.

Glazer, W. M., and Dickson, R. A. 1998. Clozapine reduces violence and persistent aggression in schizophrenia. *Journal of Clinical Psychiatry, 59 (Suppl. 3)*, 8–14.

Goldman, L.S., Genel, M., Bezman, R. J., and Slanetz, P. J. 1998. Diagnosis and treatment of attention-deficit/hyperactivity disorder in children and adolescents. *Journal of the American Medical Association, 279(14)*, 1100–1107.

Goldstein, A. J., and Chambless, D. L. 1978. A re-analysis of agoraphobia. *Behavior Therapy*, 9, 47–59.

Gonsiorek, J. C. 1991. The empirical basis for the demise of the illness model of homosexuality. In J. C. Gonsiorek and J. D. Weinrich (Eds.), *Homosexuality: Research implications for public policy*. Newbury Park, CA: Sage.

———. 1995. Gay male identities: Concepts and issues. In A. R. D'Augelli and C. J. Patterson (Eds.), *Lesbian, gay, and bisexual identities over the lifespan: Psychological perspectives*. New York: Oxford University Press.

Goodman, R., and Stevenson, J. 1989. A twin study of hyperactivity: I. An examination of hyperactivity scores and categories derived from Rutter Teacher and Parent Questionnaires. II. The etiological role of genes, family relationships, and perinatal adversity. *Journal of Child Psychology and Psychiatry, 30*, 671–710.

Goodwin, G. M., and Jamison, K. R. 1990. *Manic-depressive illness*. New York: Oxford University Press.

Gorton, G., and Ahktar, S. 1990. The literature on personality disorders, 1985–1988: Trends, issues, and controversies. *Hospital and Community Psychiatry, 41, (1)* 39–51.

Goskin, L. O., Lazzarini, Z., Jones, T. S., and Flaherty, K. 1997. Prevention of HIV/AIDS and other blood-borne diseases among injection drug users: A national survey on the regulation of syringes and needles. *Journal of the American Medical Association, 277, (1)* 53–62.

Gottesman, I. I. 1991. *Schizophrenia genesis: The origins of madness*. New York: W. H. Freeman and Co.

Green, R. 1987. *The "sissy boy" syndrome and the development of homosexuality*. New Haven: Yale University Press.

Greene, B. A. 1985. Considerations in the treatment of black patients by white therapists. *Psychotherapy, 22(2S)*, 389–93.

Gregoire, A. 1992. New treatments for erectile impotence. *British Journal of Psychiatry, 160*, 315–326.

Guggenheim, F. G., and Smith, G. R. 1995. Somatoform disorders. In H. I. Kaplan and B. J. Saddock (Eds.), *Comprehensive textbook of psychiatry: 6th edition*. Baltimore: Williams & Wilkins.

Gunderson, J. G. 1994. Building structure for the borderline construct. *Acta Psychiatrica Scandinavica, 89 (Suppl 379)*, 12–18.

Gunderson, J. G., Ronningstam, E. F., and Bodkin, A. 1990. The diagnostic interview for narcissistic patients. *Archives of General Psychiatry, 47, (7)* 676–680.

Haley, W. E., Roth, D. L., Coleton, M. I., Ford, G. R., West, C. A., Collins, R. P., and Isoba, T. L., 1996. Appraisal, coping, and social support as mediators of well-being in black and white family caregivers of patients with Alzheimer's disease. *Journal of Consulting and Clinical Psychology, 64 (1)*, 121–129.

Hartmann, H. 1950/1964. Comments on the psychoanalytic theory of the ego. In *Essays on ego psychology*. New York: International Universities Press, pp. 113–141.

Hartnoll, R. L. 1994. Opiates: Prevalence and demographic factors. *Addiction, 89, 11*, 1377–1383.

Harvey, M. R. 1996. An ecological view of psychological trauma and trauma recovery. *Journal of Traumatic Stress, 9, 1, 3–23.*

Hawton, K., Catalan, J., and Fagg, J. 1992. Sex therapy for erectile dysfunction: Characteristics of couples, treatment outcomes, and prognostic factors. *Archives of Sexual Behavior, 21(2)*, 161–172.

Hebert, R., Leclerc, G., Bravo, G., and Girouard, G. 1994. Efficacy of a support group programme for caregivers of demented patients in the community: A randomized control trial. *Archives of Gerontology and Geriatrics, 18, 1–14.*

Heiman, J. R., and Lo Piccolo, J. 1988. *Becoming orgasmic: A sexual and personal growth program for women.* New York: Prentice-Hall.

Herek, G. M. 1995. Psychological heterosexism in the United States. In A. R. D'Augelli and C. J. Patterson (Eds.), *Lesbian, gay, and bisexual identities over the lifespan: Psychological perspectives.* New York: Oxford University Press.

Herman, J. L. 1992. *Trauma and recovery.* New York: Basic Books.

Herman, J. L., Perry, J. C., and van der Kolk, B. A. 1989. Childhood trauma in borderline personality disorder. *American Journal of Psychiatry, 146, (4) 490–995.*

Hollon, S. D., Shelton, R. C., and Davis, D. D. 1993. Cognitive therapy for depression: Conceptual issues and clinical efficacy. *Journal of Consulting and Clinical Psychology, 61(2)*, 270–275.

Hooker, E. 1957. The adjustment of the male overt homosexual. *Journal of Projective Techniques, 21*, 18–30.

Horney, K. 1950. *The neurotic personality of our time.* New York: Norton.

Horowitz, M. 1976. *Stress response syndromes.* New York: Jason Aronson.

Hser, Y. I., Anglin, D., and Powers, K. 1993. A 24-year follow-up of California narcotic addicts. *Archives of General Psychiatry, 50*, 577–584.

Institute of Medicine 1985. Research on mental illness and addictive disorders: Progress and prospects. A report of the board on mental health and behavioral medicine. *American Journal of Psychiatry, 142, (7 Suppl.)*, 1–41.

Jacobsen, E. 1938. *Progressive relaxation.* Chicago: University of Chicago Press.

Jamison, K. R. 1993. *Touched with fire: Manic depressive illness and temperament.* New York: Free Press.

Janoff-Bulman, R. 1992. *Shattered assumptions: Toward a new psychology of trauma.* New York: Free Press.

Jefferson, J. W. 1997. Antidepressants in panic disorder. *Journal of Clinical Psychiatry, 58(Suppl 2)*, 20–25.

Jenkins, S. Y. 1996. Psychotherapy and black female conflicts. *Women and Therapy, 18, 1*, 59–74.

Johnson, B. 1994. Food, bodies, and growing up female: Childhood lessons about culture, race, and class. In P. Fallon, M. A. Katzman, and S. C. Wooley (Eds.), *Feminist perspectives on eating disorders.* New York: Guilford.

Jordan, J. V., Kaplan, A. G., Miller, J. B., Stiver, I. P., and Surrey, J. L. 1991. *Women's growth in connection: Writings from the Stone Center.* New York: Guilford.

Josephs, L. 1994. Psychoanalytic and related interpretations. In B. B. Wolman and G. Stricker (Eds.), *Anxiety and related disorders: A handbook.* New York: Wiley.

Kabat-Zinn, J., Massion, A. O., Kristseller, J., Peterson, L. G., Fletcher, K. E., Pbert, L., Lenderking, W. R., and Santorelli, S. F. 1992. Effectiveness of a meditation-based stress reduction program in the treatment of anxiety disorders. *American Journal of Psychiatry, 149,* 936–942.

Kafka, M. P. 1994. Sertraline pharmacotherapy for paraphilias and paraphilia-related disorders: An open trial. *Annals of Clinical Psychiatry, 6, (3)* 189–195.

Kagan, J., and Zentner, M. 1996. Early childhood predictors of adult psychopathology. *Harvard Review of Psychiatry, 3, (6),* 341–350.

Kaplan, E. H., Khoshnood, K., and Heimer, R. 1994. A decline in HIV-infected needles returned to New Haven's needle exchange program: Client shift or needle exchange? *American Journal of Public Health, 84, (12),* 1991–1994.

Kaplan, H. S. 1974. *The new sex therapy: Active treatment of sexual dysfunctions.* New York: Brunner/Mazel.

Kass, F., Spitzer, R. L., and Williams, J. B. W. 1983. An empirical study of the issue of sex bias in the diagnostic criteria of DSM-III Axis II personality disorders. *American Psychologist, 38, (7)* 799–803.

Katon, W. 1993. Somatization disorder, hypochondriasis, and conversion disorder. In D. Dunner (Ed)., *Current psychiatric therapy.* Philadelphia: Saunders.

Katzman, M. A., and Lee, S. 1997. Beyond body image: The integration of feminist and transcultural theories in the understanding of self-starvation. *International Journal of Eating Disorders, 22, (4),* 385–394.

Katzman, M. A., Wolchik, S. A., and Braver, S. 1984. The prevalence of bulimia nervosa and binge eating in a college sample. *International Journal of Eating Disorders, 3(3),* 53–61.

Keane, T. M., Fairbank, C. L., Caddell, J. M., Zimering, R. T., and Bender, M. E. 1985. A behavioral approach to assessing and treating post-traumatic stress disorder in Vietnam veterans. In C. R. Figley (Ed.), *Trauma and its wake: The study and treatment of posttraumatic stress disorder.* New York: Brunner/Mazel, Psychosocial Stress, Vol 4 Vol I.

Keel, P. K., and Mitchell, J. E. 1997. Outcome in bulimia nervosa. *American Journal of Psychiatry, 154, (3)* 313–321.

Kendall, R. E., Chalmers, J. C., and Platz, C. 1987. Epidemiology of puerperal psychoses. *British Journal of Psychiatry, 150,* 662–673.

Kendler, K. S., MacLean, C., Neale, M., Kessler, R. C., Heath, A., and Eaves, L. 1991. The genetic epidemiology of bulimia nervosa. *American Journal of Psychiatry, 148, (12)* 1627–1637.

Kent, D. A., Tomasson, K., and Coryell, W. 1995. Course and outcome of conversion and somatization disorders: A four-year follow-up. *Psychosomatics, 36(2),* 138–144.

Kernberg, O. F. 1984. *Severe personality disorders: Psychotherapeutic strategies.* New Haven: Yale University Press.

———. 1975. *Borderline conditions and pathological narcissism.* (Master Work Series) New York: Jason Aronson.

———. 1980. *Internal world and external reality: Object relations theory applied.* New York: Jason Aronson.

Kernberg, P. F. 1997. Developmental aspects of normal and pathological narcissism. In E. F. Ronningstam (Ed.), *Disorders of narcissism: Diagnostic, clinical, and empirical implications.* Washington, DC: American Psychiatric Press, pp. 103–120.

Kessler, R. C., McGonagle, K. A., Zhao, S., Nelson, C. B., Hughes, M., Eshleman, S., Wittchen, H., and Kendler, K. S. 1994. Lifetime and 12-month prevalence of DSM-III-

R psychiatric disorders in the United States: Results from the National Comorbidity Survey. *Archives of General Psychiatry, 51, (1)* 8–19.

Kilpatrick, D. G., and Best, C. L. 1992. *Rape in America: A report to the nation.* Arlington, VA: National Victim Center.

Klein, M. 1964. *Contributions to psychoanalysis.* New York: McGraw-Hill.

———. 1940/1948. Mourning and its relation to manic-depressive states. In *Contributions to psycho-analysis, 1921–1945.* London: Hogarth Press, pp. 311–338.

Kleinman, A. 1988. *Rethinking psychiatry: From cultural category to personal experience.* New York: Free Press.

Klerman, G. L., Weissman, M. M., Rounsaville, B. J., and Chevron, E. S. 1984. *Interpersonal psychotherapy of depression.* New York: Basic Books.

Klerman, G. L., Hirschfeld, R. M. A., Weissman, M. M., Pelicier, Y., Ballenger, J. C., Costa e Silva, J. A., Judd, L. L., and Keller, M. B. (Eds.). 1993. *Panic anxiety and its treatments: Report of the World Psychiatric Association Presential Educational Program Task Force.* Washington DC: American Psychiatric Press.

Klerman, G. L., Weissman, M. M., Ouellette, R., Johnson, J., and Greenwald, S. 1991. Panic attacks in the community: Social morbidity and health care utilization. *Journal of the American Medical Association, 265, (6)* 742–746.

Klinger, R. L., and Stein, T. S. 1996. Impact of violence, childhood sexual abuse, and domestic violence and abuse on lesbians, bisexuals, and gay men. In (R. P. Cabaj and T. S. Stein, Eds.), *Textbook of homosexuality and mental health* Washington DC: American Psychiatric Press, pp. 801–818.

Kluft, R. P. 1996. Dissociative identity disorder. In (L. K. Michelson and W. J. Ray, Eds.), *Handbook of dissociation: Theoretical, empirical, and clinical perspectives.* New York: Plenum, pp. 337–366.

Knight, R. 1953. Borderline states. *Bulletin of the Menninger Clinic, 17,* 1–12.

Knutson, B., Wolkowitz, O. M., Cole, S. W., Chan, T., Moore, E. A., Johnson, R. C., Terpstra, J., Turner, R. A., and Reus, V. I. 1998. Selective alteration of personality and social behavior by serotonergic intervention. *American Journal of Psychiatry, 155 (3)*, 373–379.

Koegel, P., Burnam, M. A., and Farr, R. K. 1990. Subsistence adaptation among homeless adults in the inner city of Los Angeles. *Journal of Social Issues, 46(4)*, 83–107.

Kog, E., and Vandereycken, W. 1989. The speculations: An overview of theories about eating disorder families. In W. Vandereycken, E. Kog, and J. Vanderlind (Eds.), *The family approach to eating disorders: Assessment and treatment of anorexia nervosa and bulimia.* New York: PMA, pp. 7–24.

Kohut, H. 1971. *The analysis of the self: A systematic approach to the psychoanalytic treatment of narcissistic personality disorders.* New York: International Universities Press.

———. 1977. *The restoration of the self.* New York: International Universities Press.

Kraft-Ebing, R. von. 1902. *Psychopathia sexualis.* Brooklyn: Physicians and Surgeons Books.

Kramer, P. D. 1993. *Listening to prozac.* New York: Viking.

Kreisman, G. J., and Straus, H. 1989. *I hate you, don't leave me.* Los Angeles: Body press.

Kroll, J., Carey, K., Sines, L., and Roth, M. 1982. Are there borderlines in Britain? A crossvalidation of U.S. findings. *Archives of General Psychiatry, 39, (1)* 60–63.

Krull, F., and Schifferdecker, M. 1990. Inpatient treatment of conversion disorder: A clinical investigation of outcome. *Psychotherapy and Psychosomatics, 53,* (1–4) 161–165.

Kulka, R. A., Schlenger, W. E., Fairbank, J. A., Hough, R. L., Jordan, B. K., Marmar, C. R., and Weiss, D. S. 1990. *Trauma and the Vietnam War generation: Report of findings from the National Vietnam Veterans Readjustment Study.* New York: Brunner/Mazel.

Kumar, V., and Cantillon, M. 1996. Update on the development of medication for memory and cognition in Alzheimer's disease. *Psychiatric Annals, 26(5)*, 280–284.

Lambert, M. J., and Bergin, A. E. 1994. The effectiveness of psychotherapy. In A. E. Bergin and S. L. Garfield (Eds.), *Handbook of psychotherapy and behavior change* (4th ed). New York: Wiley and Sons, pp. 143–189.

Lang, P. J. 1979. Presidential address, 1978. A bioinformational theory of emotional imagery. *Psychophysiology, 16, (6)* 495–512.

Lasch, C. 1978. *The culture of narcissism.* New York: Norton.

Leibenluft, E. 1996. Women with bipolar illness: Clinical and research issues. *American Journal of Psychiatry, 153, (2)* 163–173.

Lewine, R. R. 1981. Sex differences in schizophrenia: Timing or subtypes? *Psychological Bulletin, 90, (3)* 432–444.

Lewinsohn, P. M. 1974. A behavioral approach to depression. In R. J. Friedman and M. M. Katz (Eds.), *The psychology of depression: Contemporary theory and research.* New York: Wiley, pp. 157–185.

Lifton, R. J. 1980. The concept of the survivor. In J. E. Dimsdale (Ed.), *Survivors, victims, and perpetrators: Essays on the Nazi holocaust.* Washington, DC: Hemisphere.

Lilenfeld, L. R., Kaye, W. H., Greeno, C. G., Merikangas, K. R., Plotnicov, K., Pollice, C., Rao, R., Strober, M., Bulik, C. M., and Nagy, L. 1997. Psychiatric disorders in women with bulimia nervosa and their first degree relatives: Effects of comorbid substance abuse. *International Journal of Eating Disorders, 22,* 253–264.

Linehan, M. M. 1993. *Cognitive-behavioral treatment of borderline personality disorder: The dialectics of effective treatment.* New York: Guilford.

Linet, O. I., and Ogrinc, F. G. 1996. Efficacy and safety of intracavernosal Alprostadil in men with erectile dysfunction. *New England Journal of Medicine, 334, (14)* 873–877.

Links, P. S., Heslegrave, R., and van Reekum, R. 1998. Prospective follow-up study of borderline personality disorder: Prognosis, prediction outcome, and Axis II comorbidity. *Canadian Journal of Psychiatry, 43(3),* 265–270.

Livesley, W. J., and Jackson, D. N. 1991. Construct validity and classification of personality disorders. In J. Oldham (Ed.), *Personality disorders: New perspectives on diagnostic validity.* Washington, DC: American Psychiatric Press.

Livesley, W. J., and Schroeder, M. L. 1990. Dimensions of personality disorder: The DSM-III-R cluster A diagnoses. *Journal of Nervous and Mental Disease, 178, 10,* 627–635.

Lo Piccolo, J. 1992. Postmodern sex therapy for erectile failure. In R. Rosen and S. Leiblum (Eds.), *Erectile disorders: Assessment and treatment.* New York: Guilford.

Loftus, E. F. 1993. The reality of repressed memories. *American Psychologist, 48,* 518–537.

Loos, C., and Bowd, A. 1997. Caregivers of persons with Alzheimer's disease: Some neglected implications of the experience of personal loss and grief. *Death Studies, 21(5),* 501–514.

Loranger, A. W., Oldham, J. M., and Tulis, E. H. 1982. Familial transmission of DSM-III borderline personality disorder. *Archives of General Psychiatry, 39, (7)* 795–799.

Lorys-Vernon, A. R., Hynd, G. W., Lyytinen, J., and Hern, K. 1993. Etiology of attention-deficit/hyperactivity disorder. In J. L. Matson (Ed.), *Handbook of hyperactivity in children* Boston: Allyn and Bacon, pp. 47–65.

Mace, N. L., and Rabins, P. V. 1991. *The 36-hour day: A family guide to caring for persons with Alzheimer's disease, related dementing illness, and memory loss in later life.* Baltimore: Johns Hopkins Press.

Mahler, M., Bergman, A., and Pine, F. 1975. *The psychological birth of the human infant: Symbiosis and individuation.* New York: Basic Books.

Maj, J. 1992. Clinical prediction of response to lithium prophylaxis in bipolar patients: A critical update. *Lithium, 3,* 15–21.

Marchand, A., Goyer, L. R., Dupuis, G., and Mainguy, N. 1998. Personality disorders and the outcome of treatment of panic disorder with agoraphobia. *Canadian Journal of Behavioral Science, 30, 1,* 14–23.

Marcus, R. N., and Katz, J. L. 1990. Inpatient care of the substance-abusing patient with a concomitant eating disorder. *Hospital and Community Psychiatry, 41, (1)* 59–63.

Marder, S. R. 1998. Facilitating compliance with antipsychotic medication. *Journal of Clinical Psychiatry, 59 (Suppl. 3),* 21–25.

Marks, M. N., Wieck, A., Checkley, S. A., and Kumar, R. 1992. Contribution of psychological and social factors to psychotic and non-psychotic relapse after childbirth in women with previous histories of affective disorder. *Journal of Affective Disorders, 24, (4)* 253–263.

Mash, E. J., and Johnston, C. 1983. Parental perceptions of child behavior problems, parenting self-esteem, and mothers' reported stress in younger and older hyperactive and normal children. *Journal of Consulting and Clinical Psychology, 52(1),* 86–99.

Masters, W., and Johnson, V. 1970. *Human sexual inadequacy.* Boston: Little Brown.

Masters, W., Johnson, V., and Kolodny, R. 1994. *Heterosexuality.* New York: Harper Collins.

Masterson, J. F. 1976. *Psychotherapy of the borderline adult: A developmental approach.* New York: Brunner/Mazel.

McCann, I. L., Sakheim, D. K., and Abrahamson, D. J. 1988. Trauma and victimization: A model of psychological adaptation. *Counseling Psychologist, 16,* 531–594.

McFarlane, A. C. 1988. The longitudinal course of posttraumatic morbidity: The range of outcomes and their predictors. *Journal of Nervous and Mental Diseases, 176, (1)* 30–39.
———. 1994. Individual psychotherapy for post-traumatic stress disorder. *Psychiatric Clinics of North America, 17(2),* 393–408.

McGlashen, T. H. 1986. The Chestnut Lodge follow-up study: III. Long-term outcome of borderline personalities. *Archives of General Psychiatry, 43, (1)* 20–30.

McGrath, E., Keita, G. P., Strickland, B. R., and Russo, N. F. (Eds.). 1990. *Women and depression: Risk factors and treatment issues (Final report of the American Psychological Association's national task force on women and depression).* Washington, DC: American Psychological Association.

McLellan, A. T., Arndt, I. O., Metzger, D. S., Woody, G. E., and O'Brien, C. P. 1993. The effects of psychosocial services in substance abuse treatment. *Journal of the American Medical Association, 269, (15)* 1953–1959.

McLellan, A. T., Grossman, D. S., Blaine, J. D., and Haverkos, H. W. 1993. Acupuncture treatment for drug use: A technical review. *Journal of Substance Abuse Treatment, 10, 6,* 569–576.

Mead, G. H. 1934. *Mind, self, and society.* Chicago: University of Chicago Press.

Mendelson, W. B., Johnson, N. E., and Stewart, M. A. 1971. Hyperactive children as teenagers: A follow-up study. *Journal of Nervous and Mental Disease, 153, (4)* 273–279.

Meyer, R. G., and Deitsch, S. E. 1996. *The clinician's handbook: Integrated diagnostics, assessment, and intervention in adult and adolescent psychopathology.* Boston: Allyn and Bacon.

Michelson, L., June, K., Vives, A., Testa, S. and Marchione, N. 1998. The role of trauma and dissociation in cognitive-behavioral psychotherapy outcome and maintenance for panic disorder with agoraphobia. *Behavior Research and Therapy, 36(11),* 1011–1050.

Michelson, L. K., and Marchione, K. 1991. Behavioral, cognitive, and pharmacological treatments of panic disorder with agoraphobia: Critique and synthesis. *Journal of Consulting and Clinical Psychology, 59,* 100–114.

Miklowitz, D. J., Goldstein, M. J., Nuechterlein, K. S., Snyder, K. S., and Mintz, J. 1988. Family factors and bipolar depression. *Archives of General Psychiatry, 45, (3)* 225–231.

Miller, A. 1981. *The drama of the gifted child.* New York: Basic Books.

Millet, K. 1990. *The looney-bin trip.* New York: Simon and Schuster.

Millon, T. 1997. DSM narcissistic personality disorder. In E. F. Ronningstam (Ed.), *Disorders of narcissism: Diagnostic, clinical, and empirical implications.* Washington, DC: American Psychiatric Press, pp. 75–101.

Minde, K., Weiss, G., and Mendelson, N. 1972. A 5-year follow-up of 91 hyperactive school children. *Journal of the American Academy of Child Psychiatry, 11, (3)* 595–610.

Minuchin, S., Rosman, B. L., and Baker, L. 1978. *Psychosomatic families: Anorexia nervosa in context.* Cambridge MA: Harvard University Press.

Mischel, W. 1968. *Personality and assessment.* New York: Wiley.

Mohr, D., and Beutler, L. 1990. Erectile dysfunction: A review of diagnostic and treatment procedures. *Clinical Psychology Review, 10,* 123–150.

Moolchan, E. T., and Hoffman, J. A. 1994. Phases of treatment: A practical approach to methadon maintenance treatment. *International Journal of Addictions, 151,* 165–168.

Morey, L. C., and Jones, J. K. 1997. Empirical studies of the construct validity of narcissistic personality disorder. In E. F. Ronningstam (Ed.), *Disorders of narcissism: Diagnostic, clinical, and empirical implications.* Washington, DC: American Psychiatric Press, pp. 351–374.

Morgentaler, A. 1993. *The male body: A physician's guide to what every man should know about his sexual health.* New York: Simon and Schuster.

Morrissey, J. P. 1989. The charging role of the public mental health hospital. In (D. A. Rochefort, Ed.), *Handbook on mental health policy in the United States.* New York: Greenwood, pp. 311–338.

Mowrer, O. H. 1960. *Learning theory and behavior.* New York: Wiley.

Najavits, L. M., and Gunderson, J. G. 1995. Better than expected: Improvements in borderline personality disorder in a 3-year prospective outcome study. *Comprehensive Psychiatry, 36, 4,* 296–302.

Nolen-Hoeksema, S. 1990. *Sex differences in depression.* Stanford, CA: Stanford University Press.

North, C. S., Ryall, J. M., Ricci, D. A., and Wetzel, R. D. 1993. *Multiple personalities, multiple disorders: Psychiatric classification and media influence.* (Oxford monographs on psychiatry, no. 1) New York: Oxford University Press.

Norton, G. R., Dorward, J., and Cox, B. J. 1986. Factors associated with panic attacks in nonclinical subjects. *Behavior Therapy, 17,* 239–252.

Nuechterlein, K. L., Dawson, M. E., Gitlin, M., Ventura, J., Goldstein, M. J., Snyder, K. S., Yee, C. M., and Mintz, J. 1992. Developmental processes in schizophrenic disorders: Longitudinal studies of vulnerability and stress. *Schizophrenia Bulletin, 18(3),* 387–425.

Nuland, S. B. 1994. *How we die: Reflections on life's final chapter.* New York: Knopf.

Office of National Drug Control Policy. 1996. Treatment protocol efectiveness study: A white paper of the Office of the National Drug Control Policy. *Journal of Substance Abuse Treatment, 13, 4,* 295–319.

Olivardia, R., Pope, H. G. Jr., Mangweth, B., and Hudson, J. I. 1995. Eating disorders in college men. *American Journal of Psychiatry, 152, 9,* 1279–1285.

Paris, J. 1997. Antisocial and borderline personality disorders: Two separate diagnoses or two aspects of the same psychopathology? *Comprehensive Psychiatry, 38, 4,* 237–242.

Parsons, T. 1951. *The social system.* Glencoe, IL: Free Press.

Pelham, W. E. 1993. Pharmacotherapy for children with attention-deficit hyperactivity disorder. *School Psychology Review, 22,* 199–227.

Pelham, W. E., and Murphy, H. A. 1986. Behavioral and pharmacological treatment of attention deficit and conduct disorders. In M. Hersen (Ed.), *Pharmacological and behavioral treatment: An integrative approach.* New York: John Wiley, pp. 108–148.

Penn, D. L., and Mueser, K. T. 1996. Research update on the psychosocial treatment of schizophrenia. *American Journal of Psychiatry, 153, (5)* 607–617.

240   References

Perlberg, M. April 1979. Adapted from trauma at Tenerife: The psychic aftershocks of a jet disaster. *Human Behavior*, 49–50.

Perlick, D., and Silverstein, B. 1994. Faces of female discontent: Depression, disordered eating, and changing gender roles. In (P. Fallon, M. A. Katzman, and S. C. Wooley (Eds.) *Feminist perspectives on eating disorders*. New York: Guilford, pp. 77–93.

Perna, G., Caldirola, D., Arancio, C., and Bellodi, L. 1997. Panic attacks: A twin study. *Psychiatry Research*, 66, 1, 69–71.

Pfiffner, L. J., and O'Leary, S. G. 1993. School-based psychological treatments. In J. L. Matson (Ed.), *Handbook of hyperactivity in children*. Boston: Allyn and Bacon, pp. 234–255.

Pine, F. 1990. The four psychologies of psychoanalysis. In *Drive, ego, object, and self: A synthesis for clinical work*. New York: Basic Books, pp. 22–41.

Pollack, M. H., and Otto, M. W. 1997. Long-term course and outcome of panic disorder. *Journal of Clinical Psychiatry*, 58 (Suppl 2), 57–60.

Pollack, W. S. 1988. Borderline personality disorder: Psychotherapy. In A. S. Bellack and M. Hersen (Eds.), *Handbook of comparative treatments for adult disorders*. New York: Wiley.

Pope, H. G. Jr., Hudson, J. I., Jonas, J. M., and Yurgelon-Todd, D. 1983. Bulimia treated with imipramine: A placebo-controlled double-blind study. *American Journal of Psychiatry*, 140, (5) 554–558.

Post, R. M. 1992. Transduction of psychosocial stress into the neurobiology of recurrent affective disorder. *American Journal of Psychiatry*, 149, (8) 999–1010.

Powis, B., Griffiths, P., Gossop, M., and Strang J. 1996. The differences between male and female drug users: Community samples of heroin and cocaine users compared. *Substance Use and Misuse*, 31, 5, 529–543.

Prochaska, J. O., DiClemente, C. C., and Norcross, J. C. 1992. In search of how people change: Applications to addictive behaviors. *American Psychologist*, 47, 9, 1102–1114.

Putnam, F. W. 1988. The switch process in multiple personality disorder and other state-change disorders. *Dissociation*, 1, 24–32.

———. 1989. *Diagnosis and treatment of multiple personality disorder*. New York: The Guilford Press.

Putnam, F. W., Guroff, J. J., Silberman, E. K., Barban, L., and Post, R. M. 1986. The clinical phenomenology of multiple personality disorder: Review of 100 recent cases. *Journal of Clinical Psychiatry*, 47, (6) 285–293.

Putnam, F. W., and Post, R. M. 1988. Multiple personality disorder: An analysis and review of the syndrome. Unpublished manuscript, cited in F.W. Putnam (1989), *Diagnosis and Treatment of Multiple Personality Disorder*. New York: The Guilford Press.

Rabins, P. V. 1996. Developing treatment guidelines for Alzheimer's disease and other dementias. *Journal of Clinical Psychiatry*, 57 (Suppl. 14), 37–38.

Rapport, M. D., Stoner, G., DuPaul, G. J., Kelly, K. L., Tucker, S. B., and Schoeler, T. 1988. Attention deficit disorder and methylphenidate: A multilevel analysis of dose-response effects on children's impulsivity across settings. *Journal of the American Academy of Child and Adolescent Psychiatry*, 27, (1) 60–69.

Rawson, R. A., Obert, J. L., McCann, M. J., and Marinelli-Casey, P. 1993. Relapse prevention strategies in outpatient substance abuse treatment. *Psychology of Addictive Behaviors*, 7, 2, 85–95.

Rehm, L. P. 1984. Self-management therapy for depression. *Advances in Behavior Therapy and Research*, 6, 83–98.

Reid, S. 1998. Suicide in schizophrenia: A review. *Journal of Mental Health—United Kingdom*, 7(4), 345–353.

Regier, D. A., Farmer, M. E., Raye, D. S., Locke, B. Z., Keith, S. J., Judd, L. L., and Goodwin, R. K. 1990. Comorbidity of mental disorders with drug and alcohol abuse: Results from the Epidemiologic Catchment Area program. *Journal of the American Medical Association*, 264, (19) 2511–2518.

Rice, J., Reich, T., Andreasen, N. C., Endicott, J., Van Eerdewegh, M., Fishman, R., Hirschfeld, R. M. A., and Klerman, G. L. 1987. The familial transmission of bipolar illness. *Archives of General Psychiatry, 44, (5)* 441–447.

Riet, G. T., Kleijnen, J., and Knipschild, P. 1990. A meta-analysis of studies into the effect of acupuncture on addiction. *British Journal of General Practice, 40, (338)* 379–382.

Rimm, D. C., and Somervill, J. W. 1977. *Abnormal psychology*. New York: Academic Press.

Rivera-Arzola, M., and Ramos-Grenier, J. 1997. Anger, ataques de nervios, and la mujer puertorriquena: Sociocultural considerations and treatment implications. In J. G. Garcia, M. C. Zea, et al. (Eds.), *Psychological interventions and research with Latino populations*. Boston: Allyn and Bacon, pp. 125–141.

Robins, R. L., and Regier, D. A. (Eds). 1991. *Psychiatric disorders in America: The epidemiologic catchment area study*. New York: Free Press.

Ronis, D. L., Bates, E. W., Garfein, A. J., Buit, B. K., Falcon, S. P., and Liberzon, I. 1996. Longtitudinal patterns of care for patients with posttraumatic stress disorder. *Journal of Traumatic Stress, 9(4)*, 763–781.

Ronningstam, E. F. 1997. Narcissistic personality disorder and pathological narcissism: Long-term stability and presence in Axis I disorders. In E. F. Ronningstam (Ed.), *Disorders of narcissism: Diagnostic, clinical, and empirical implications*. Washington, DC: American Psychiatric Press, pp. 375–414.

Rosen, R., and Leiblum, S. 1992. Erectile disorders: An overview of historical trends and clinical perspectives. In R. Rosen and S. Leiblum (Eds.), *Erectile disorders: Assessment and treatment*. New York: Guilford.

Rosenthal, R., and Rosnow, R. L. 1984. *Essentials of behavioral research: Methods and data analyses*. New York: McGraw-Hill.

Ross, C. A. 1989. *Multiple personality disorder: Diagnosis, clinical features, and treatment*. New York, Wiley.

———. 1997. *Dissociative identity disorder: Diagnosis, clinical features, and treatment of multiple personality (second edition)*. New York: Wiley and sons.

Ross, J. L. 1977. Anorexia nervosa: An overview. *Bulletin of the Menninger Clinic, 41, (5)* 418–436.

Rossi, P. H. 1990. The old homeless and the new homelessness in historical perspective. *American Psychologist, 45, (8)* 954–959.

Rothbaum, B. O., and Foa, E. B. 1996. Cognitive-behavioral therapy for posttraumatic stress disorder. In B. A. van der Kolk, A. C. McFarlane, et al. (Eds.), *Traumatic stress: The effects of overwhelming experience on mind, body, and society*. New York: Guilford, pp. 491–509.

Roy-Byrne, P. P., Geraci, M., and Uhde, T. W. 1986. Life events and the onset of panic disorder. *American Journal of Psychiatry, 143*, 1424–1427.

Rubonis, A. V., and Bickman, L. 1991. Psychological impairment in the wake of disaster: The disaster-psychopathology relationship. *Psychological Bulletin, 109, (3)* 384–399.

Rupp, A., and Keith, S. J. 1993. The costs of schizophrenia: Assessing the burden. *Psychiatric Clinics of North America, (2)* 413–423.

Russell, D. E. H. 1986. *The secret trauma: Incest in the lives of girls and women*. New York: Basic Books.

Sabo, A. N. 1997. Etiological significance of associations between childhood trauma and borderline personality disorder: Conceptual and clinical implications. *Journal of Personality Disorders, 11, 1*, 50–70.

Safer, D. J., and Krager, J. M. 1988. A survey of medication treatment for hyperactive/inattentive students. *Journal of the American Medical Association, 260, (15)* 2256–2259.

Safer, D. J., Zito, J. M., and Fine, E. M. 1996. Increased methylphenidate usage for attention-deficit hyperactivity disorder in the 1990s. *Pediatrics, 98*, 1084–1088.

Satterfield, J. H., Cantwell, D. P., Schell, A., and Blaschke, T. 1979. Growth of hyperactive children treated with methylphenidate. *Archives of General Psychiatry, 36, (2)* 212–217.

Schachar, R., Taylor, E., Wieselberg, M., Thorley, G., and Rutter, M. 1987. Changes in family functioning and relationships in children who respond to methylphenidate. *Journal of the Academy of Child and Adolescent Psychiatry, 26,* 728–732.

Schilling, R. F., Schinke, S. P., and El-Bassel, N. 1993. Substance abuse. In A. S. Bellack and M. Hersen (Eds.), *Psychopathology in adulthood.* Boston: Allyn and Bacon.

Schmidt, C. 1995. Sexual psychopathology and DSM-IV. In J. Oldham and M. Riba (Eds.), *Review of psychiatry.* Washington DC: American Psychiatric Press.

Schneider, K. 1959. *Clinical psychopathology.* New York: Grune and Stratton. Translated by M. W. Hamilton.

Schoenbaum, E. E., Hartel, D. M., and Gourevitch, M. N. 1996. Needle exchange use among a cohort of injecting drug users. *AIDS, 10, 14,* 1729–1734.

Schoenewolf, G. 1996. The persistence of the belief that madness is hereditary. *Journal of Contemporary Psychotherapy, 26, 4,* 379–390.

Schuckit, M. 1995. *Drug and alcohol abuse: A clinical guide to diagnosis and treatment* (4th ed.). New York: Plenum Medical Books.

Schwartz, R. S. 1991. Mood brighteners, affect tolerance, and the blues. *Psychiatry, 54, (4)* 397–403.

Scott, J. E., and Dixon, L. B. 1995. Psychological interventions for schizophrenia. *Schizophrenia Bulletin, 21, 4,* 621–630.

Seivewright, N., and Daly, C. 1997. Personality disorder and drug use: A review. *Drug and Alcohol Review, 16, 3,* 235–250.

Shalev, A. Y., Bonne, O., and Eth, S. 1996. Treatment of posttraumatic stress disorder: A review. *Psychosomatic Medicine, 58(2),* 165–182.

Shea, M. T., Elkin, I., Imber, S. D., Sotsky, S. M., Watkins, J.T., Collins, J. F., Pilkonis, P. A., Beckham, E., Glass, D. R., Dolan, R. T., and Parloff, M. B. 1992. Course of depressive symptoms over follow-up: Findings from the National Institute of Mental Health Treatment of Depression Collaborative Research Program. *Archives of General Psychiatry, 49, (10)* 782–787.

Shear, M. K. 1996. Factors in the etiology and pathogenesis of panic disorder: Revisiting the attachment-separation paradigm. *American Journal of Psychiatry, 153 (7 Suppl.),* 125–136.

Shearin, E. N., and Linehan, M. M. 1994. Dialectical behavior therapy for borderline personality disorder: Theoretical and empirical foundations. *Acta Psychiatrica Scandinavica, 89 (Suppl 379),* 61–68.

Sheehan, D. V., and Harnett-Sheehan, K. 1996. The role of SSRIs in panic disorder. *Journal of Clinical Psychiatry, 57 (Suppl 10),* 51–60.

Shisslak, C. M., Crago, M., and Estes, L. S. 1995. The spectrum of eating disturbances. *International Journal of Eating Disorders, 18, 3,* 209–219.

Shore, J. H., Tatum, E. L., and Vollmer, W. M. 1986. Psychiatric reactions to disaster: The Mount Saint Helen's Experience. *American Journal of Psychiatry, 143, (5)* 590–595.

Snowdon, D. A., Greiner, L. H., Mortimer, J. A., Riley, K. P., Greiner, P. A., and Markesbery, W. R. 1997. Brain infarction and the clinical expression of Alzheimer's disease. *Journal of the American Medical Association, 277, 10,* 813–817.

Sobell, L. C., Sobell, M. B., Toncatto, T., and Leo, G. I. 1993. What triggers the resolution of alcohol problems without treatment? *Alcohol: Clinical and Experimental Research, 17,* 217–224.

Solomon, P. R., Hirschoff, A., Kelly, B., Relin, M., Brush, M., DeVeaux, R. D., and Pendlebury, W. W. 1998. A 7-minute neurocognitive screening battery highly sensitive to Alzheimer's disease. *Archives of Neurology, 55, (3)* 349–355.

Spector, I. P., and Carey, M. P. 1990. Incidence and prevalence of the sexual dysfunctions: A critical review of the empirical literature. *Archives of Sexual Behavior, 19,4,* 389–408.

Steele, R. E. 1978. Relationship of race, sex, social class, and social mobility to depression in normal adults. *Journal of Social Psychology, 104,* 37–47.

Steiner-Adair, C. 1986. The body politic: Normal female adolescent development and development of eating disorders. *Journal of the American Academy of Psychoanalysis, 1,* 95–114.

Stermac, L. 1990. Clinical management of nontranssexual patients. In R. Blanchard and B. W. Steiner (Eds.), *Clinical management of gender identity disorders in children and adults.* Washington DC: American Psychiatric Press.

Stern, A. 1938. Psychoanalytic investigation of and therapy in the borderline group of neuroses. *Psychoanalytic Quarterly, 7,* 467–489.

Stiver, I. 1988. Developmental psychopathology: Introducing a consultant in the treatment of borderline patients. *McLean Hospital Journal, 13,* 89–113.

Stoller, R. J. 1968. *Sex and gender: On the development of masculinity and femininity.* Science House: New York.

Stone, M. 1980. *The borderline syndromes.* New York: McGraw-Hill.

Stone, M. H., Hurt, S. W., and Stone, D. K. 1987. The PI 500: Long-term follow-up of borderline inpatients meeting DSM-III criteria: I. Global Outcome. *Journal of Personality Disorders, 1,* 291–298.

Strober, M., and Humphrey, L. L. 1987. Familial contributions to the etiology and course of anorexia nervosa and bulimia. *Journal of Consulting and Clinical Psychology, 55, (5)* 654–659.

Sue, S., Zane, N., and Young, K. 1994. Research on psychotherapy with culturally diverse populations. In A. E. Bergin and S. L. Garfield (Eds.), *Handbook of psychotherapy and behavior change* (4th ed). New York: Wiley & Sons, pp. 783–817.

Sullivan, P. F., Bulik, C. M., and Kendler, K. S. 1998. The epidemiology and classification of bulimia nervosa. *Psychological Medicine, 28(3),* 599–610.

Suppes, T., Baldessarini, R. J., Faedda, G. L., and Tohen, M. 1991. Risk of recurrence following discontinuation of lithium treatment in bipolar disorder. *Archives of General Psychiatry, 48, (12)* 1082–1088.

Szatmari, P., Offord, D. R., and Boyle, M. H. 1989. Ontario child health study: Prevalence of attention deficit disorder with hyperactivity. *Journal of Child Psychology and Psychiatry, 30,* 219–230.

Tallmadge, J., and Barkley, R. A. 1983. The interactions of hyperactive and normal boys with their mothers and fathers. *Journal of Abnormal Child Psychology, 11, (4)* 565–579.

Terr, L. 1990. *Too scared to cry: Psychic trauma in childhood.* Grand Rapids, MI: Harper and Row.

Thorpe, G. L., and Hecker, J. E. 1991. Psychosocial aspects of panic disorder. In J. R. Walker, G. R. Norton, and C. A. Ross (Eds.), *Panic disorder and agoraphobia: A comprehensive guide for the practitioner.* Pacific Grove, CA: Brooks/Cole.

Torem, M. S. 1996. Psychopharmacology. In (L. K. Michelson and W. J. Ray, Eds.), *Handbook of dissociation: Theoretical, empirical, and clinical perspectives.* New York: Plenum, pp. 545–568.

Torgerson, S. 1983. Genetic factors in anxiety disorders. *Archives of General Psychiatry, 40, (10)* 1085–1089.

Torrey, E. F. 1997. *Out of the shadows: Confronting America's mental illness crisis.* New York: Wiley and Sons.

Torrey, E. F., Bower, A. E., Taylor, E. H., and Gottesman, I. I. 1994. *Schizophrenia and manic-depressive disorder: The biological roots of mental illness revealed by the landmark study of identical twins.* New York: Basic Books.

Tran, P. V., Hamilton, S. H., Kuntz, A. J., Potvin, J. H., Andersen, S. W., Beasley, C. Jr., and Tollefson, G. D. 1997. Double-blind comparison of olanzapine versus risperidone in the treatment of schizophrenia and other psychotic disorders. *Journal of Clinical Psychopharmacology, 17, 5,* 407–418.

Travin, S., and Protter, B. 1993. *Sexual perversions: Integrative treatment approaches for the clinician.* New York: Plenum.

Ursano, R. J., Boydstun, J. A., and Wheatley, R. D. 1981. Psychiatric illness in U.S. Air Force Vietnam prisoners of war: A five-year follow up. *American Journal of Psychiatry, 138, (3)* 310–314.

van Boemel, G. B., and Rozee, P. D. 1992. Treatment for psychosomatic blindness among Cambodian refugee women. *Women and Therapy, 13(3),* 239–266.

Vaughn, C. E., and Leff, J. P. 1976. The influence of family and social factors on the course of psychiatric illness: A comparison of schizophrenics and depressed neurotic patients. *British Journal of Psychiatry, 129,* 125–137.

Wall, T. W. 1984. Hypnotic phenomena. In W. C. Wester and A. H. Smith (Eds.), *Clinical hypnosis: A multidisciplinary approach.* Philadelphia: J.B. Lippincott.

Waller, G. 1993. Childhood sexual abuse and borderline personality disorder in eating-disordered women. *International Journal of Eating Disorders, 13, (3)* 259–263.

Wallerstein, J. S., Corbin, S. B., and Lewis, J. M. 1988. Children of divorce: A 10-year study. In E. M. Hetherington and J. D. Arasteh (Eds.), *Impact of divorce, single parenting, and stepparenting on children.* Hillsdale, NJ: Lawrence Erlbaum.

Ward, J., Mattick, R. P., and Hall, W. 1994. The effectiveness of methadone maintenance treatment: An overview. *Drug and Alcohol Review, 13, 3,* 327–336.

Watters, J. K. 1996. Impact of HIV risk and infection and the role of prevention services. *Journal of Substance Abuse Treatment, 13, 5,* 375–385.

Wechsler, D. 1991. *Wechsler Intelligence Scale for Children: Third edition.* Psychological Corporation. San Antonio: Harcourt Brace Jovanovich.

Wehr, T. A., Sack, D. A., and Rosenthal, N. E. 1987. Sleep reduction as a final common pathway in the genesis of mania. *American Journal of Psychiatry, 144, (2)* 201–204.

Weinstein, M. R. 1976. The international register of lithium babies. *Drug Information Journal, 10(2),* 94–100.

Weiss, G., and Hechtman, L. T. 1993. *Hyperactive children grown up: ADHD in children, adolescents, and adults* (2nd ed.). New York: The Guilford Press.

Weiss, G., Minde, K., Werry, J. S., Douglas, V., and Nemeth, E. 1971. Studies on the hyperactive child: VII. Five-year follow-up. *Archives of General Psychiatry, 24, (5)* 409–414.

Whalen, C. K. 1989. Attention deficit and hyperactivity disorders. In T. Ollendick and M. Hersen (Eds.), *Handbook of child psychopathology.* New York: Plenum Press.

Whalen, C. K., Henker, B., and Granger, D. A. 1990. Social judgment processes in hyperactive boys: Effects of methylphenidate and comparisons with normal peers. *Journal of Abnormal Child Psychology, 18, (3)* 297–316.

Widiger, T. A., and Frances, A. J. 1988. Personality disorders. In J. A. Talbott, R. E. Hales, and S. C. Yudofsky (Eds.), *Textbook of psychiatry.* Washington DC: American Psychiatric Press.

Widiger, T. A., and Trull, T. J. 1993. Borderline and narcissistic personality disorders. In P. B. Sutker and H. E. Adams (Eds.), *Comprehensive handbook of psychopathology* (2nd ed.). New York: Plenum.

Wilbur, C. B. 1984. Treatment of multiple personality. *Psychiatric Annals, 14,* 27–31.

Wilkinson, A. 1994. A changed vision of God. *The New Yorker, 69, 47,* 52–68.

Williams, A. L. 1996. Skin color in psychotherapy. In R. Perez-Foster, M. Moskowitz, and R. Javier (Eds.), *Reaching across the boundaries of culture and class: Widening the scope of psychotherapy*. Northvale, NJ: Jason Aronson.

Williams, L. M. 1994. Recall of childhood trauma: Prospective study of women's memories of child sexual abuse. *Journal of Consulting and Clinical Psychology, 62, (6)* 1167–1176.

Williamson, L. 1998. Eating disorders and the cultural forces behind the drive for thinness: Are African-American women really protected? *Social Work in Health Care, 28(1)*, 61–73.

Wilson, T. G. 1995. Psychological treatment of binge eating and bulimia nervosa. *Journal of Mental Health–U.K., 4, 5*, 451–457.

Winnicott, D. W. 1971. *Playing and reality*. Middlesex, England: Penguin.

Wolf, E. S. 1988. *Treating the self: Elements of clinical self psychology*. New York: Guilford.

Wonderlich, S. A., Swift, W. J., Slotnick, H. B., and Goodman, S. 1990. DSM-III-R personality disorders in eating-disorder subtypes. *International Journal of Eating Disorders, 9*, 607–616.

Wooley, S. C. 1994. Sexual abuse and eating disorders: The concealed debate. In P. Fallon, M. A. Katzman, and S. C. Wooley (Eds.), *Feminist perspectives on eating disorders*. New York: Guilford.

Worell, J., and Remer, P. 1992. *Feminist perspectives in therapy: An empowerment model for women*. New York: Wiley.

World Health Organization. 1992. *ICD-10 classification of mental and behavioral disorders: Clinical descriptions and diagnostic guidelines*. Geneva: Author.

Wyatt, R. J., and Henter, I. D. 1998. The effects of early and sustained intervention on the long-term morbidity of schizophrenia. *Journal of Psychiatric Research, 32(30–4)*, 169–177.

Young, L. T., Warsh, J. J., Kish, S. J., and Shannak, K., and Hornykeiwicz, O. 1994. Reduced brain 5-HT and elevated NE turnover and metabolites in bipolar affective disorder. *Biological Psychiatry, 35, (2)* 121–127.

Zahn, T. P., Moraga, R., and Ray, W. J. 1996. Psychophysiological assessment of dissociative disorders. In L. K. Michelson, W. J. Ray (Eds.), *Handbook of dissociation: Theoretical, empirical, and clinical perspectives*. New York: Plenum.

Zametkin, A. J., Nordahl, T. E., Gross, M., King, A. C., Semple, W. E., Rumsey, J., Hamburger, S., and Cohen, R. M. 1990. Cerebral glucose metabolism in adults with hyperactivity of childhood onset. *New England Journal of Medicine, 323, (20)* 1361–1366.

Zanarini, M. C., and Gunderson, J. G. 1997. Differential diagnosis of antisocial and borderline personaltiy disorders. In J. Brieling et al. (Eds.), *Handbook of antisocial behavior*. New York: Wiley, pp. 83–91.

Zanarini, M. C., Gunderson, J. G., Frankenburg, F. R., and Chauncey, D. L. 1990. Discriminating borderline personality disorder from other Axis II disorders. *American Journal of Psychiatry, 147, (2)* 161–167.

Zanarini, M. C., Gunderson, J. G., Marino, M. F., Schwartz, E. O., and Frankenburg, F. R. 1989. Childhood experiences of borderline patients. *Comprehensive Psychiatry, 30, 1*, 18–25.

Zanarini, M. C., Williams, A. A., Lewis, R. E., Reich, R. B., Vera, S. C., Marino, M. F., Levin, A., Yong, L., and Frankenburg, F. R. 1997. Reported pathological childhood experiences associated with the development of borderline personality disorder. *American Journal of Psychiatry, 154, 8*, 1101–1106.

Zilbergeld, B. 1992. *The new male sexuality*. New York: Bantam Books.

Zornberg, G. L. 1998. Identifying critical periods of neurodevelopmental risk: The turning point in schizophrenia research. *Harvard Review of Psychiatry, 6(3)*, 171–174.

Zubin, J., and Spring, B. J. 1977. Vulnerability: A new view of schizophrenia. *Journal of Abnormal Psychology*, 86, *(2)* 103–126.

Zucker, K. J., and Blanchard, R. 1997. Transvestic fetishism: Psychopathology and theory. In (D. R. Laws and W. O'Donohue, Eds.), *Sexual deviance: Theory, assessment, and treatment*. New York: Guilford, pp. 253–279.